CAN'T STOP Cursing YOU 1

Art: NATSUKO URUMA

Original Story: KENSUKE KOBA

Translation: Christina Rose

Lettering: Rachel J. Pierce

DAREKA WO NOROWAZUNI IRARENAI KONO SEKAI DE Volume 1
©2019 Kensuke Koba, Natsuko Uruma/ SQUARE ENIX CO., LTD. First published in Japan in 2019 by SQUARE ENIX CO., LTD. English translation rights arranged with SQUARE ENIX CO., LTD. and Yen Press, LLC through Tuttle-Mori Agency, Inc.

English translation ©2021 by SQUARE ENIX CO., LTD.

Yen Press
150 West 30th St, 19th Floor
New York, NY 10001

Visit us at yenpress.com ✳ facebook.com/yenpress ✳ twitter.com/yenpress ✳ yenpress.tumblr.com ✳ instagram.com/yenpress

First Yen Press Edition: March 2021

Yen Press is an imprint of Yen Press, LLC. The Yen Press name and logo are trademarks of Yen Press, LLC.

The publisher is not responsible for websites (or their content) that are not owned by the publisher.

Library of Congress Control Number: 2020951852

ISBNs: 978-1-9753-2168-0 (paperback)
       978-1-9753-2169-7 (ebook)

10 9 8 7 6 5 4 3 2 1

BVG

Printed in the United States of America

IM
Great Priest Imhotep

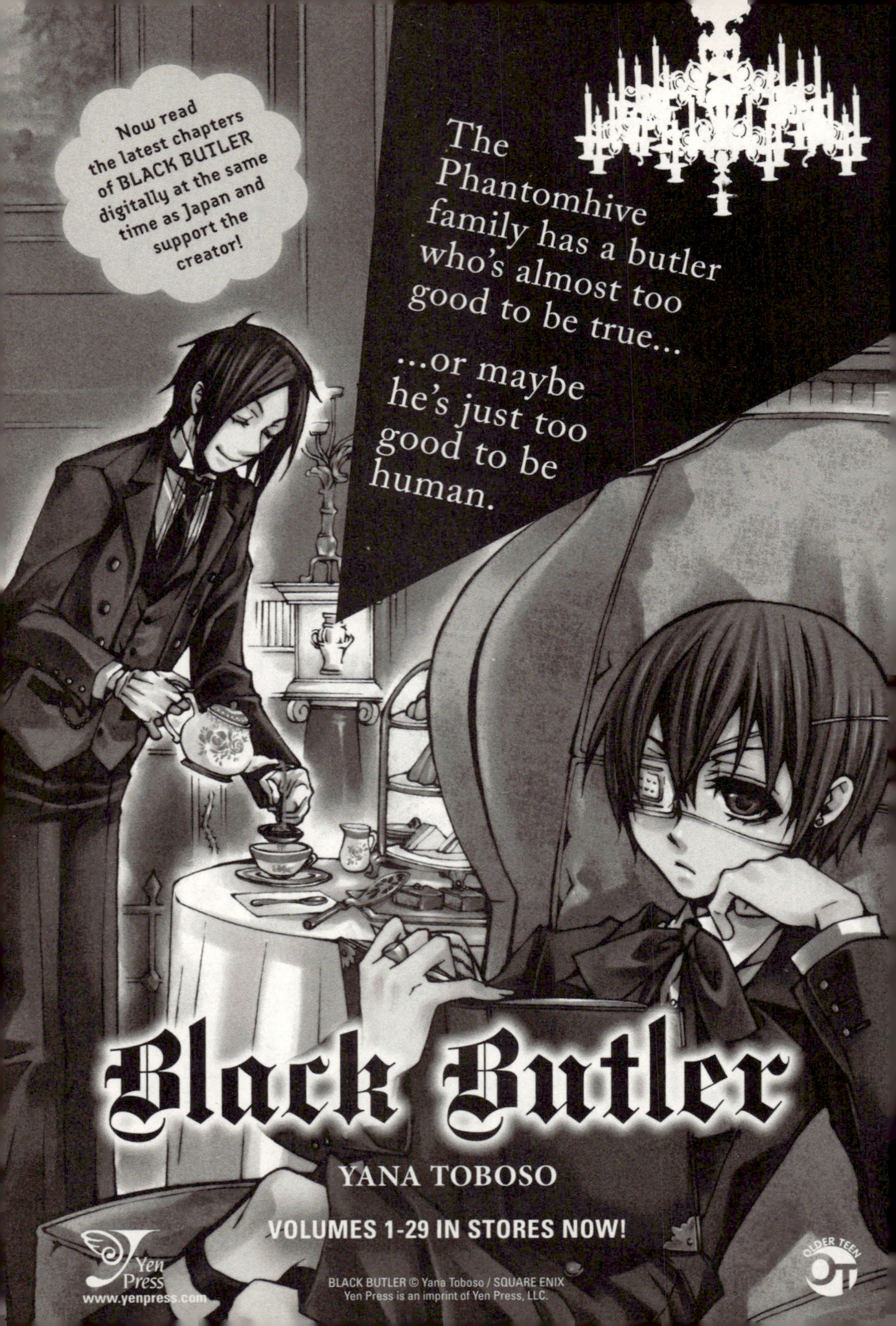
Now read the latest chapters of BLACK BUTLER digitally at the same time as Japan and support the creator!
The Phantomhive family has a butler who's almost too good to be true...
...or maybe he's just too good to be human.
Black Butler
YANA TOBOSO
VOLUMES 1-29 IN STORES NOW!
Yen Press
www.yenpress.com
OLDER TEEN
OT
BLACK BUTLER © Yana Toboso / SQUARE ENIX
Yen Press is an imprint of Yen Press, LLC.

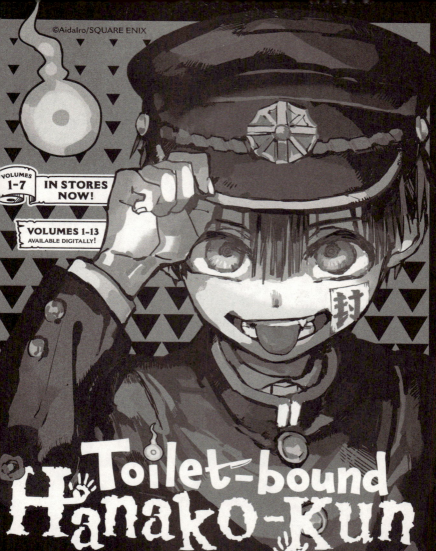

©AidaIro/SQUARE ENIX

VOLUMES 1-7 IN STORES NOW!

VOLUMES 1-13 AVAILABLE DIGITALLY!

Toilet-bound Hanako-Kun

At Kamome Academy, rumors abound about the school's Seven Mysteries, one of which is Hanako-san. Said to occupy the third stall of the third floor girls' bathroom in the old school building, Hanako-san grants any wish when summoned. Nene Yashiro, an occult-loving high school girl who dreams of romance, ventures into this haunted bathroom...but the Hanako-san she meets there is nothing like she imagined! Kamome Academy's Hanako-san...is a boy!

Yen Press

For more information visit www.yenpress.com

MURDERER
IN THE STREETS, KILLER
IN THE SHEETS!

MURCIÉLAGO
VOLUMES 1-16
AVAILABLE
NOW!

Mass murderer Kuroko Koumori has two passions in life: taking lives and pleasuring ladies. This doesn't leave her with many career prospects, but Kuroko actually has the perfect gig—as a hit woman for the police!

www.YenPress.com

Murciélago © Yoshimurakana / SQUARE ENIX

Common Honorifics

-san: The Japanese equivalent of Mr./Mrs./Miss. If a situation calls for politeness, this is the fail-safe honorific.

-kun: Used most often when referring to boys, this indicates affection or familiarity. Occasionally used by older men among their peers, but it may also be used by anyone referring to a person of lower standing.

-chan: An affectionate honorific indicating familiarity used mostly in reference to girls; also used in reference to cute persons or animals of either gender.

-sensei: A respectful term for teachers, artists, or high-level professionals.

-sama: Conveys great respect; may also indicate that the social status of the speaker is lower than that of the addressee.

-chin: A very informal suffix meant to sound cute.

no honorific: Indicates familiarity or closeness; if used without permission or reason, addressing someone in this manner would constitute an insult.

Translation Notes

Page 9: Classes: Instead of students traveling to the teachers' classrooms depending on the subject, Japanese students generally stay in the same classroom with teachers rotating depending on the subject. Each class is generally assigned a two-part number, like 2-9, to differentiate from other classes. The first number indicates which school year—first, second, or third—while the second number is used to distinguish them from other classes in the same year.

Page 124: *Warabi mochi*: A jellylike confection made from bracken—a type of fern—starch and covered or dipped in *kinako*, or sweet toasted soybean flour. It is most often enjoyed in the summertime.

Page 219: *Katakirauwa*: Malicious spirit from Japanese folklore. They take the form of piglets with one ear and red eyes. They do not possess a shadow, but their skin is black. *Katakirauwa* can steal a person's soul by running through their legs. However, if a person's legs are crossed, they will fail to steal said soul.

BONUS COMICS ②

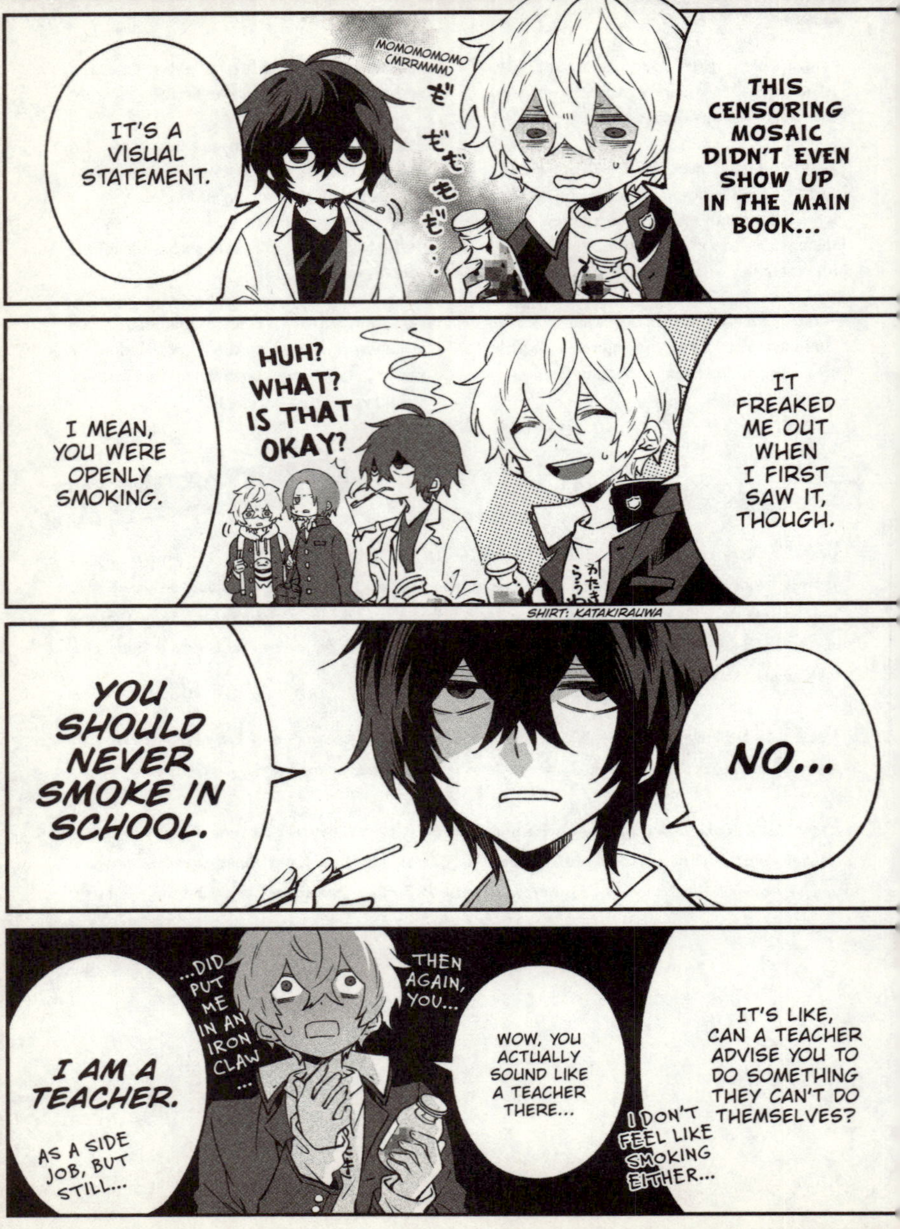
THIS CENSORING MOSAIC DIDN'T EVEN SHOW UP IN THE MAIN BOOK...
MOMOMOMOMO (MRRMMM)
IT'S A VISUAL STATEMENT.
IT FREAKED ME OUT WHEN I FIRST SAW IT, THOUGH.
HUH? WHAT? IS THAT OKAY?
I MEAN, YOU WERE OPENLY SMOKING.
SHIRT: KATAKIRAUWA
NO...
YOU SHOULD NEVER SMOKE IN SCHOOL.
IT'S LIKE, CAN A TEACHER ADVISE YOU TO DO SOMETHING THEY CAN'T DO THEMSELVES?
I DON'T FEEL LIKE SMOKING EITHER...
WOW, YOU ACTUALLY SOUND LIKE A TEACHER THERE...
THEN AGAIN, YOU...
...DID PUT ME IN AN IRON CLAW...
I AM A TEACHER.
AS A SIDE JOB, BUT STILL...

BONUS COMICS ①

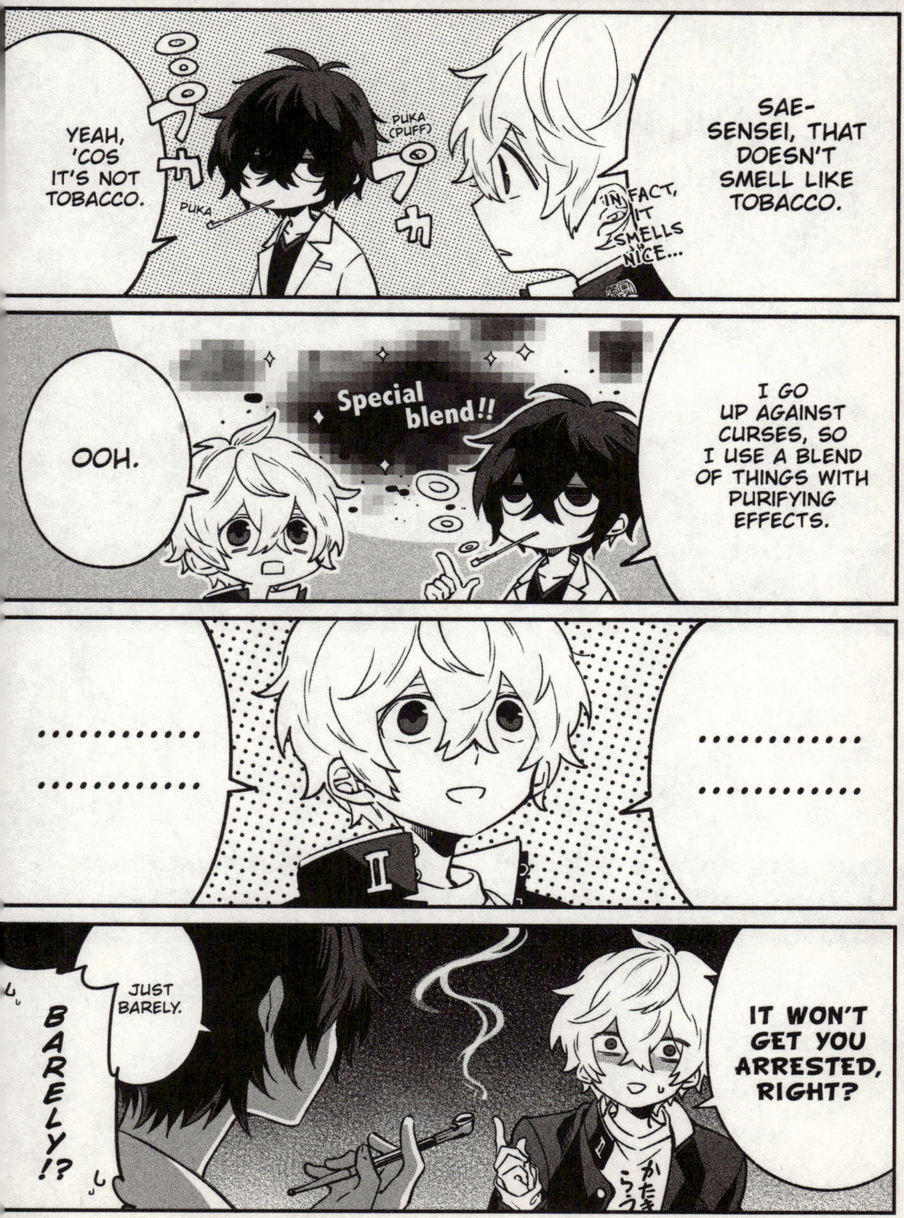

SAE-SENSEI, THAT DOESN'T SMELL LIKE TOBACCO.
IN FACT, IT SMELLS NICE...
PUKA (PUFF)
YEAH, 'COS IT'S NOT TOBACCO.
PUKA
I GO UP AGAINST CURSES, SO I USE A BLEND OF THINGS WITH PURIFYING EFFECTS.
Special blend!!
OOH.
....
....
....
....
IT WON'T GET YOU ARRESTED, RIGHT?
JUST BARELY.
BARELY!?

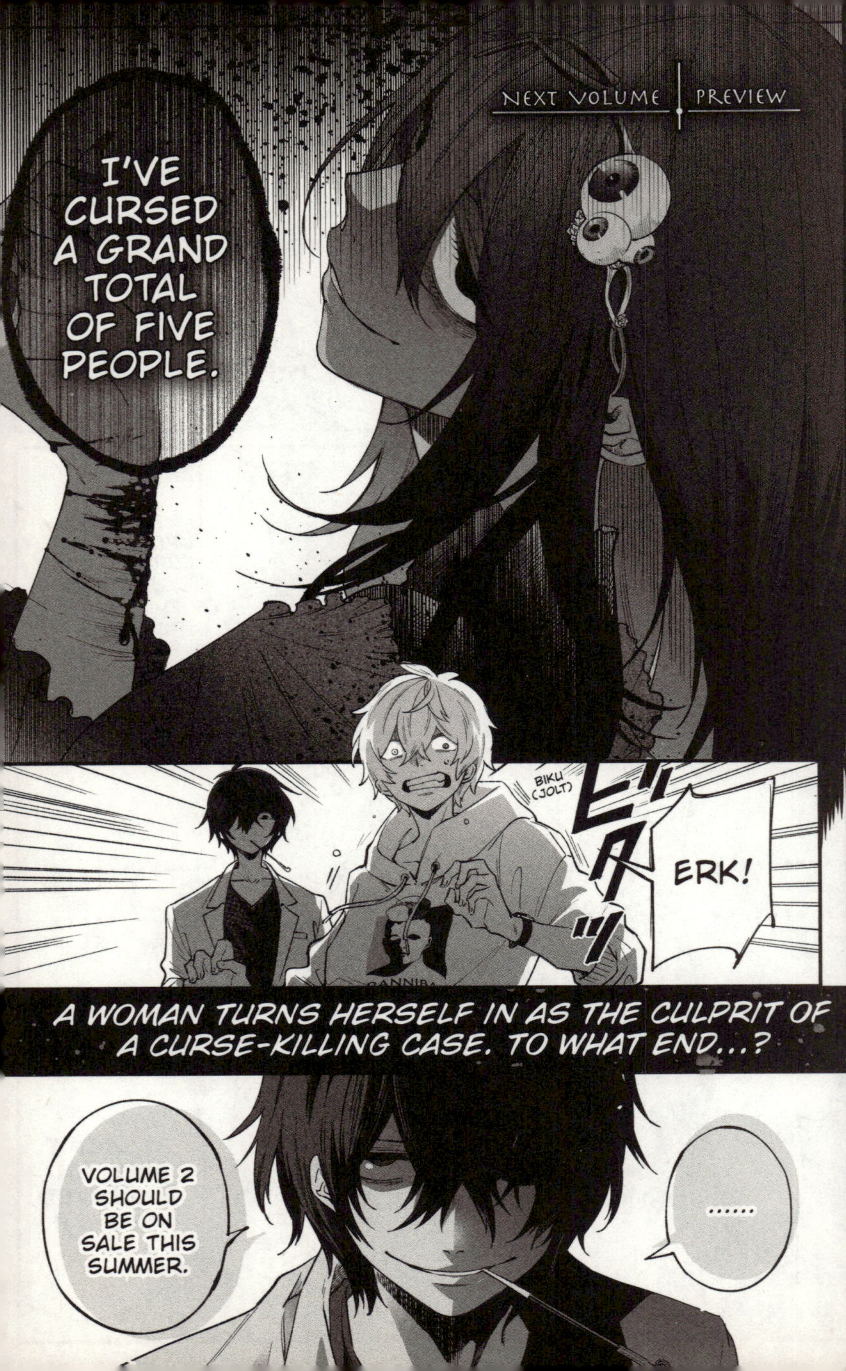
NEXT VOLUME PREVIEW
I'VE CURSED A GRAND TOTAL OF FIVE PEOPLE.
ERK!
BIKU (JOLT)
A WOMAN TURNS HERSELF IN AS THE CULPRIT OF A CURSE-KILLING CASE. TO WHAT END...?
......
VOLUME 2 SHOULD BE ON SALE THIS SUMMER.

Gods of curses...

We stand not in opposition...

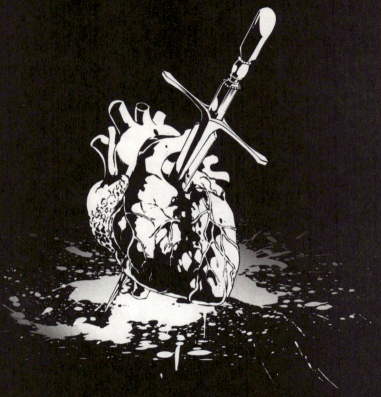

...but in indulgence of your games.

Curse-Breaker Association Founder

Luberry Crowley

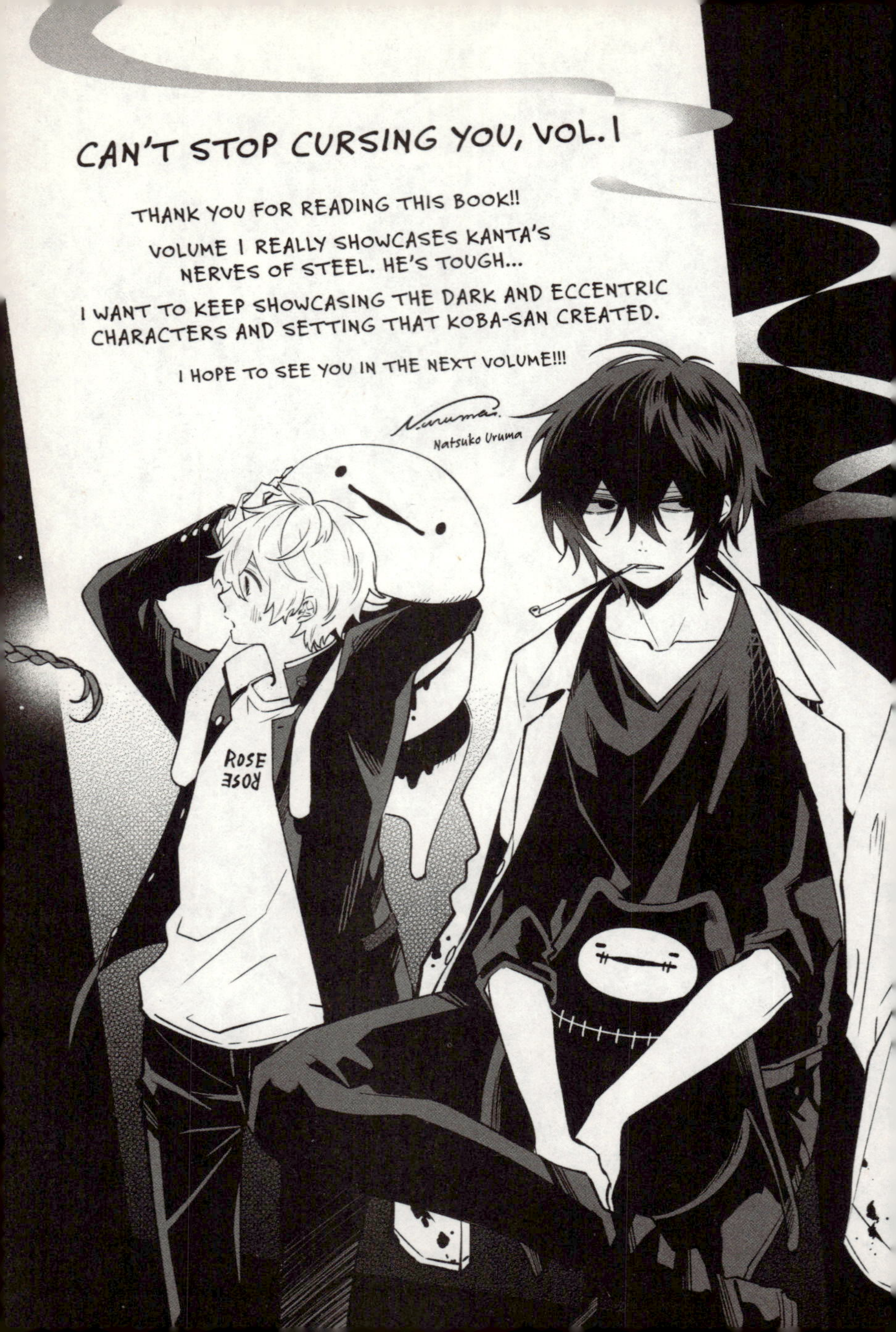
CAN'T STOP CURSING YOU, VOL. 1
THANK YOU FOR READING THIS BOOK!!
VOLUME 1 REALLY SHOWCASES KANTA'S NERVES OF STEEL. HE'S TOUGH...
I WANT TO KEEP SHOWCASING THE DARK AND ECCENTRIC CHARACTERS AND SETTING THAT KOBA-SAN CREATED.
I HOPE TO SEE YOU IN THE NEXT VOLUME!!!
Natsuko Uruma
ROSE
ROSE

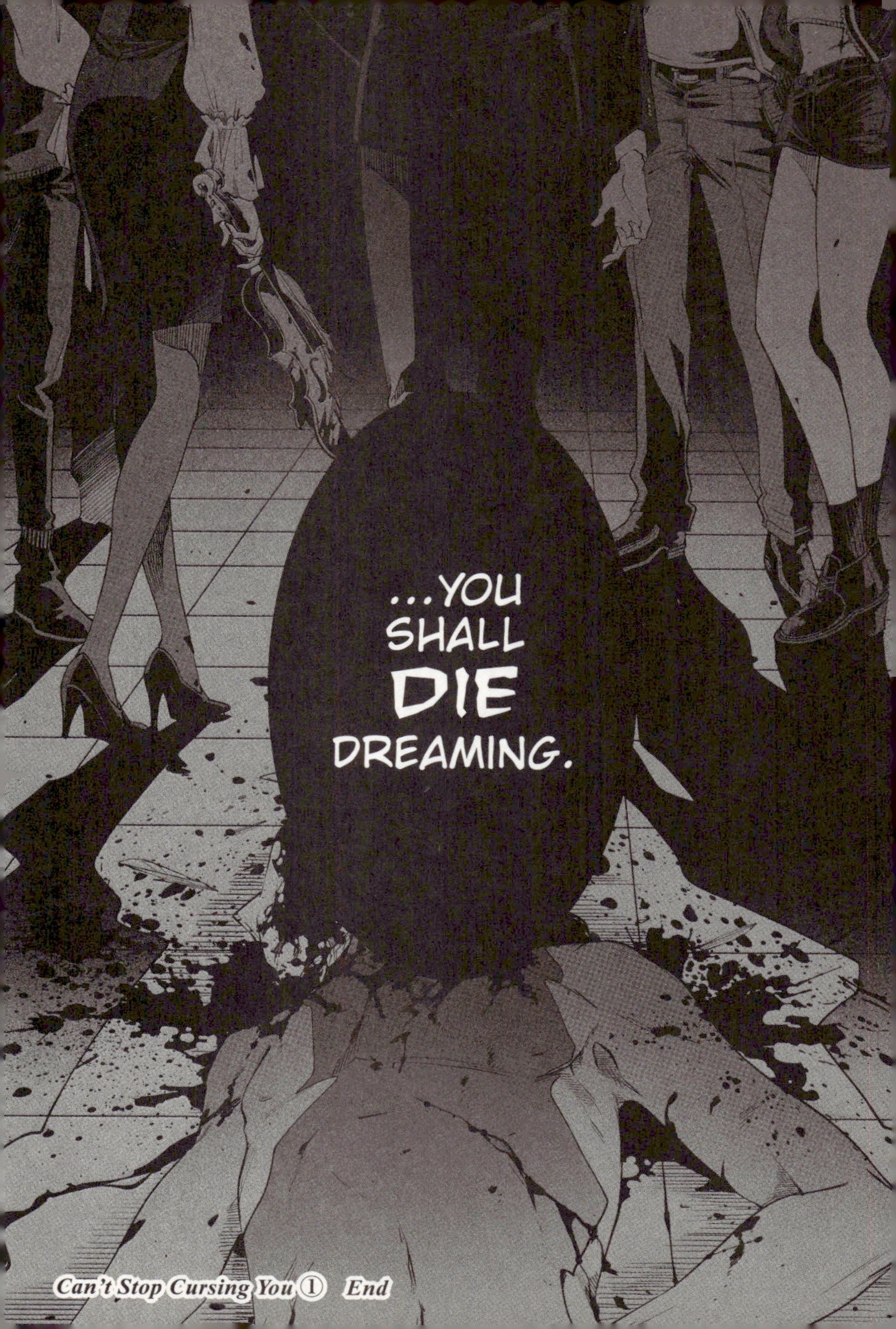
...YOU SHALL DIE DREAMING.
Can't Stop Cursing You ① End

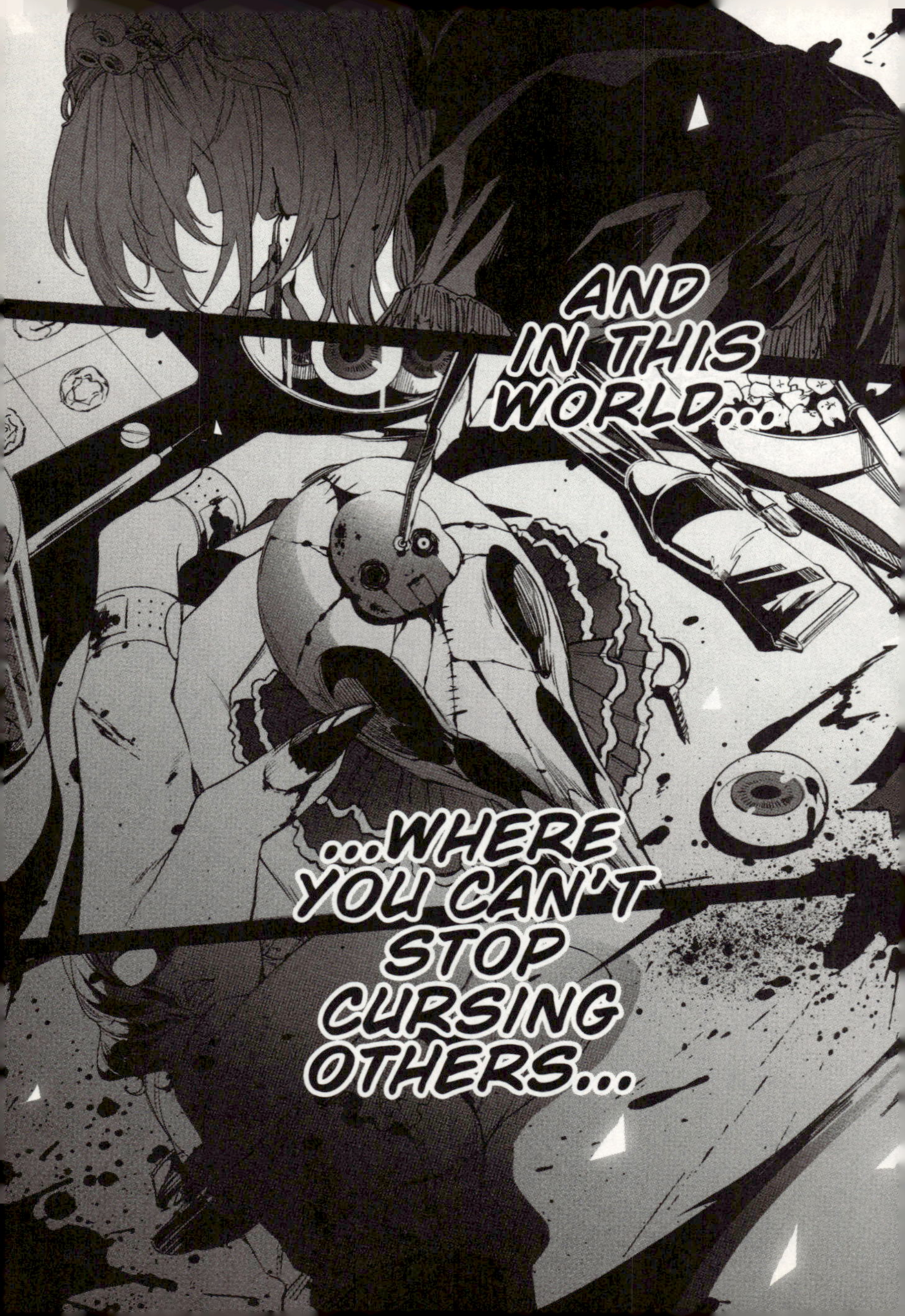
AND IN THIS WORLD...
...WHERE YOU CAN'T STOP CURSING OTHERS...

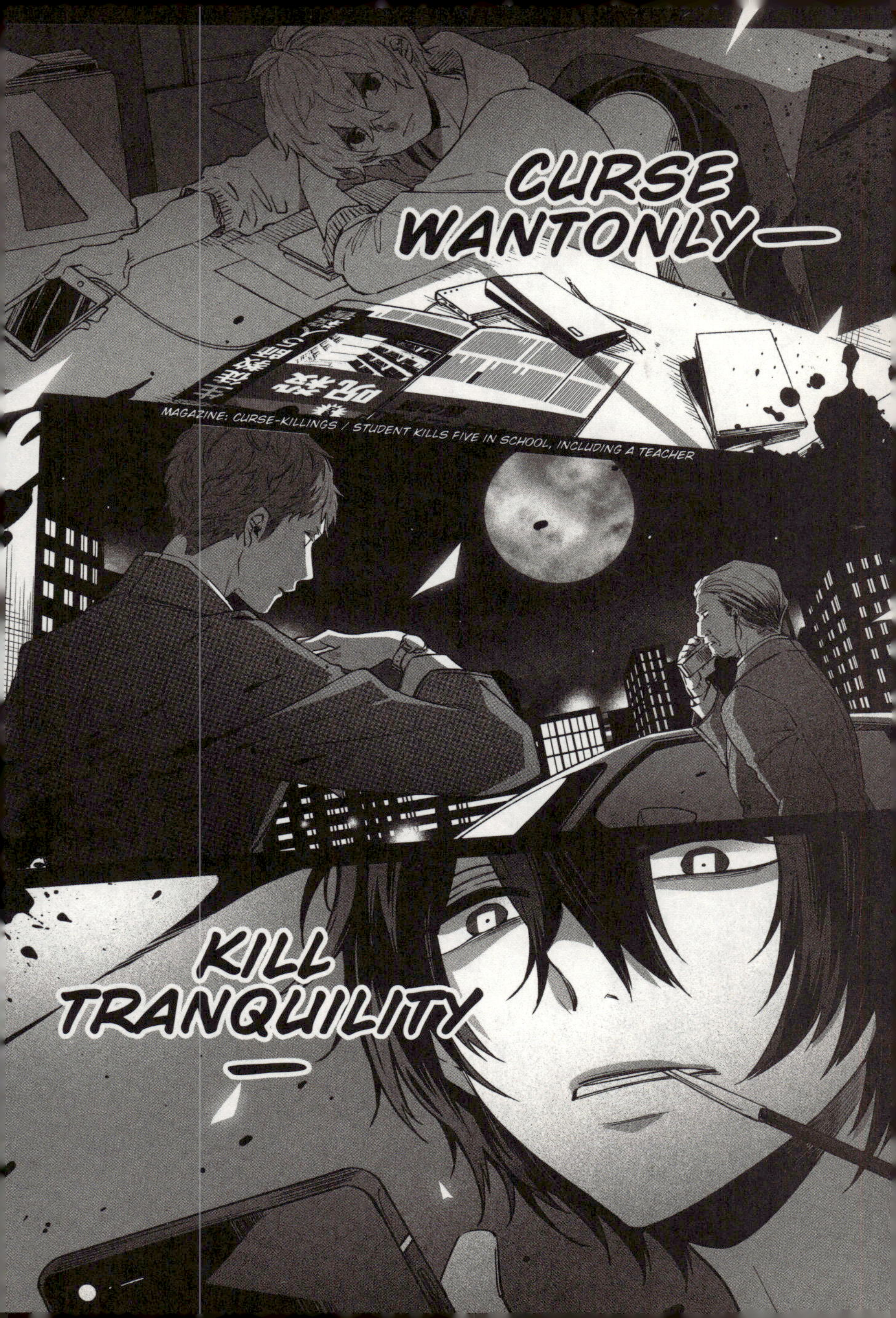
CURSE WANTONLY—
MAGAZINE: CURSE-KILLINGS / STUDENT KILLS FIVE IN SCHOOL, INCLUDING A TEACHER
KILL TRANQUILITY—

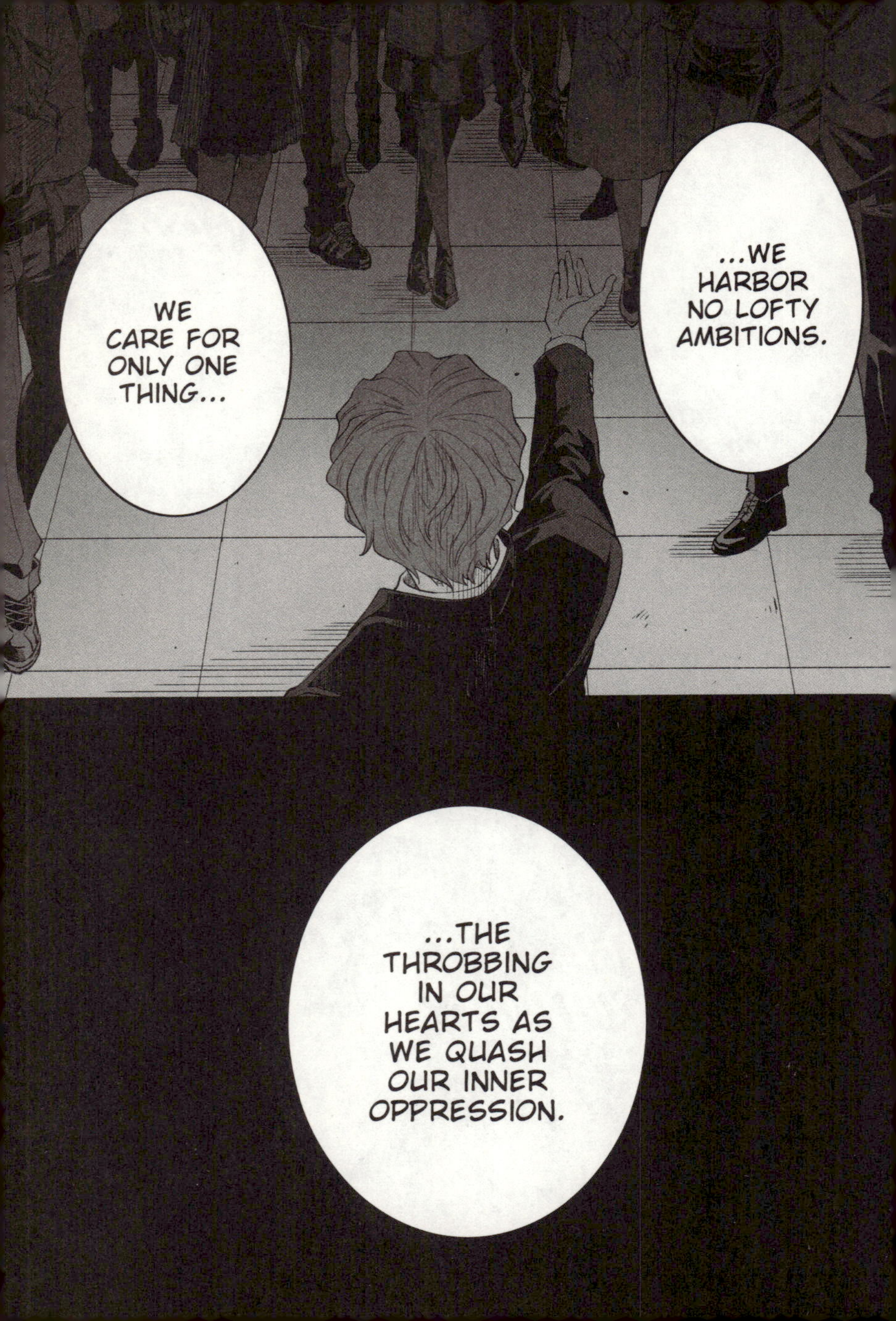
...WE HARBOR NO LOFTY AMBITIONS.
WE CARE FOR ONLY ONE THING...
...THE THROBBING IN OUR HEARTS AS WE QUASH OUR INNER OPPRESSION.

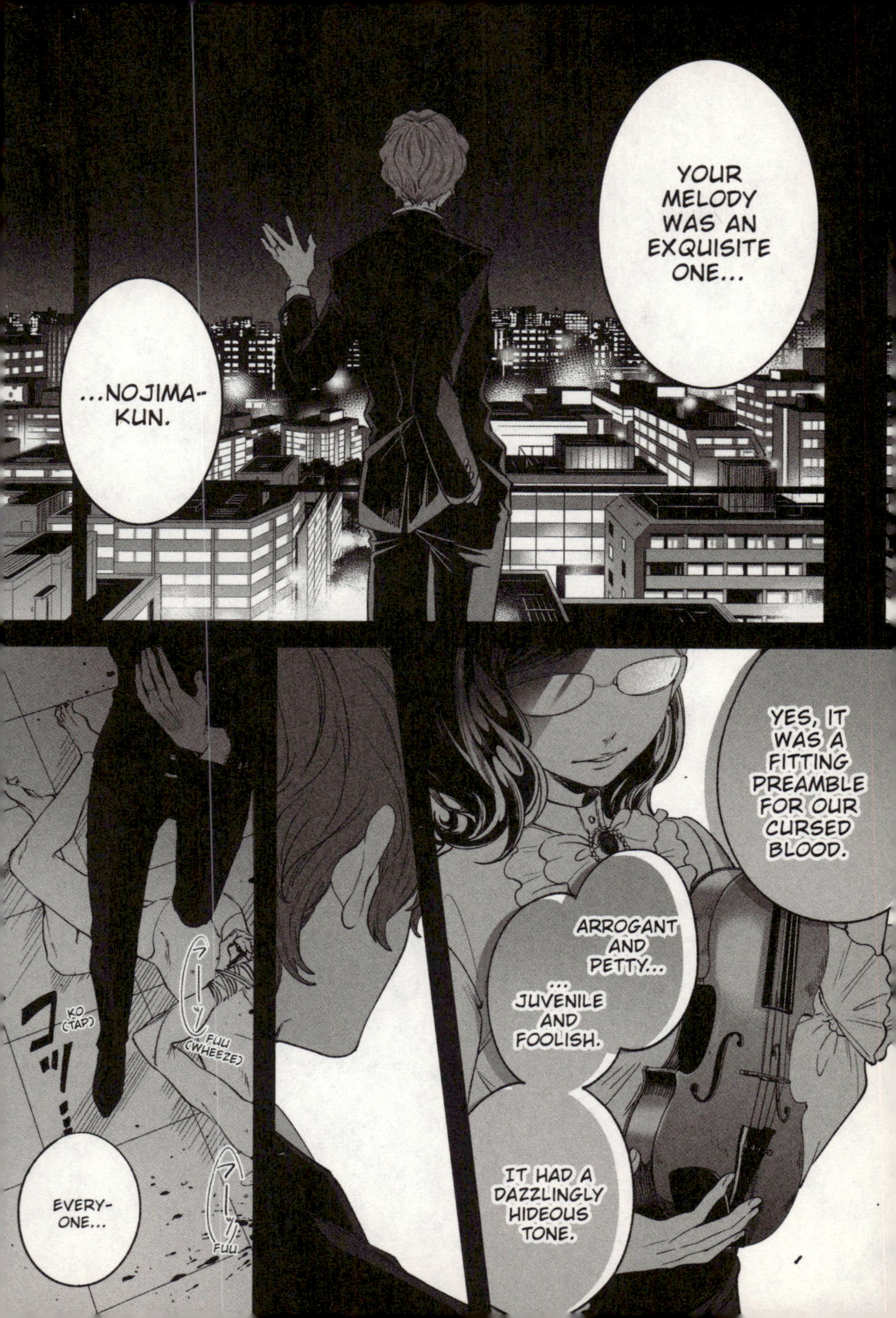
YOUR MELODY WAS AN EXQUISITE ONE...
...NOJIMA-KUN.
YES, IT WAS A FITTING PREAMBLE FOR OUR CURSED BLOOD.
ARROGANT AND PETTY... ...JUVENILE AND FOOLISH.
IT HAD A DAZZLINGLY HIDEOUS TONE.
FUU (WHEEZE)
KO (TAP)
FUU
EVERY-ONE...

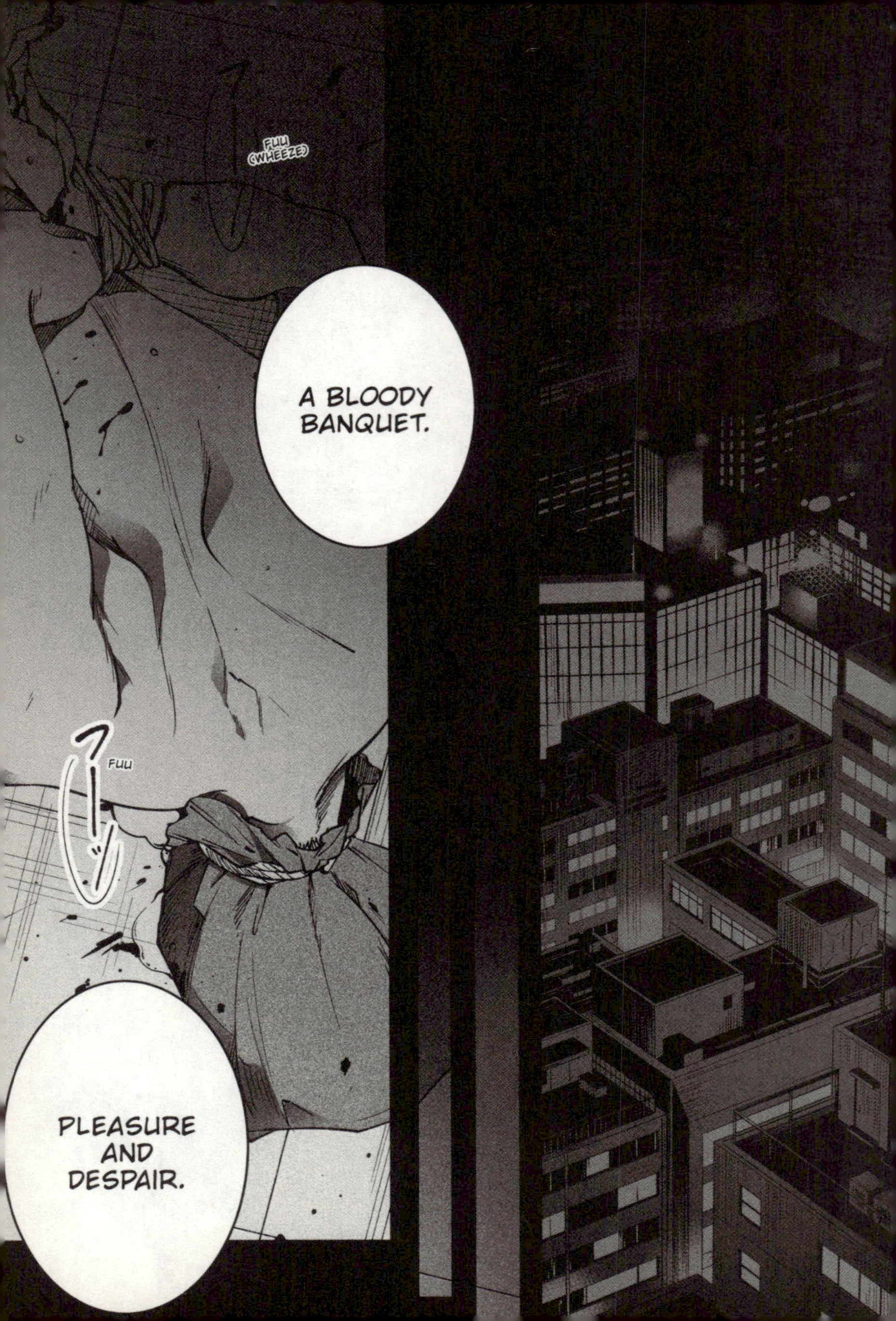
FUU (WHEEZE)
A BLOODY BANQUET.
FUU
PLEASURE AND DESPAIR.

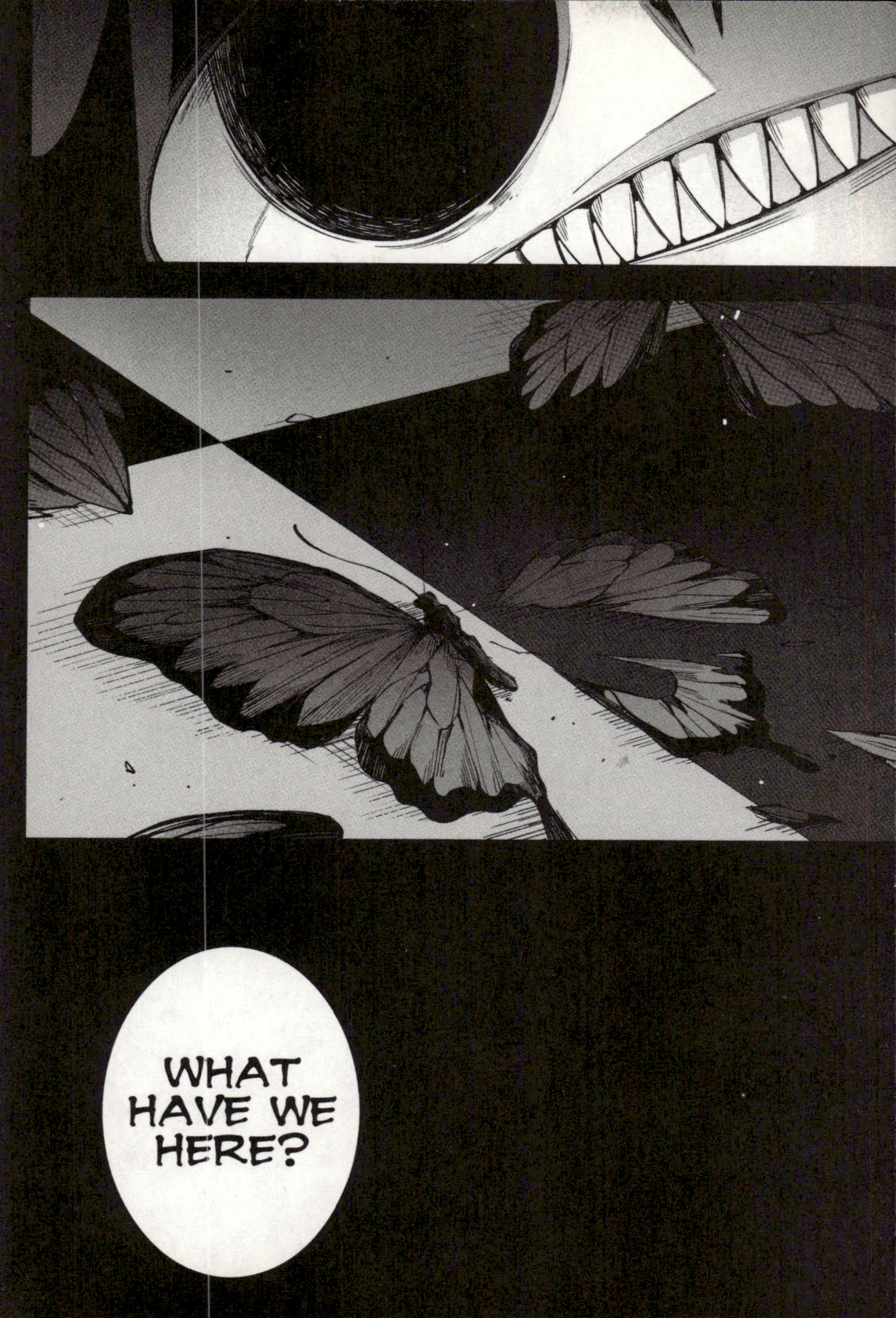
WHAT HAVE WE HERE?

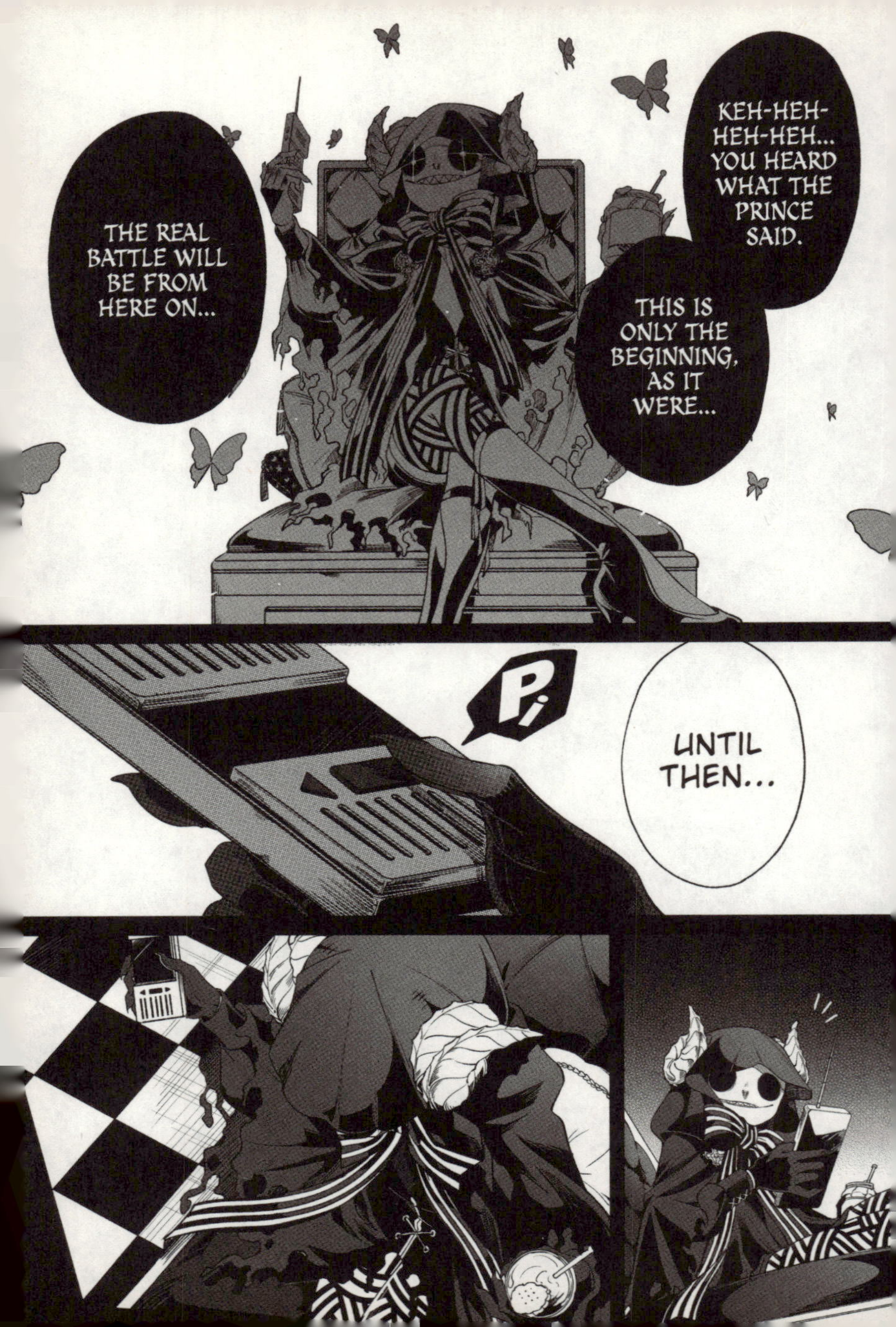
KEH-HEH-HEH-HEH... YOU HEARD WHAT THE PRINCE SAID.
THIS IS ONLY THE BEGINNING, AS IT WERE...
THE REAL BATTLE WILL BE FROM HERE ON...
UNTIL THEN...
Pi

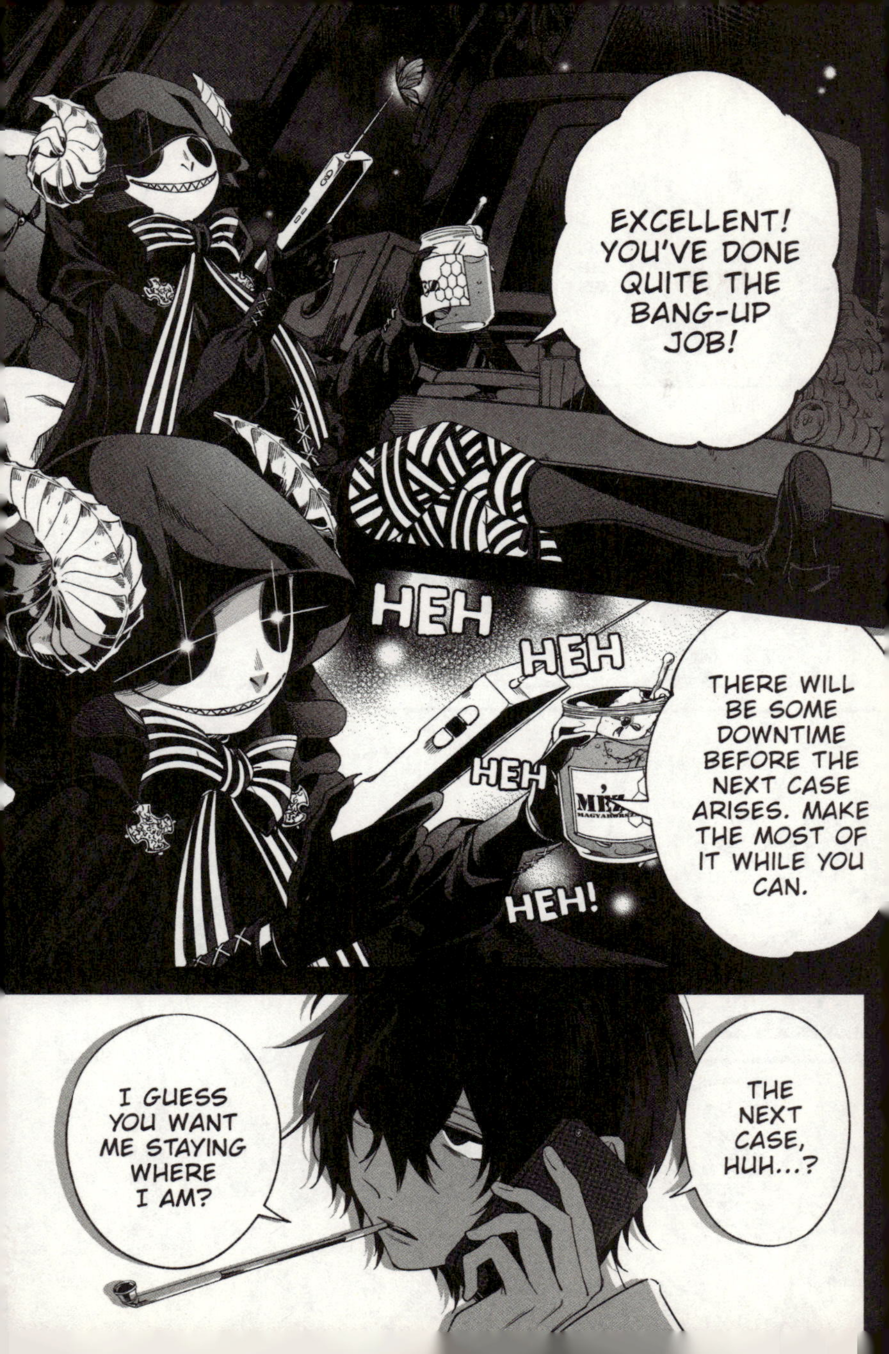
EXCELLENT! YOU'VE DONE QUITE THE BANG-UP JOB!
HEH
HEH
HEH
HEH!
THERE WILL BE SOME DOWNTIME BEFORE THE NEXT CASE ARISES. MAKE THE MOST OF IT WHILE YOU CAN.
THE NEXT CASE, HUH...?
I GUESS YOU WANT ME STAYING WHERE I AM?

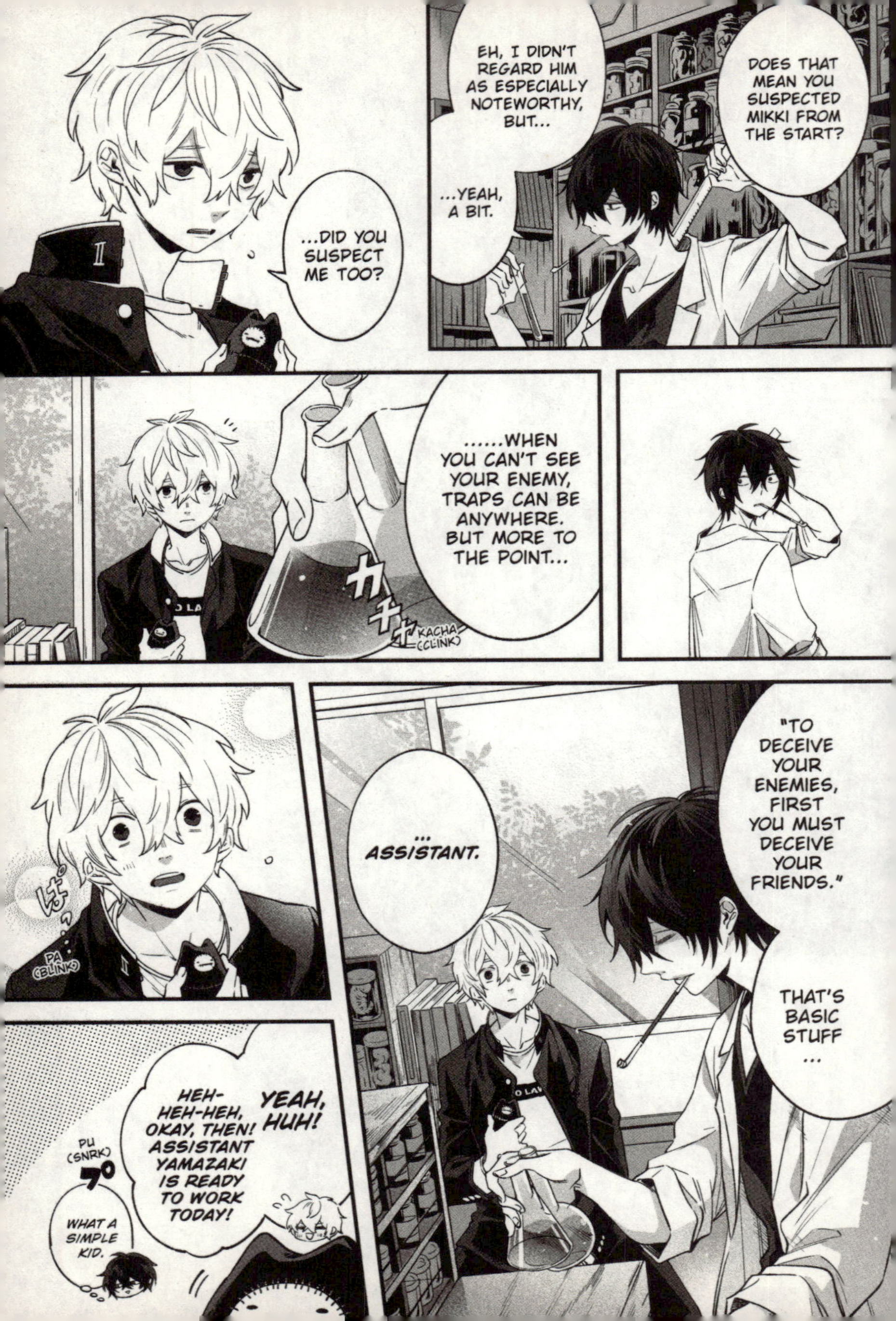
DOES THAT MEAN YOU SUSPECTED MIKKI FROM THE START?
EH, I DIDN'T REGARD HIM AS ESPECIALLY NOTEWORTHY, BUT...
...YEAH, A BIT.
...DID YOU SUSPECT ME TOO?
......WHEN YOU CAN'T SEE YOUR ENEMY, TRAPS CAN BE ANYWHERE. BUT MORE TO THE POINT...
KACHA (CLINK)
"TO DECEIVE YOUR ENEMIES, FIRST YOU MUST DECEIVE YOUR FRIENDS."
... ASSISTANT.
THAT'S BASIC STUFF ...
PA (BLINK)
YEAH, HUH!
HEH-HEH-HEH, OKAY, THEN! ASSISTANT YAMAZAKI IS READY TO WORK TODAY!
PU (SNRK)
WHAT A SIMPLE KID.

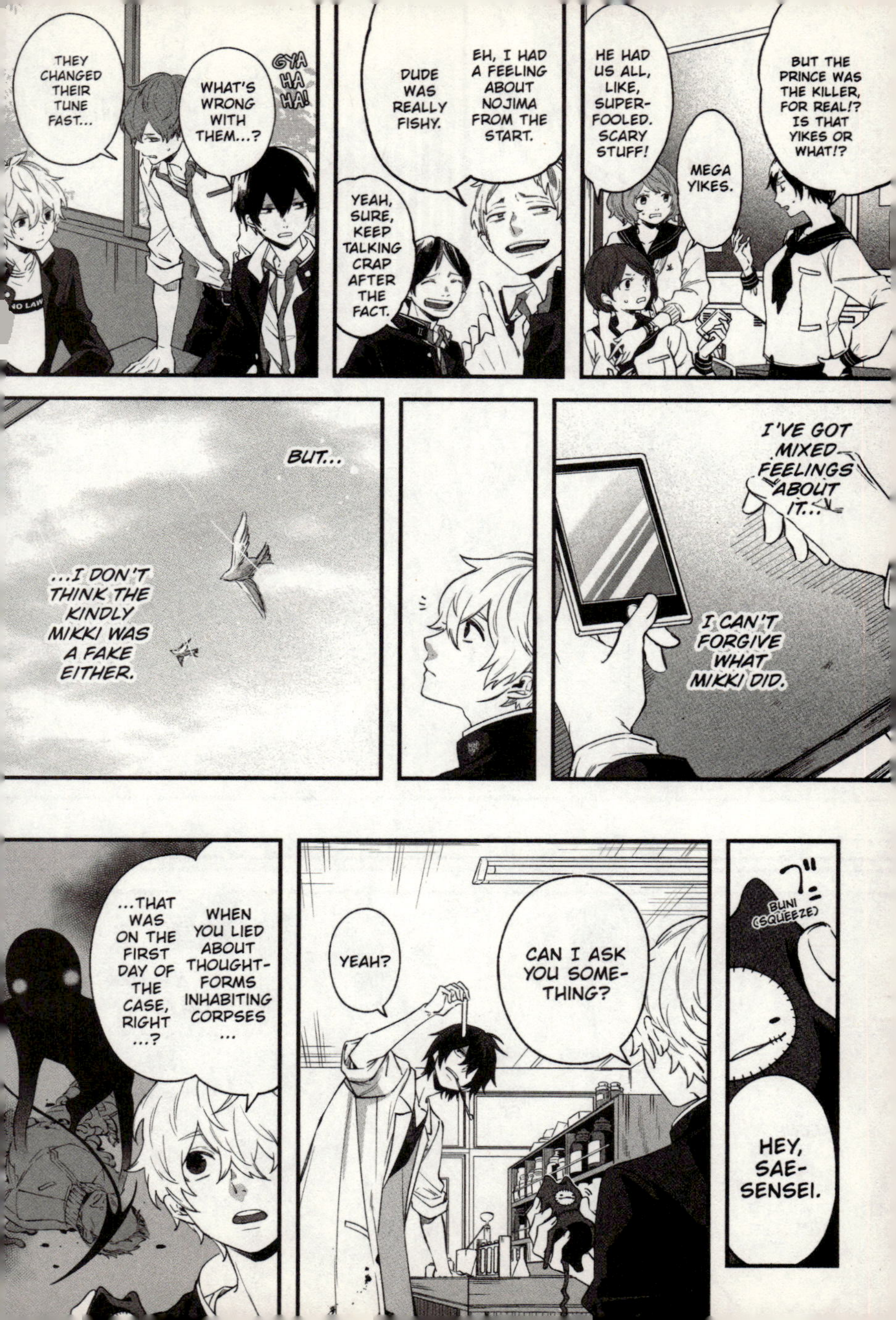
BUT THE PRINCE WAS THE KILLER, FOR REAL!? IS THAT YIKES OR WHAT!?
HE HAD US ALL, LIKE, SUPER-FOOLED. SCARY STUFF!
MEGA YIKES.
EH, I HAD A FEELING ABOUT NOJIMA FROM THE START.
DUDE WAS REALLY FISHY.
YEAH, SURE, KEEP TALKING CRAP AFTER THE FACT.
GYA HA HA!
WHAT'S WRONG WITH THEM...?
THEY CHANGED THEIR TUNE FAST...
NO LAW
I'VE GOT MIXED FEELINGS ABOUT IT...
I CAN'T FORGIVE WHAT MIKKI DID.
BUT...
...I DON'T THINK THE KINDLY MIKKI WAS A FAKE EITHER.
BUNI (SQUEEZE)
HEY, SAE-SENSEI.
CAN I ASK YOU SOMETHING?
YEAH?
WHEN YOU LIED ABOUT THOUGHT-FORMS INHABITING CORPSES...
...THAT WAS ON THE FIRST DAY OF THE CASE, RIGHT...?

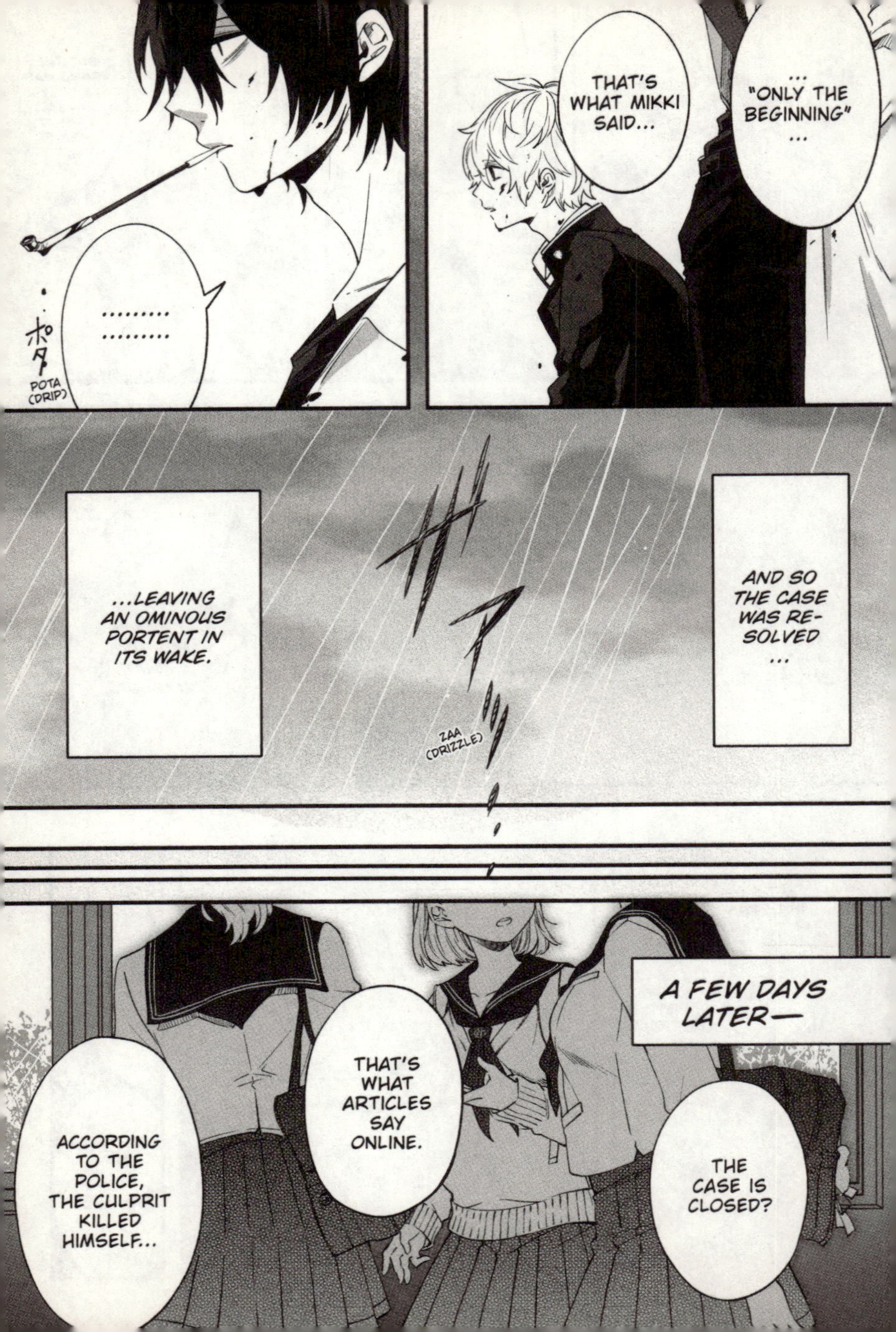
... "ONLY THE BEGINNING" ...
THAT'S WHAT MIKKI SAID...
....
ポタ
POTA (DRIP)
AND SO THE CASE WAS RE-SOLVED ...
ZAA (DRIZZLE)
...LEAVING AN OMINOUS PORTENT IN ITS WAKE.
A FEW DAYS LATER—
THE CASE IS CLOSED?
THAT'S WHAT ARTICLES SAY ONLINE.
ACCORDING TO THE POLICE, THE CULPRIT KILLED HIMSELF...

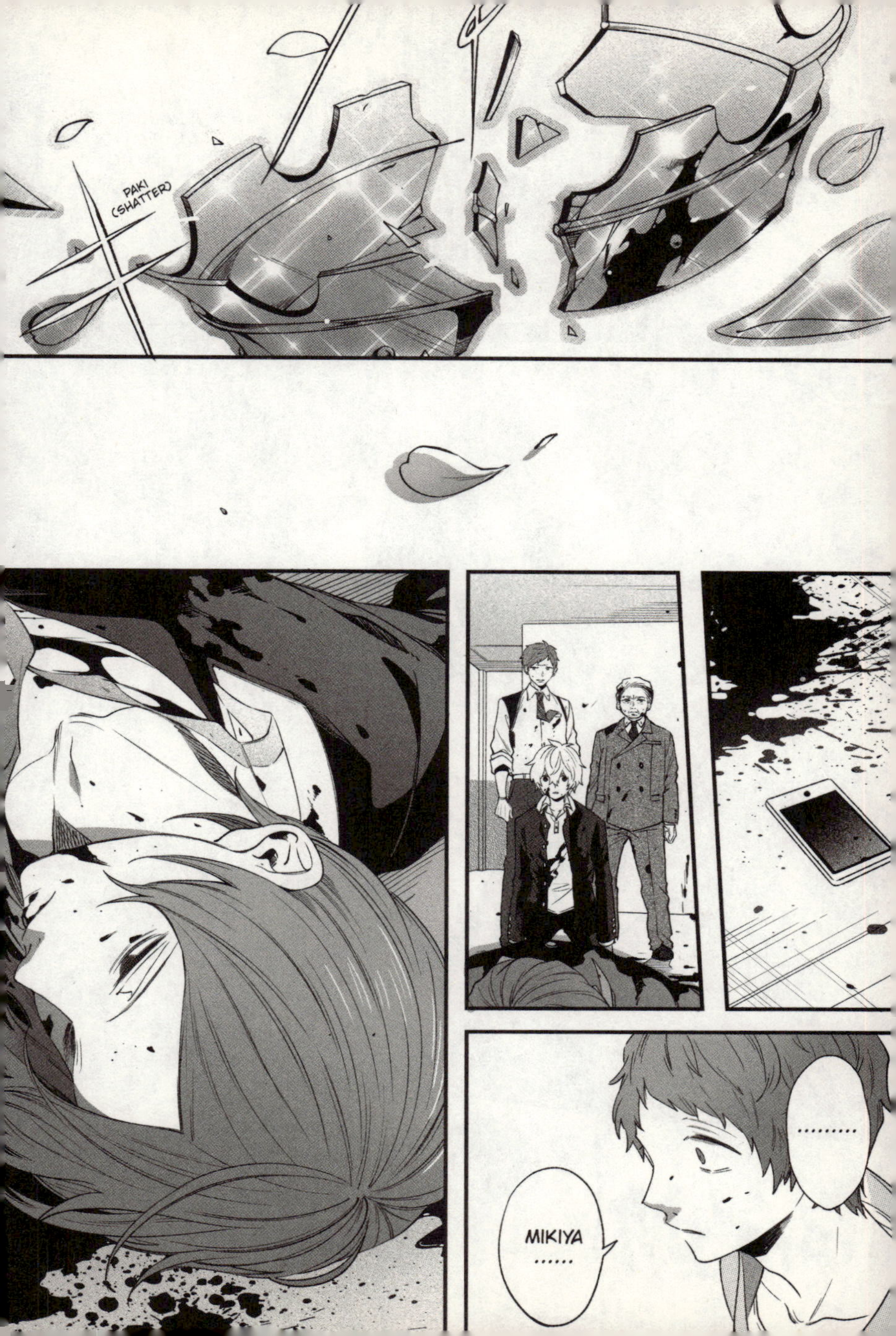
PAKI (SHATTER)
....
MIKIYA ......

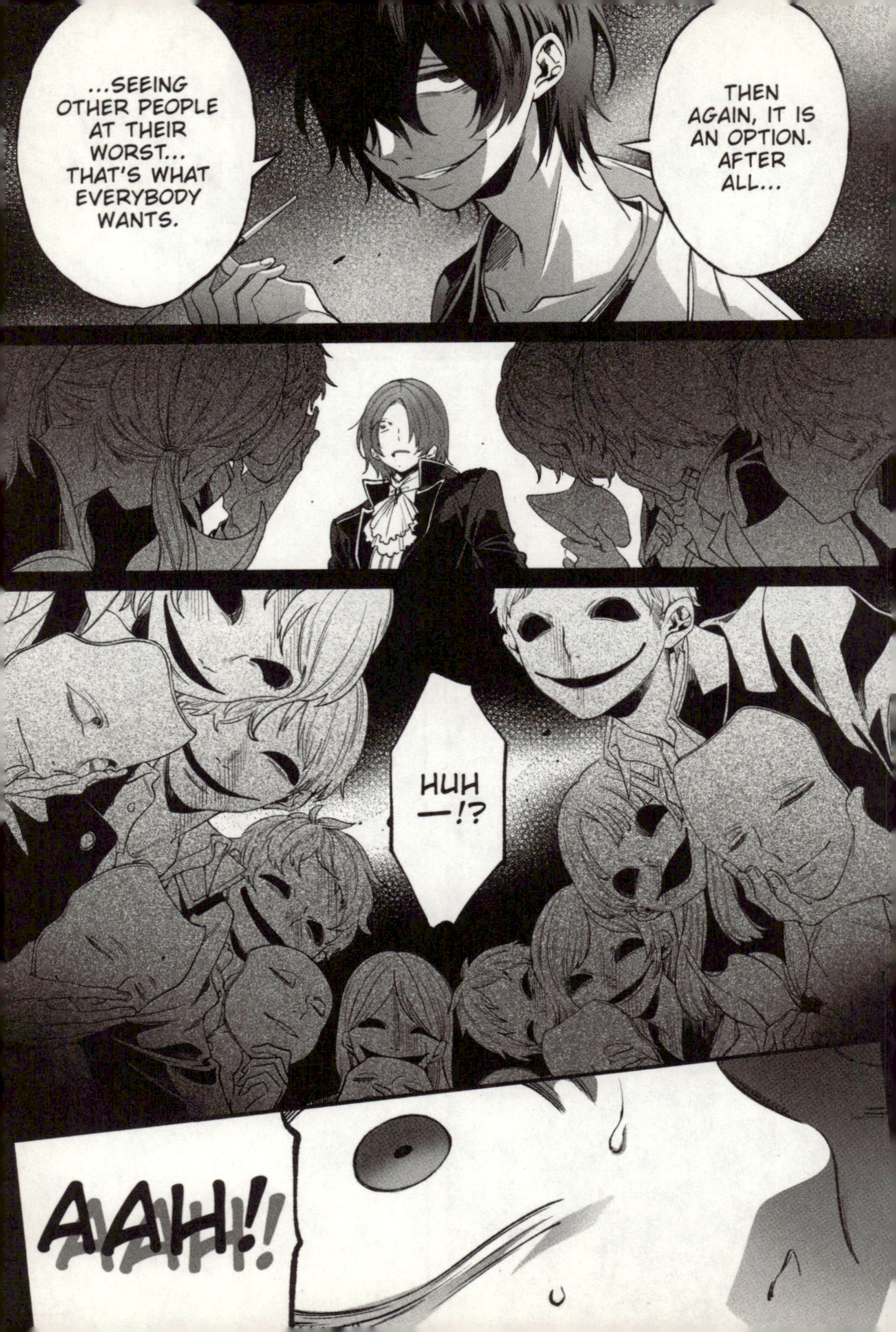
THEN AGAIN, IT IS AN OPTION. AFTER ALL...
...SEEING OTHER PEOPLE AT THEIR WORST... THAT'S WHAT EVERYBODY WANTS.
HUH—!?
AAH!!

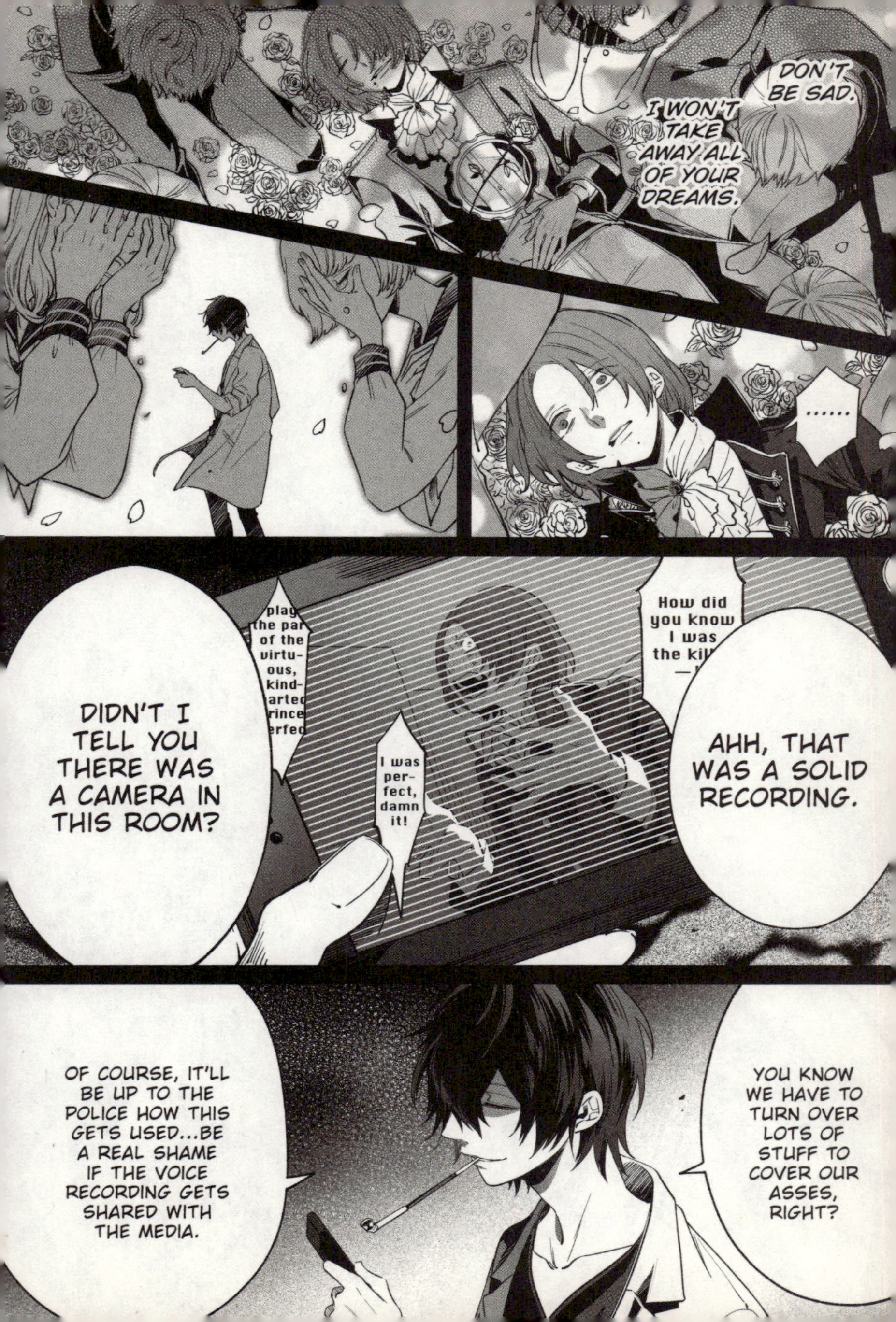
DON'T BE SAD.
I WON'T TAKE AWAY ALL OF YOUR DREAMS.
......
How did you know I was the kil —I
AHH, THAT WAS A SOLID RECORDING.
I was perfect, damn it!
pla the par of the virtu-ous, kind-arted rince erfec
DIDN'T I TELL YOU THERE WAS A CAMERA IN THIS ROOM?
YOU KNOW WE HAVE TO TURN OVER LOTS OF STUFF TO COVER OUR ASSES, RIGHT?
OF COURSE, IT'LL BE UP TO THE POLICE HOW THIS GETS USED...BE A REAL SHAME IF THE VOICE RECORDING GETS SHARED WITH THE MEDIA.

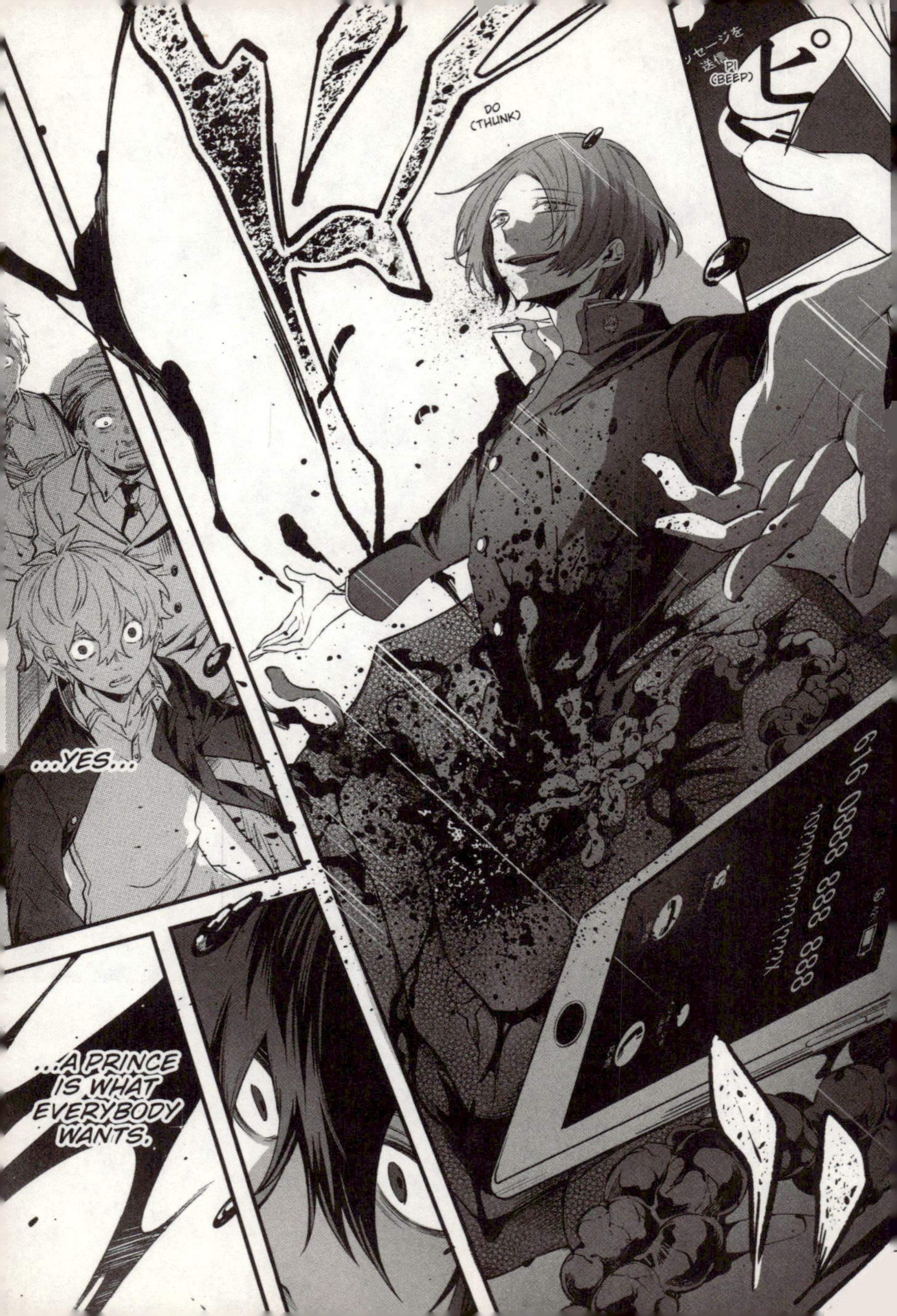
ッセージを
送信
PI
(BEEP)
DO
(THUNK)
...YES...
...A PRINCE IS WHAT EVERYBODY WANTS.

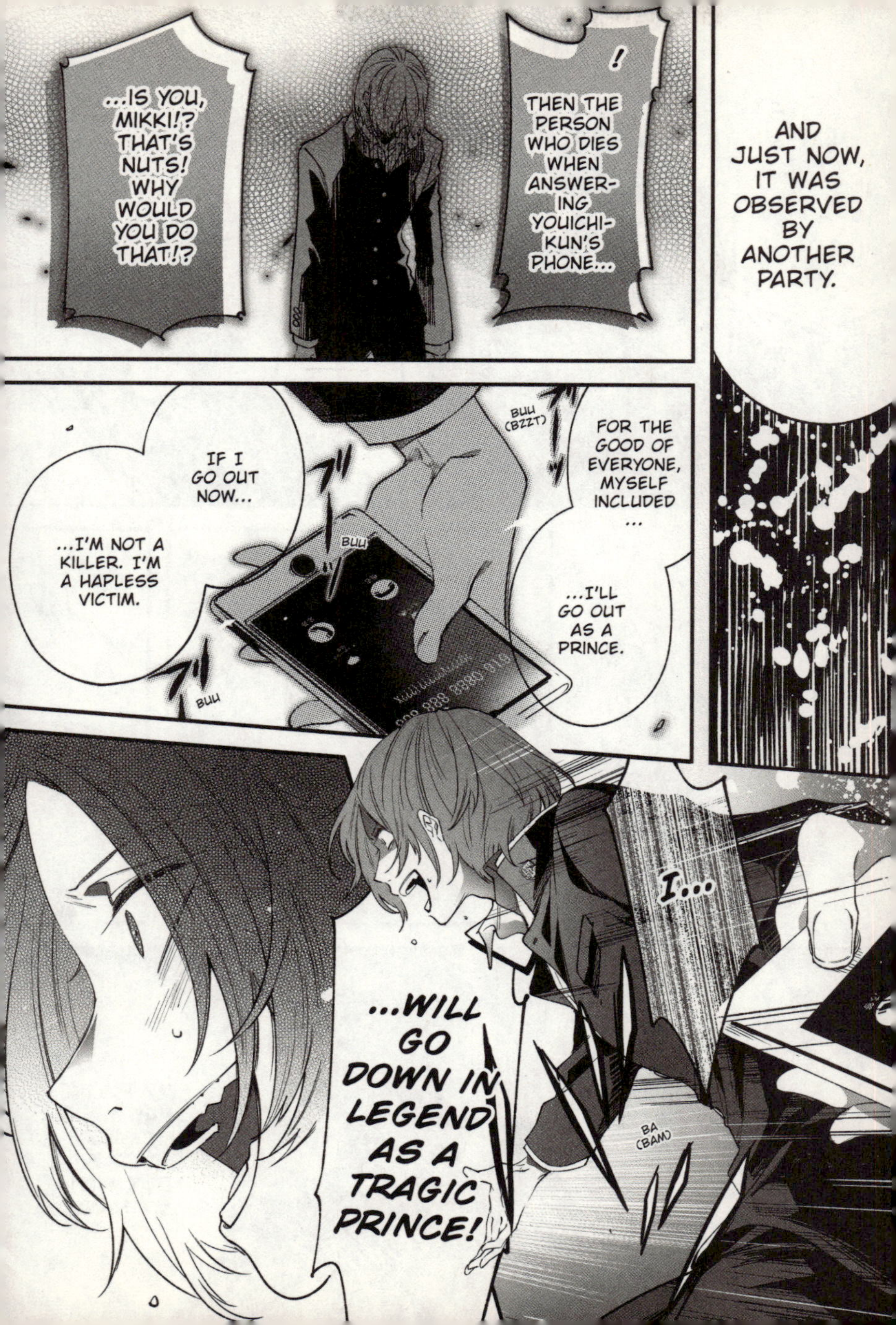
AND JUST NOW, IT WAS OBSERVED BY ANOTHER PARTY.
!
THEN THE PERSON WHO DIES WHEN ANSWERING YOUICHI-KUN'S PHONE...
...IS YOU, MIKKI!? THAT'S NUTS! WHY WOULD YOU DO THAT!?
BUU (BZZT)
FOR THE GOOD OF EVERYONE, MYSELF INCLUDED...
...I'LL GO OUT AS A PRINCE.
BUU
IF I GO OUT NOW...
...I'M NOT A KILLER. I'M A HAPLESS VICTIM.
BUU
I...
...WILL GO DOWN IN LEGEND AS A TRAGIC PRINCE!
BA (BAM)

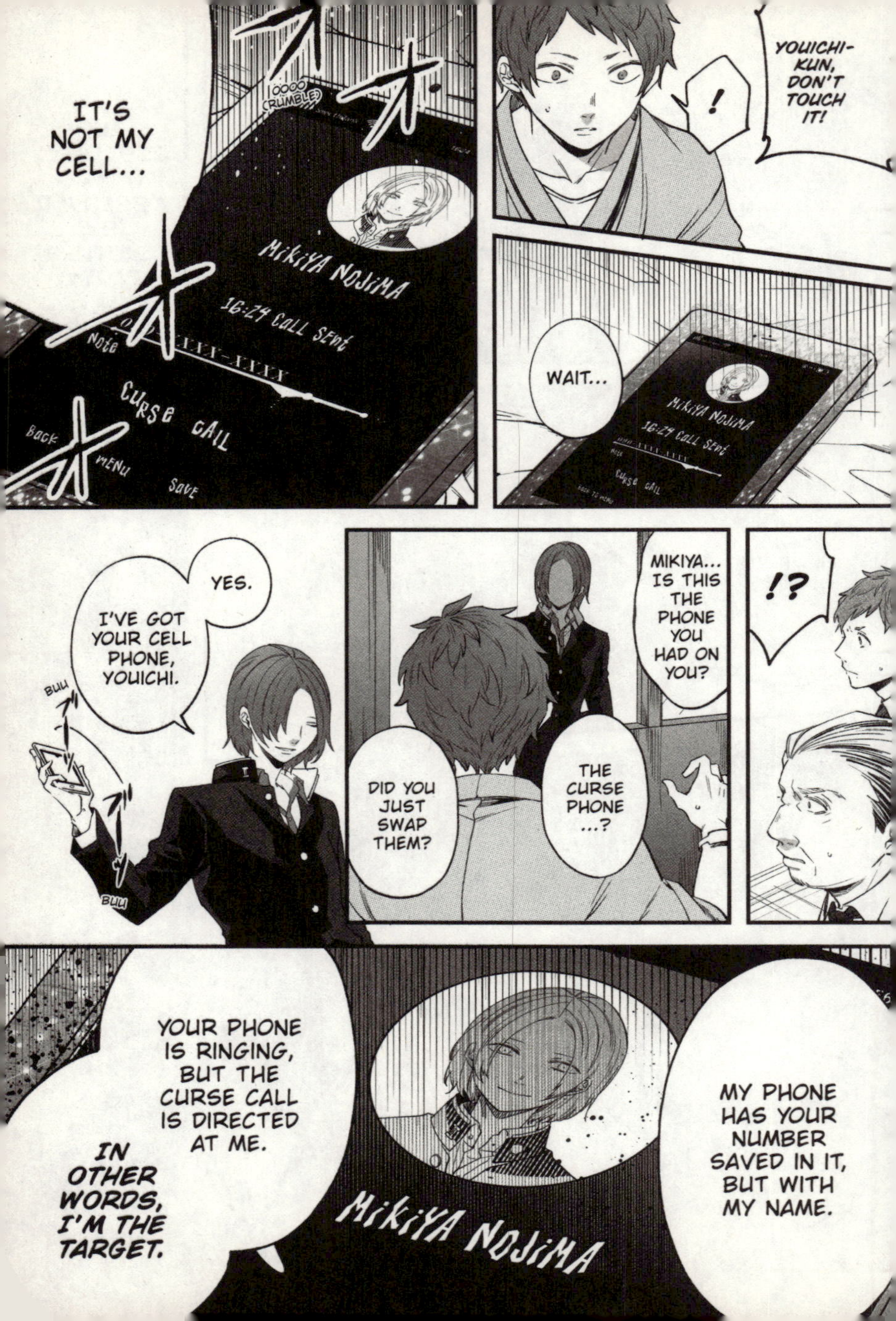
YOUICHI-KUN, DON'T TOUCH IT!
!
WAIT...
RUMBLE
IT'S NOT MY CELL...
MiKiYA NOJiMA
16:24 CALL SENT
Note
CURSE CALL
Back
MENU
SAVE
!?
MIKIYA... IS THIS THE PHONE YOU HAD ON YOU?
THE CURSE PHONE ...?
DID YOU JUST SWAP THEM?
YES.
I'VE GOT YOUR CELL PHONE, YOUICHI.
BUU
BUU
MY PHONE HAS YOUR NUMBER SAVED IN IT, BUT WITH MY NAME.
MiKiYA NOJiMA
YOUR PHONE IS RINGING, BUT THE CURSE CALL IS DIRECTED AT ME.
IN OTHER WORDS, I'M THE TARGET.

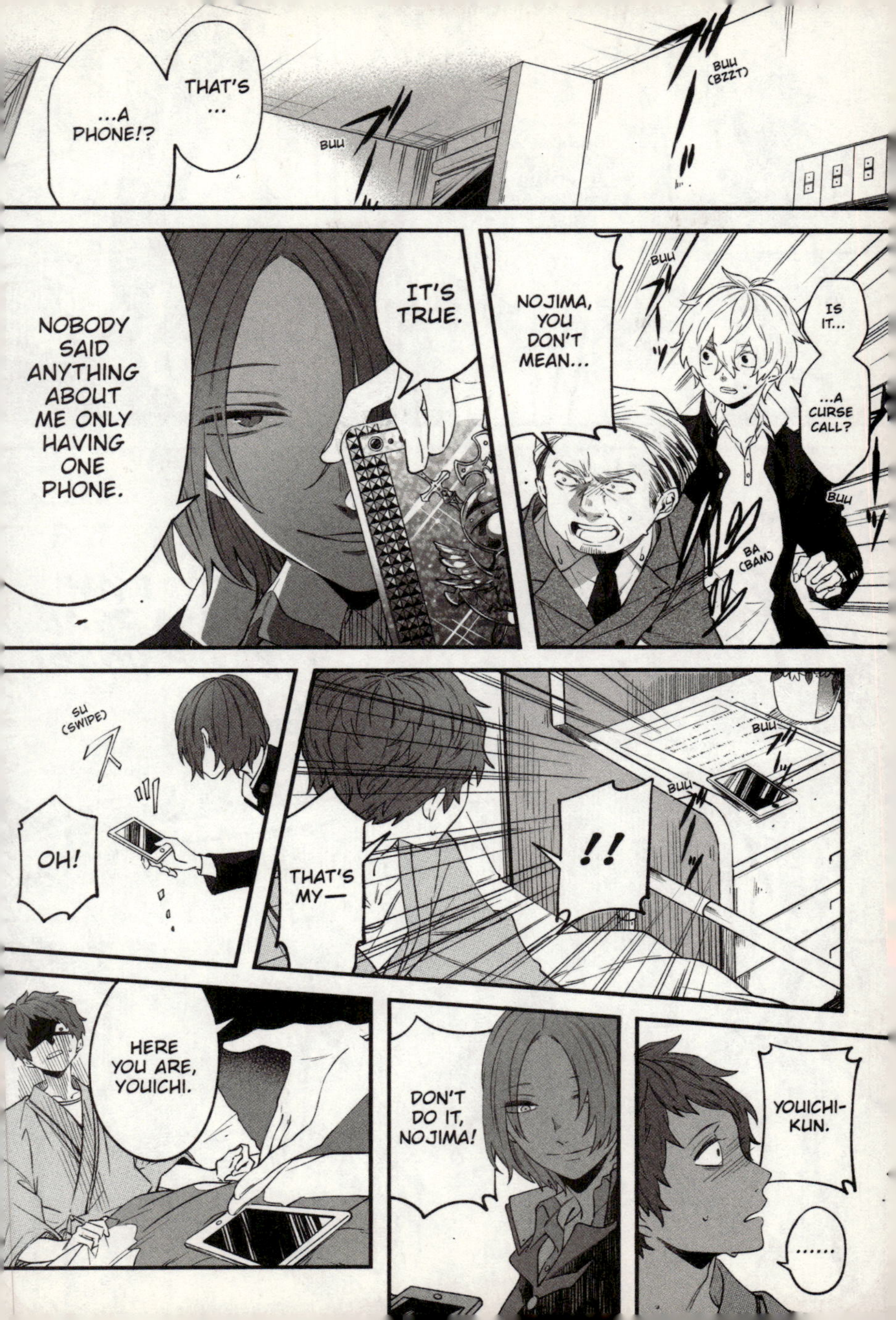
BUU (BZZT)
BUU
THAT'S ...
...A PHONE!?
IS IT...
...A CURSE CALL?
NOJIMA, YOU DON'T MEAN...
BUU
BUU
BA (BAM)
IT'S TRUE.
NOBODY SAID ANYTHING ABOUT ME ONLY HAVING ONE PHONE.
BUU
BUU
!!
THAT'S MY—
SU (SWIPE)
OH!
YOUICHI-KUN.
......
DON'T DO IT, NOJIMA!
HERE YOU ARE, YOUICHI.

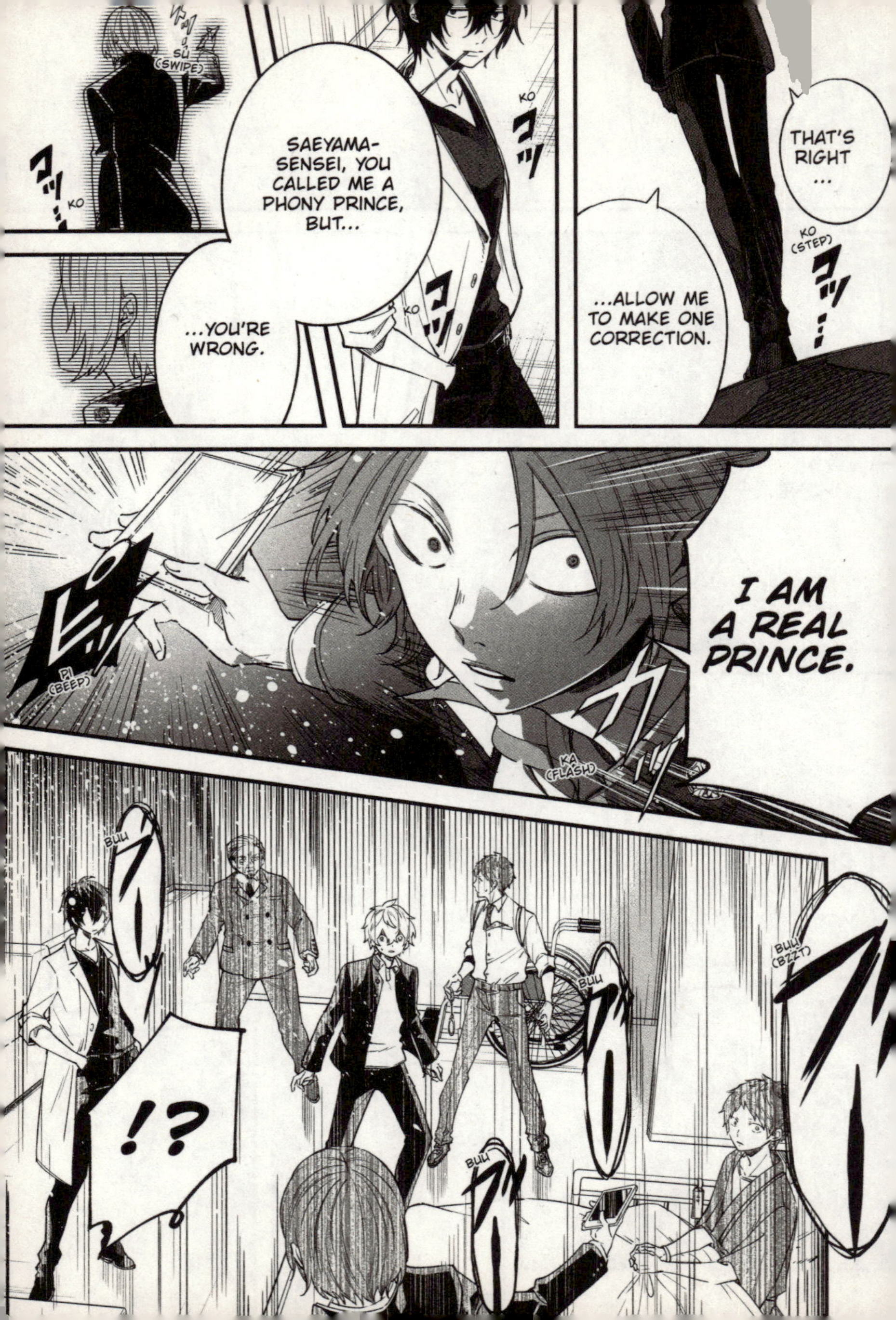
THAT'S RIGHT ...
KO (STEP)
...ALLOW ME TO MAKE ONE CORRECTION.
KO
SAEYAMA-SENSEI, YOU CALLED ME A PHONY PRINCE, BUT...
KO
...YOU'RE WRONG.
SU (SWIPE)
KO
I AM A REAL PRINCE.
KA (FLASH)
PI (BEEP)
BUU (BZZT)
BUU
BUU
!?
BUU

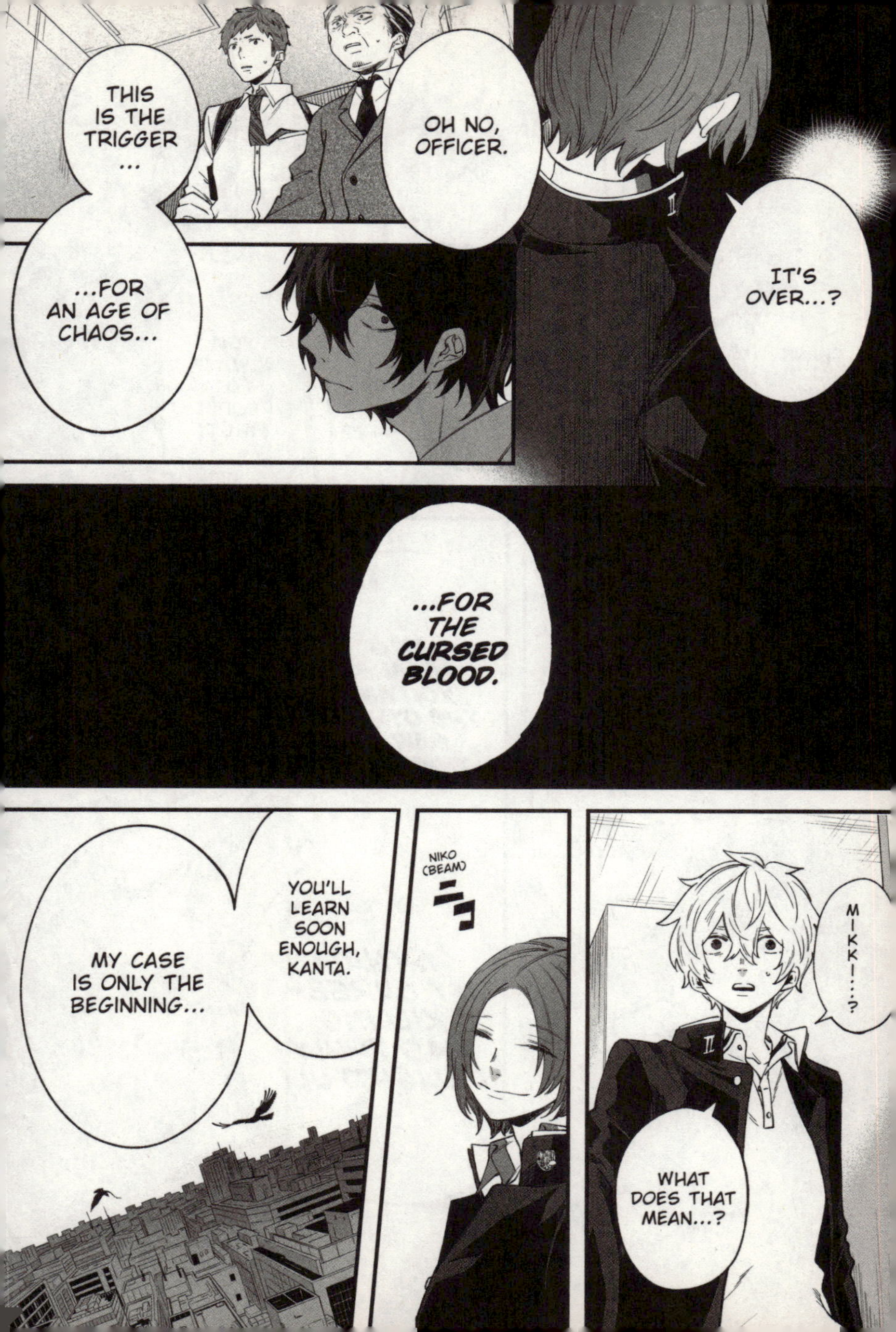
IT'S OVER...?
OH NO, OFFICER.
THIS IS THE TRIGGER ...
...FOR AN AGE OF CHAOS...
...FOR THE CURSED BLOOD.
MIKKI...?
WHAT DOES THAT MEAN...?
NIKO (BEAM)
YOU'LL LEARN SOON ENOUGH, KANTA.
MY CASE IS ONLY THE BEGINNING...

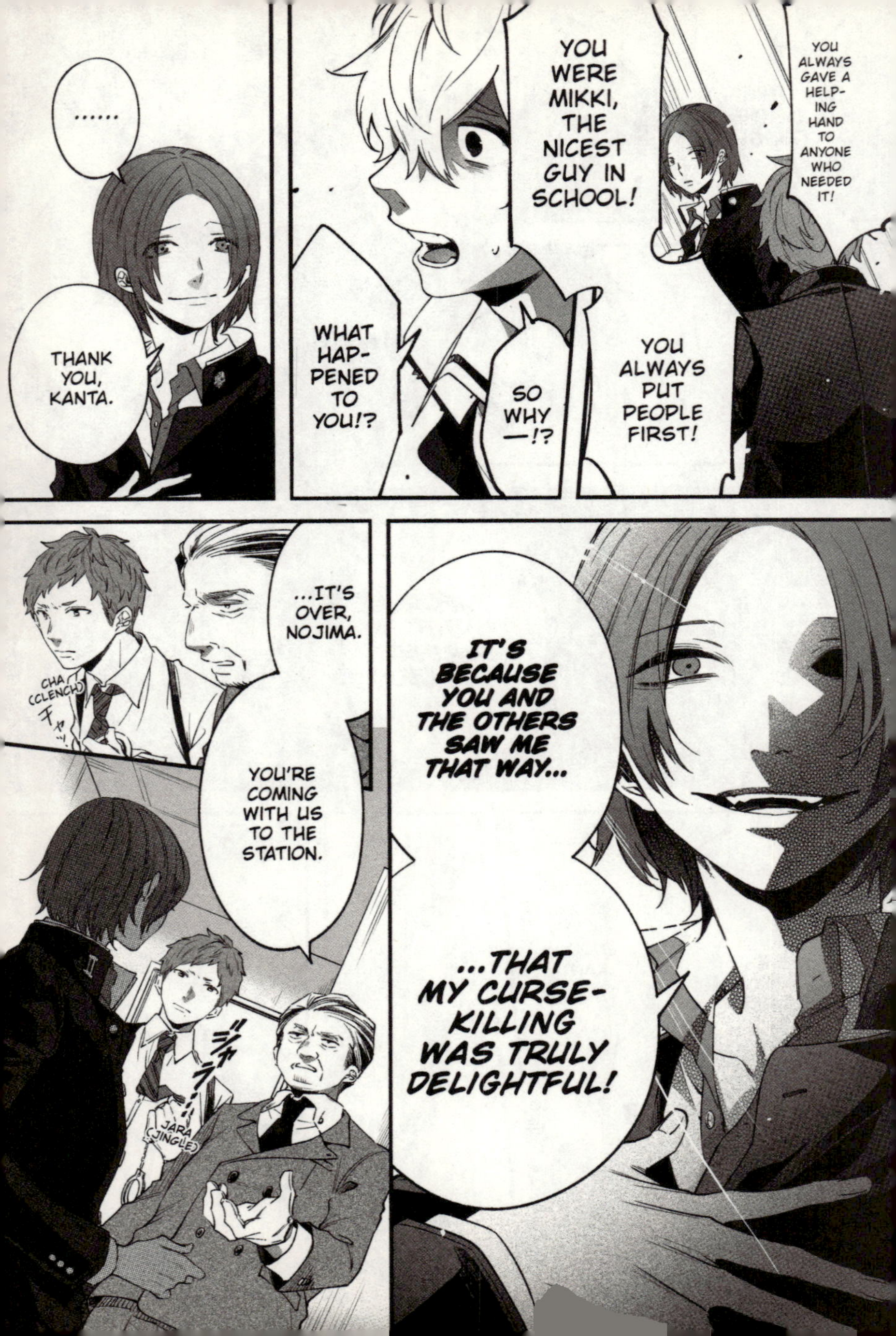
YOU ALWAYS GAVE A HELPING HAND TO ANYONE WHO NEEDED IT!
YOU ALWAYS PUT PEOPLE FIRST!
YOU WERE MIKKI, THE NICEST GUY IN SCHOOL!
SO WHY—!?
WHAT HAPPENED TO YOU!?
......
THANK YOU, KANTA.
IT'S BECAUSE YOU AND THE OTHERS SAW ME THAT WAY...
...THAT MY CURSE-KILLING WAS TRULY DELIGHTFUL!
...IT'S OVER, NOJIMA.
CHA (CLENCH)
YOU'RE COMING WITH US TO THE STATION.
JARA (JINGLE)

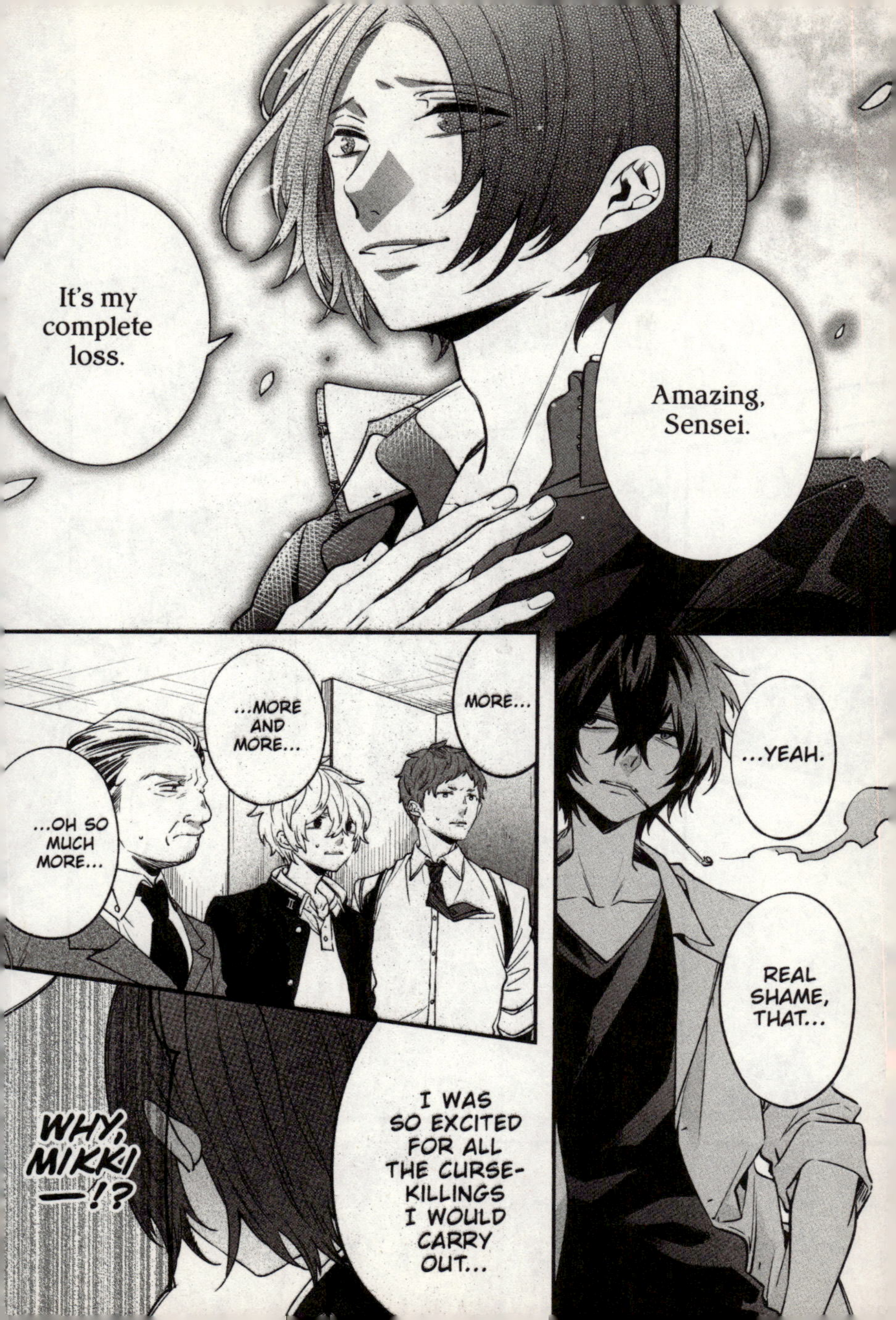
Amazing, Sensei.
It's my complete loss.
...YEAH.
REAL SHAME, THAT...
MORE...
...MORE AND MORE...
...OH SO MUCH MORE...
I WAS SO EXCITED FOR ALL THE CURSE-KILLINGS I WOULD CARRY OUT...
WHY, MIKKI—!?

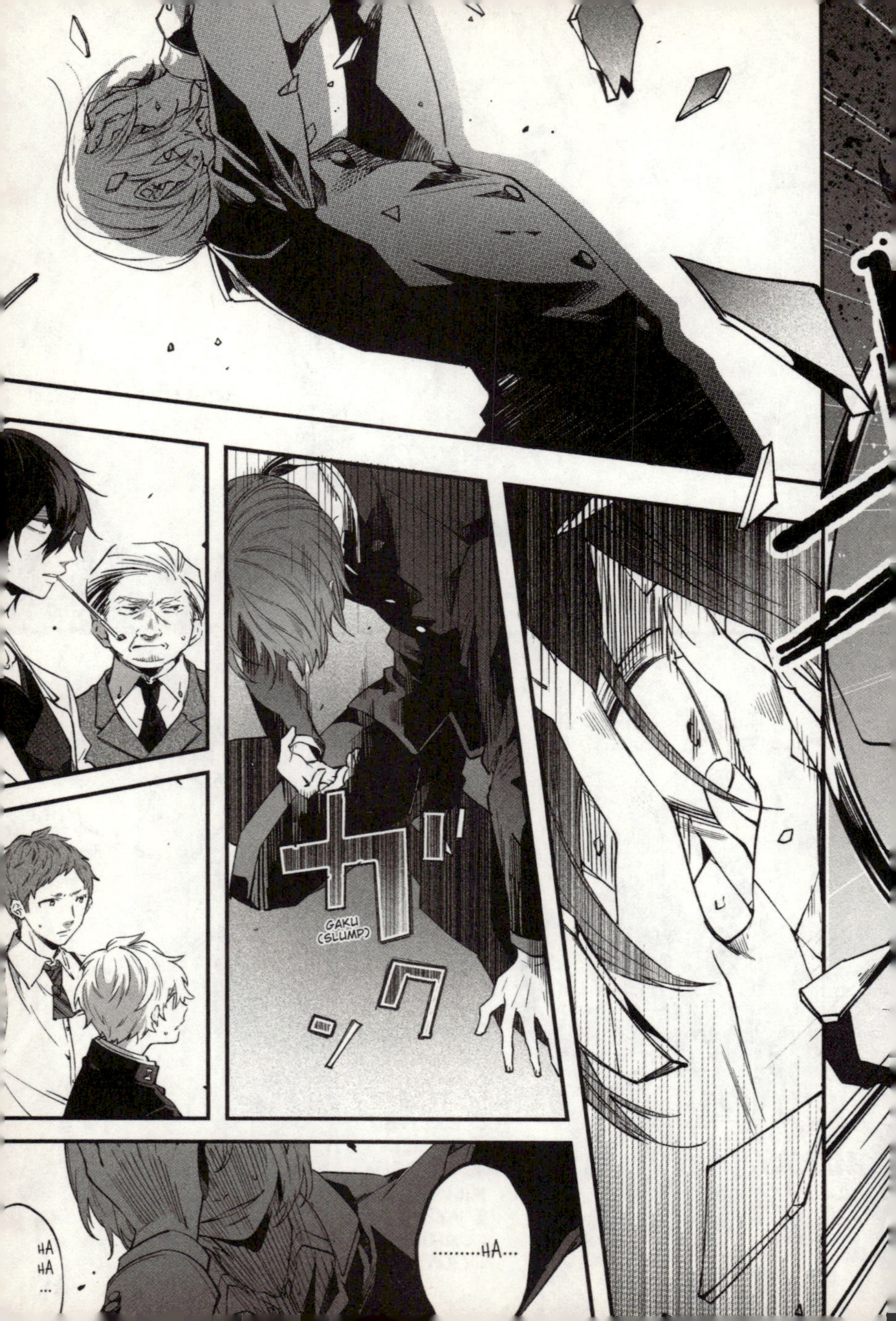
GAKU (SLUMP)
.........HA...
HA HA ...

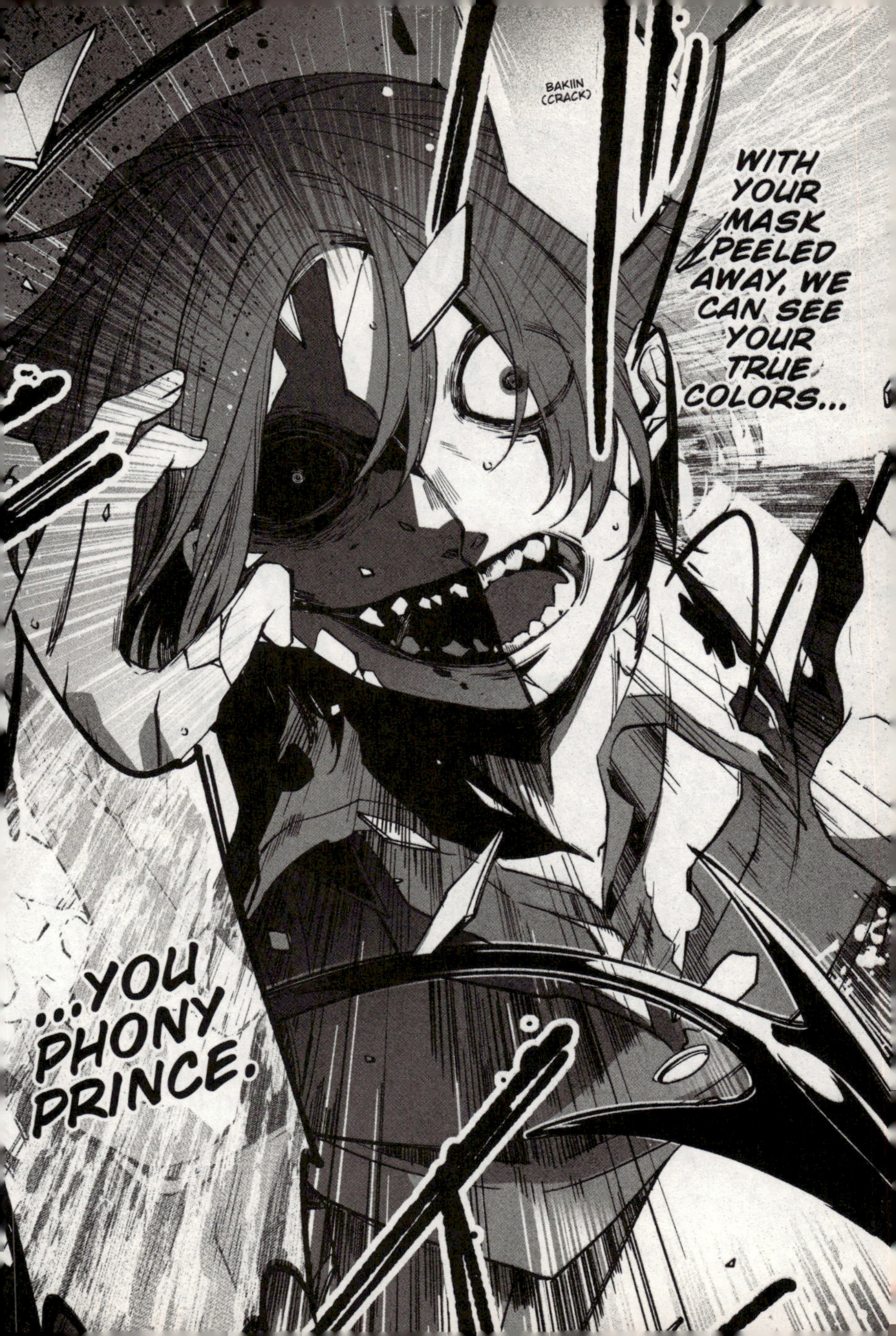
BAKIIN (CRACK)
WITH YOUR MASK PEELED AWAY, WE CAN SEE YOUR TRUE COLORS...
...YOU PHONY PRINCE.

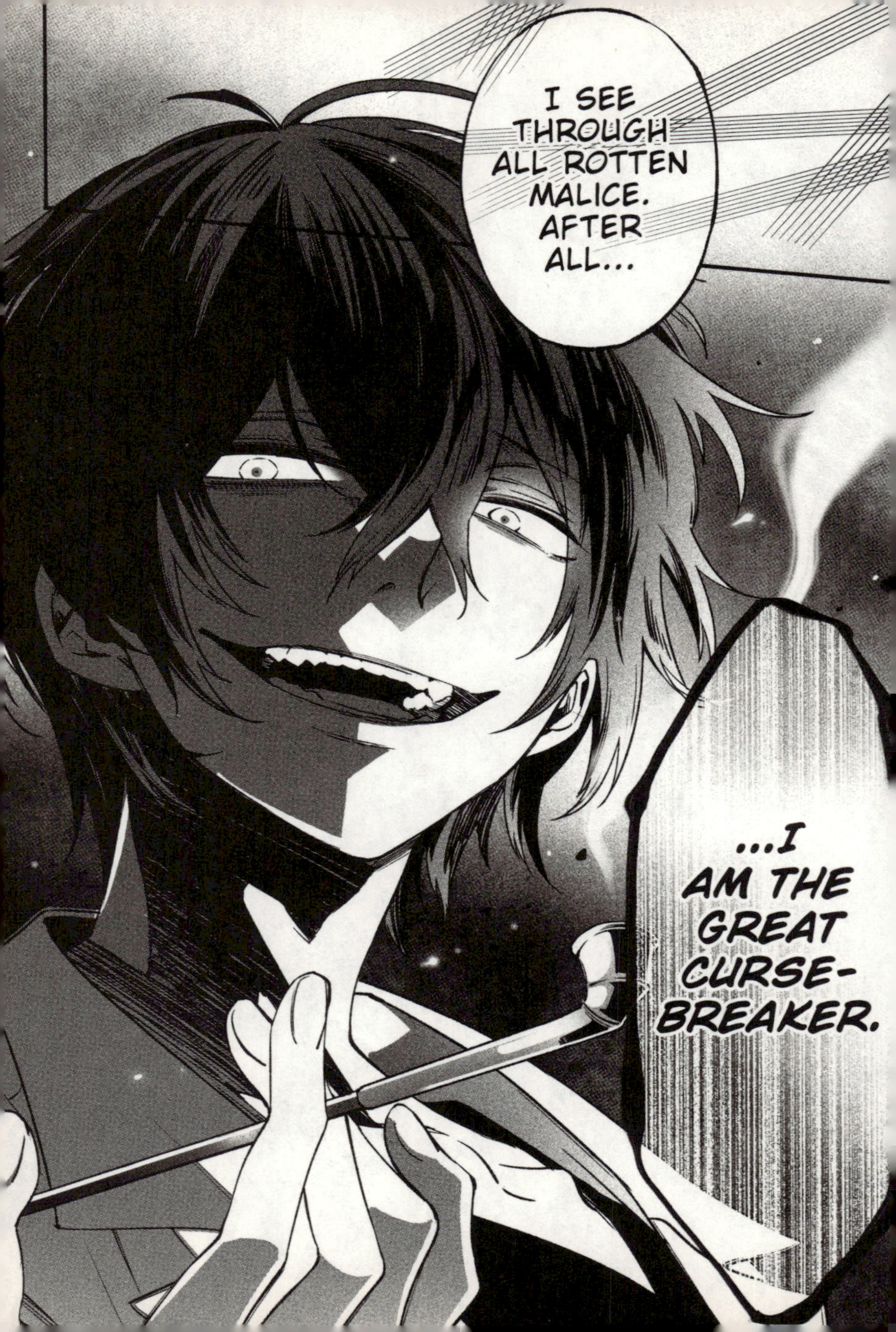
I SEE THROUGH ALL ROTTEN MALICE. AFTER ALL...
...I AM THE GREAT CURSE-BREAKER.

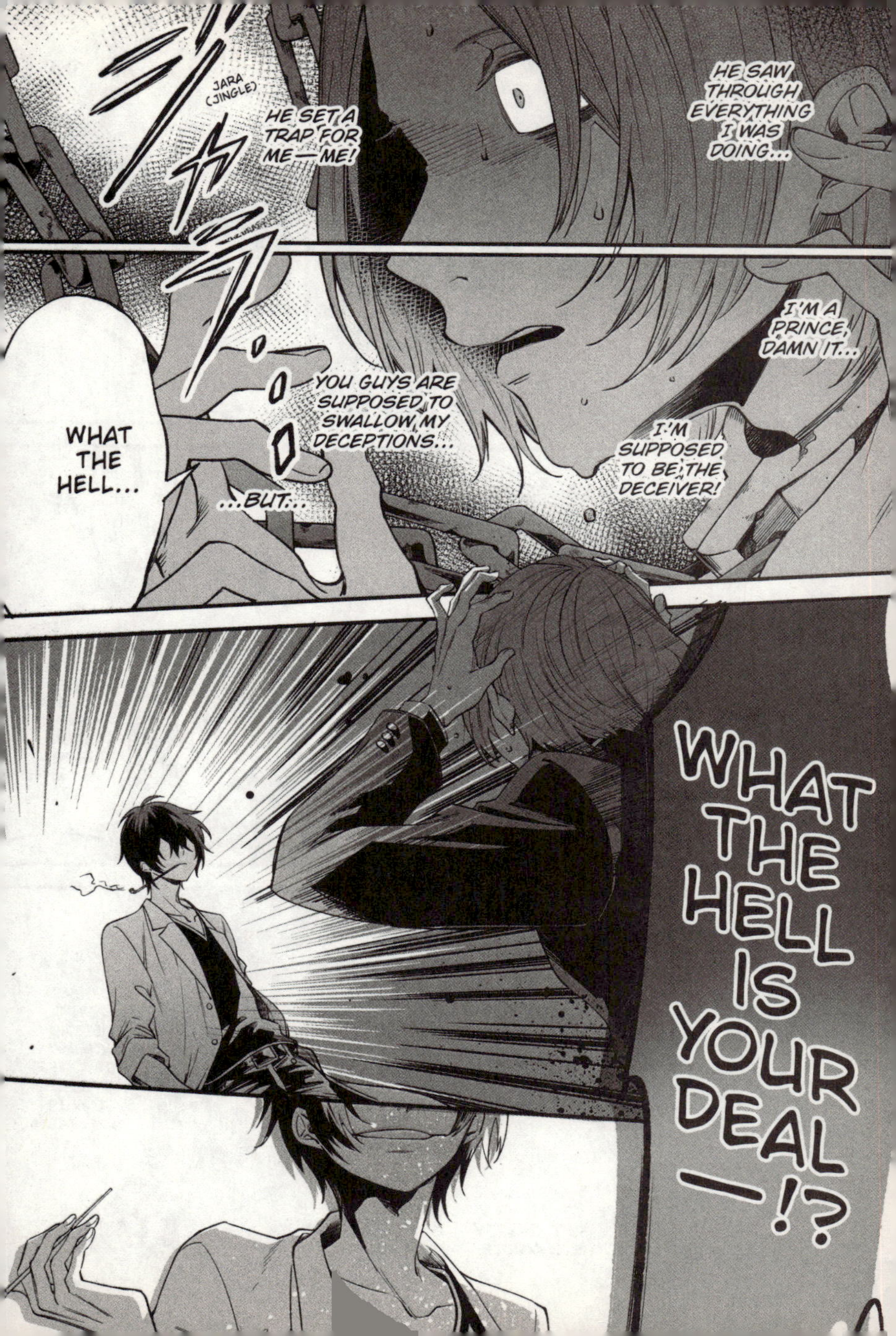
HE SAW THROUGH EVERYTHING I WAS DOING...
HE SET A TRAP FOR ME—ME!
JARA (JINGLE)
I'M A PRINCE, DAMN IT...
I'M SUPPOSED TO BE THE DECEIVER!
YOU GUYS ARE SUPPOSED TO SWALLOW MY DECEPTIONS...
...BUT...
WHAT THE HELL...
WHAT THE HELL IS YOUR DEAL—!?

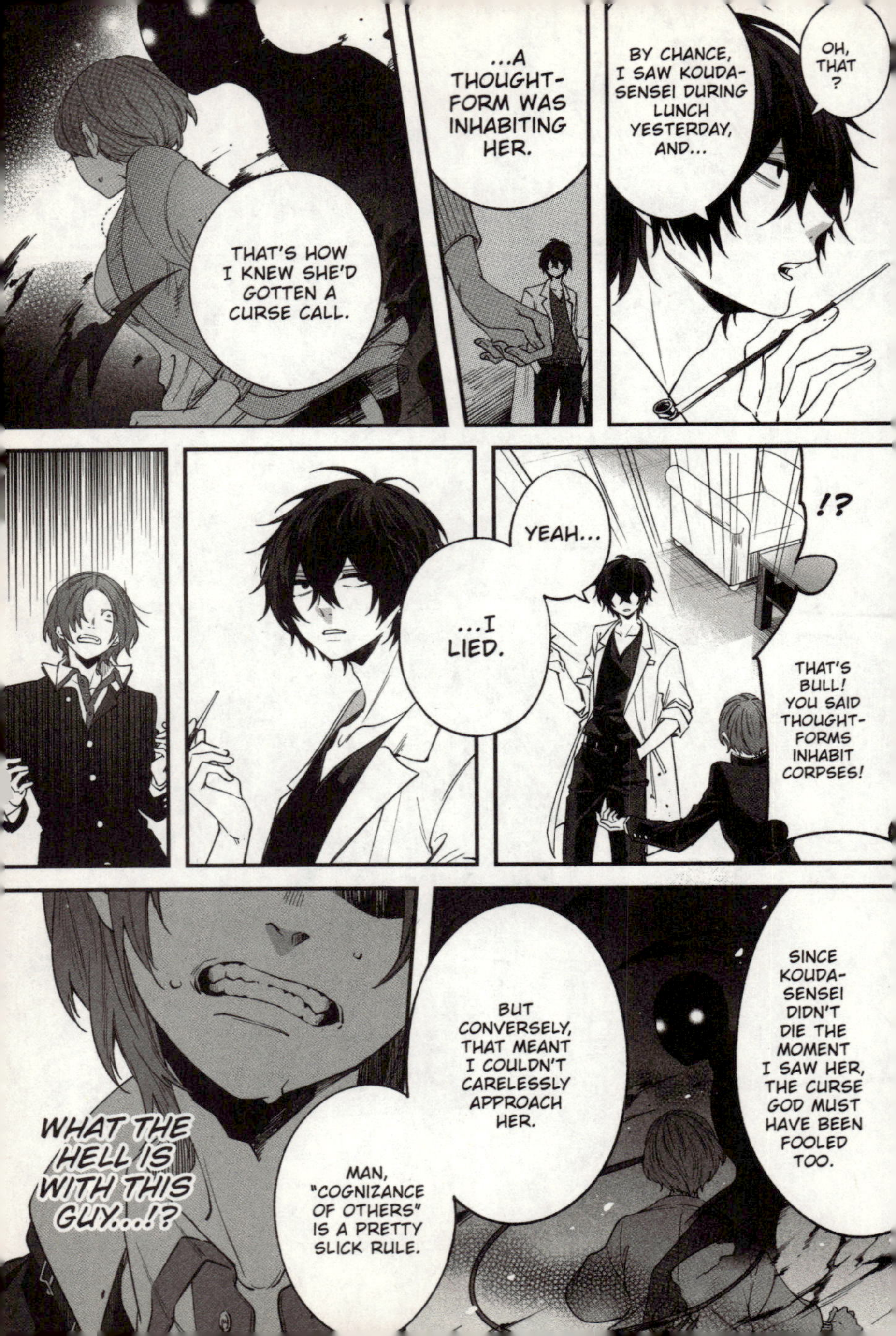
OH, THAT?
BY CHANCE, I SAW KOUDA-SENSEI DURING LUNCH YESTERDAY, AND...
...A THOUGHT-FORM WAS INHABITING HER.
THAT'S HOW I KNEW SHE'D GOTTEN A CURSE CALL.
!?
THAT'S BULL! YOU SAID THOUGHT-FORMS INHABIT CORPSES!
YEAH...
...I LIED.
SINCE KOUDA-SENSEI DIDN'T DIE THE MOMENT I SAW HER, THE CURSE GOD MUST HAVE BEEN FOOLED TOO.
BUT CONVERSELY, THAT MEANT I COULDN'T CARELESSLY APPROACH HER.
MAN, "COGNIZANCE OF OTHERS" IS A PRETTY SLICK RULE.
WHAT THE HELL IS WITH THIS GUY...!?

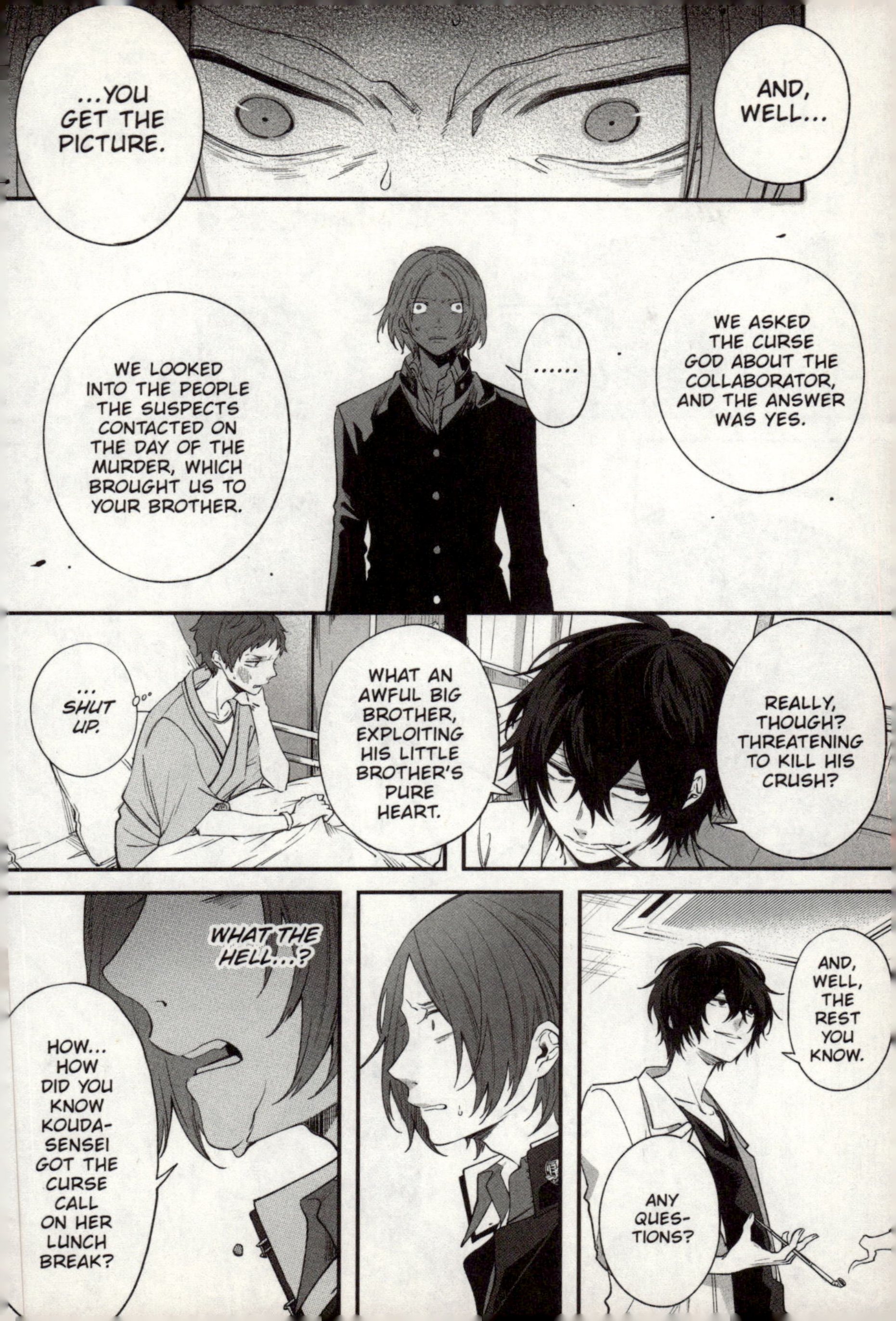
AND, WELL...
...YOU GET THE PICTURE.
WE ASKED THE CURSE GOD ABOUT THE COLLABORATOR, AND THE ANSWER WAS YES.
......
WE LOOKED INTO THE PEOPLE THE SUSPECTS CONTACTED ON THE DAY OF THE MURDER, WHICH BROUGHT US TO YOUR BROTHER.
REALLY, THOUGH? THREATENING TO KILL HIS CRUSH?
WHAT AN AWFUL BIG BROTHER, EXPLOITING HIS LITTLE BROTHER'S PURE HEART.
... SHUT UP.
AND, WELL, THE REST YOU KNOW.
ANY QUES-TIONS?
WHAT THE HELL...?
HOW... HOW DID YOU KNOW KOUDA-SENSEI GOT THE CURSE CALL ON HER LUNCH BREAK?

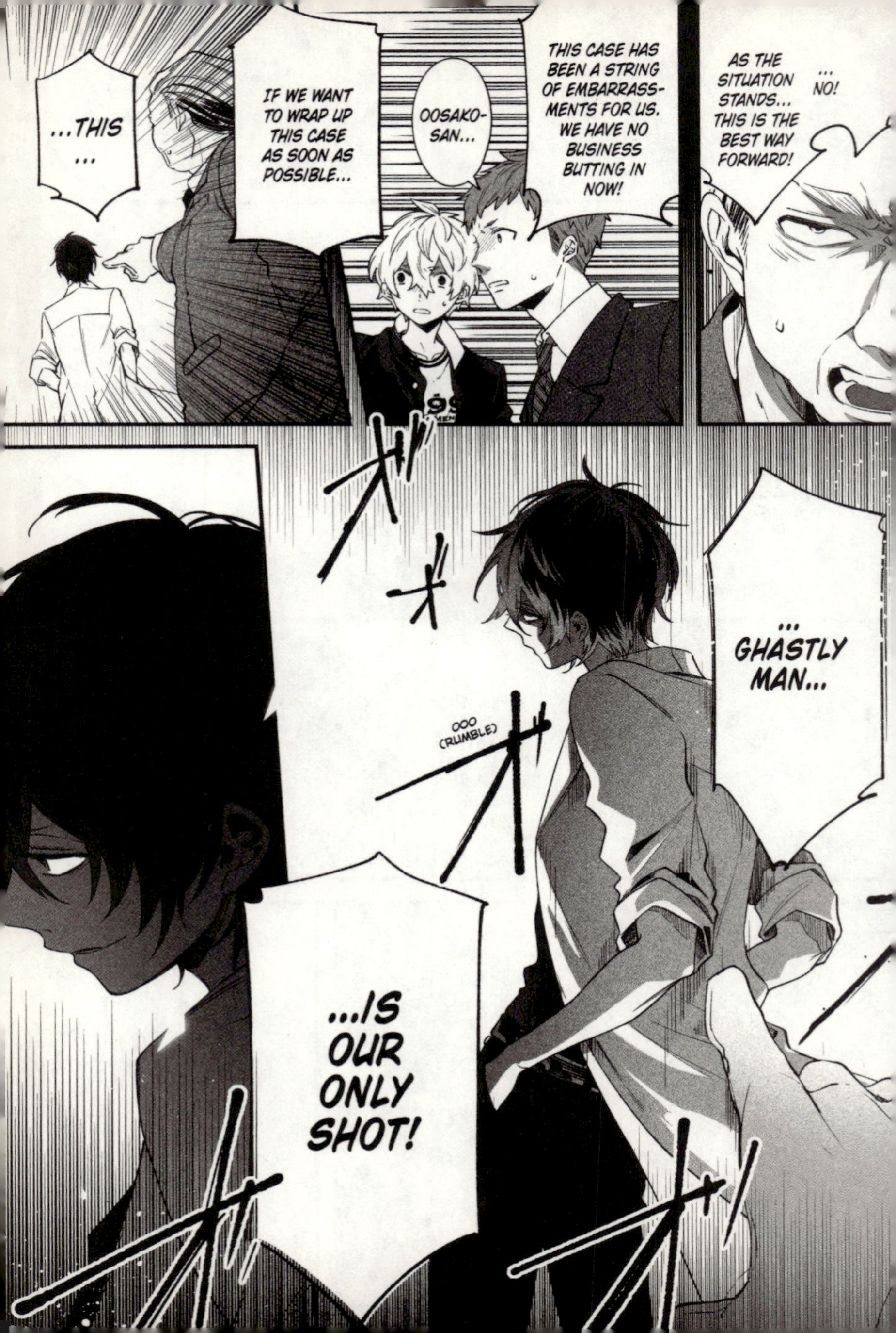
... NO!
AS THE SITUATION STANDS... THIS IS THE BEST WAY FORWARD!
THIS CASE HAS BEEN A STRING OF EMBARRASS-MENTS FOR US. WE HAVE NO BUSINESS BUTTING IN NOW!
OOSAKO-SAN...
IF WE WANT TO WRAP UP THIS CASE AS SOON AS POSSIBLE...
...THIS ...
... GHASTLY MAN...
OOO (RUMBLE)
...IS OUR ONLY SHOT!

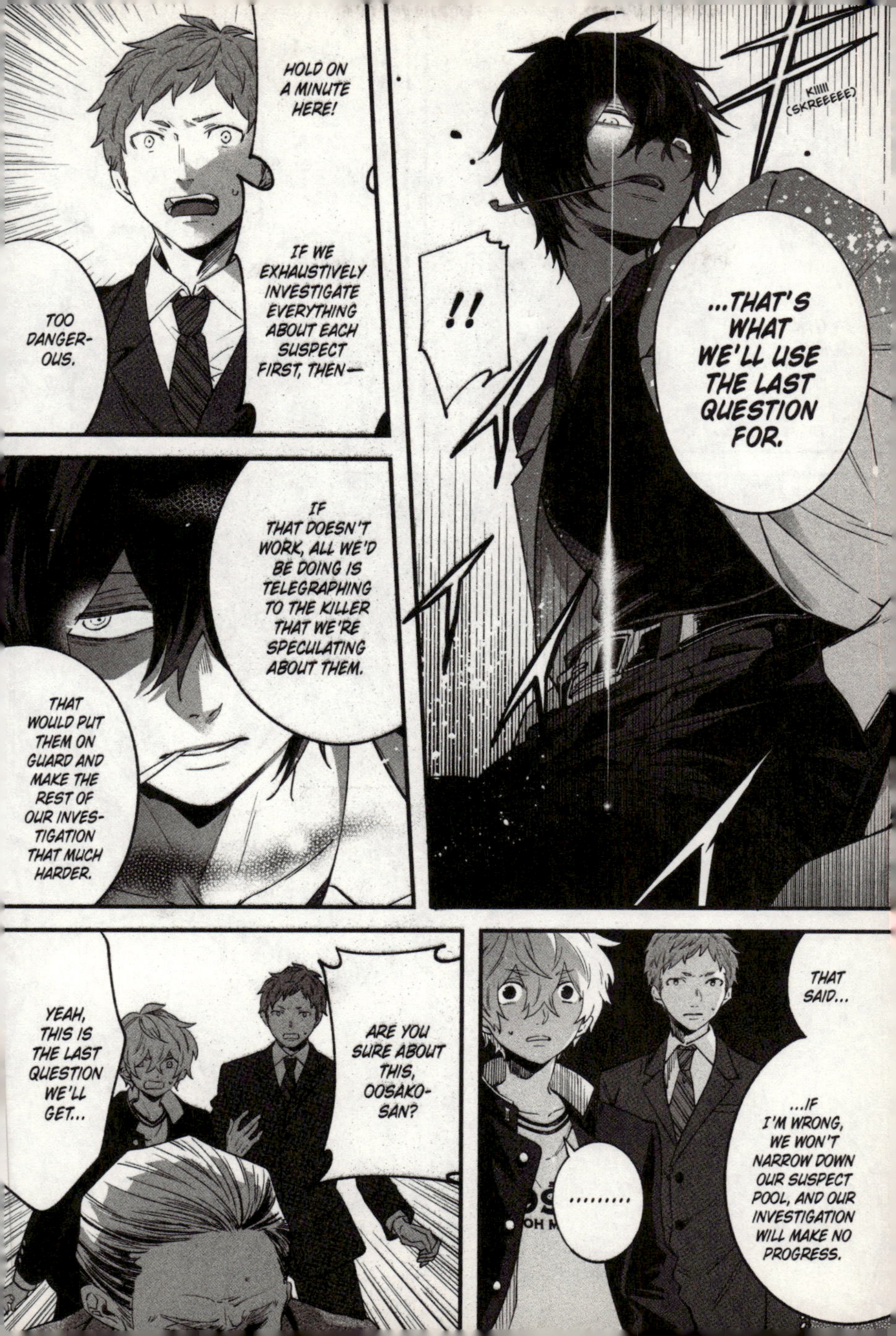
KIIIII (SKREEEEEE)
!!
...THAT'S WHAT WE'LL USE THE LAST QUESTION FOR.
HOLD ON A MINUTE HERE!
IF WE EXHAUSTIVELY INVESTIGATE EVERYTHING ABOUT EACH SUSPECT FIRST, THEN—
TOO DANGEROUS.
IF THAT DOESN'T WORK, ALL WE'D BE DOING IS TELEGRAPHING TO THE KILLER THAT WE'RE SPECULATING ABOUT THEM.
THAT WOULD PUT THEM ON GUARD AND MAKE THE REST OF OUR INVESTIGATION THAT MUCH HARDER.
THAT SAID...
...IF I'M WRONG, WE WON'T NARROW DOWN OUR SUSPECT POOL, AND OUR INVESTIGATION WILL MAKE NO PROGRESS.
....
ARE YOU SURE ABOUT THIS, OOSAKO-SAN?
YEAH, THIS IS THE LAST QUESTION WE'LL GET...

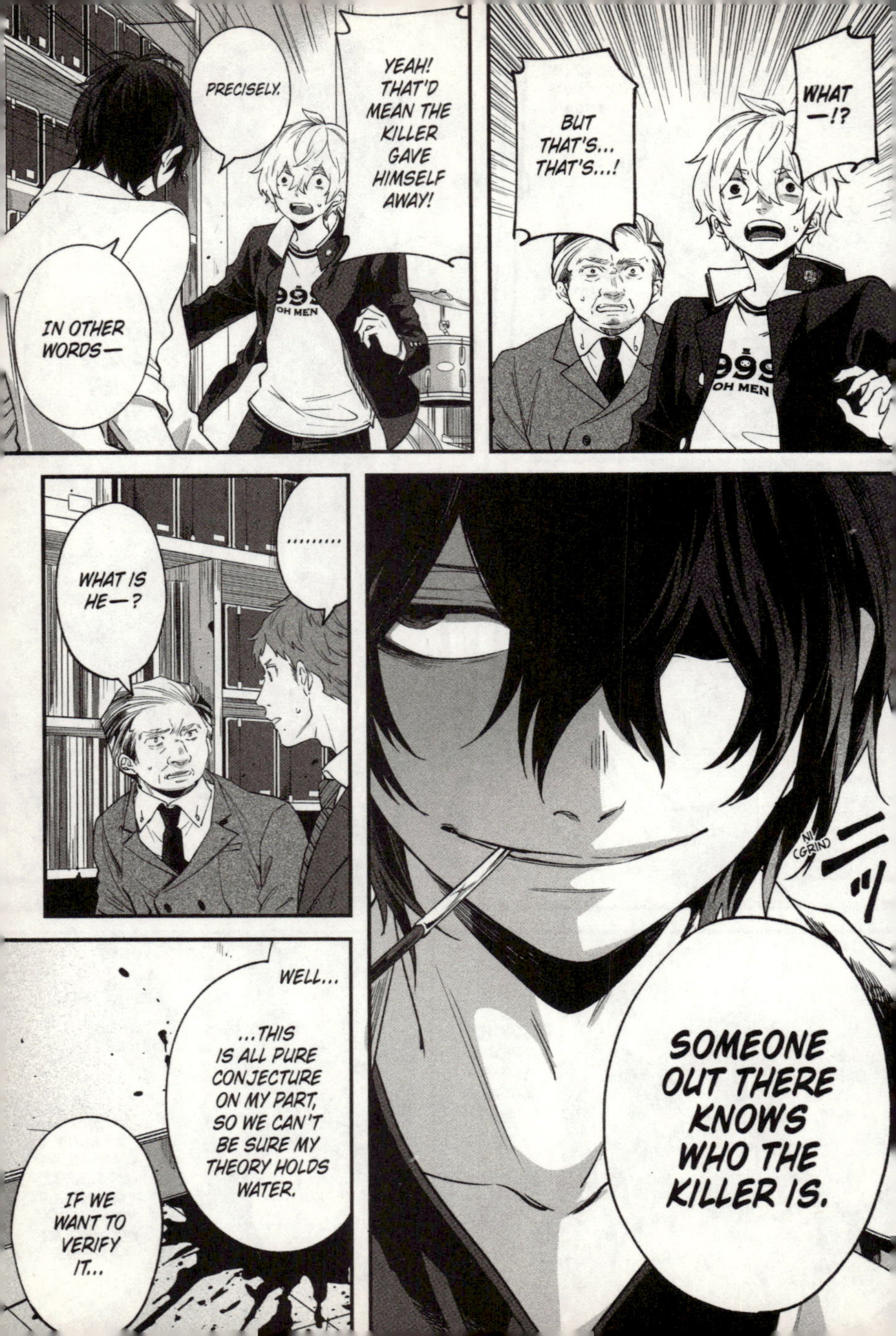
WHAT—!?
BUT THAT'S... THAT'S...!
YEAH! THAT'D MEAN THE KILLER GAVE HIMSELF AWAY!
PRECISELY.
IN OTHER WORDS—
ニッ
NI (GRIN)
SOMEONE OUT THERE KNOWS WHO THE KILLER IS.
....
WHAT IS HE—?
WELL...
...THIS IS ALL PURE CONJECTURE ON MY PART, SO WE CAN'T BE SURE MY THEORY HOLDS WATER.
IF WE WANT TO VERIFY IT...

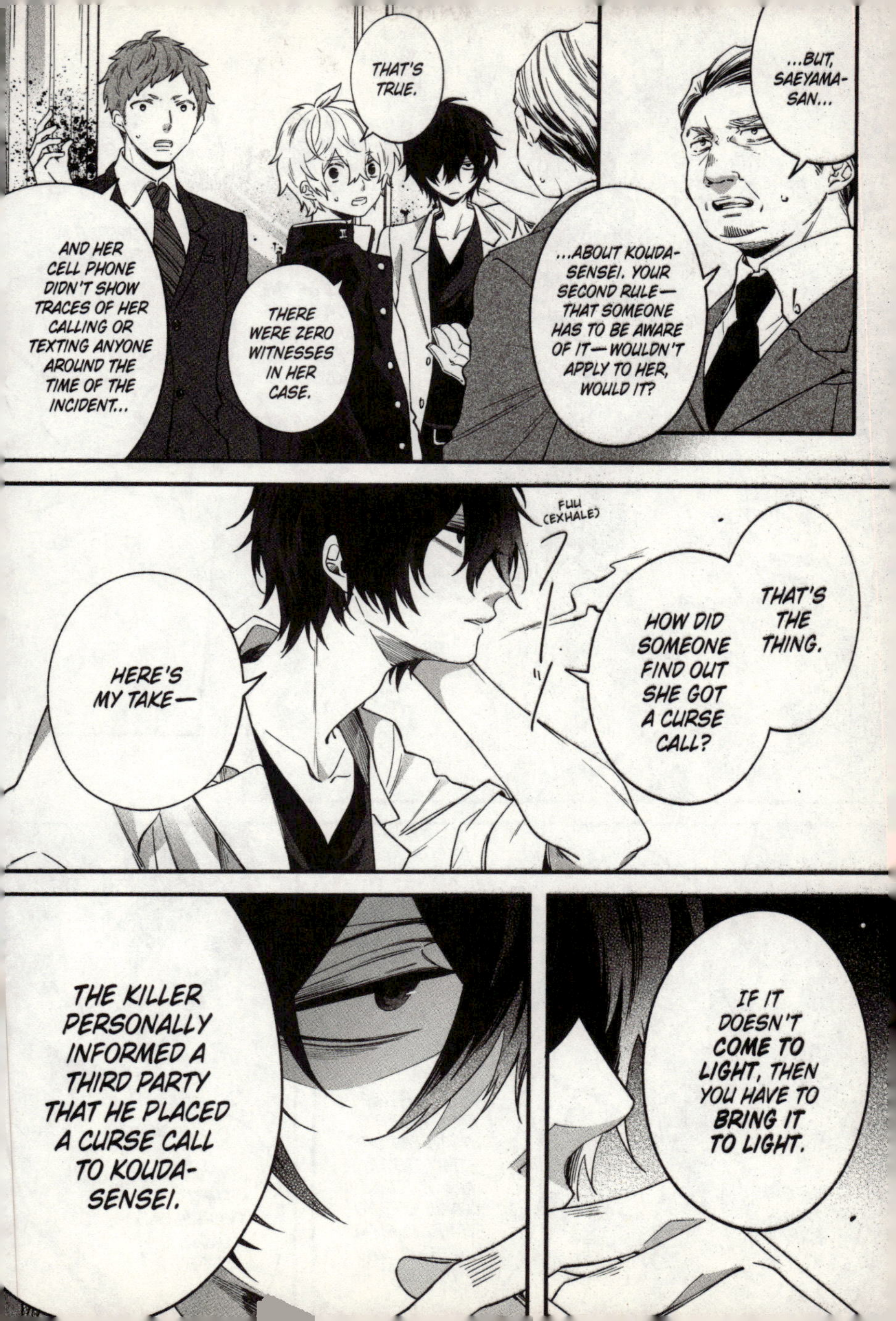
...BUT, SAEYAMA-SAN...
...ABOUT KOUDA-SENSEI. YOUR SECOND RULE—THAT SOMEONE HAS TO BE AWARE OF IT—WOULDN'T APPLY TO HER, WOULD IT?
THAT'S TRUE.
THERE WERE ZERO WITNESSES IN HER CASE.
AND HER CELL PHONE DIDN'T SHOW TRACES OF HER CALLING OR TEXTING ANYONE AROUND THE TIME OF THE INCIDENT...
FUU (EXHALE)
THAT'S THE THING.
HOW DID SOMEONE FIND OUT SHE GOT A CURSE CALL?
HERE'S MY TAKE—
IF IT DOESN'T COME TO LIGHT, THEN YOU HAVE TO BRING IT TO LIGHT.
THE KILLER PERSONALLY INFORMED A THIRD PARTY THAT HE PLACED A CURSE CALL TO KOUDA-SENSEI.

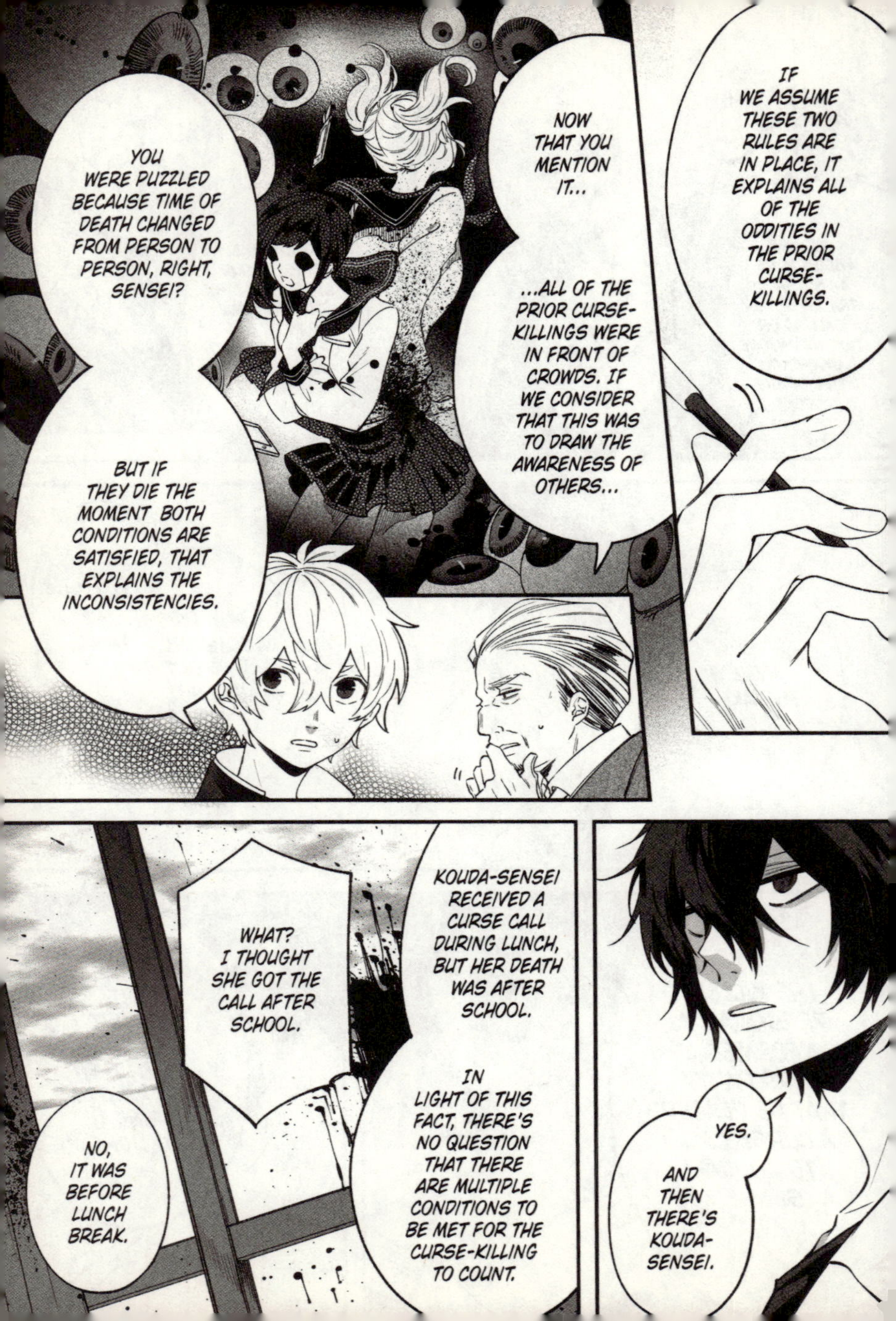
IF WE ASSUME THESE TWO RULES ARE IN PLACE, IT EXPLAINS ALL OF THE ODDITIES IN THE PRIOR CURSE-KILLINGS.
NOW THAT YOU MENTION IT...
...ALL OF THE PRIOR CURSE-KILLINGS WERE IN FRONT OF CROWDS. IF WE CONSIDER THAT THIS WAS TO DRAW THE AWARENESS OF OTHERS...
YOU WERE PUZZLED BECAUSE TIME OF DEATH CHANGED FROM PERSON TO PERSON, RIGHT, SENSEI?
BUT IF THEY DIE THE MOMENT BOTH CONDITIONS ARE SATISFIED, THAT EXPLAINS THE INCONSISTENCIES.
YES.
AND THEN THERE'S KOUDA-SENSEI.
KOUDA-SENSEI RECEIVED A CURSE CALL DURING LUNCH, BUT HER DEATH WAS AFTER SCHOOL.
WHAT? I THOUGHT SHE GOT THE CALL AFTER SCHOOL.
IN LIGHT OF THIS FACT, THERE'S NO QUESTION THAT THERE ARE MULTIPLE CONDITIONS TO BE MET FOR THE CURSE-KILLING TO COUNT.
NO, IT WAS BEFORE LUNCH BREAK.

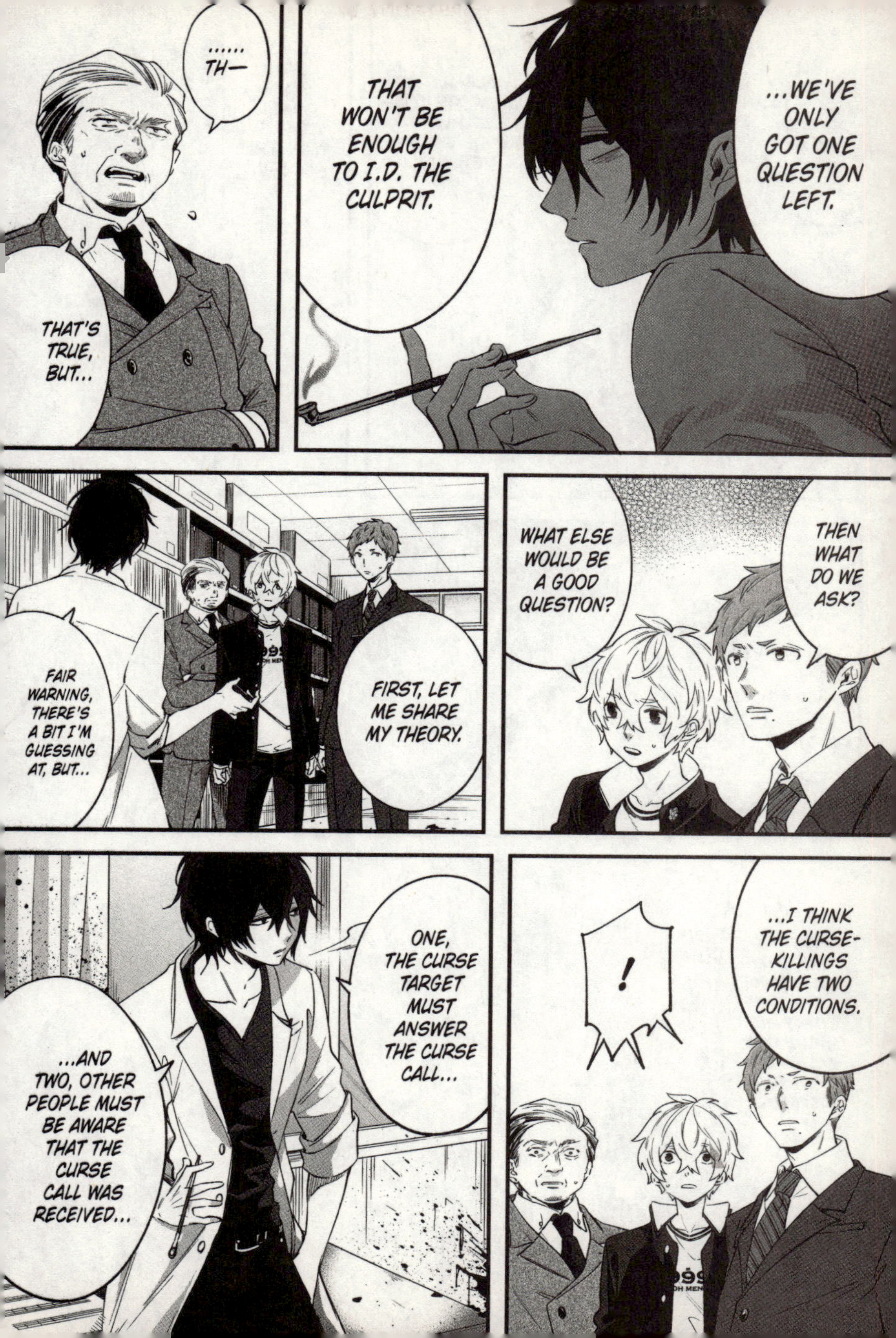
...WE'VE ONLY GOT ONE QUESTION LEFT.
THAT WON'T BE ENOUGH TO I.D. THE CULPRIT.
......TH—
THAT'S TRUE, BUT...
THEN WHAT DO WE ASK?
WHAT ELSE WOULD BE A GOOD QUESTION?
FIRST, LET ME SHARE MY THEORY.
FAIR WARNING, THERE'S A BIT I'M GUESSING AT, BUT...
...I THINK THE CURSE-KILLINGS HAVE TWO CONDITIONS.
!
ONE, THE CURSE TARGET MUST ANSWER THE CURSE CALL...
...AND TWO, OTHER PEOPLE MUST BE AWARE THAT THE CURSE CALL WAS RECEIVED...

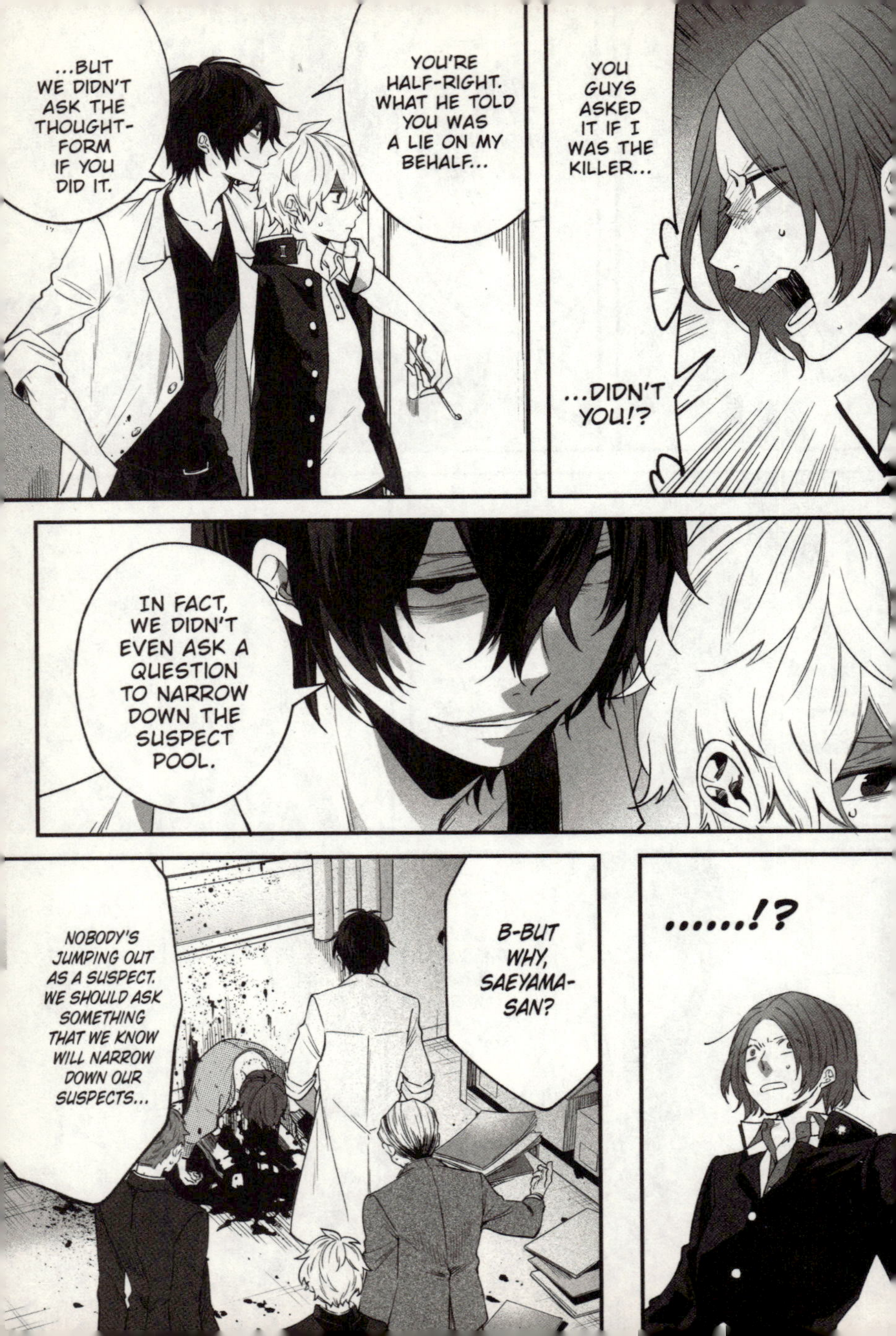
YOU GUYS ASKED IT IF I WAS THE KILLER...
...DIDN'T YOU!?
YOU'RE HALF-RIGHT. WHAT HE TOLD YOU WAS A LIE ON MY BEHALF...
...BUT WE DIDN'T ASK THE THOUGHT-FORM IF YOU DID IT.
IN FACT, WE DIDN'T EVEN ASK A QUESTION TO NARROW DOWN THE SUSPECT POOL.
......!?
B-BUT WHY, SAEYAMA-SAN?
NOBODY'S JUMPING OUT AS A SUSPECT. WE SHOULD ASK SOMETHING THAT WE KNOW WILL NARROW DOWN OUR SUSPECTS...

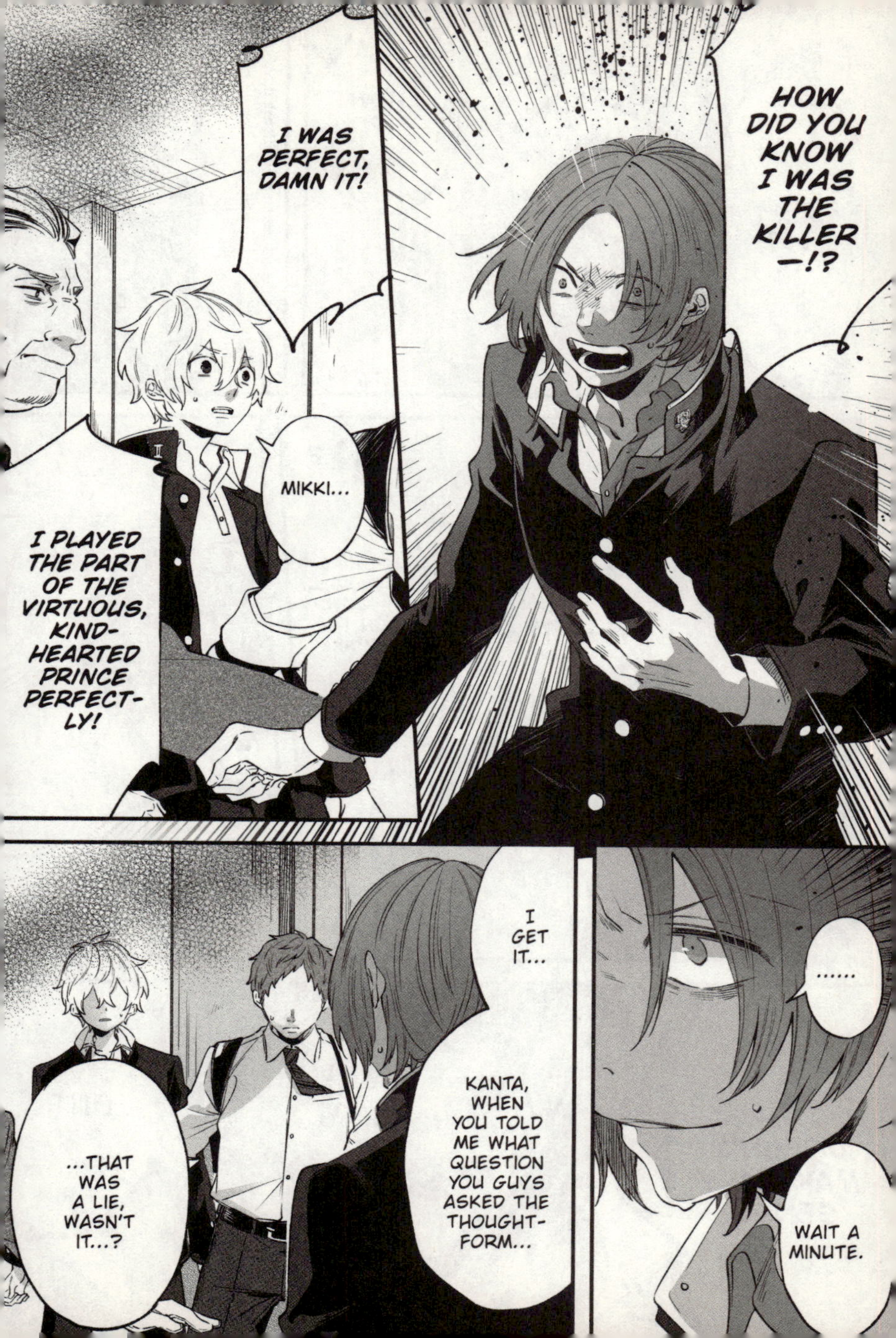
HOW DID YOU KNOW I WAS THE KILLER—!?
I WAS PERFECT, DAMN IT!
MIKKI...
I PLAYED THE PART OF THE VIRTUOUS, KIND-HEARTED PRINCE PERFECTLY!
......
WAIT A MINUTE.
I GET IT...
KANTA, WHEN YOU TOLD ME WHAT QUESTION YOU GUYS ASKED THE THOUGHT-FORM...
...THAT WAS A LIE, WASN'T IT...?

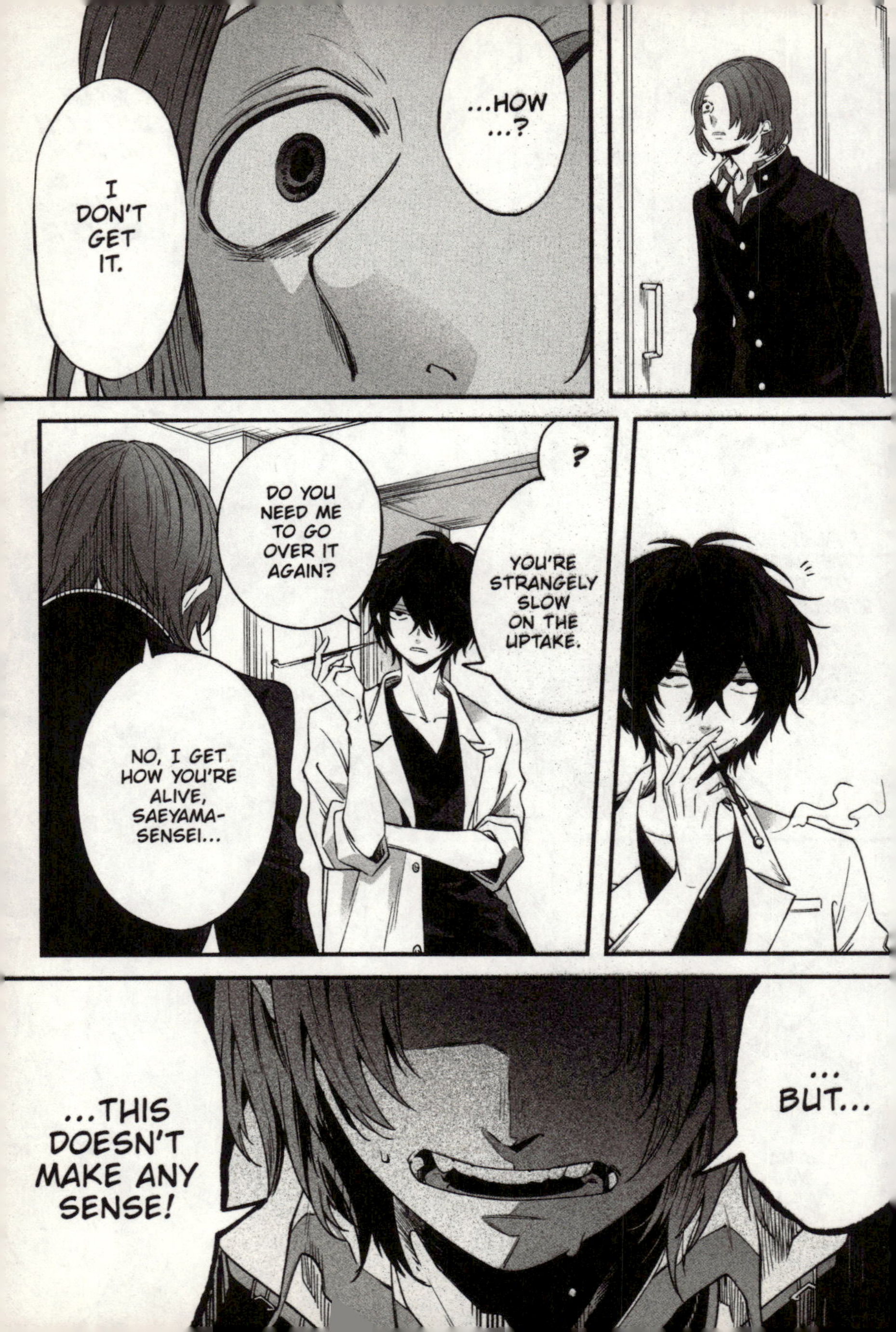
...HOW ...?
I DON'T GET IT.
?
YOU'RE STRANGELY SLOW ON THE UPTAKE.
DO YOU NEED ME TO GO OVER IT AGAIN?
NO, I GET HOW YOU'RE ALIVE, SAEYAMA-SENSEI...
... BUT...
...THIS DOESN'T MAKE ANY SENSE!

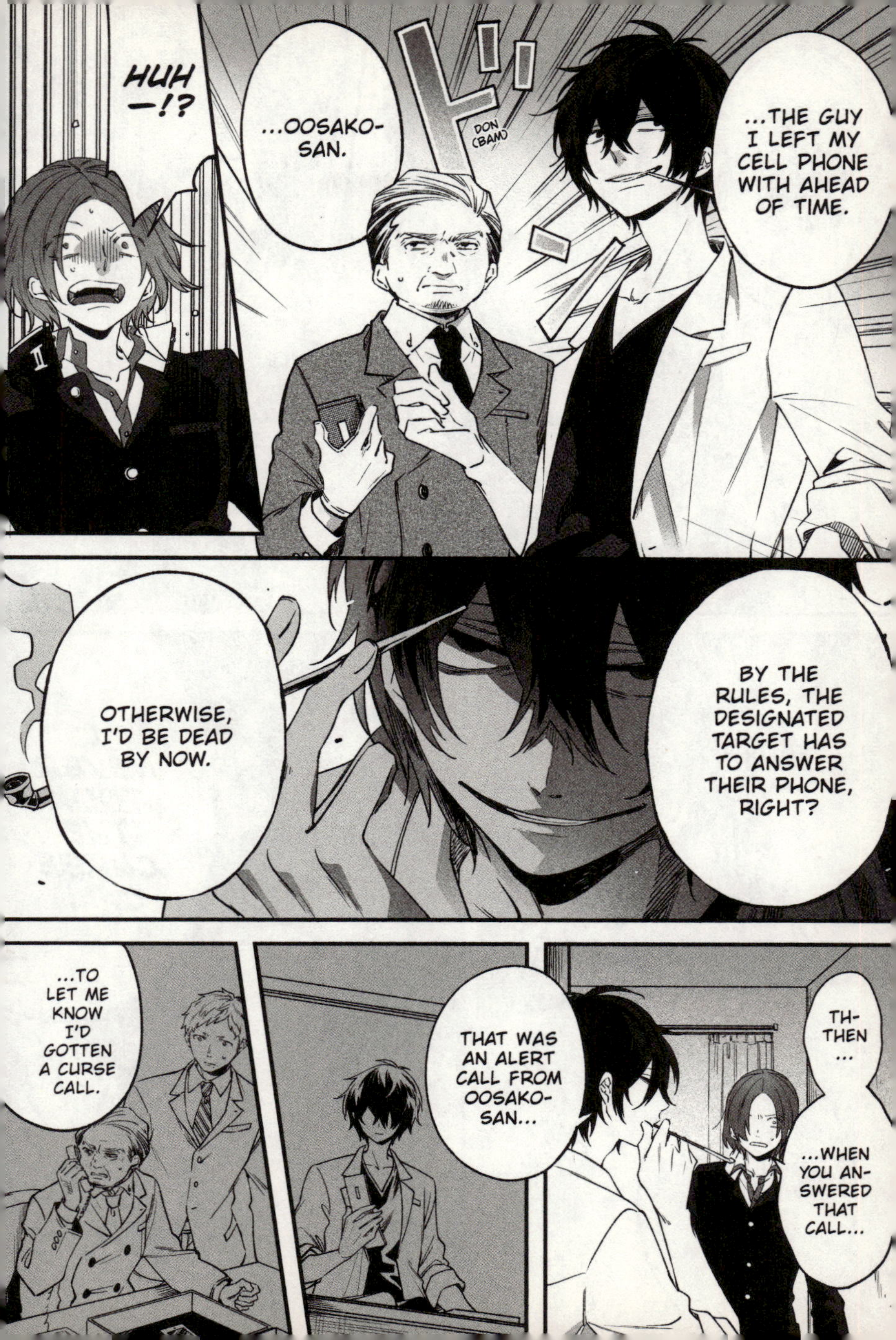
...THE GUY I LEFT MY CELL PHONE WITH AHEAD OF TIME.
DON (BAM)
...OOSAKO-SAN.
HUH—!?
BY THE RULES, THE DESIGNATED TARGET HAS TO ANSWER THEIR PHONE, RIGHT?
OTHERWISE, I'D BE DEAD BY NOW.
TH-THEN...
...WHEN YOU ANSWERED THAT CALL...
THAT WAS AN ALERT CALL FROM OOSAKO-SAN...
...TO LET ME KNOW I'D GOTTEN A CURSE CALL.

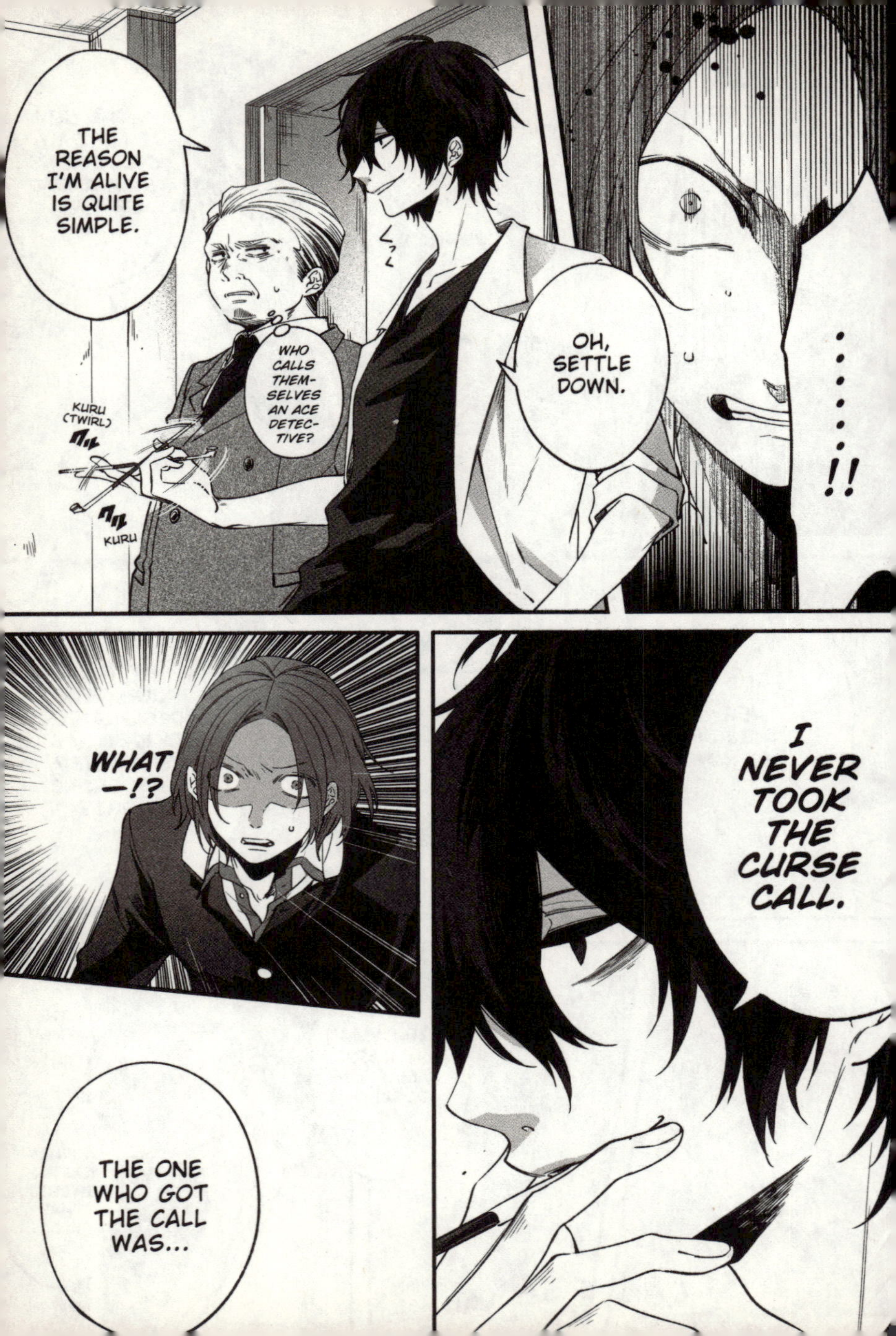
......!!
OH, SETTLE DOWN.
THE REASON I'M ALIVE IS QUITE SIMPLE.
WHO CALLS THEMSELVES AN ACE DETECTIVE?
KURU (TWIRL)
KURU
I NEVER TOOK THE CURSE CALL.
WHAT—!?
THE ONE WHO GOT THE CALL WAS...

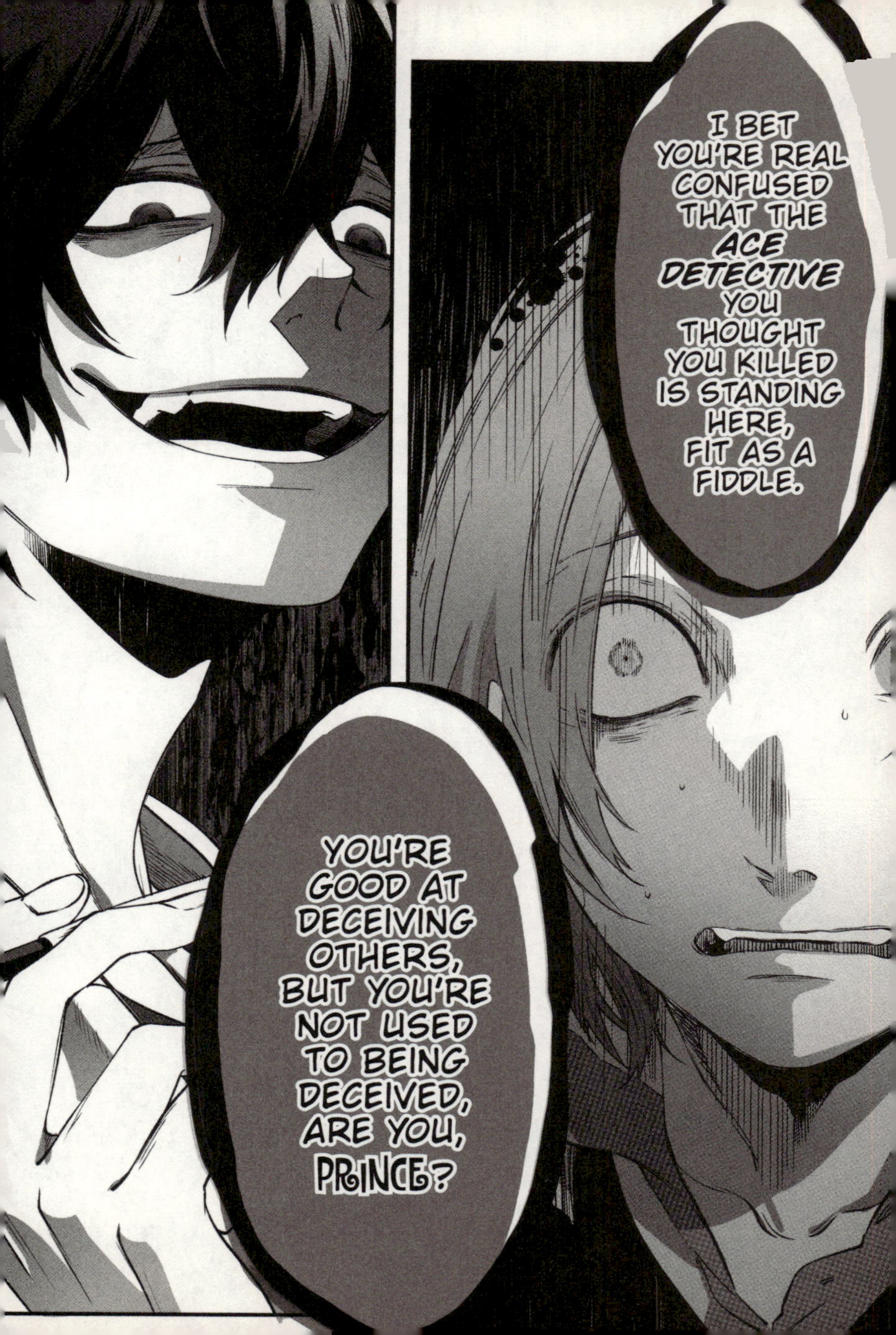
I BET YOU'RE REAL CONFUSED THAT THE ACE DETECTIVE YOU THOUGHT YOU KILLED IS STANDING HERE, FIT AS A FIDDLE.
YOU'RE GOOD AT DECEIVING OTHERS, BUT YOU'RE NOT USED TO BEING DECEIVED, ARE YOU, PRINCE?

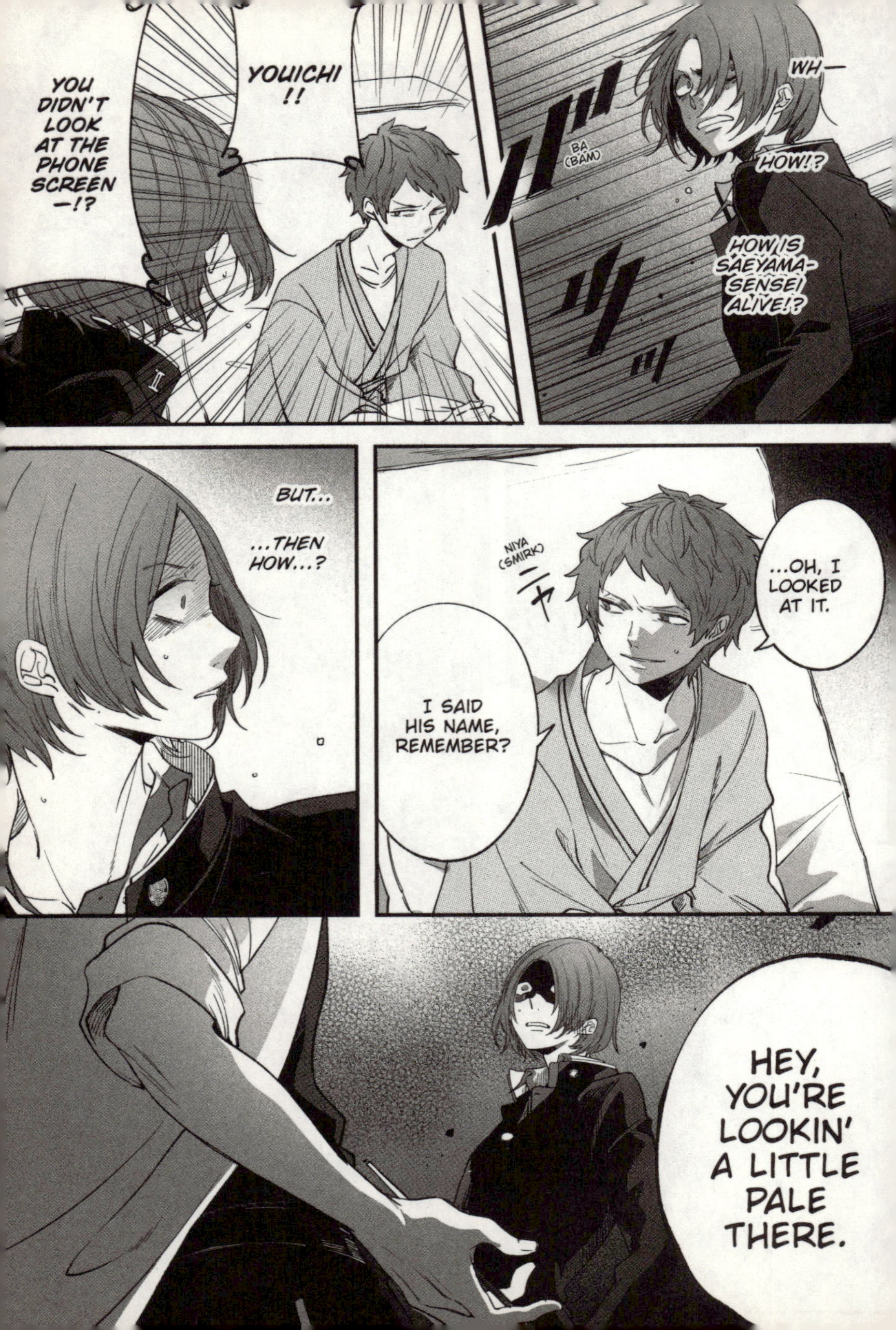
WH—
BA (BAM)
HOW!?
HOW IS SAEYAMA-SENSEI ALIVE!?
YOUICHI !!
YOU DIDN'T LOOK AT THE PHONE SCREEN—!?
...OH, I LOOKED AT IT.
NIYA (SMIRK)
ニヤ
I SAID HIS NAME, REMEMBER?
BUT...
...THEN HOW...?
HEY, YOU'RE LOOKIN' A LITTLE PALE THERE.

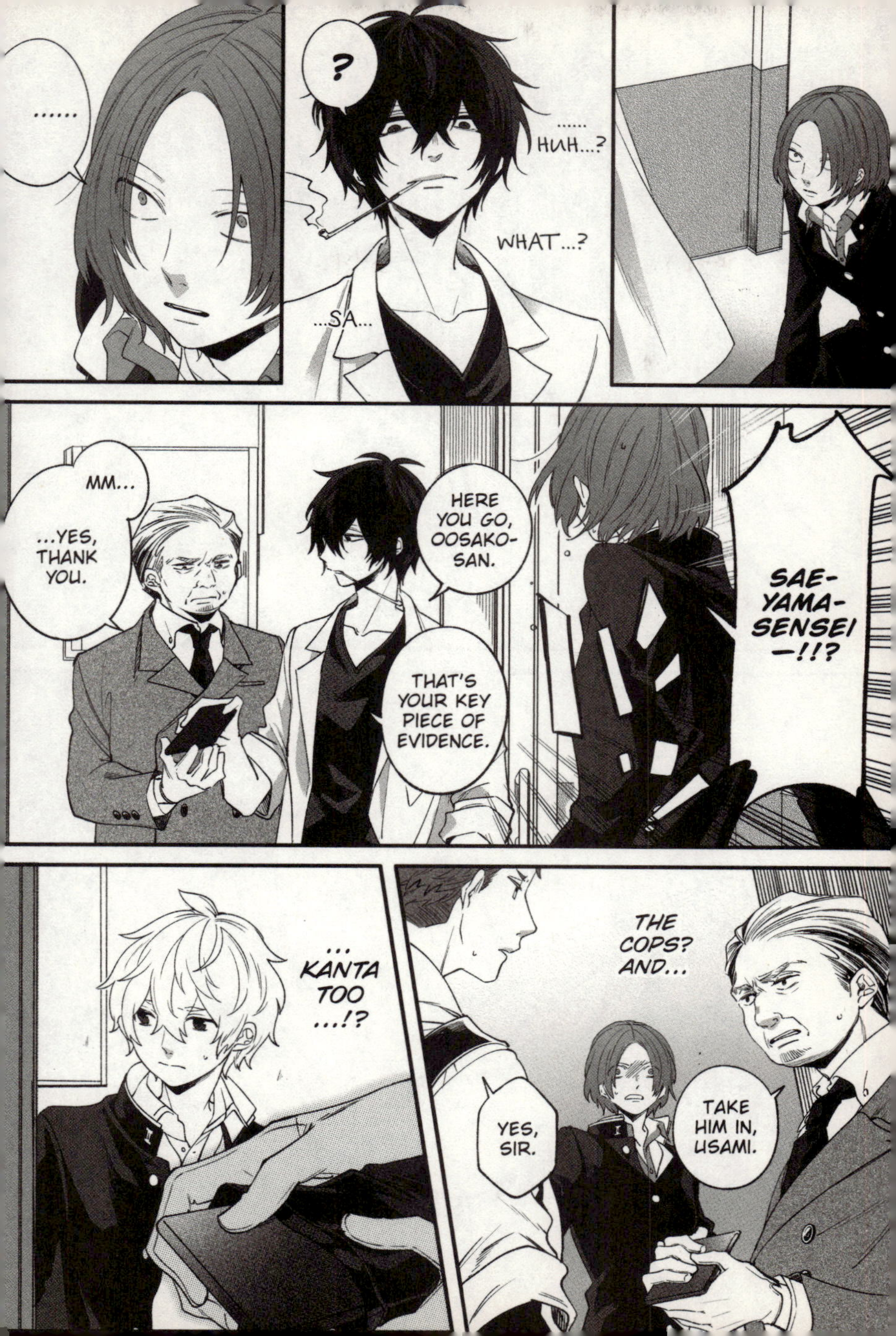
?
...... HUH...?
WHAT...?
...SA...
......
SAE-YAMA-SENSEI—!!?
HERE YOU GO, OOSAKO-SAN.
THAT'S YOUR KEY PIECE OF EVIDENCE.
MM...
...YES, THANK YOU.
THE COPS? AND...
TAKE HIM IN, USAMI.
YES, SIR.
... KANTA TOO ...!?

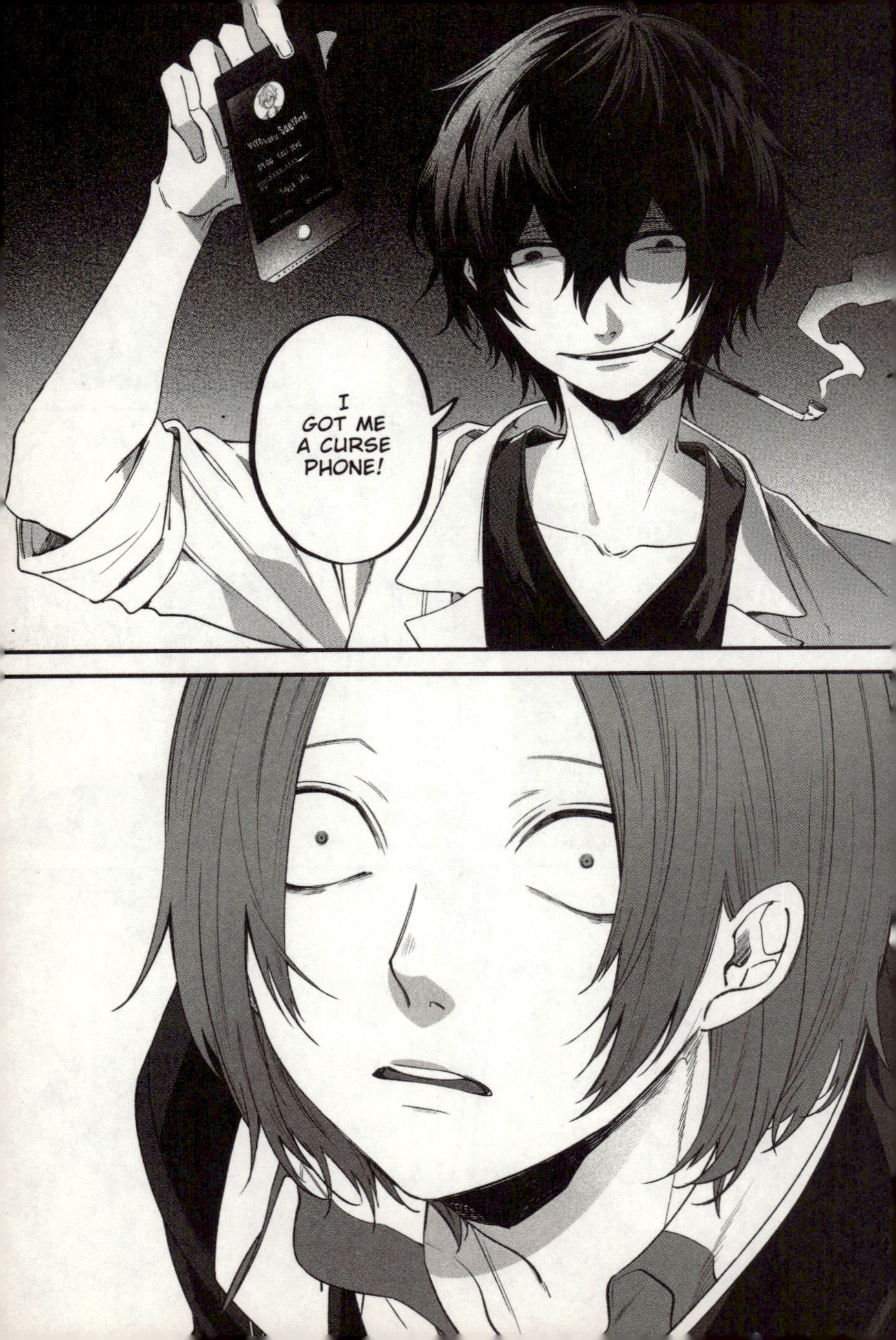
I GOT ME A CURSE PHONE!

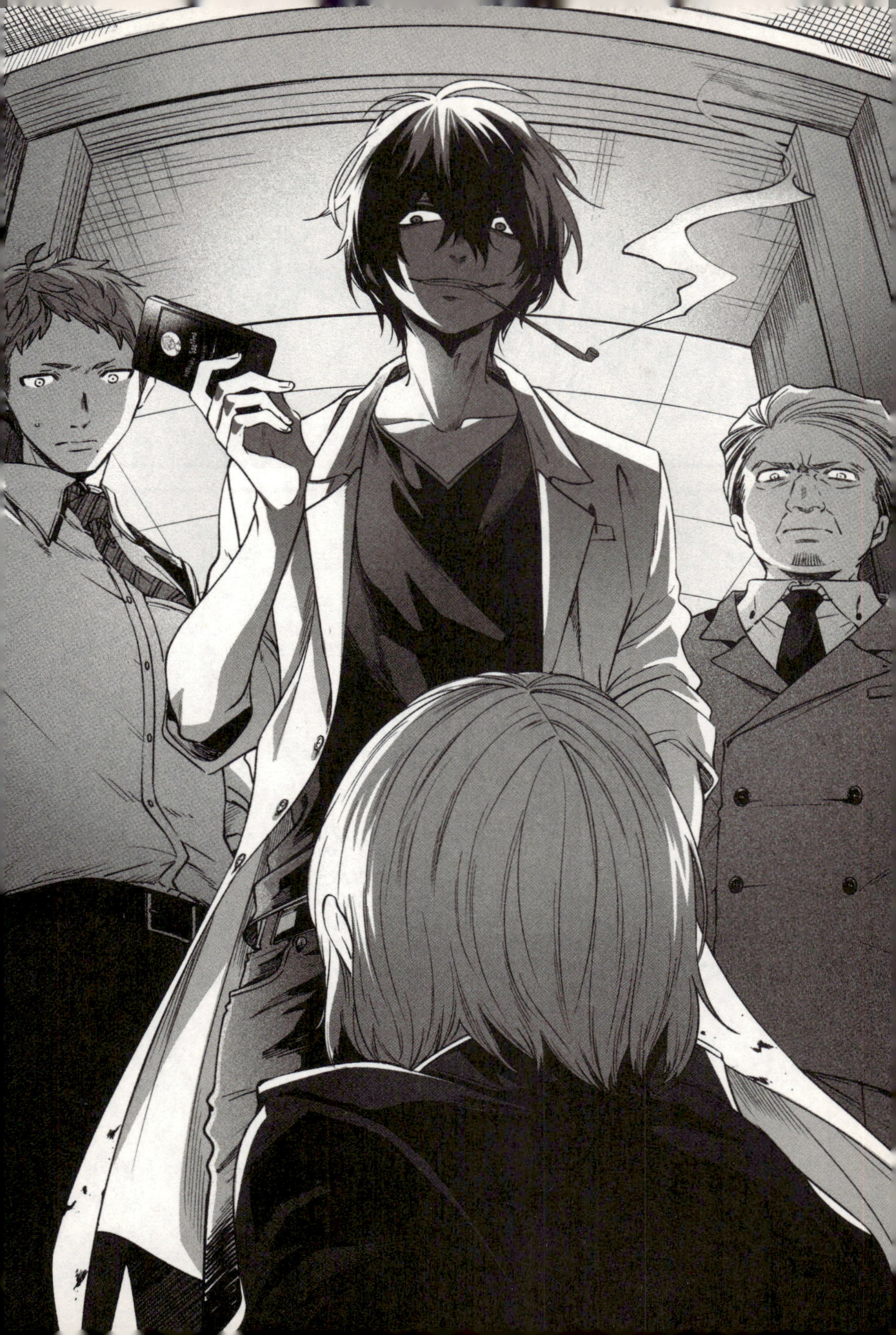

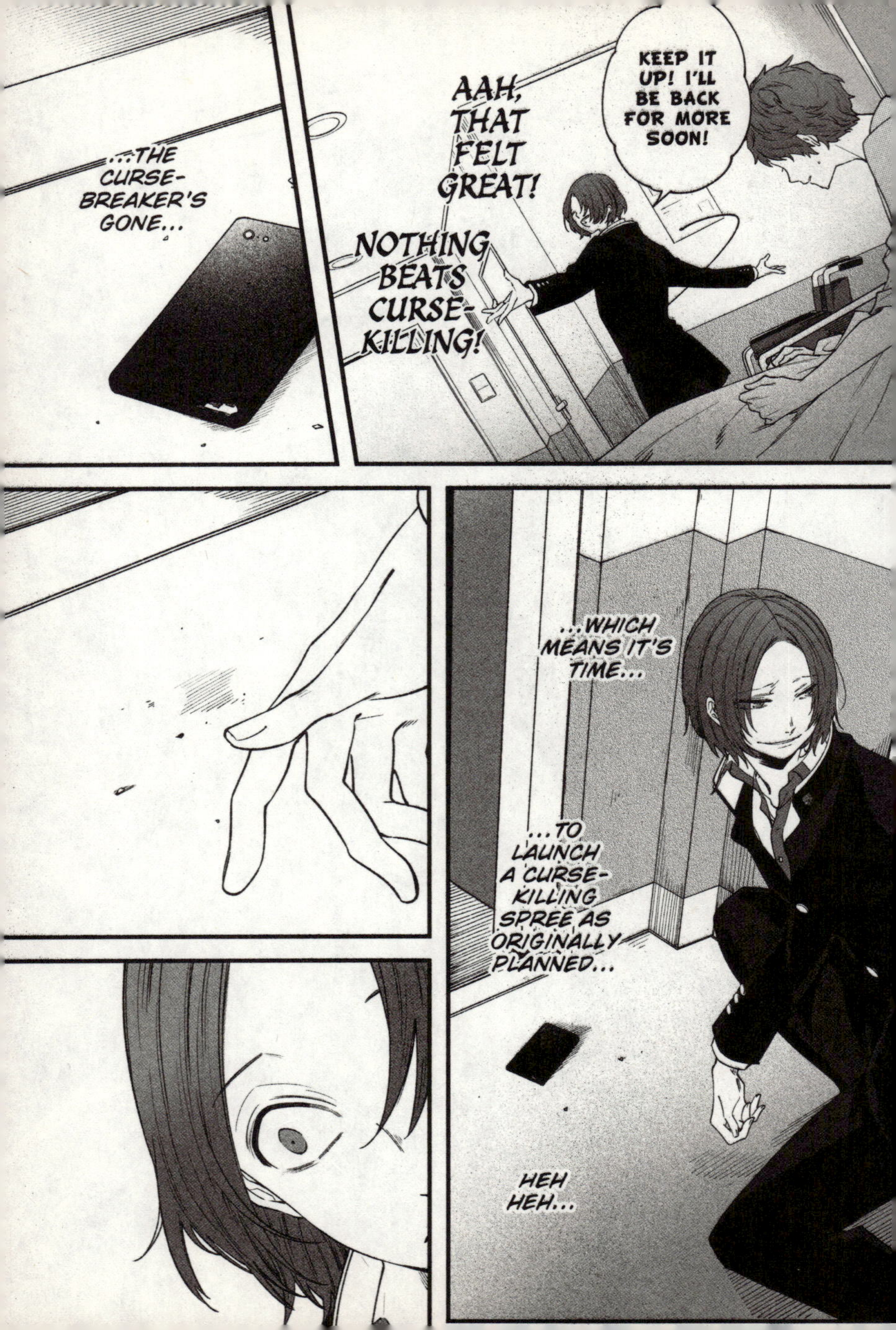
KEEP IT UP! I'LL BE BACK FOR MORE SOON!
AAH, THAT FELT GREAT!
NOTHING BEATS CURSE-KILLING!
...THE CURSE-BREAKER'S GONE...
...WHICH MEANS IT'S TIME...
...TO LAUNCH A CURSE-KILLING SPREE AS ORIGINALLY PLANNED...
HEH HEH...

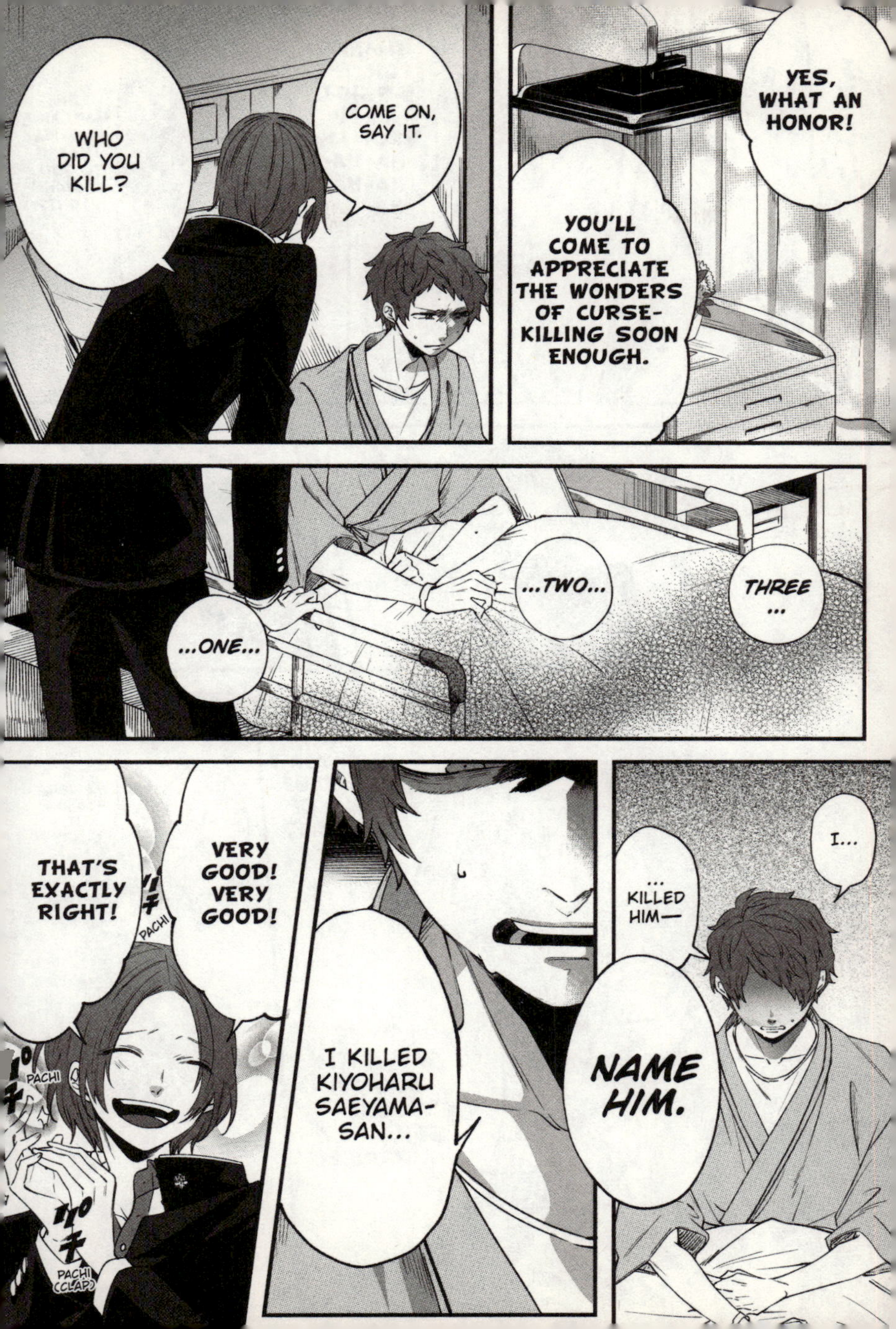
YES, WHAT AN HONOR!
YOU'LL COME TO APPRECIATE THE WONDERS OF CURSE-KILLING SOON ENOUGH.
COME ON, SAY IT.
WHO DID YOU KILL?
THREE...
...TWO...
...ONE...
I...
...KILLED HIM—
NAME HIM.
I KILLED KIYOHARU SAEYAMA-SAN...
VERY GOOD! VERY GOOD!
THAT'S EXACTLY RIGHT!
PACHI
PACHI
PACHI (CLAP)

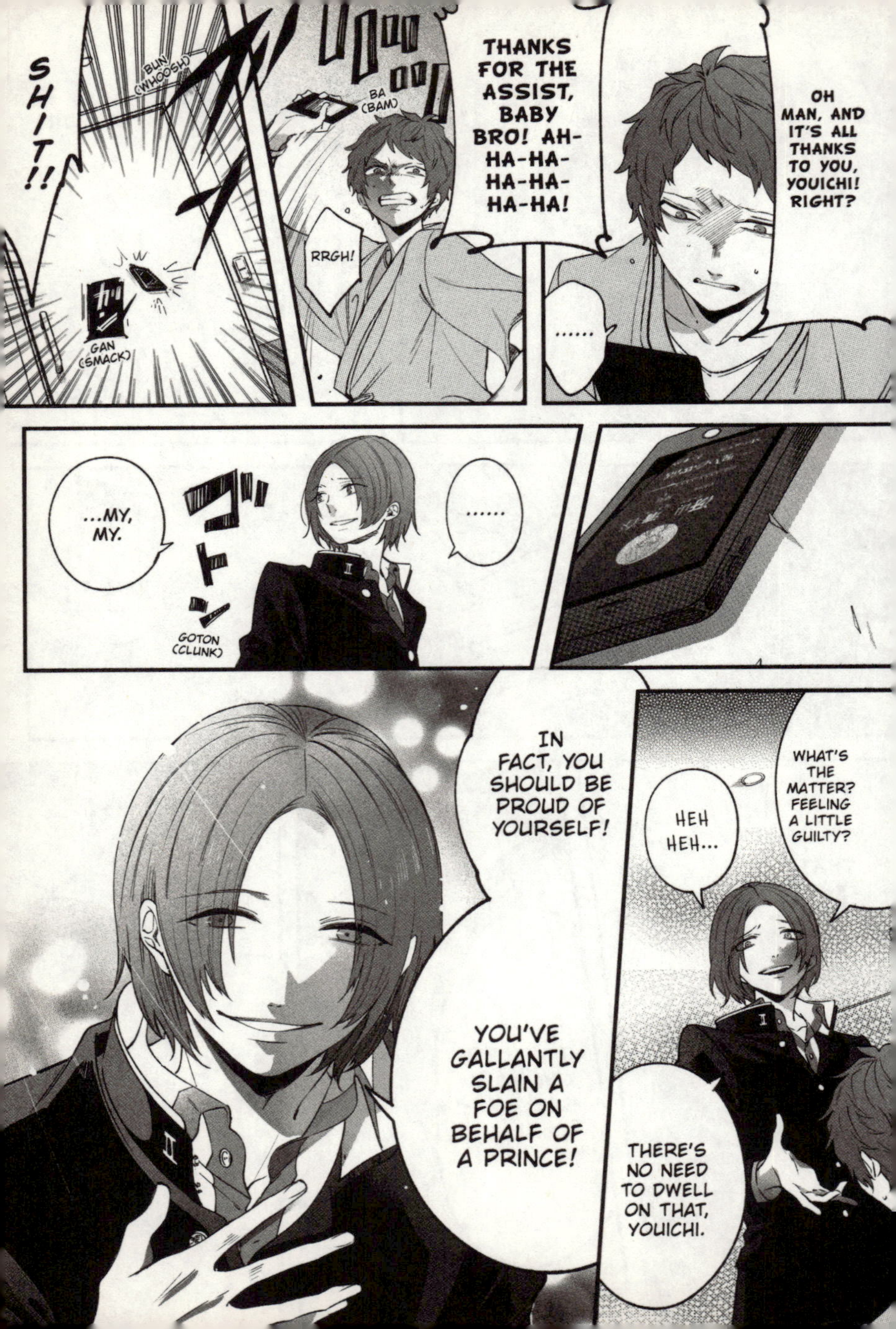
OH MAN, AND IT'S ALL THANKS TO YOU, YOUICHI! RIGHT?
THANKS FOR THE ASSIST, BABY BRO! AH-HA-HA-HA-HA-HA-HA!
......
BA (BAM)
RRGH!
SHIT!!
BUN (WHOOSH)
GAN (SMACK)
......
GOTON (CLUNK)
...MY, MY.
WHAT'S THE MATTER? FEELING A LITTLE GUILTY?
HEH HEH...
THERE'S NO NEED TO DWELL ON THAT, YOUICHI.
IN FACT, YOU SHOULD BE PROUD OF YOURSELF!
YOU'VE GALLANTLY SLAIN A FOE ON BEHALF OF A PRINCE!

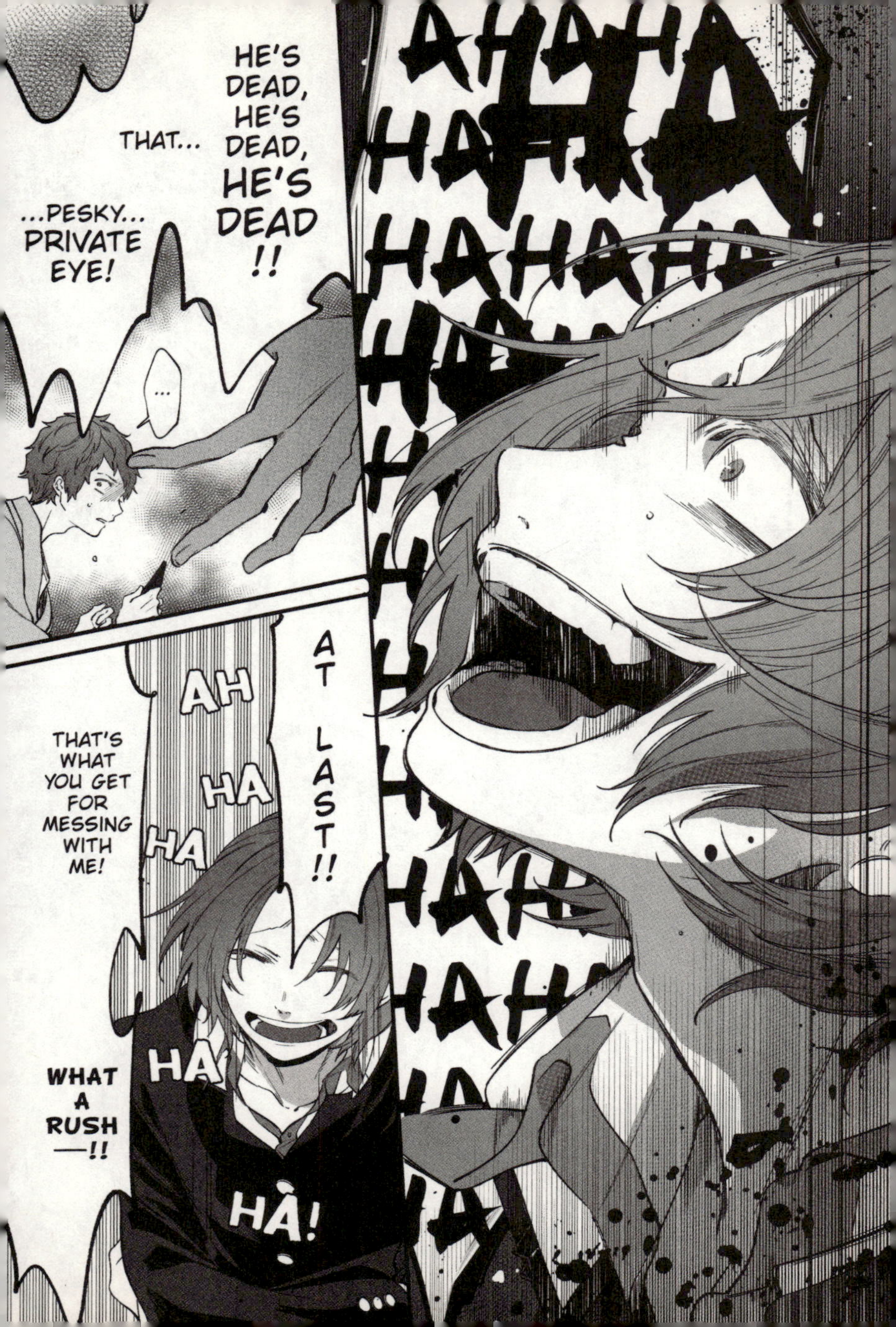
AHAHA
HAHA
HAHAHA
HE'S DEAD, HE'S DEAD, HE'S DEAD!!
THAT...
...PESKY... PRIVATE EYE!
...
AT LAST!!
AH
THAT'S WHAT YOU GET FOR MESSING WITH ME!
HA
HA
HA
WHAT A RUSH—!!
HA!

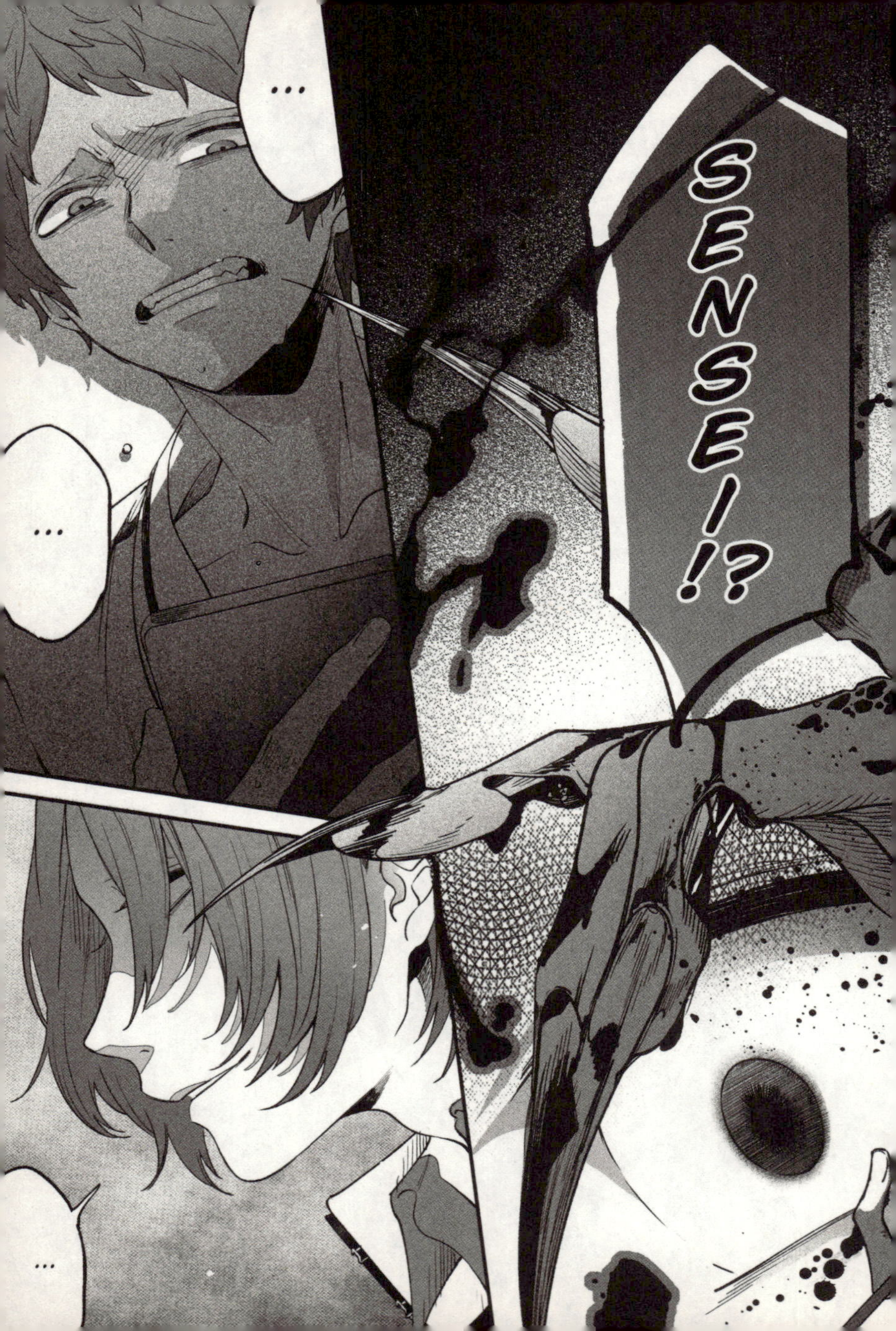
SENSEI!?
...
...
...

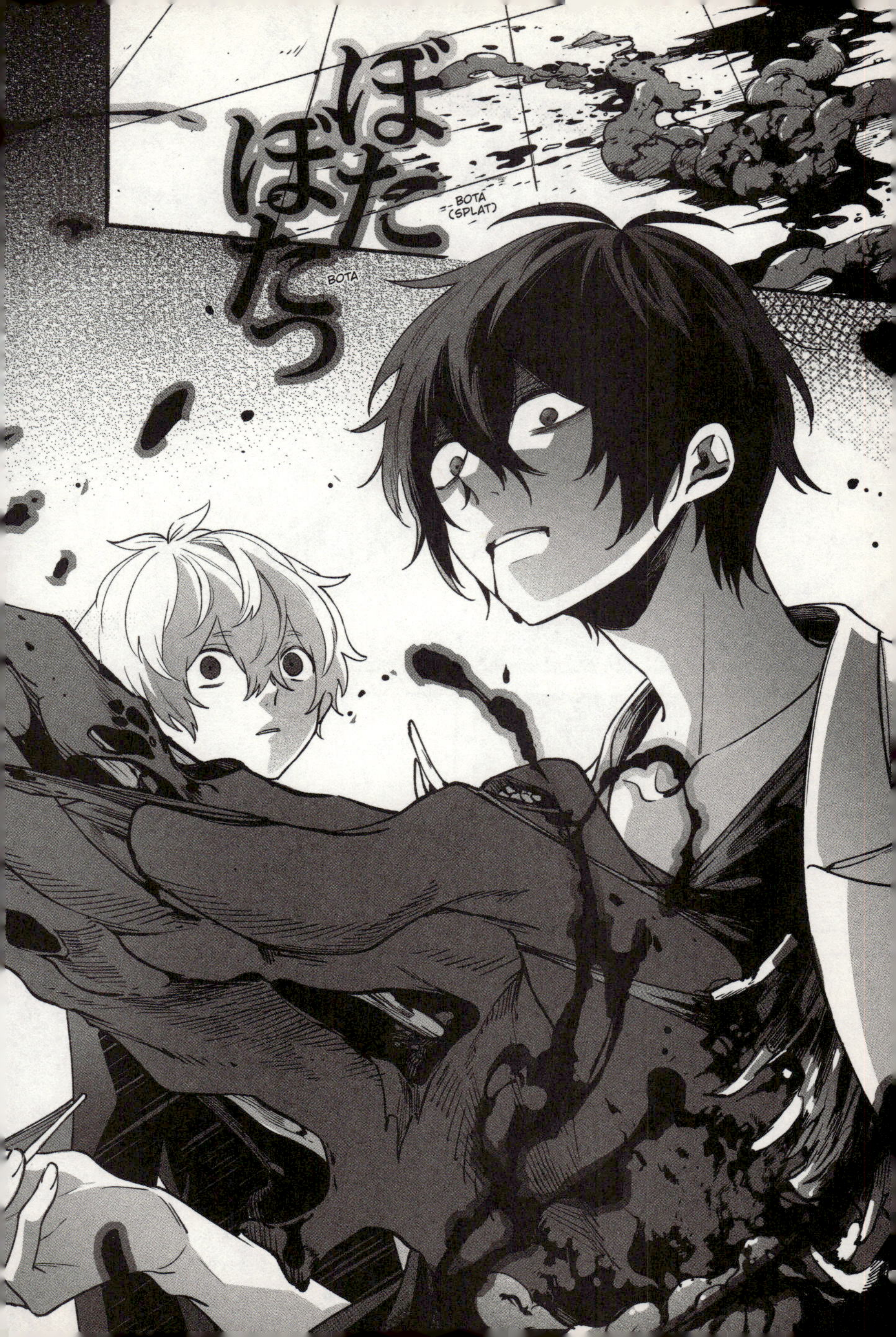
ぼた
BOTA (SPLAT)
ぼたっ
BOTA

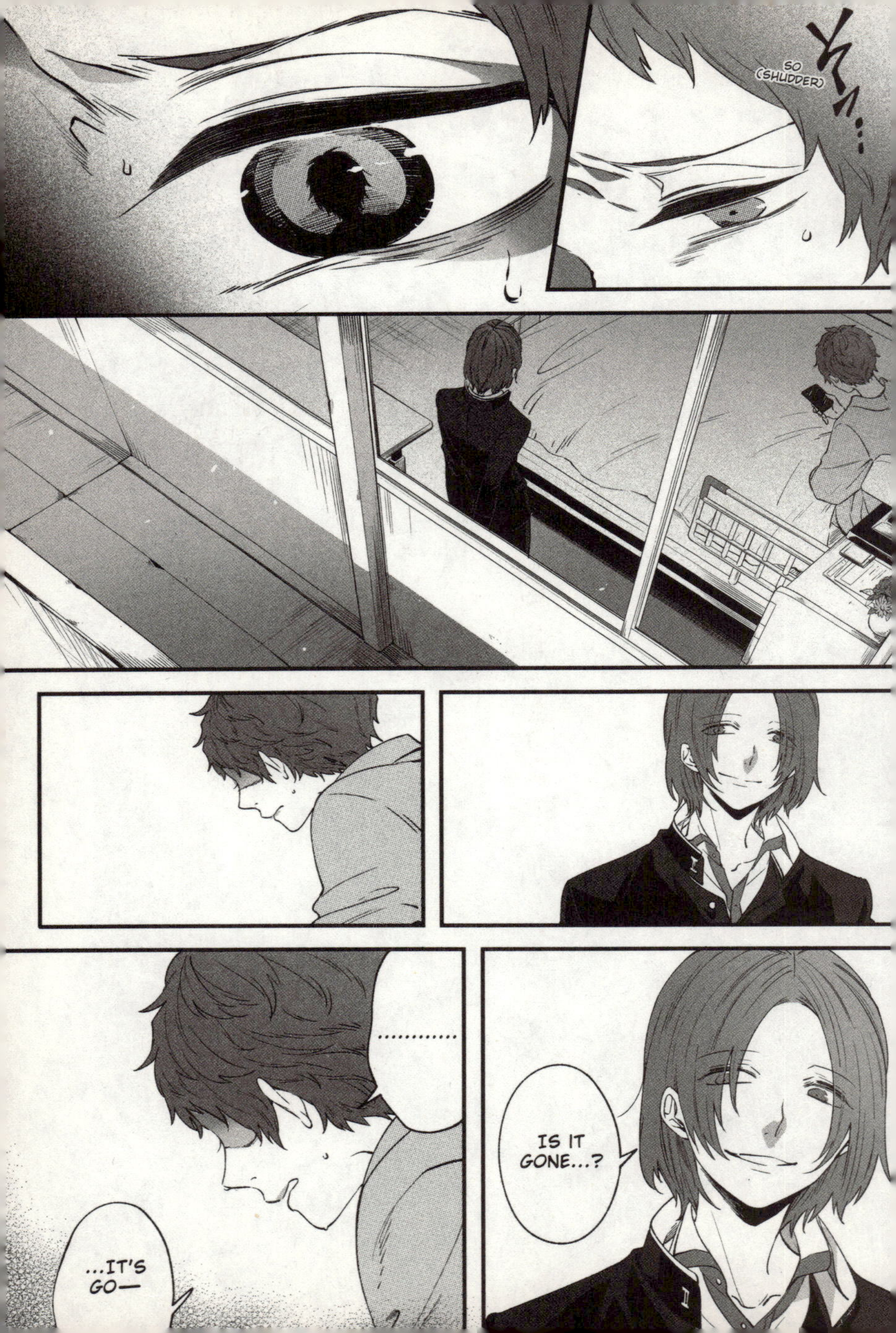
SO (SHUDDER)
....
IS IT GONE...?
...IT'S GO—

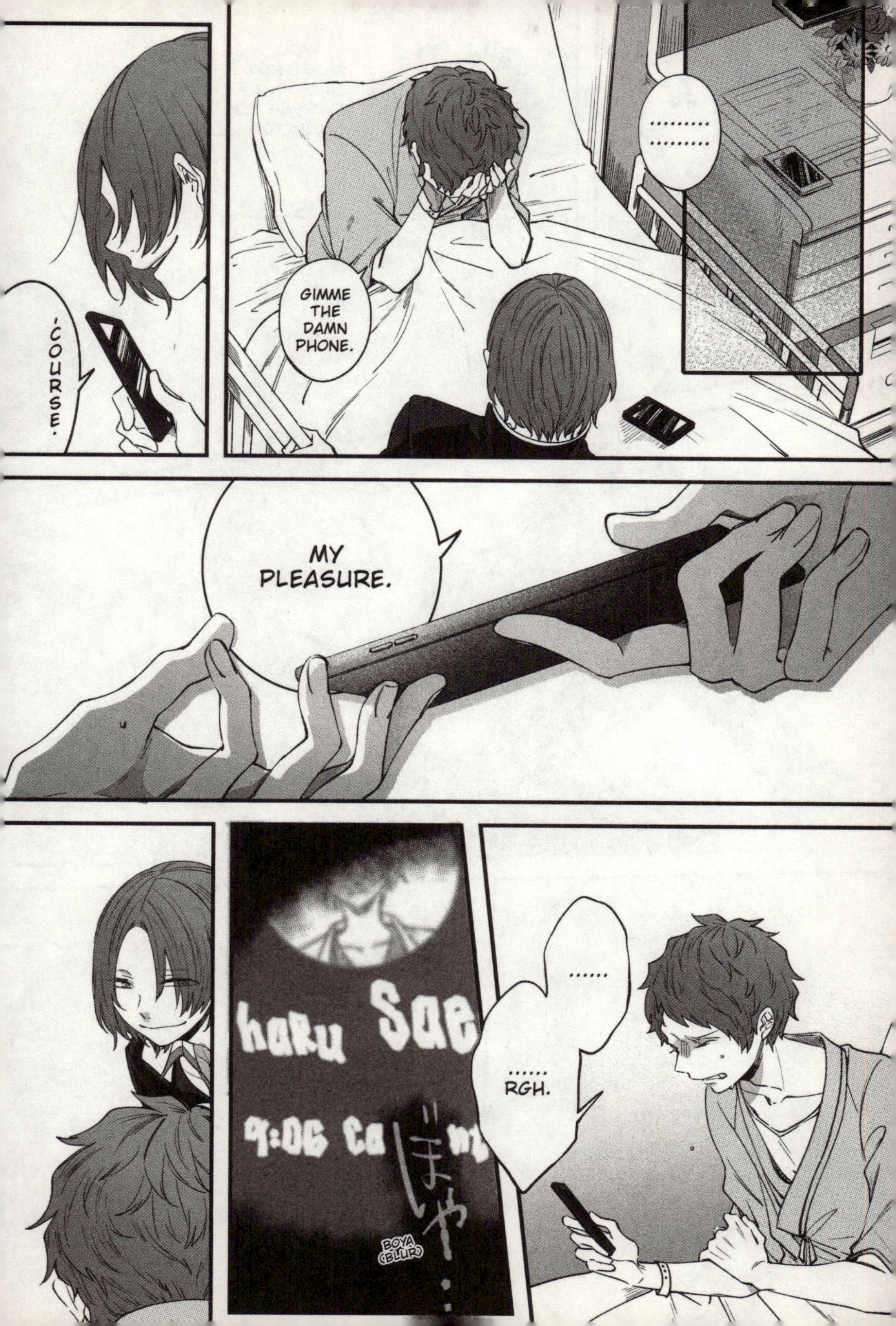
....
....
GIMME THE DAMN PHONE.
'COURSE.
MY PLEASURE.
......
...... RGH.
haku Sae
9:06
ぼや
BOYA (BLUR)

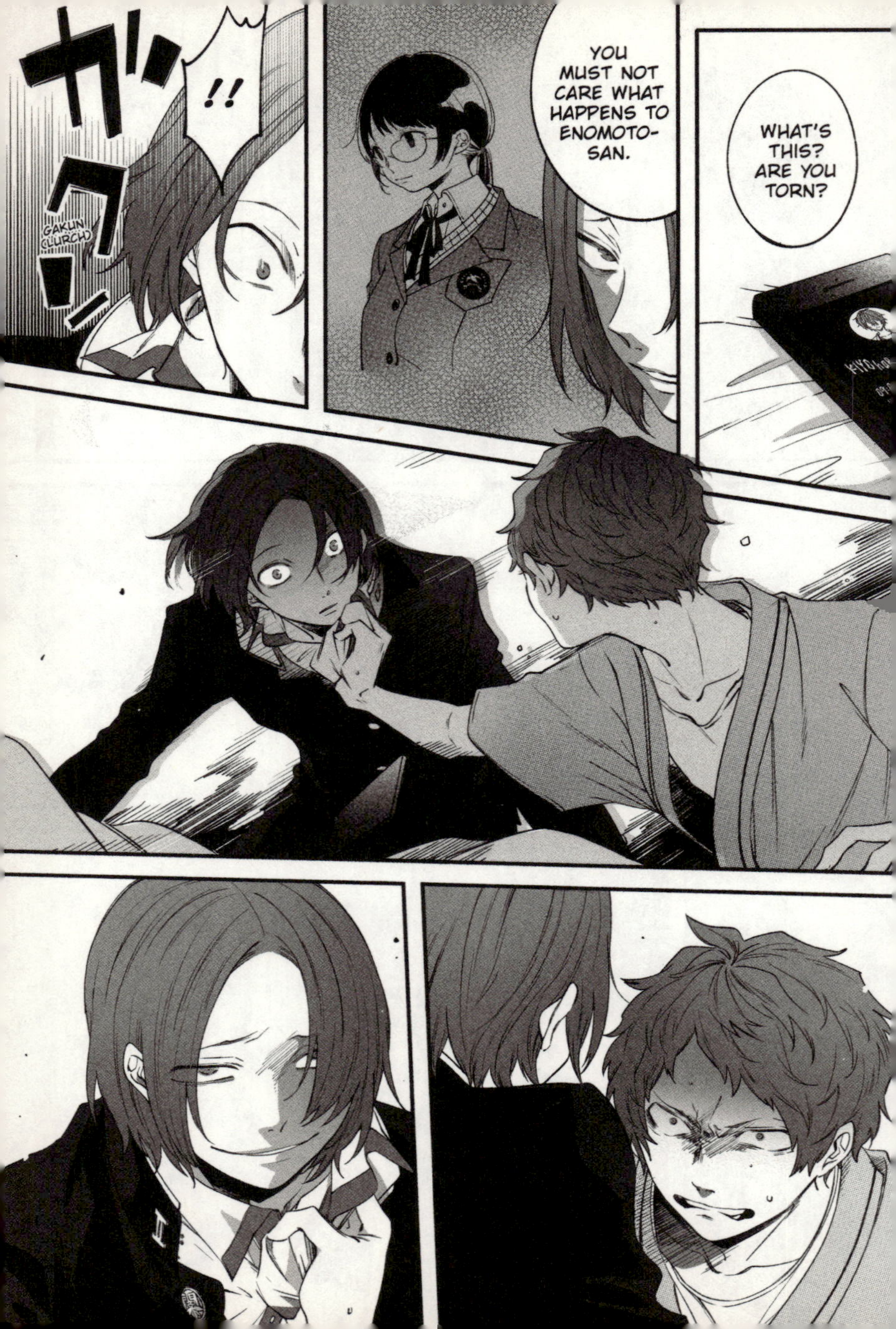
WHAT'S THIS? ARE YOU TORN?
YOU MUST NOT CARE WHAT HAPPENS TO ENOMOTO-SAN.
!!
GAKUN (LURCH)

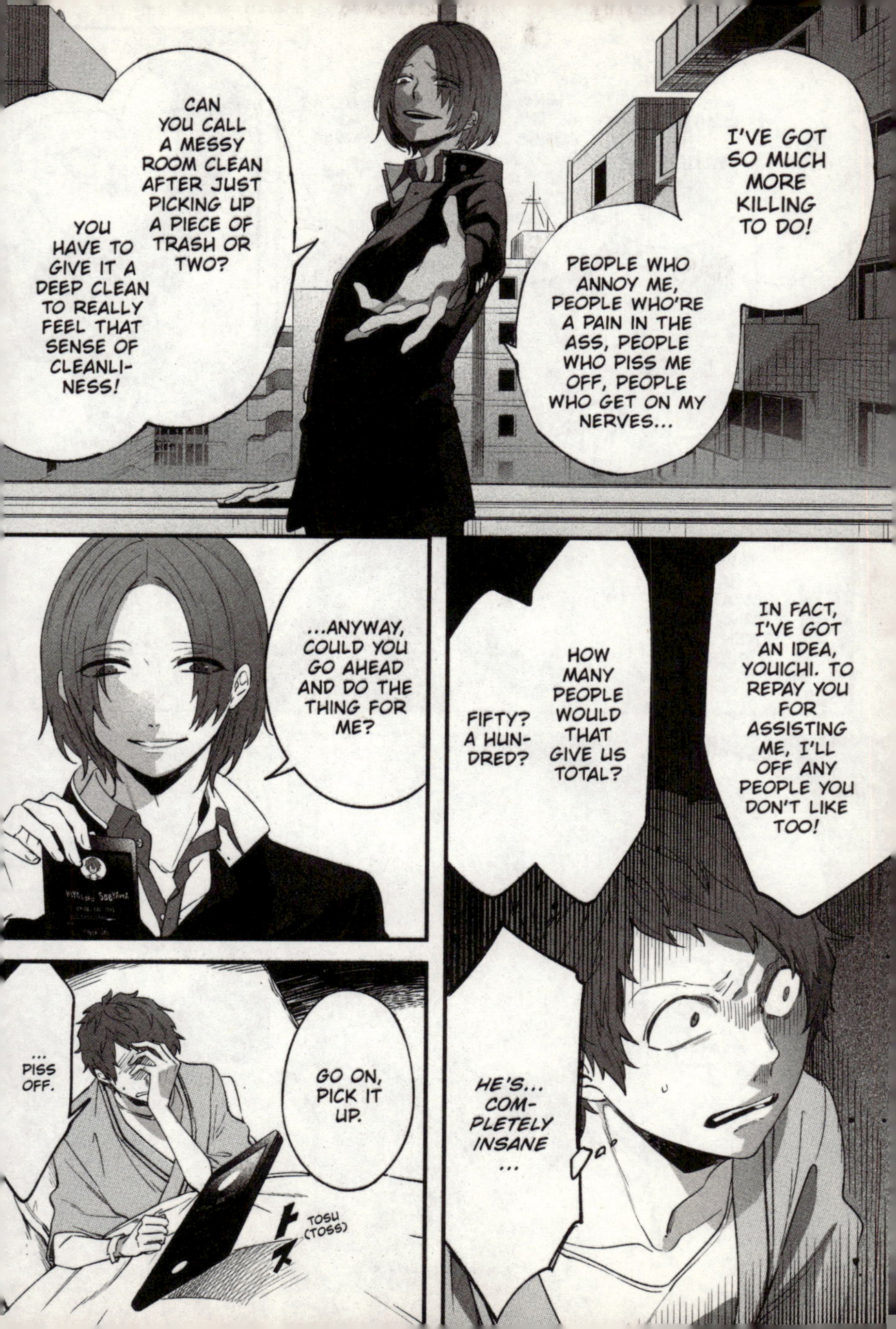
I'VE GOT SO MUCH MORE KILLING TO DO!
PEOPLE WHO ANNOY ME, PEOPLE WHO'RE A PAIN IN THE ASS, PEOPLE WHO PISS ME OFF, PEOPLE WHO GET ON MY NERVES...
CAN YOU CALL A MESSY ROOM CLEAN AFTER JUST PICKING UP A PIECE OF TRASH OR TWO?
YOU HAVE TO GIVE IT A DEEP CLEAN TO REALLY FEEL THAT SENSE OF CLEANLI-NESS!
IN FACT, I'VE GOT AN IDEA, YOUICHI. TO REPAY YOU FOR ASSISTING ME, I'LL OFF ANY PEOPLE YOU DON'T LIKE TOO!
HOW MANY PEOPLE WOULD THAT GIVE US TOTAL?
FIFTY? A HUN-DRED?
HE'S... COM-PLETELY INSANE...
...ANYWAY, COULD YOU GO AHEAD AND DO THE THING FOR ME?
GO ON, PICK IT UP.
... PISS OFF.
TOSU (TOSS)

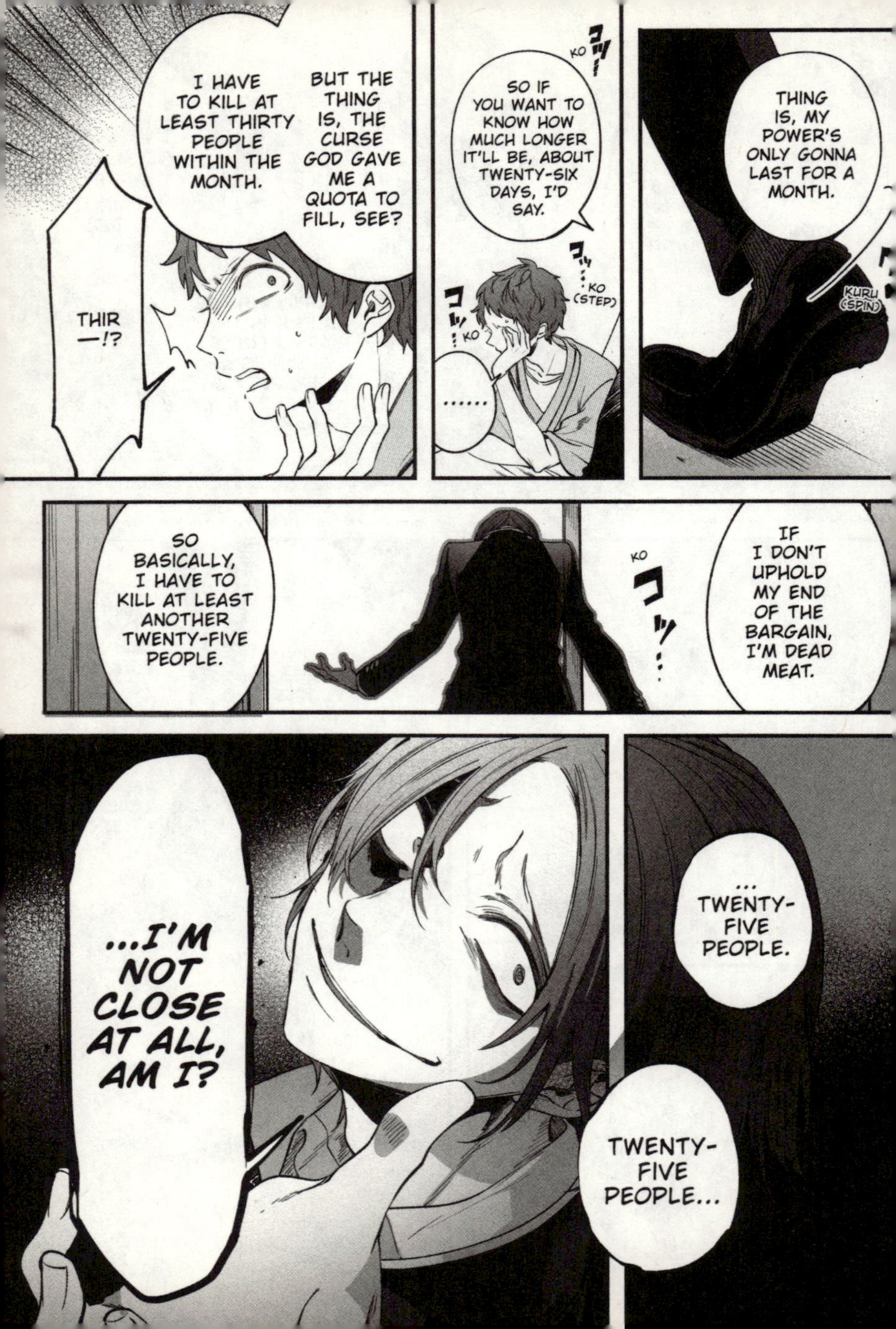
THING IS, MY POWER'S ONLY GONNA LAST FOR A MONTH.
KURU (SPIN)
KO
SO IF YOU WANT TO KNOW HOW MUCH LONGER IT'LL BE, ABOUT TWENTY-SIX DAYS, I'D SAY.
KO (STEP)
KO
......
BUT THE THING IS, THE CURSE GOD GAVE ME A QUOTA TO FILL, SEE?
I HAVE TO KILL AT LEAST THIRTY PEOPLE WITHIN THE MONTH.
THIR—!?
IF I DON'T UPHOLD MY END OF THE BARGAIN, I'M DEAD MEAT.
KO
SO BASICALLY, I HAVE TO KILL AT LEAST ANOTHER TWENTY-FIVE PEOPLE.
...TWENTY-FIVE PEOPLE.
TWENTY-FIVE PEOPLE...
...I'M NOT CLOSE AT ALL, AM I?

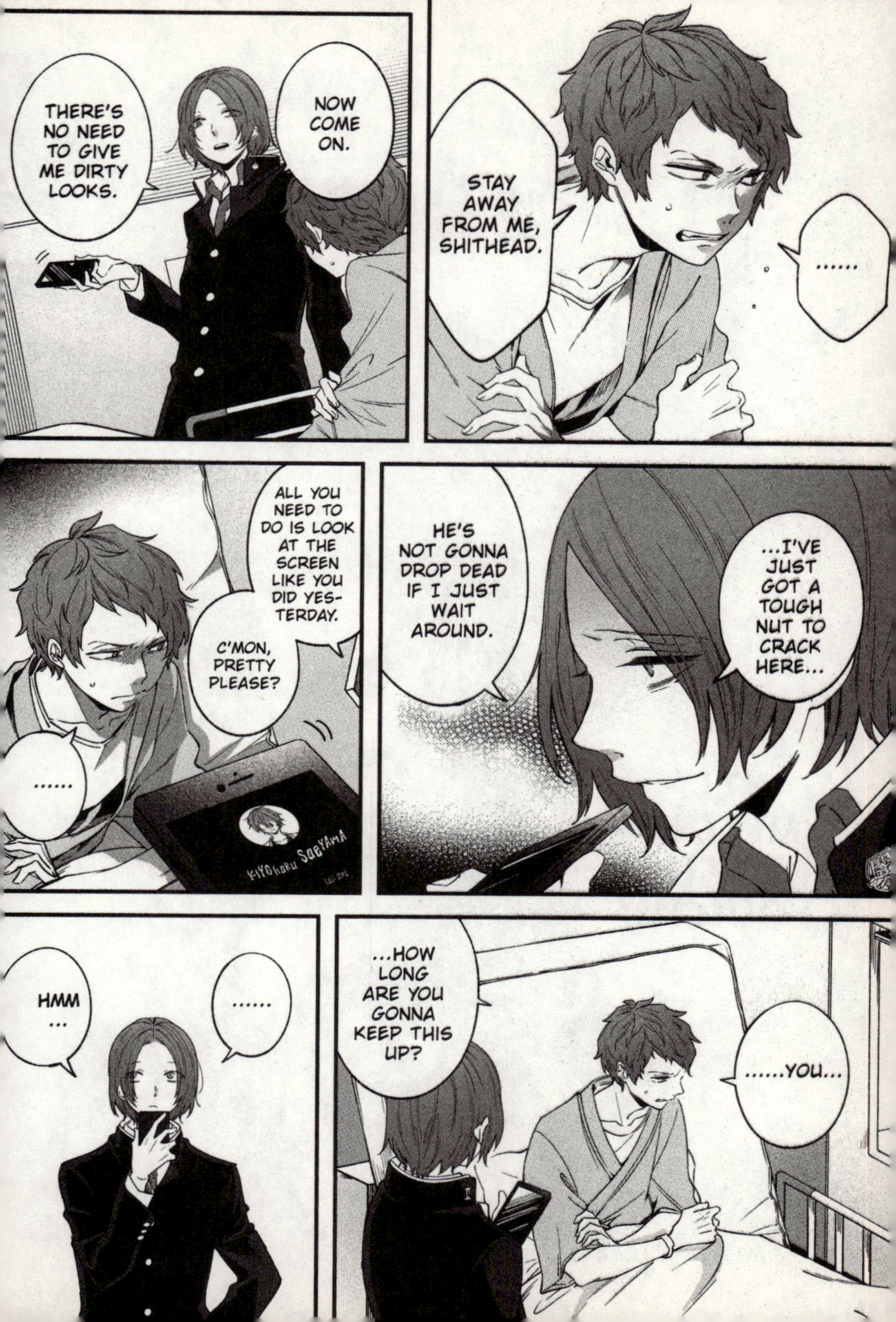
......
STAY AWAY FROM ME, SHITHEAD.
NOW COME ON.
THERE'S NO NEED TO GIVE ME DIRTY LOOKS.
...I'VE JUST GOT A TOUGH NUT TO CRACK HERE...
HE'S NOT GONNA DROP DEAD IF I JUST WAIT AROUND.
ALL YOU NEED TO DO IS LOOK AT THE SCREEN LIKE YOU DID YES-TERDAY.
C'MON, PRETTY PLEASE?
KIYOharu SaeYAMA
......
......YOU...
...HOW LONG ARE YOU GONNA KEEP THIS UP?
......
HMM ...

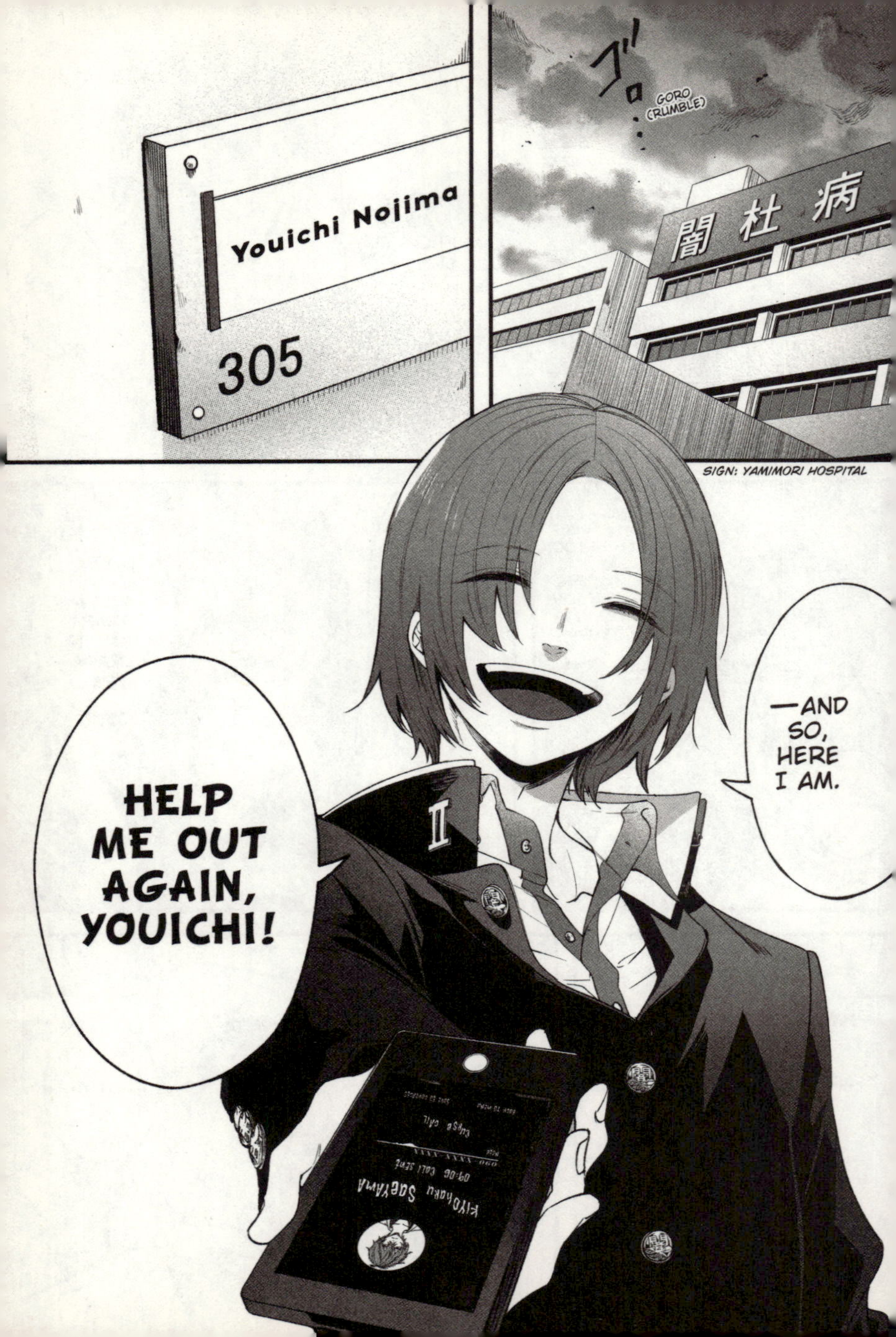
ゴロ
GORO (RUMBLE)
闇杜病
SIGN: YAMIMORI HOSPITAL
Youichi Nojima
305
—AND SO, HERE I AM.
HELP ME OUT AGAIN, YOUICHI!

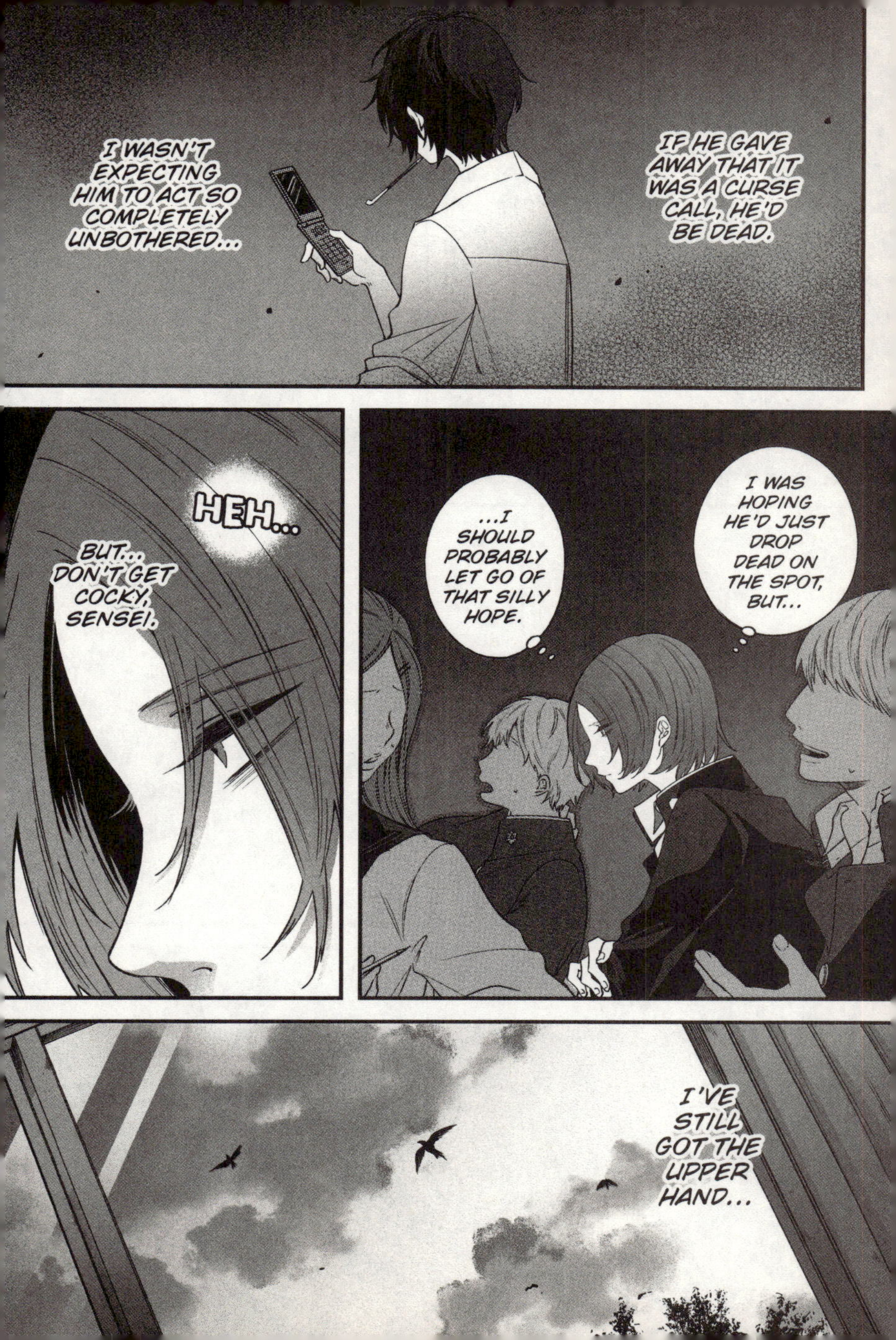
IF HE GAVE AWAY THAT IT WAS A CURSE CALL, HE'D BE DEAD.
I WASN'T EXPECTING HIM TO ACT SO COMPLETELY UNBOTHERED...
I WAS HOPING HE'D JUST DROP DEAD ON THE SPOT, BUT...
...I SHOULD PROBABLY LET GO OF THAT SILLY HOPE.
HEH...
BUT... DON'T GET COCKY, SENSEI.
I'VE STILL GOT THE UPPER HAND...

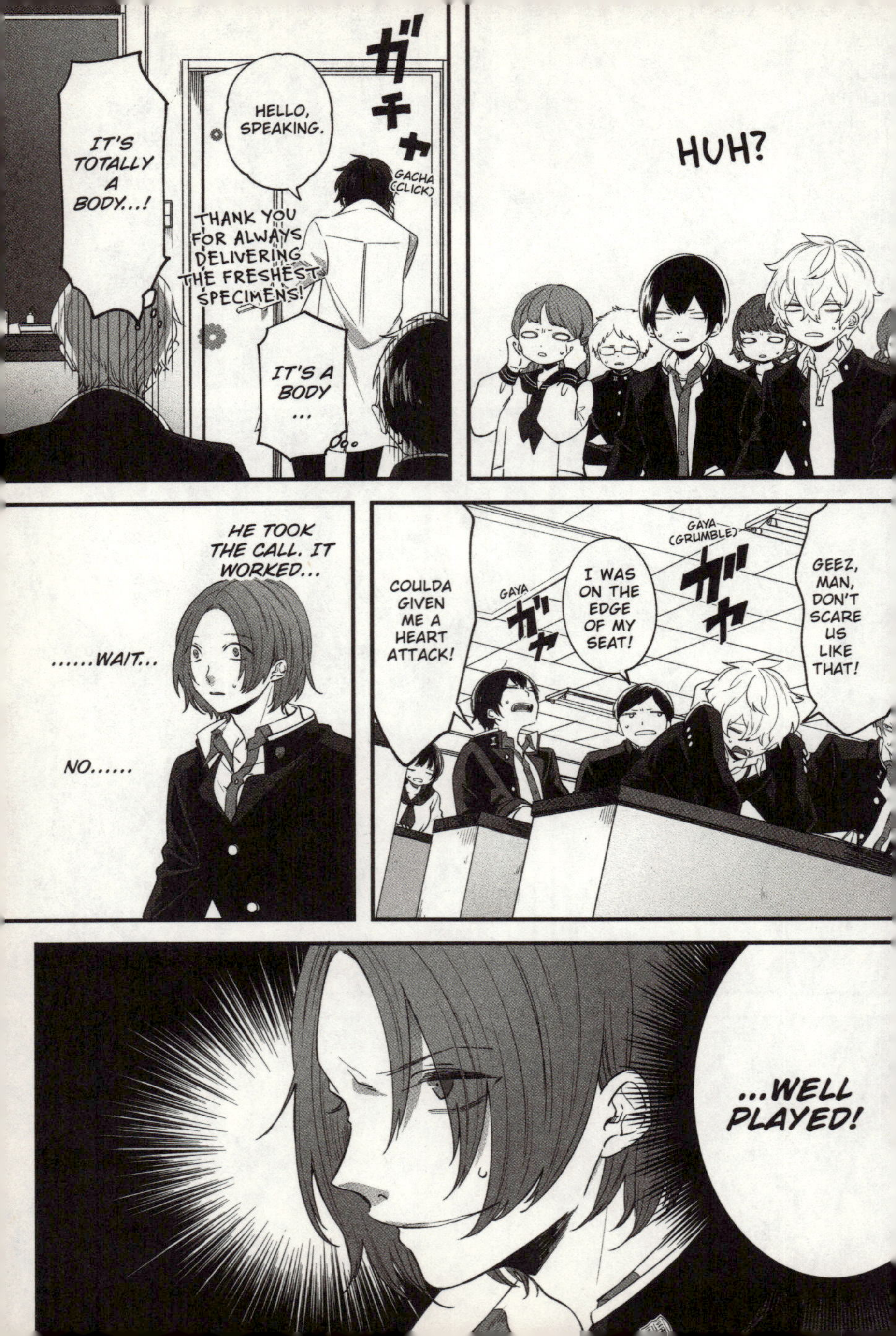
HUH?
ガチャ
GACHA (CLICK)
HELLO, SPEAKING.
THANK YOU FOR ALWAYS DELIVERING THE FRESHEST SPECIMENS!
IT'S A BODY ...
IT'S TOTALLY A BODY...!
GAYA (GRUMBLE)
ガヤ
GEEZ, MAN, DON'T SCARE US LIKE THAT!
I WAS ON THE EDGE OF MY SEAT!
GAYA
ガヤ
COULDA GIVEN ME A HEART ATTACK!
HE TOOK THE CALL. IT WORKED...
......WAIT...
NO......
...WELL PLAYED!

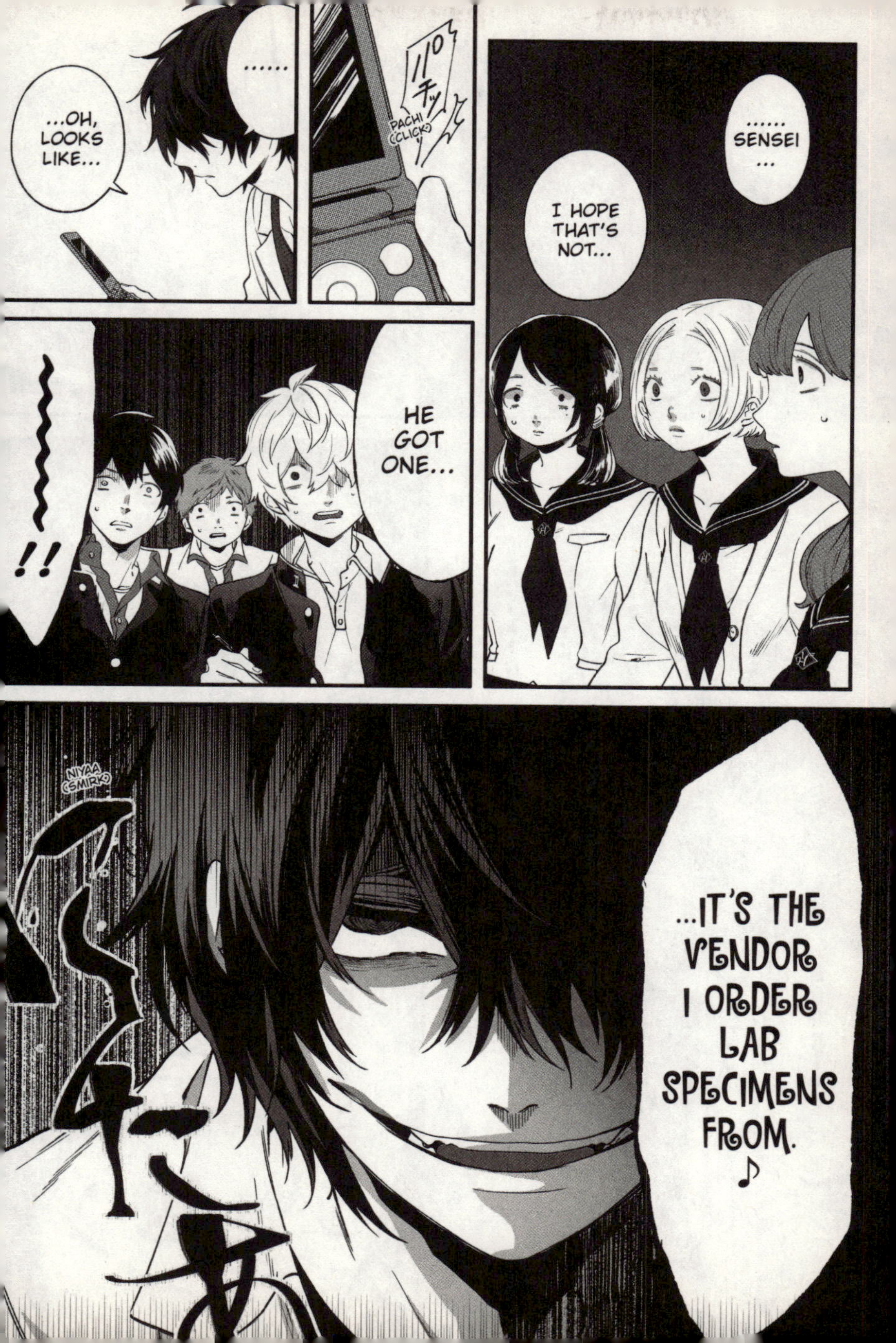
......
SENSEI
...
I HOPE THAT'S NOT...
PACHI (CLICK)
......
...OH, LOOKS LIKE...
HE GOT ONE...
!!
...IT'S THE VENDOR I ORDER LAB SPECIMENS FROM. ♪
NIYAA (SMIRK)

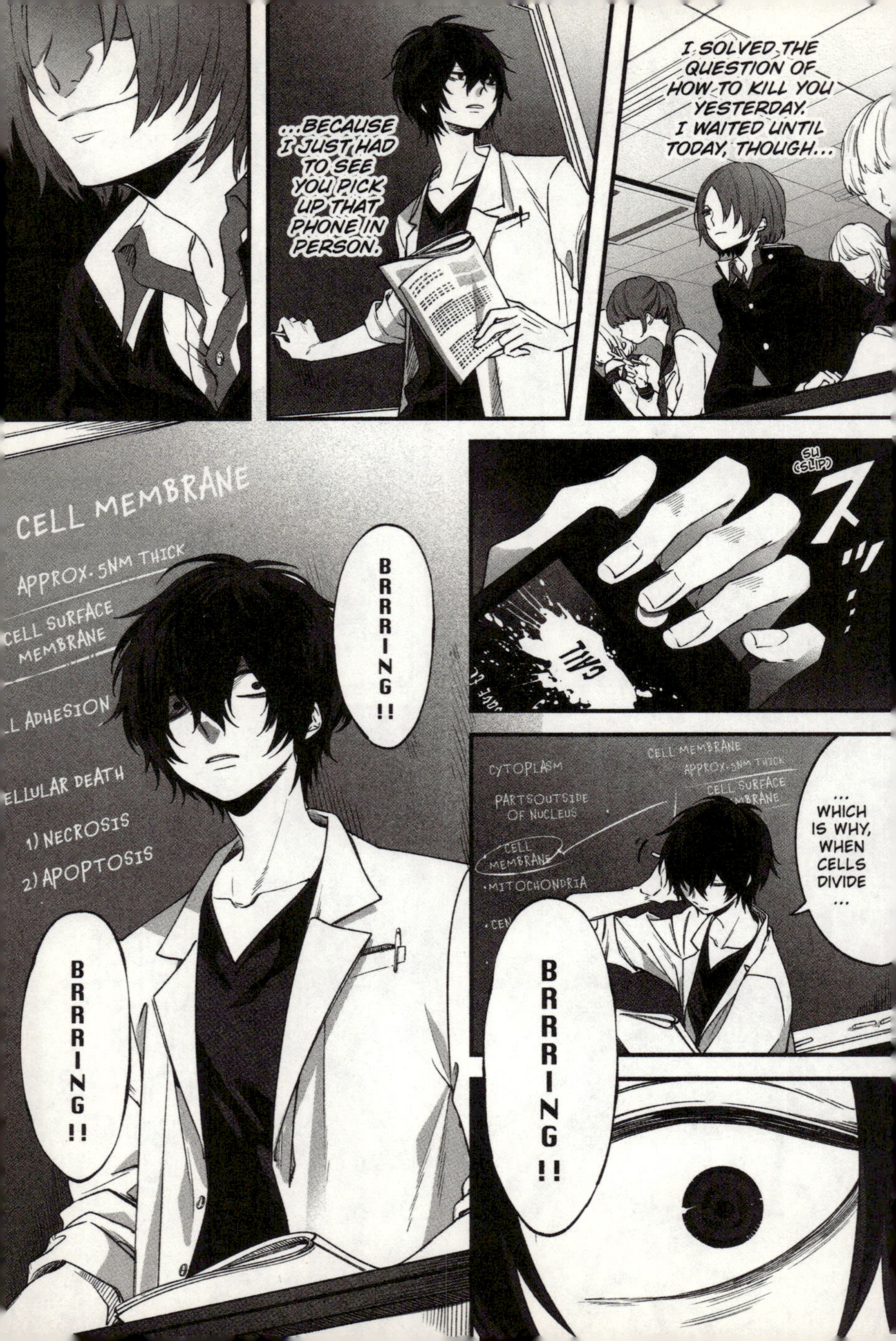
I SOLVED THE QUESTION OF HOW TO KILL YOU YESTERDAY. I WAITED UNTIL TODAY, THOUGH...
...BECAUSE I JUST HAD TO SEE YOU PICK UP THAT PHONE IN PERSON.
SU (SLIP)
CALL
CYTOPLASM
PARTSOUTSIDE OF NUCLEUS
CELL MEMBRANE
·MITOCHONDRIA
CELL MEMBRANE
APPROX. 5NM THICK
CELL SURFACE MEMBRANE
...WHICH IS WHY, WHEN CELLS DIVIDE...
BRRRING!!
CELL MEMBRANE
APPROX. 5NM THICK
CELL SURFACE MEMBRANE
L ADHESION
ELLULAR DEATH
1) NECROSIS
2) APOPTOSIS
BRRRING!!
BRRRING!!

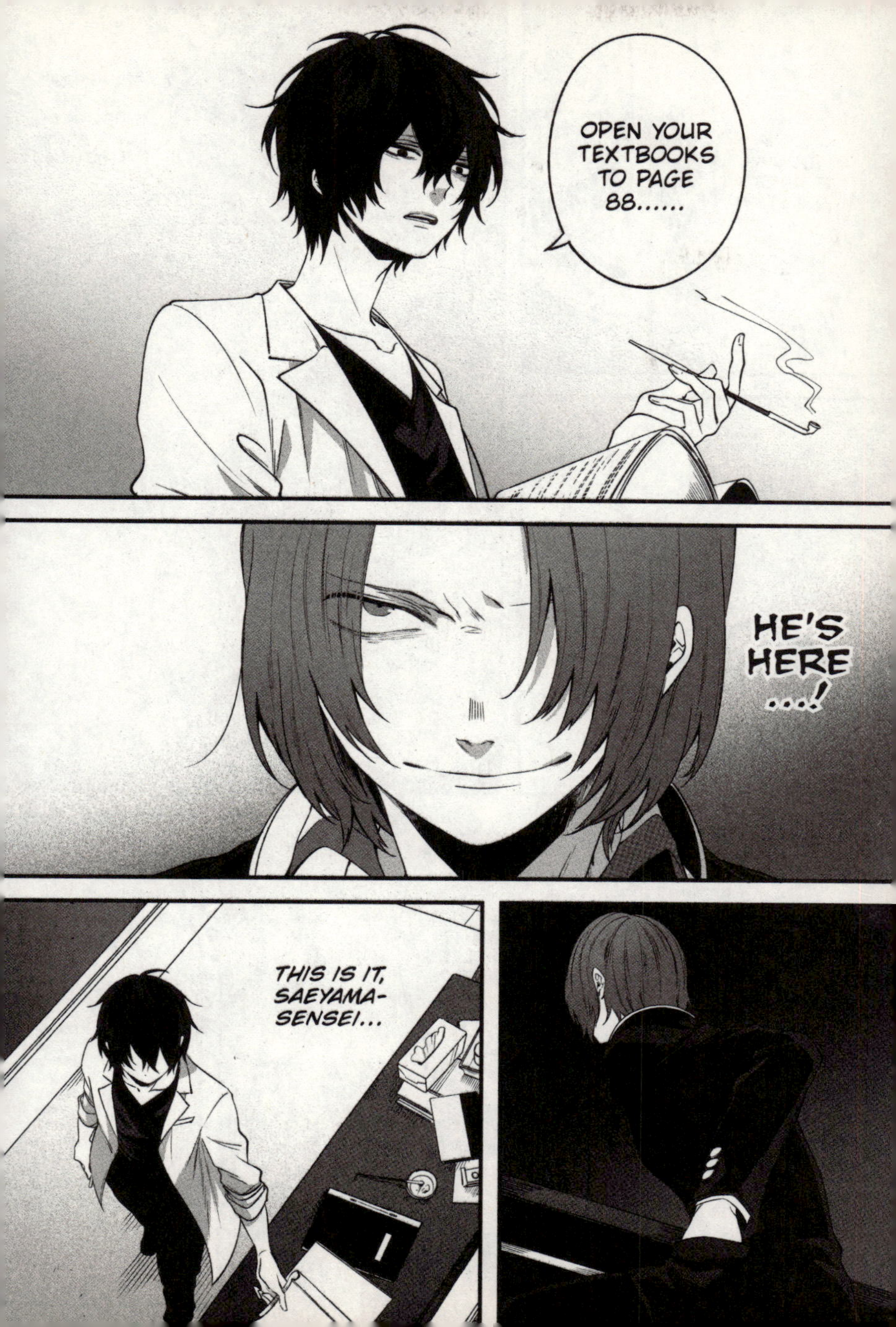
OPEN YOUR TEXTBOOKS TO PAGE 88......
HE'S HERE ...!
THIS IS IT, SAEYAMA-SENSEI...

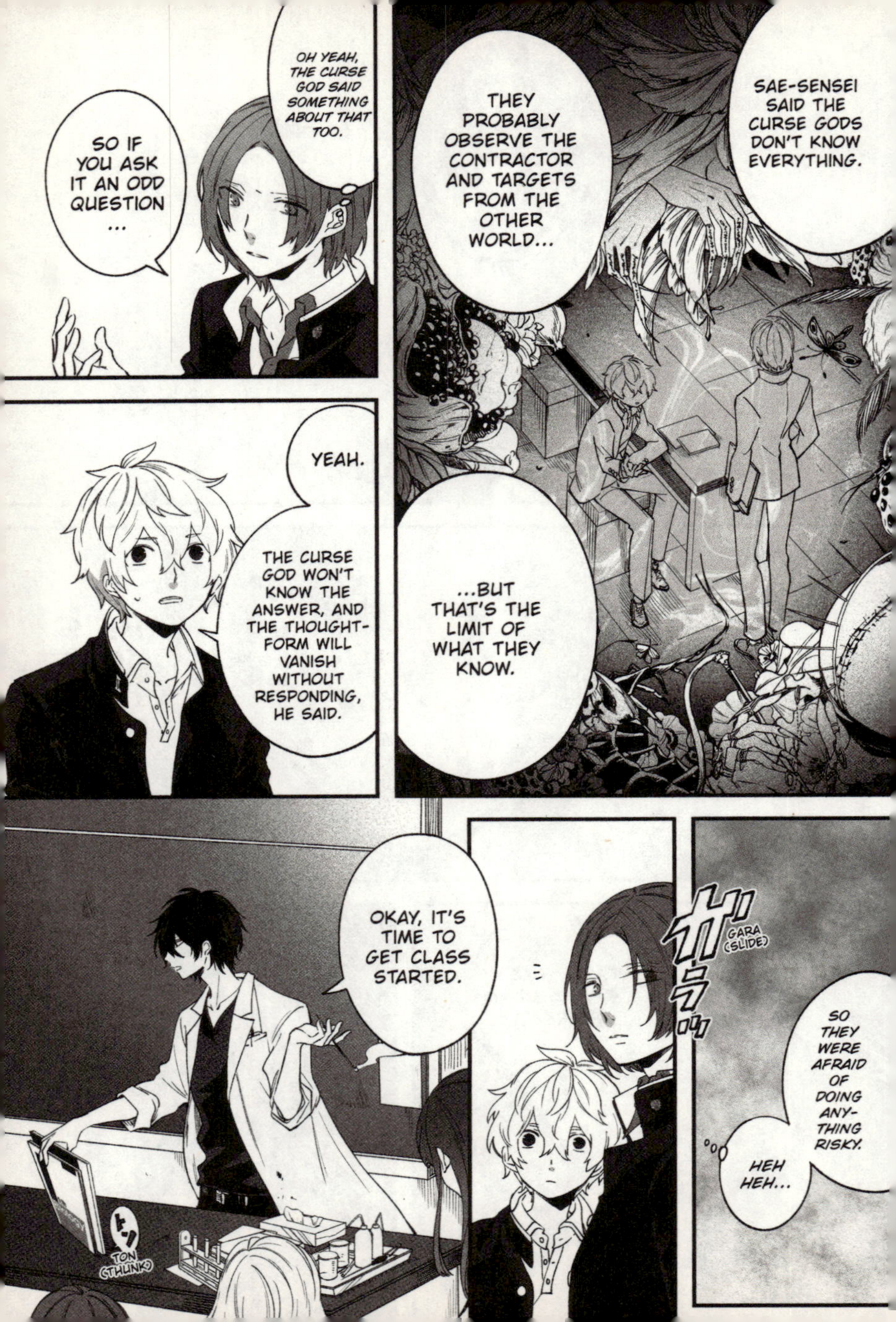
SAE-SENSEI SAID THE CURSE GODS DON'T KNOW EVERYTHING.
THEY PROBABLY OBSERVE THE CONTRACTOR AND TARGETS FROM THE OTHER WORLD...
...BUT THAT'S THE LIMIT OF WHAT THEY KNOW.
OH YEAH, THE CURSE GOD SAID SOMETHING ABOUT THAT TOO.
SO IF YOU ASK IT AN ODD QUESTION ...
YEAH.
THE CURSE GOD WON'T KNOW THE ANSWER, AND THE THOUGHT-FORM WILL VANISH WITHOUT RESPONDING, HE SAID.
SO THEY WERE AFRAID OF DOING ANY-THING RISKY.
HEH HEH...
GARA (SLIDE)
OKAY, IT'S TIME TO GET CLASS STARTED.
TON (THUNK)

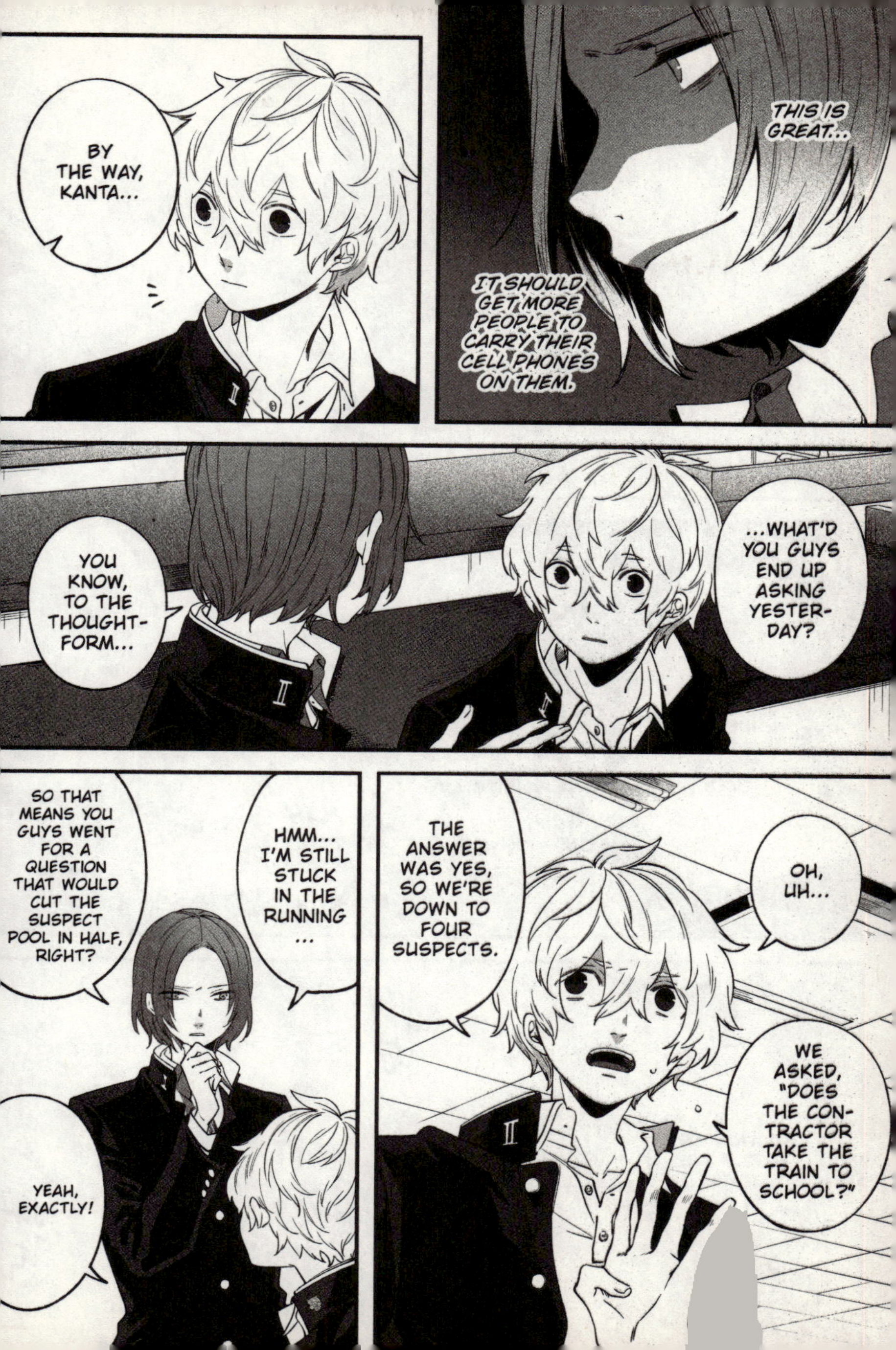
THIS IS GREAT...
IT SHOULD GET MORE PEOPLE TO CARRY THEIR CELL PHONES ON THEM.
BY THE WAY, KANTA...
...WHAT'D YOU GUYS END UP ASKING YESTER-DAY?
YOU KNOW, TO THE THOUGHT-FORM...
OH, UH...
THE ANSWER WAS YES, SO WE'RE DOWN TO FOUR SUSPECTS.
WE ASKED, "DOES THE CON-TRACTOR TAKE THE TRAIN TO SCHOOL?"
HMM... I'M STILL STUCK IN THE RUNNING ...
SO THAT MEANS YOU GUYS WENT FOR A QUESTION THAT WOULD CUT THE SUSPECT POOL IN HALF, RIGHT?
YEAH, EXACTLY!

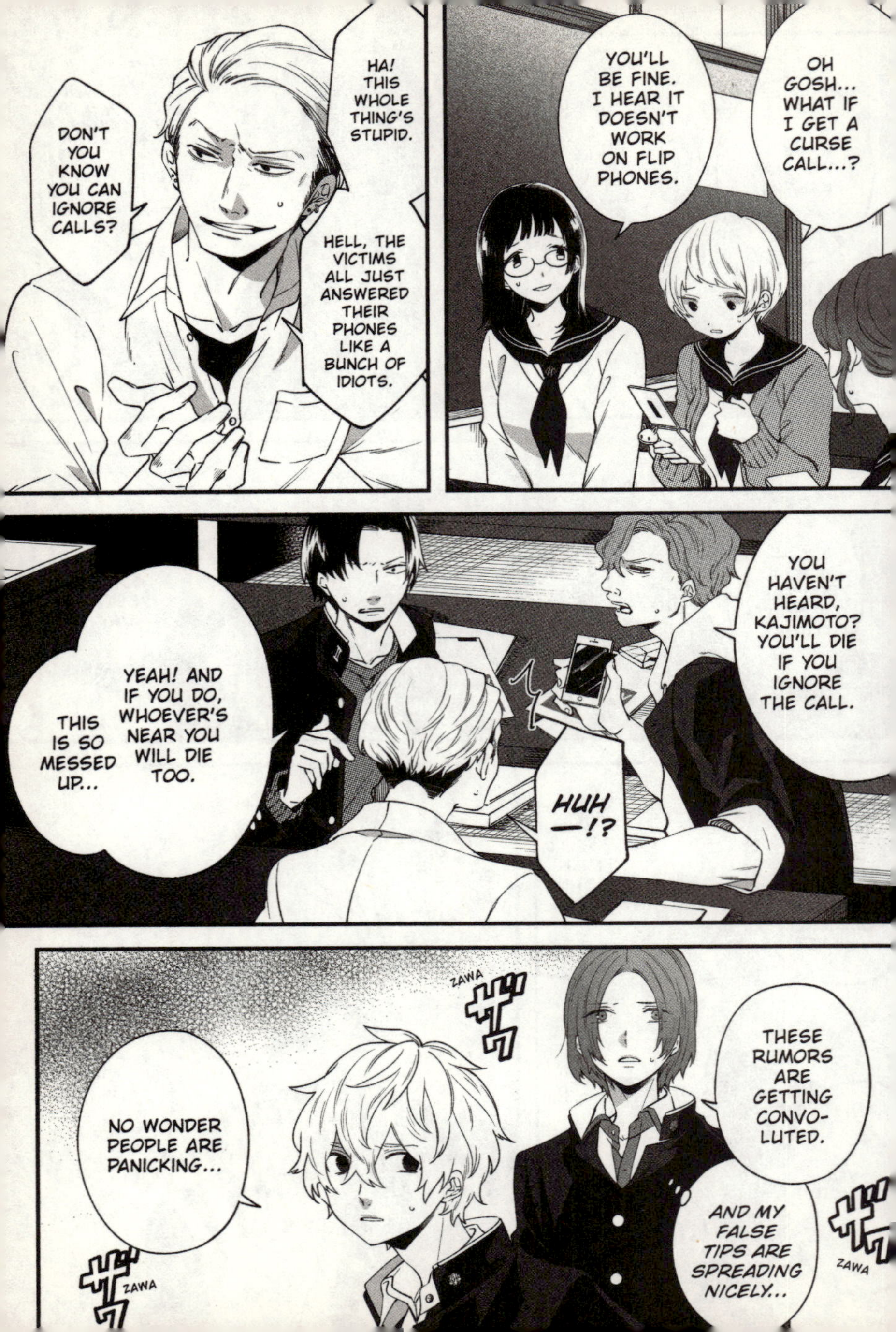
OH GOSH... WHAT IF I GET A CURSE CALL...?
YOU'LL BE FINE. I HEAR IT DOESN'T WORK ON FLIP PHONES.
HA! THIS WHOLE THING'S STUPID.
DON'T YOU KNOW YOU CAN IGNORE CALLS?
HELL, THE VICTIMS ALL JUST ANSWERED THEIR PHONES LIKE A BUNCH OF IDIOTS.
YOU HAVEN'T HEARD, KAJIMOTO? YOU'LL DIE IF YOU IGNORE THE CALL.
HUH—!?
YEAH! AND IF YOU DO, WHOEVER'S NEAR YOU WILL DIE TOO.
THIS IS SO MESSED UP...
ZAWA
THESE RUMORS ARE GETTING CONVOLUTED.
AND MY FALSE TIPS ARE SPREADING NICELY...
ZAWA
NO WONDER PEOPLE ARE PANICKING...
ZAWA

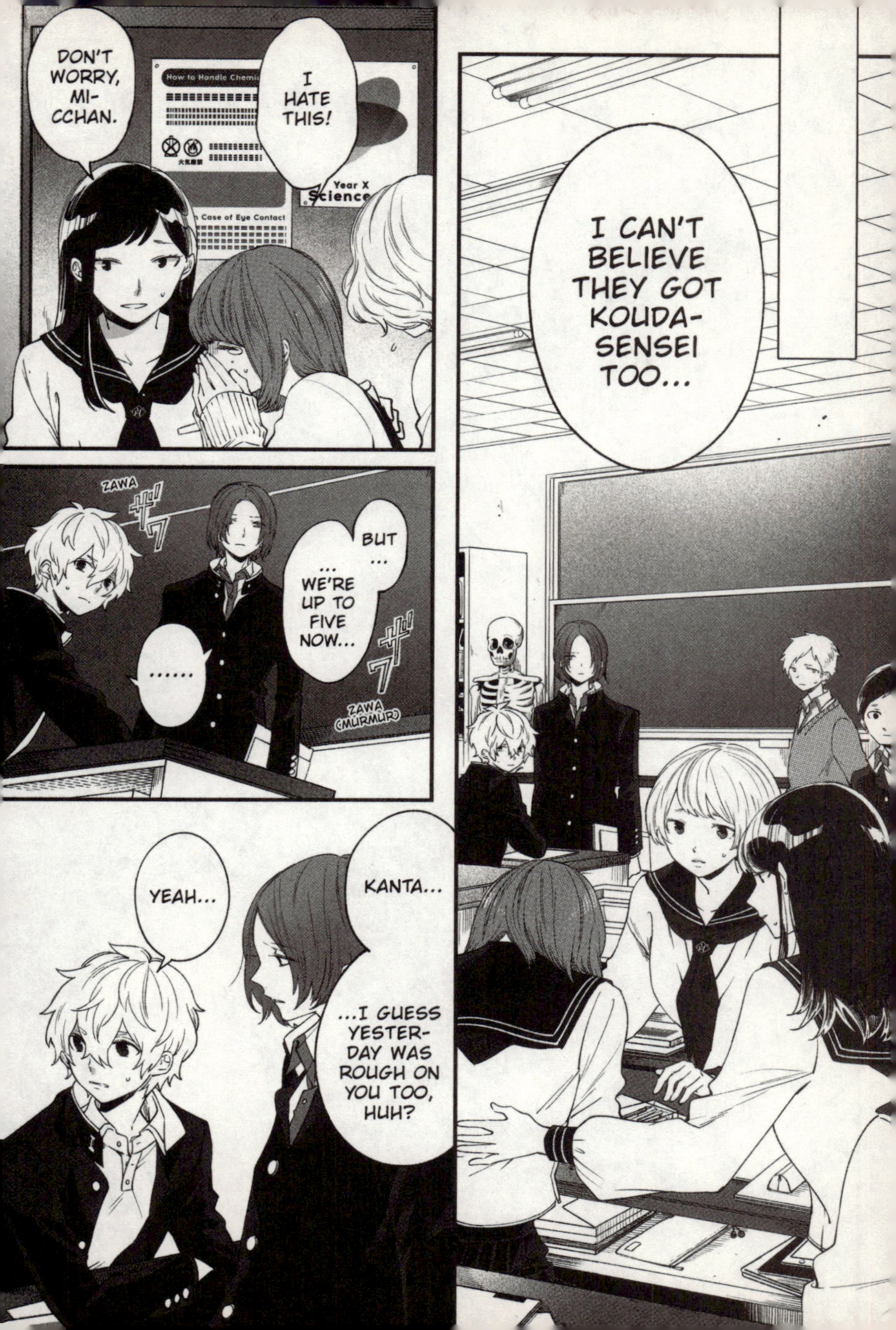
I CAN'T BELIEVE THEY GOT KOUDA-SENSEI TOO...
I HATE THIS!
DON'T WORRY, MI-CCHAN.
Year X Science
In Case of Eye Contact
BUT... ...WE'RE UP TO FIVE NOW...
ZAWA
ZAWA (MURMUR)
......
KANTA...
YEAH...
...I GUESS YESTER-DAY WAS ROUGH ON YOU TOO, HUH?

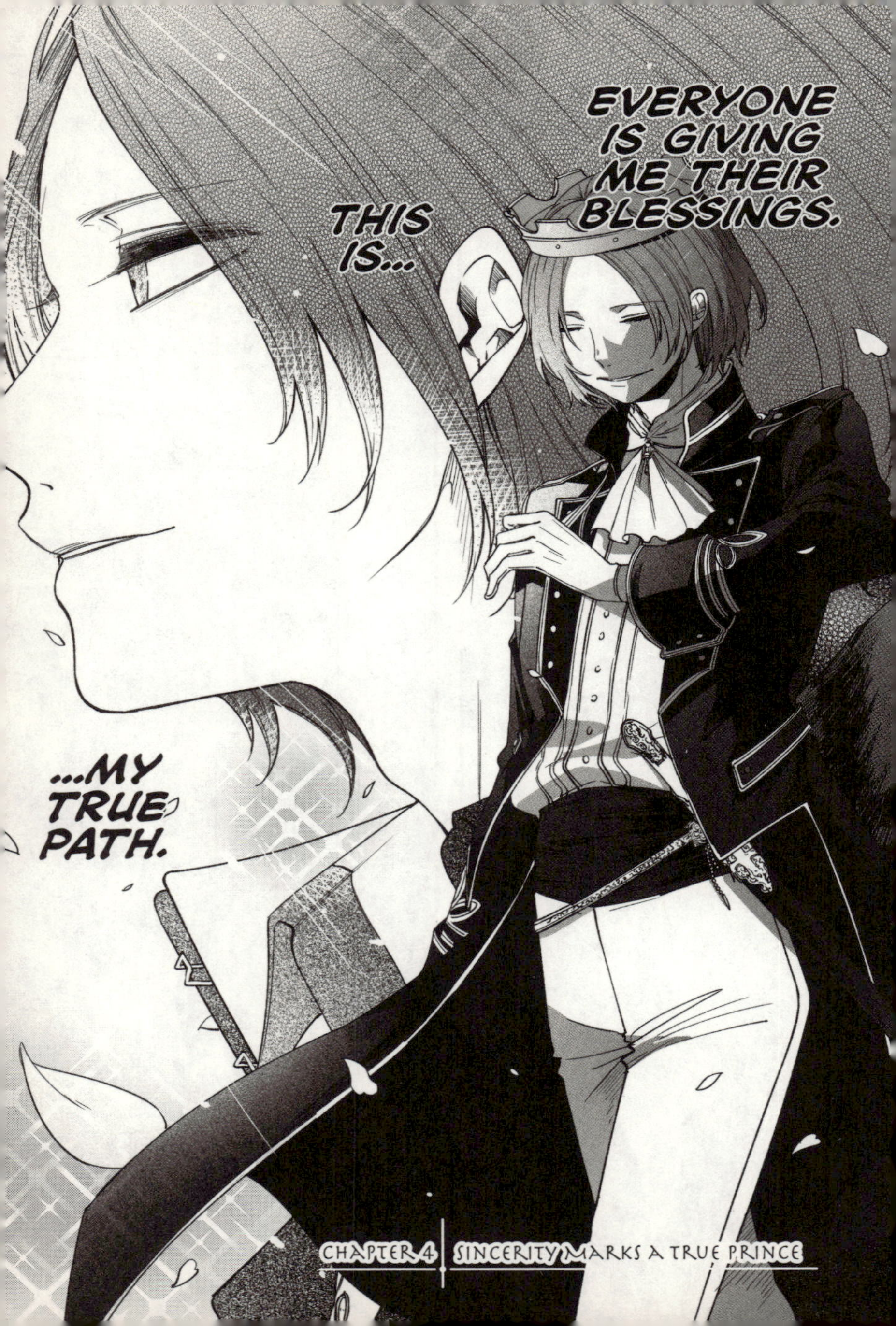
EVERYONE IS GIVING ME THEIR BLESSINGS.
THIS IS...
...MY TRUE PATH.
CHAPTER 4 SINCERITY MARKS A TRUE PRINCE

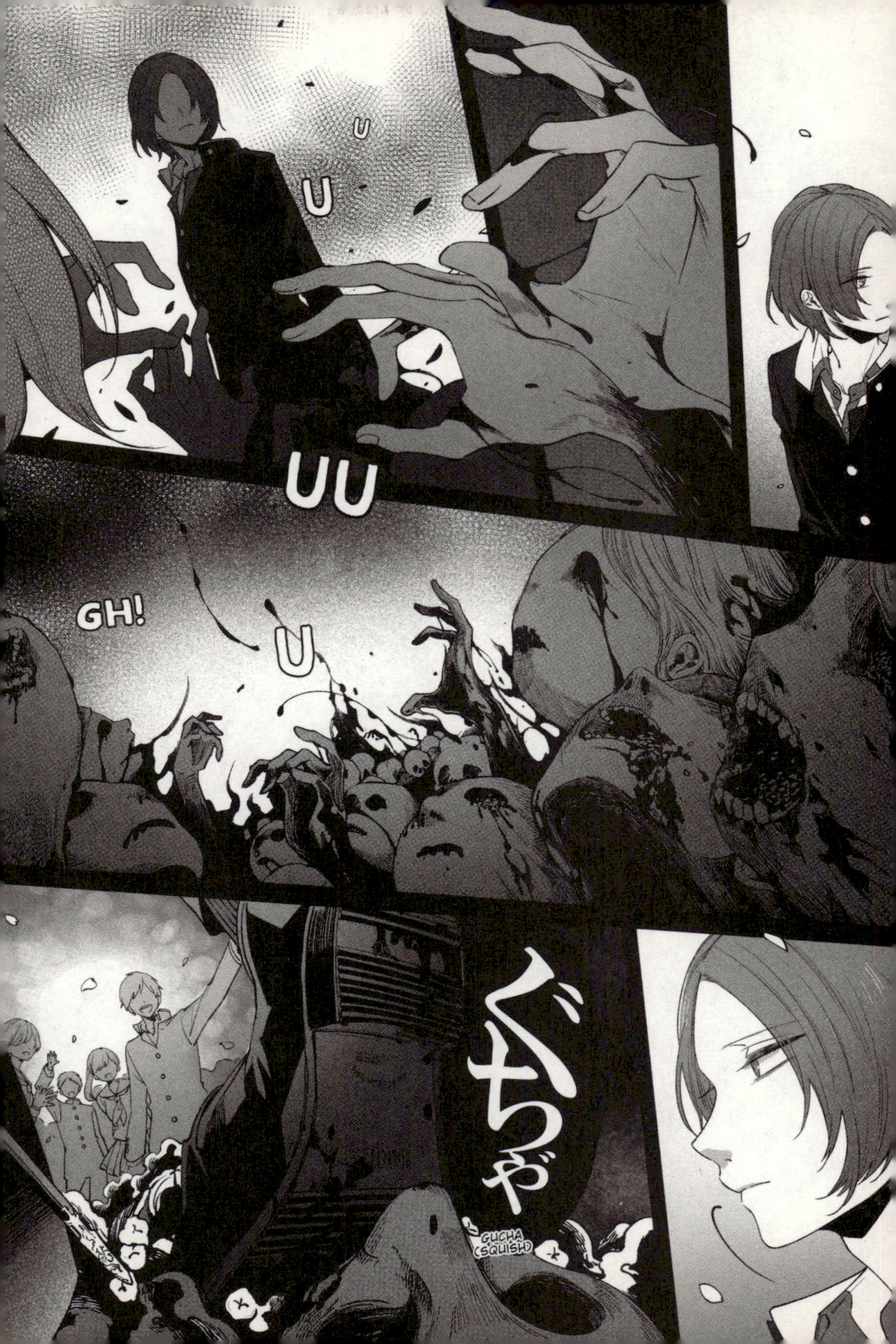

U
U
UU
GH!
U
ぐちゃ
GUCHA (SQUISH)

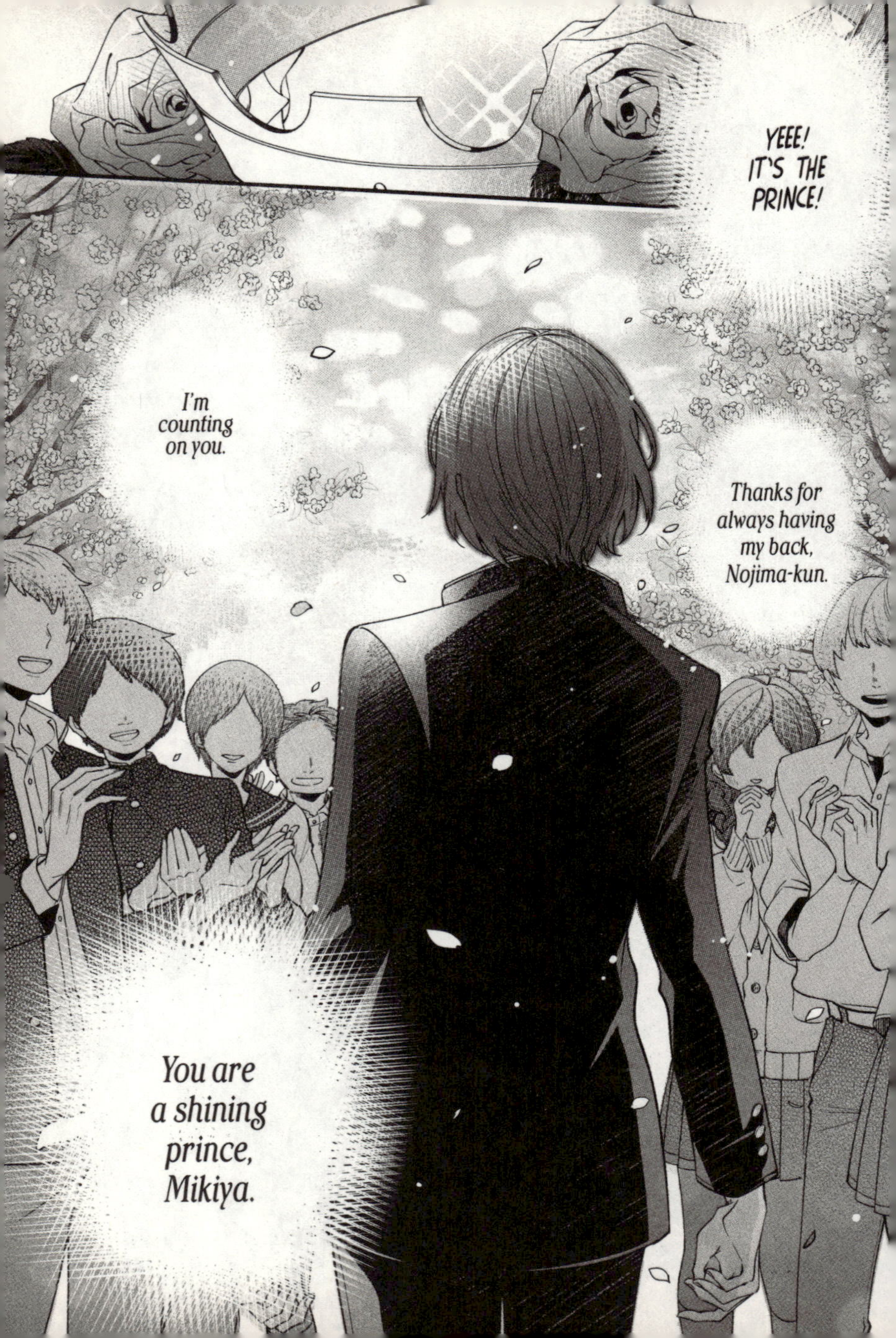
YEEE! IT'S THE PRINCE!
Thanks for always having my back, Nojima-kun.
I'm counting on you.
You are a shining prince, Mikiya.

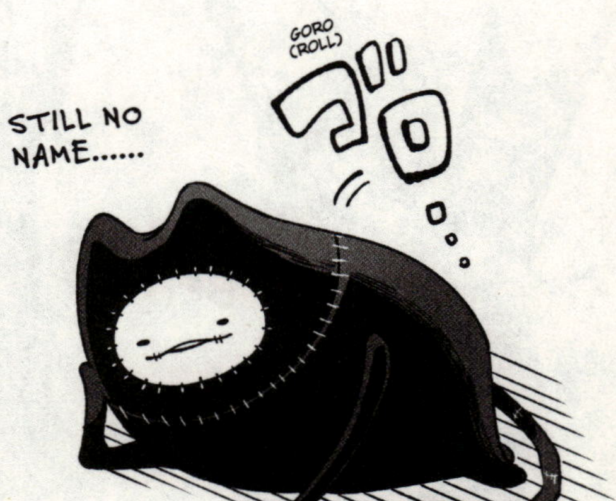
STILL NO NAME......
GORO (ROLL)
ゴロ

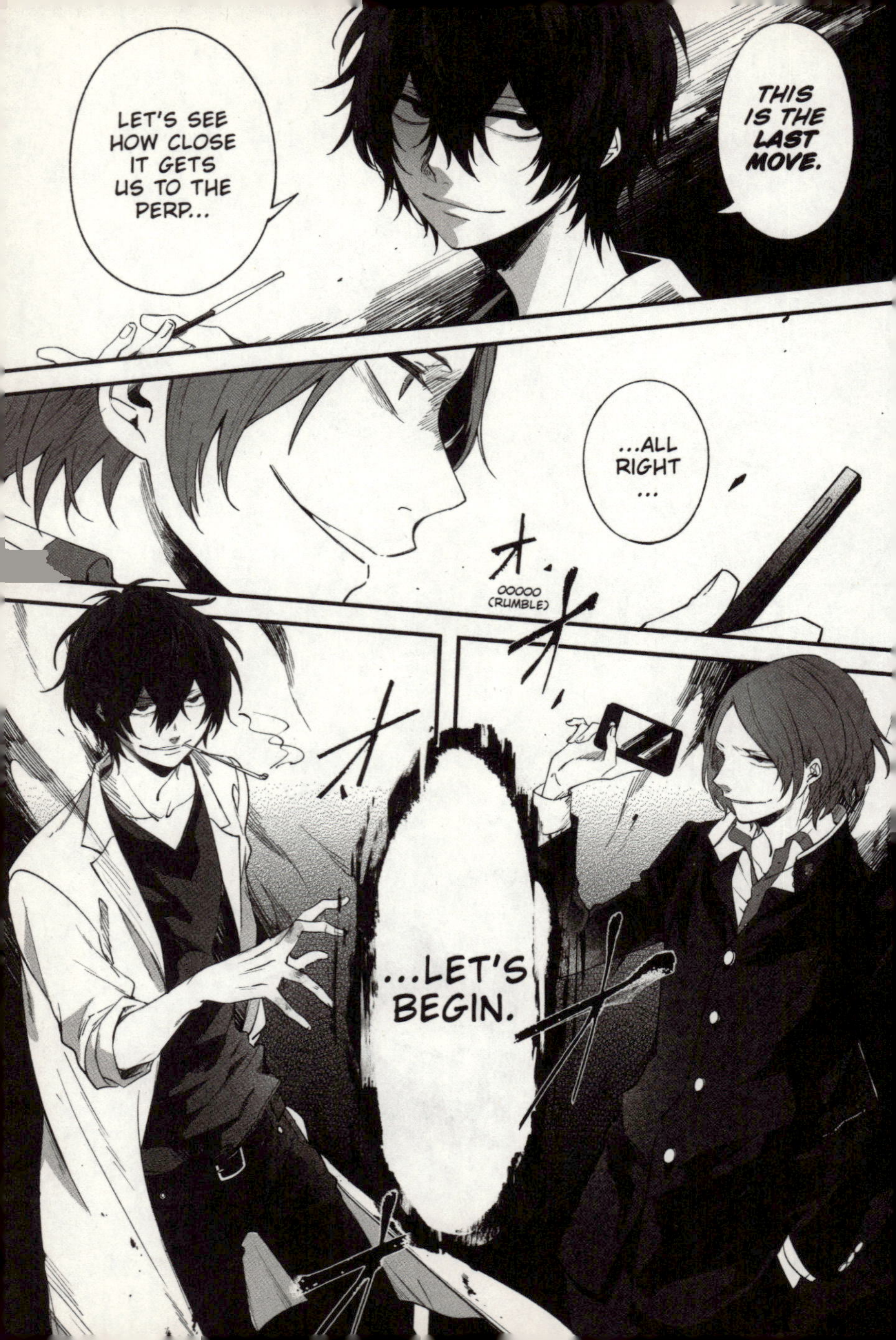
THIS IS THE LAST MOVE.
LET'S SEE HOW CLOSE IT GETS US TO THE PERP...
...ALL RIGHT ...
OOOOO (RUMBLE)
...LET'S BEGIN.

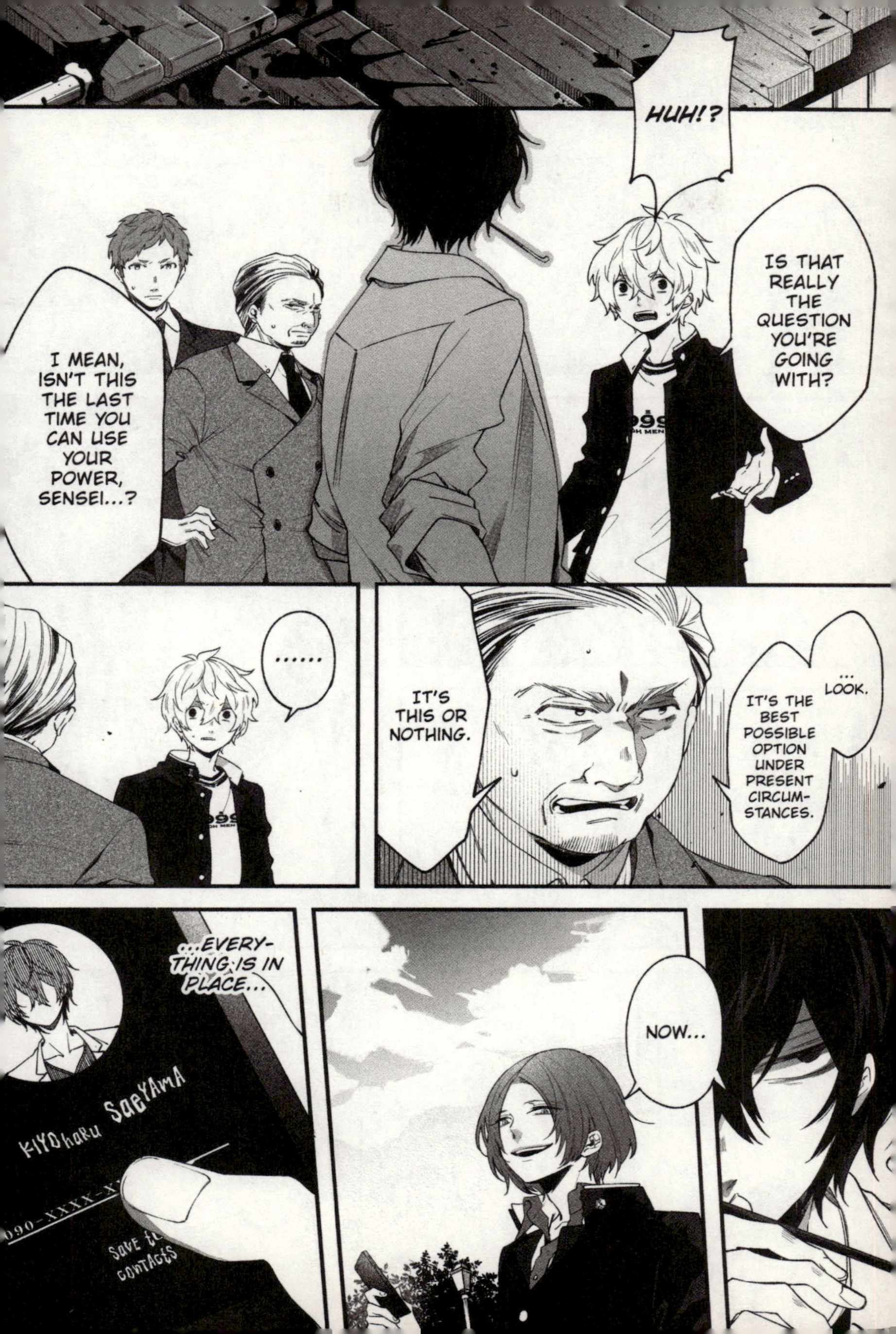
HUH!?
IS THAT REALLY THE QUESTION YOU'RE GOING WITH?
I MEAN, ISN'T THIS THE LAST TIME YOU CAN USE YOUR POWER, SENSEI...?
... LOOK.
IT'S THE BEST POSSIBLE OPTION UNDER PRESENT CIRCUM-STANCES.
IT'S THIS OR NOTHING.
......
NOW...
...EVERY-THING IS IN PLACE...
KIYOharu SaeYAmA

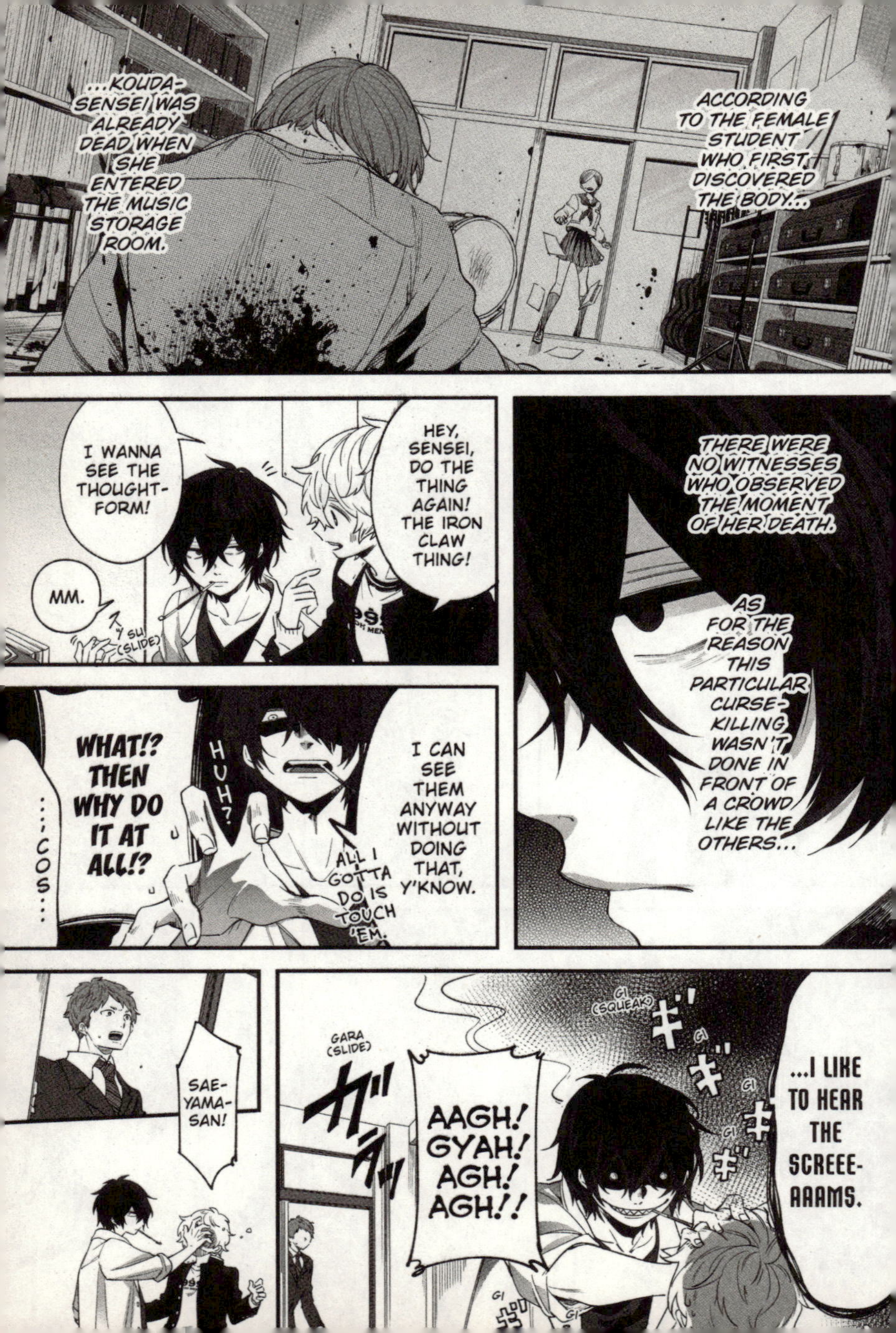
ACCORDING TO THE FEMALE STUDENT WHO FIRST DISCOVERED THE BODY...
...KOUDA-SENSEI WAS ALREADY DEAD WHEN SHE ENTERED THE MUSIC STORAGE ROOM.
THERE WERE NO WITNESSES WHO OBSERVED THE MOMENT OF HER DEATH.
AS FOR THE REASON THIS PARTICULAR CURSE-KILLING WASN'T DONE IN FRONT OF A CROWD LIKE THE OTHERS...
HEY, SENSEI, DO THE THING AGAIN! THE IRON CLAW THING!
I WANNA SEE THE THOUGHT-FORM!
MM.
SU (SLIDE)
I CAN SEE THEM ANYWAY WITHOUT DOING THAT, Y'KNOW.
ALL I GOTTA DO IS TOUCH 'EM.
HUH?
WHAT!? THEN WHY DO IT AT ALL!?
...COS...
...I LIKE TO HEAR THE SCREEE-AAAMS.
GI (SQUEAK)
GI
GI
GI
AAGH! GYAH! AGH! AGH!!
GARA (SLIDE)
GI
GI
SAE-YAMA-SAN!

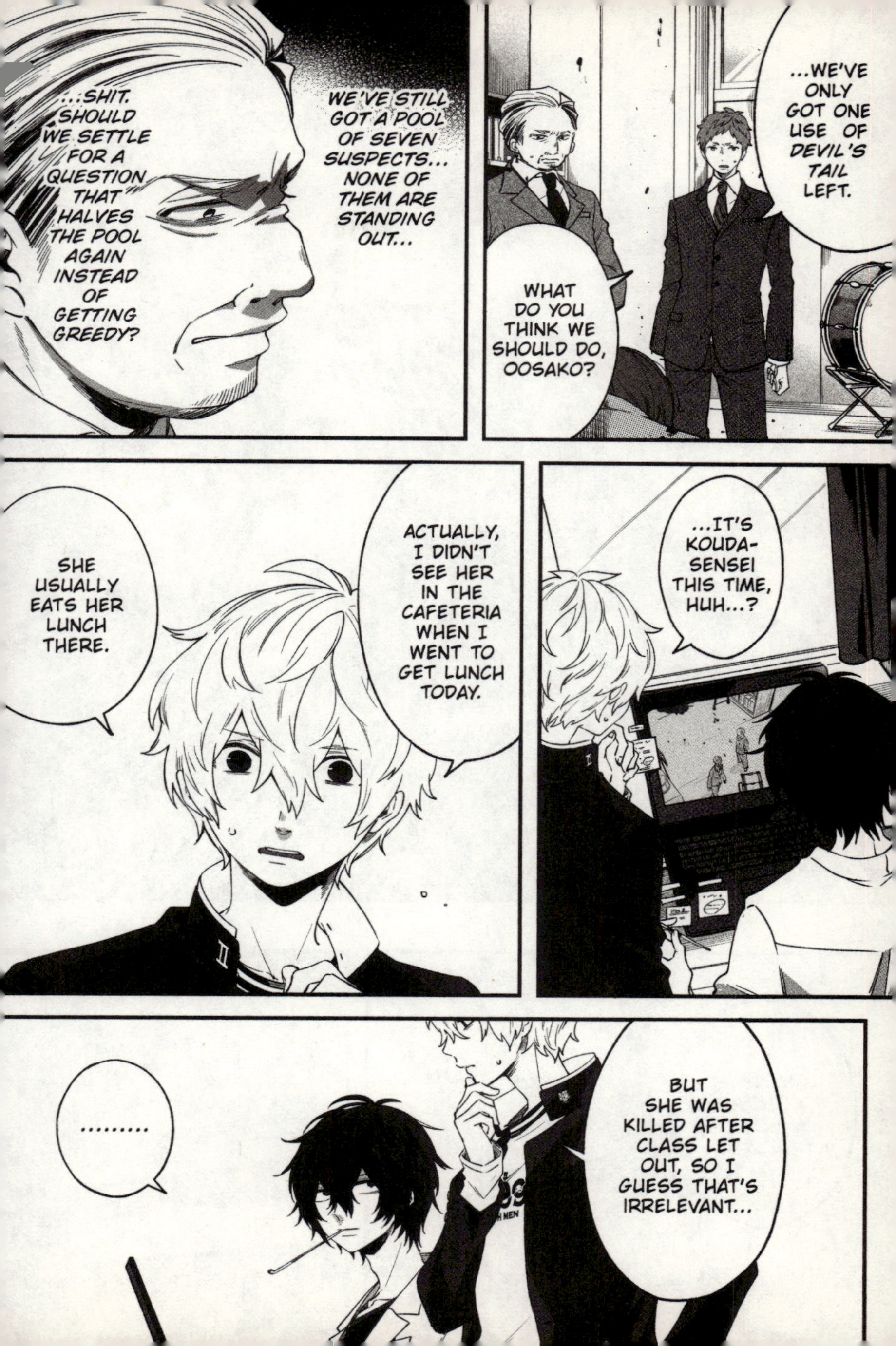
...WE'VE ONLY GOT ONE USE OF DEVIL'S TAIL LEFT.
WHAT DO YOU THINK WE SHOULD DO, OOSAKO?
WE'VE STILL GOT A POOL OF SEVEN SUSPECTS... NONE OF THEM ARE STANDING OUT...
...SHIT. SHOULD WE SETTLE FOR A QUESTION THAT HALVES THE POOL AGAIN INSTEAD OF GETTING GREEDY?
...IT'S KOUDA-SENSEI THIS TIME, HUH...?
ACTUALLY, I DIDN'T SEE HER IN THE CAFETERIA WHEN I WENT TO GET LUNCH TODAY.
SHE USUALLY EATS HER LUNCH THERE.
BUT SHE WAS KILLED AFTER CLASS LET OUT, SO I GUESS THAT'S IRRELEVANT...
....

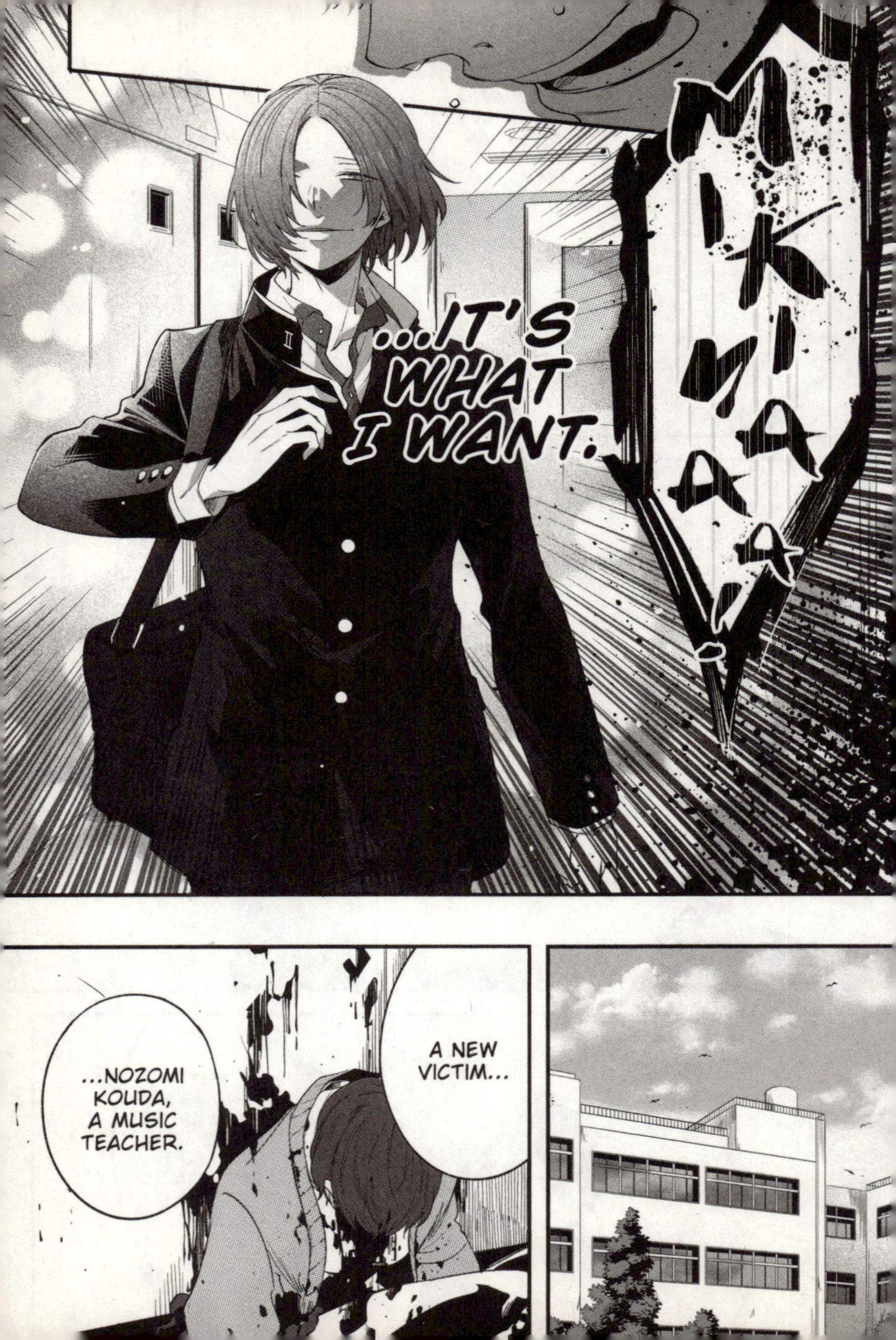
...IT'S WHAT I WANT.
A NEW VICTIM...
...NOZOMI KOUDA, A MUSIC TEACHER.

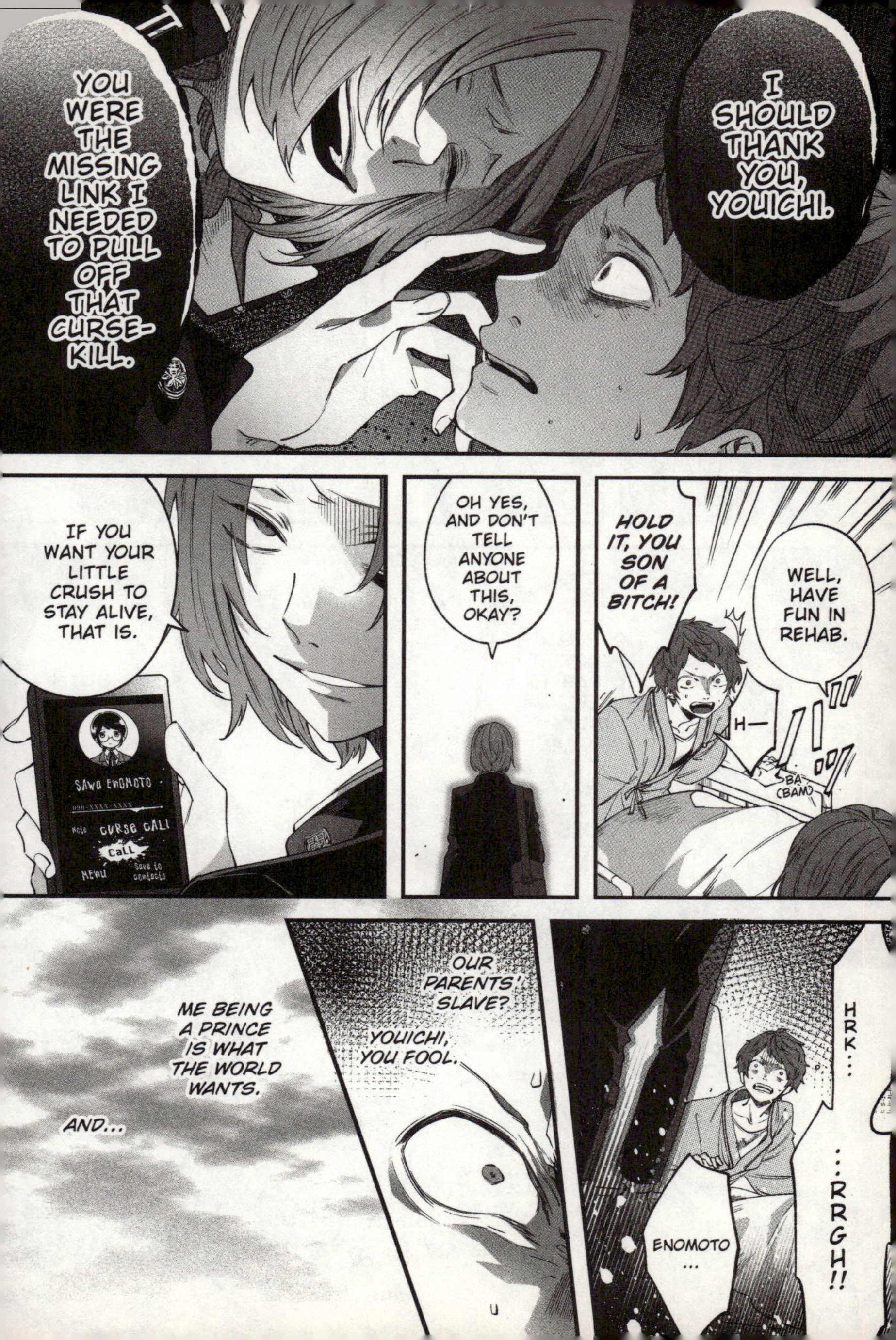
I SHOULD THANK YOU, YOUICHI.
YOU WERE THE MISSING LINK I NEEDED TO PULL OFF THAT CURSE-KILL.
WELL, HAVE FUN IN REHAB.
HOLD IT, YOU SON OF A BITCH!
H—
BA (BAM)
OH YES, AND DON'T TELL ANYONE ABOUT THIS, OKAY?
IF YOU WANT YOUR LITTLE CRUSH TO STAY ALIVE, THAT IS.
SAWA ENOMOTO
090-XXXX-XXXX
Note CURSE CALL
CaLL
Menu
Save to contacts
HRK...
...RRGH!!
ENOMOTO...
OUR PARENTS' SLAVE?
YOUICHI, YOU FOOL.
ME BEING A PRINCE IS WHAT THE WORLD WANTS.
AND...

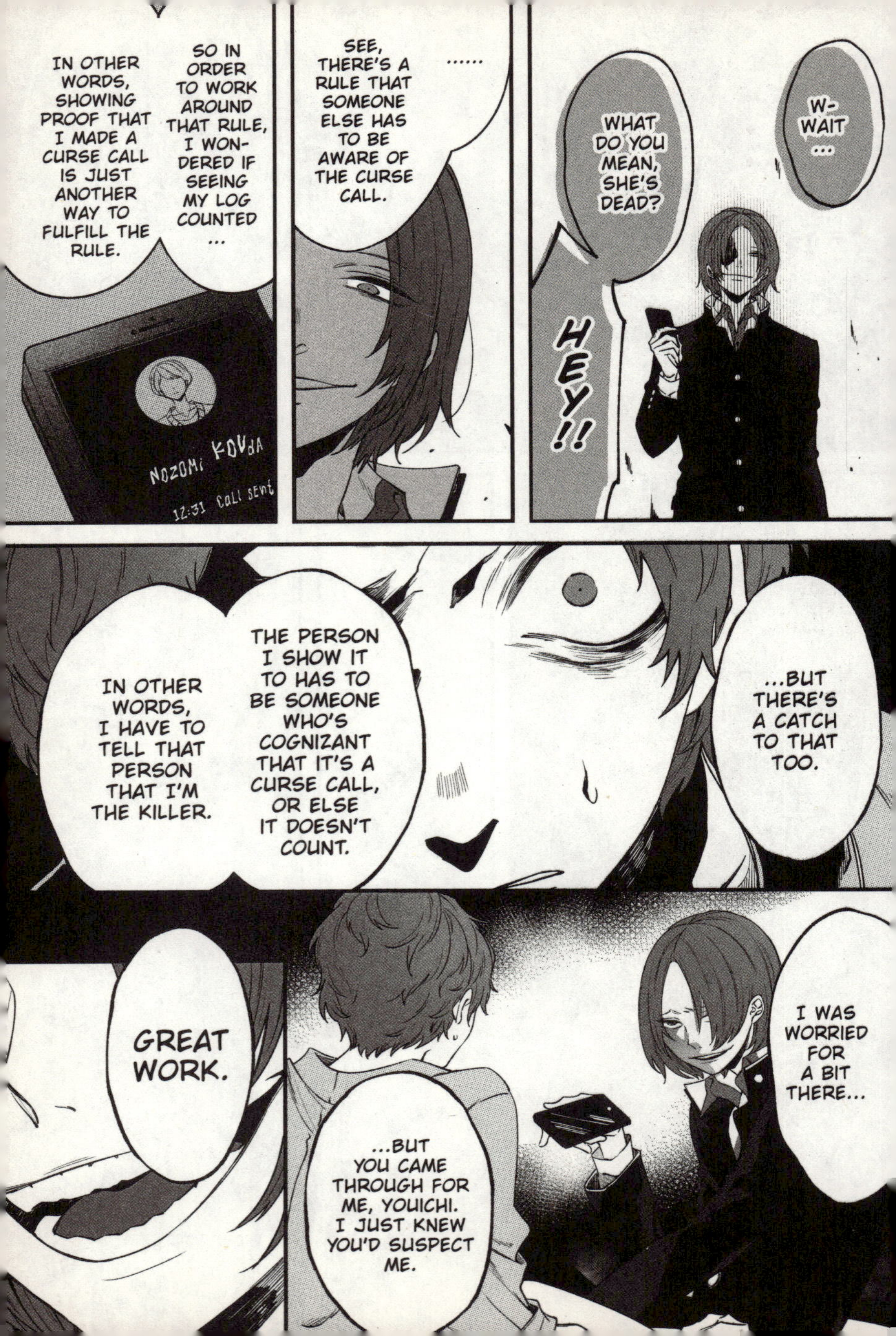
W-WAIT...
WHAT DO YOU MEAN, SHE'S DEAD?
HEY!!
......
SEE, THERE'S A RULE THAT SOMEONE ELSE HAS TO BE AWARE OF THE CURSE CALL.
SO IN ORDER TO WORK AROUND THAT RULE, I WONDERED IF SEEING MY LOG COUNTED...
IN OTHER WORDS, SHOWING PROOF THAT I MADE A CURSE CALL IS JUST ANOTHER WAY TO FULFILL THE RULE.
NOZOMi KOUdA
12:31 Call sent
...BUT THERE'S A CATCH TO THAT TOO.
THE PERSON I SHOW IT TO HAS TO BE SOMEONE WHO'S COGNIZANT THAT IT'S A CURSE CALL, OR ELSE IT DOESN'T COUNT.
IN OTHER WORDS, I HAVE TO TELL THAT PERSON THAT I'M THE KILLER.
I WAS WORRIED FOR A BIT THERE...
...BUT YOU CAME THROUGH FOR ME, YOUICHI. I JUST KNEW YOU'D SUSPECT ME.
GREAT WORK.

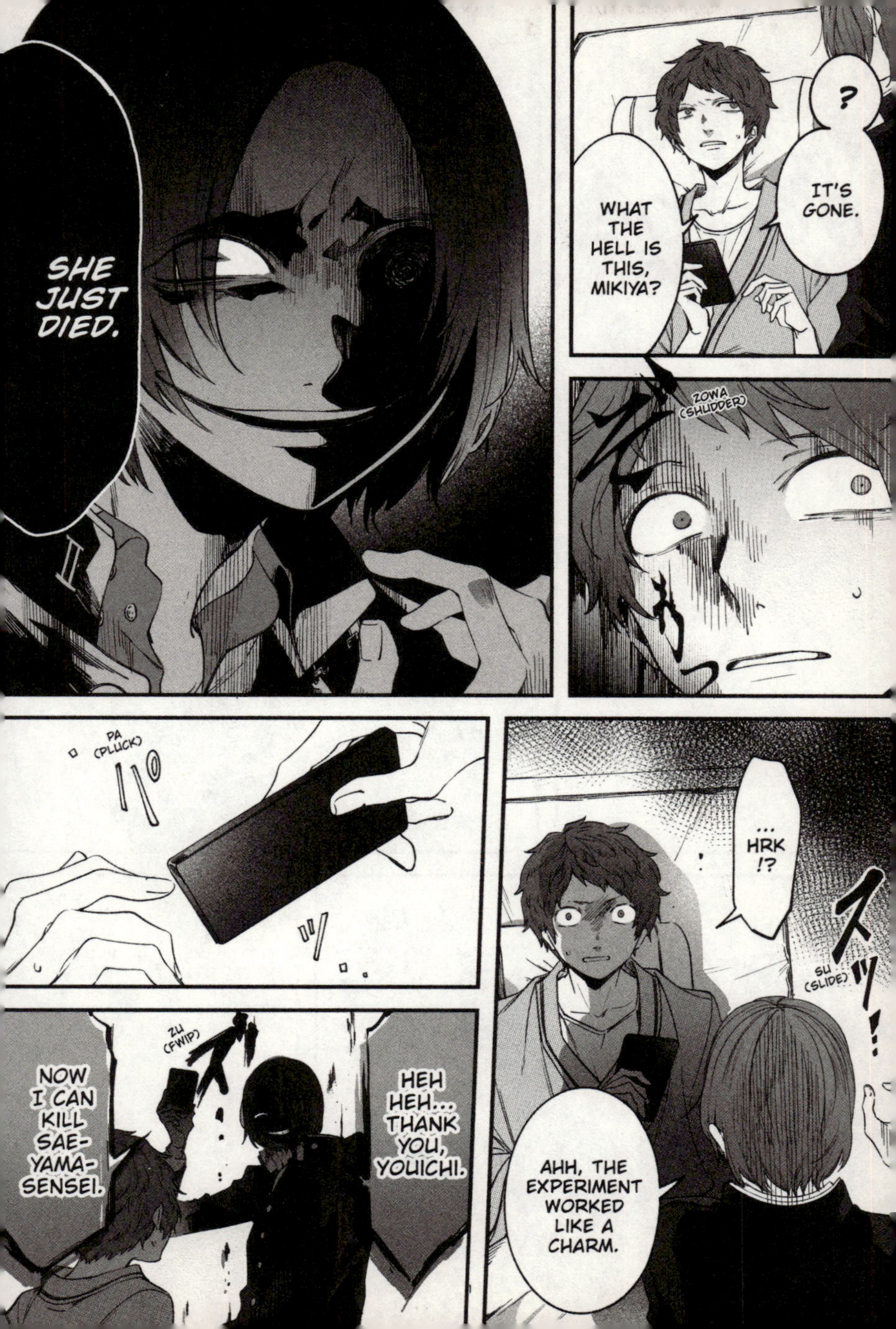
?
IT'S GONE.
WHAT THE HELL IS THIS, MIKIYA?
ZOWA (SHUDDER)
SHE JUST DIED.
...HRK !?
SU (SLIDE)
AHH, THE EXPERIMENT WORKED LIKE A CHARM.
PA (PLUCK)
ZU (FWIP)
HEH HEH... THANK YOU, YOUICHI.
NOW I CAN KILL SAE-YAMA-SENSEI.

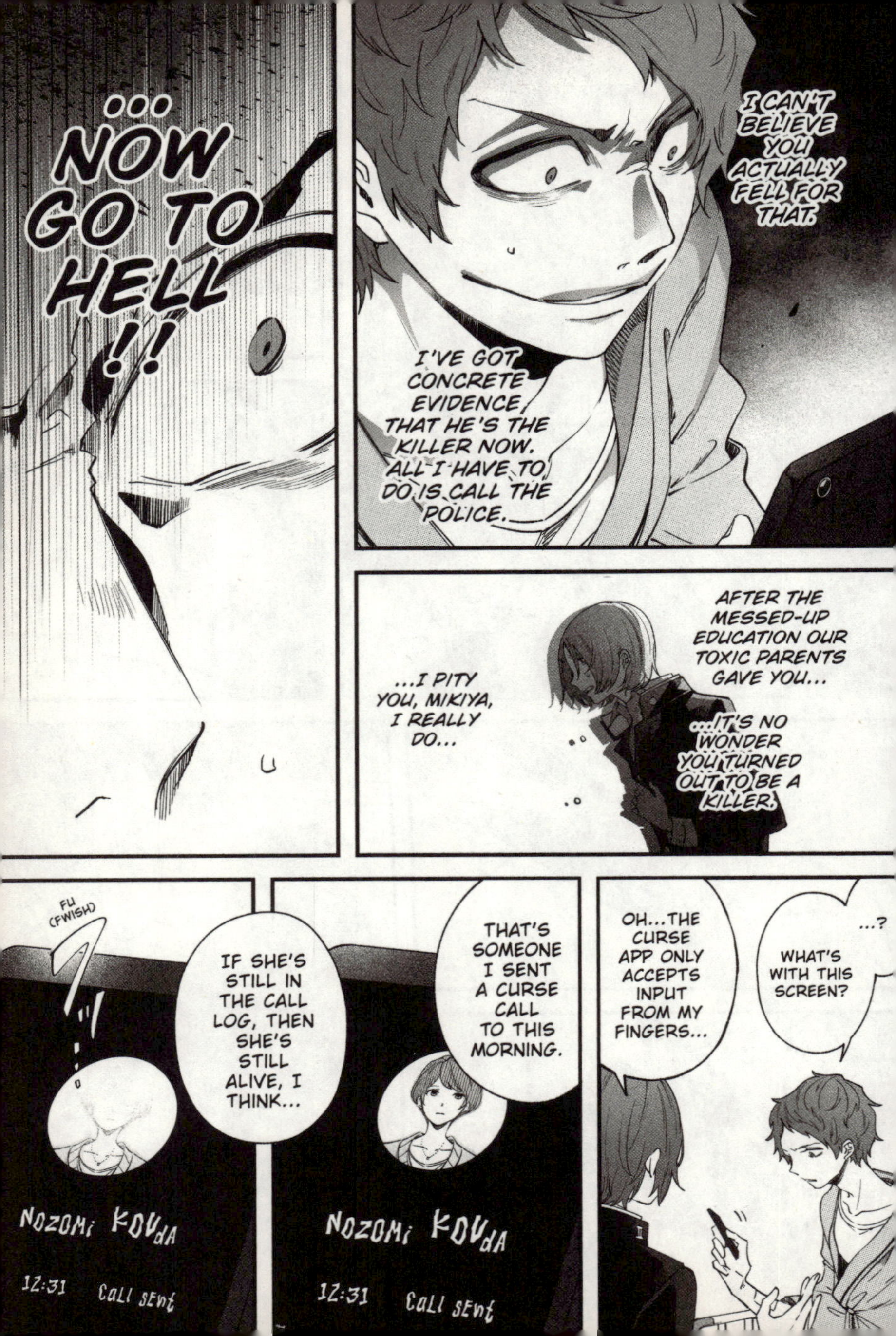
I CAN'T BELIEVE YOU ACTUALLY FELL FOR THAT.
I'VE GOT CONCRETE EVIDENCE THAT HE'S THE KILLER NOW. ALL I HAVE TO DO IS CALL THE POLICE.
AFTER THE MESSED-UP EDUCATION OUR TOXIC PARENTS GAVE YOU...
...IT'S NO WONDER YOU TURNED OUT TO BE A KILLER.
...I PITY YOU, MIKIYA, I REALLY DO...
...NOW GO TO HELL!!
...?
WHAT'S WITH THIS SCREEN?
OH...THE CURSE APP ONLY ACCEPTS INPUT FROM MY FINGERS...
THAT'S SOMEONE I SENT A CURSE CALL TO THIS MORNING.
NOZOMI KOUDA
12:31 Call sent
FU (FWISH)
IF SHE'S STILL IN THE CALL LOG, THEN SHE'S STILL ALIVE, I THINK...
NOZOMI KOUDA
12:31 Call sent

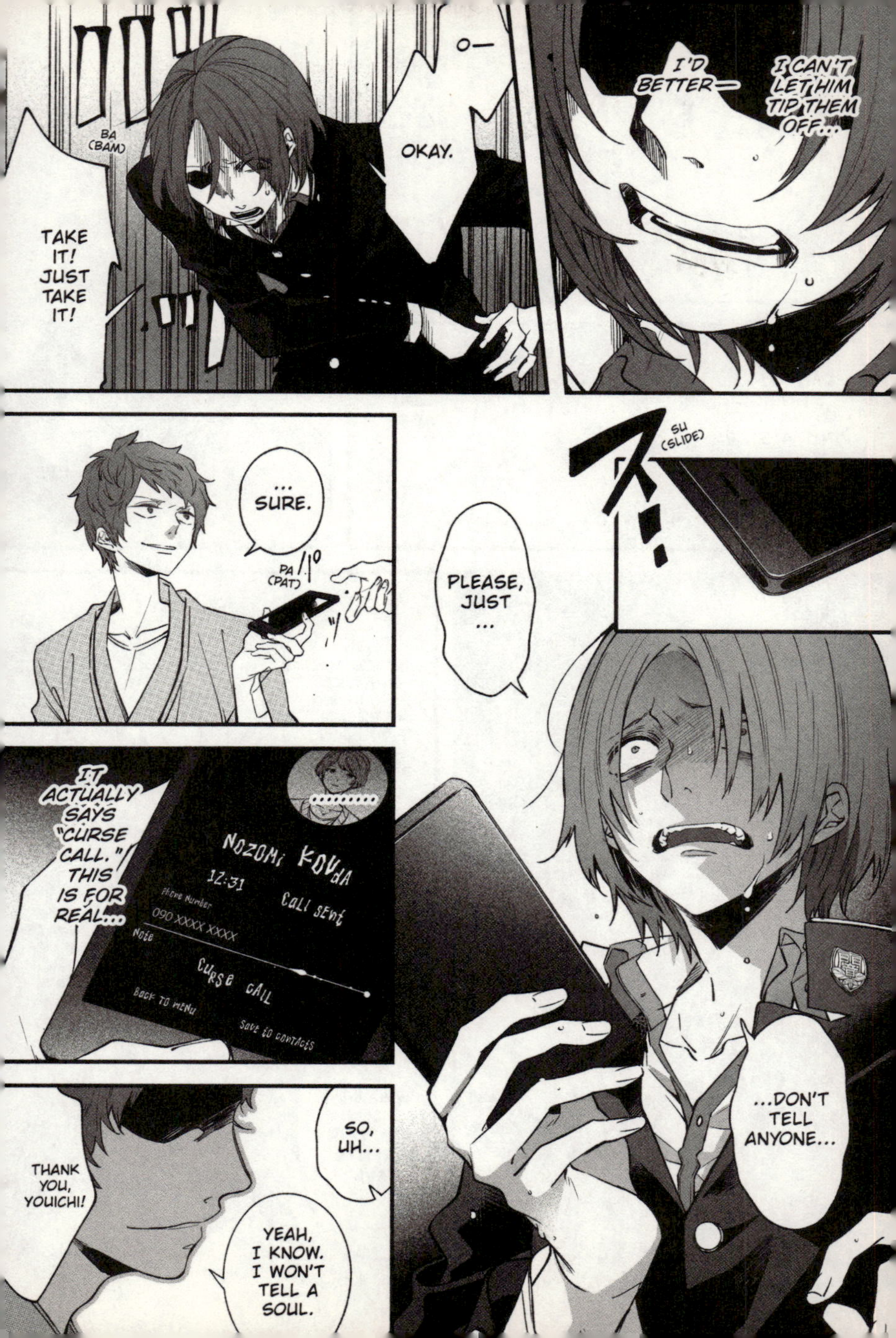
I CAN'T LET HIM TIP THEM OFF...
I'D BETTER—
O—
OKAY.
BA (BAM)
TAKE IT! JUST TAKE IT!
SU (SLIDE)
PLEASE, JUST ...
... SURE.
PA (PAT)
...DON'T TELL ANYONE...
IT ACTUALLY SAYS "CURSE CALL." THIS IS FOR REAL...
NOZOMI KOUDA
12:31
CALL SENT
Phone Number
090 XXXX XXXX
Note
CURSE CALL
BACK TO MENU
SAVE TO CONTACTS
SO, UH...
YEAH, I KNOW. I WON'T TELL A SOUL.
THANK YOU, YOUICHI!

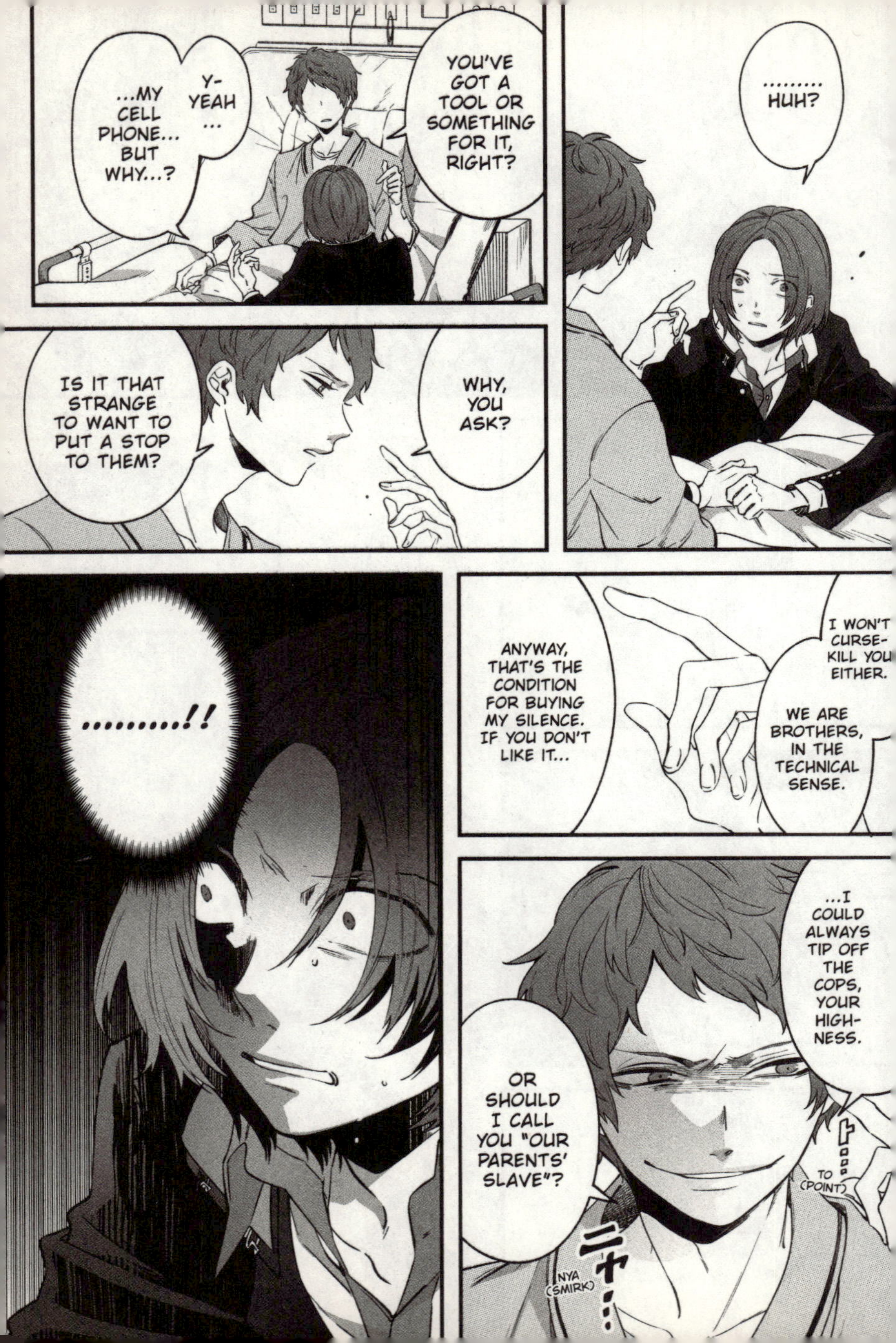
....
HUH?
YOU'VE GOT A TOOL OR SOMETHING FOR IT, RIGHT?
Y-YEAH...
...MY CELL PHONE... BUT WHY...?
WHY, YOU ASK?
IS IT THAT STRANGE TO WANT TO PUT A STOP TO THEM?
I WON'T CURSE-KILL YOU EITHER.
WE ARE BROTHERS, IN THE TECHNICAL SENSE.
ANYWAY, THAT'S THE CONDITION FOR BUYING MY SILENCE. IF YOU DON'T LIKE IT...
...I COULD ALWAYS TIP OFF THE COPS, YOUR HIGHNESS.
ト...
TO (POINT)
OR SHOULD I CALL YOU "OUR PARENTS' SLAVE"?
ニヤ...
NYA (SMIRK)
.........!!

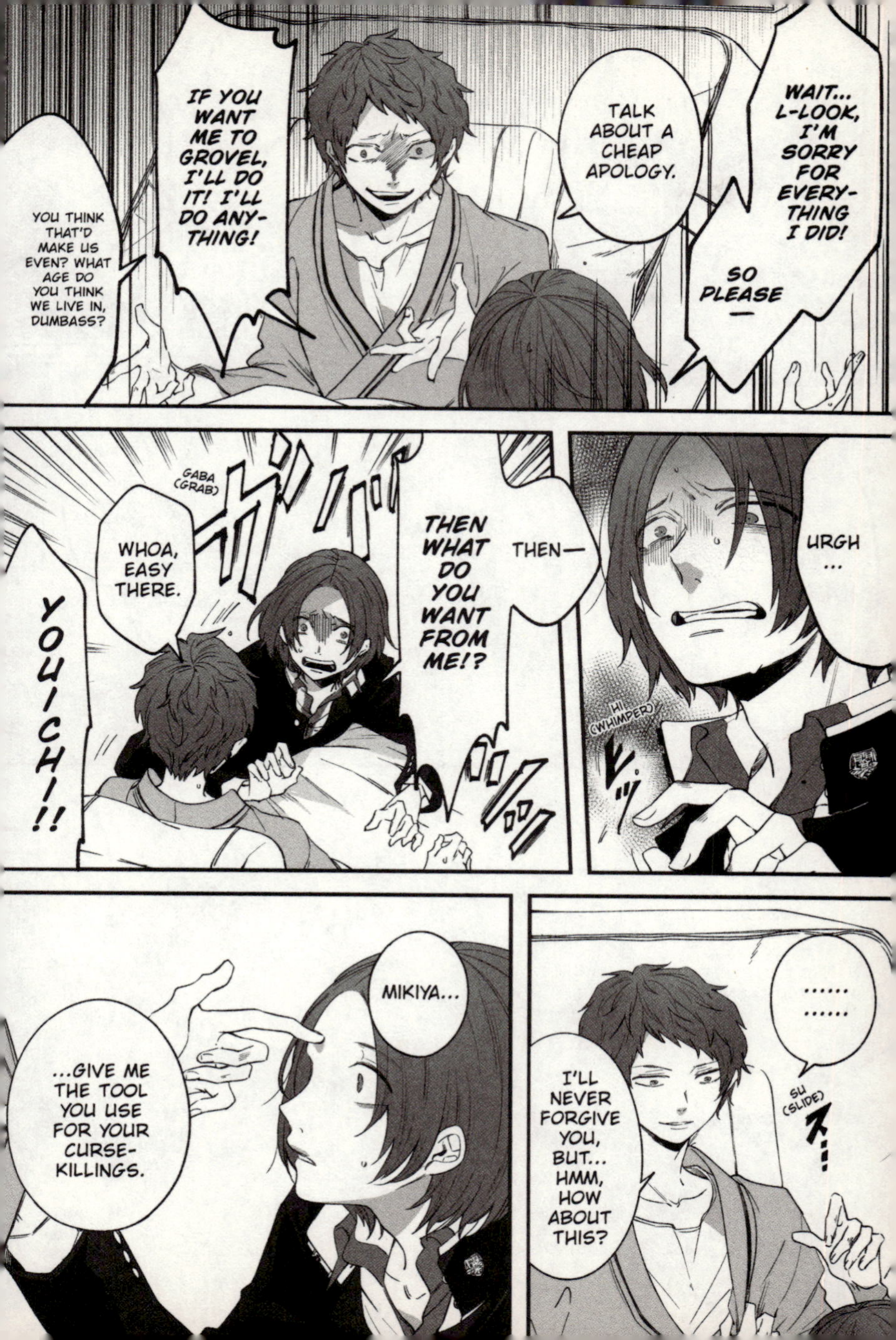
WAIT... L-LOOK, I'M SORRY FOR EVERY-THING I DID!
SO PLEASE —
TALK ABOUT A CHEAP APOLOGY.
IF YOU WANT ME TO GROVEL, I'LL DO IT! I'LL DO ANY-THING!
YOU THINK THAT'D MAKE US EVEN? WHAT AGE DO YOU THINK WE LIVE IN, DUMBASS?
URGH ...
HI (WHIMPER)
THEN—
THEN WHAT DO YOU WANT FROM ME!?
GABA (GRAB)
WHOA, EASY THERE.
YOUICHI!!
......
......
SU (SLIDE)
I'LL NEVER FORGIVE YOU, BUT... HMM, HOW ABOUT THIS?
MIKIYA...
...GIVE ME THE TOOL YOU USE FOR YOUR CURSE-KILLINGS.

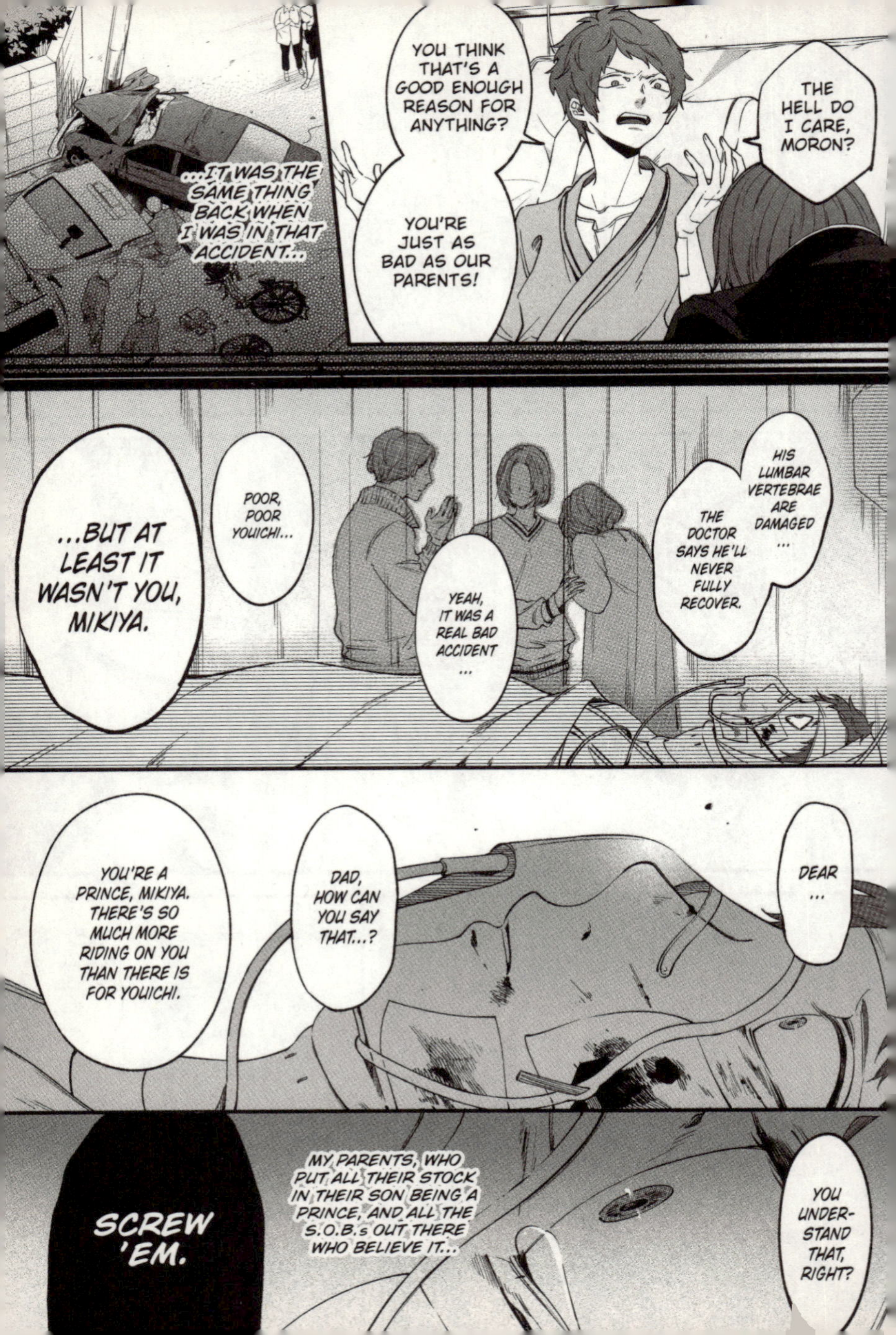
THE HELL DO I CARE, MORON?
YOU THINK THAT'S A GOOD ENOUGH REASON FOR ANYTHING?
YOU'RE JUST AS BAD AS OUR PARENTS!
...IT WAS THE SAME THING BACK WHEN I WAS IN THAT ACCIDENT...
HIS LUMBAR VERTEBRAE ARE DAMAGED...
THE DOCTOR SAYS HE'LL NEVER FULLY RECOVER.
YEAH, IT WAS A REAL BAD ACCIDENT...
POOR, POOR YOUICHI...
...BUT AT LEAST IT WASN'T YOU, MIKIYA.
DEAR...
DAD, HOW CAN YOU SAY THAT...?
YOU'RE A PRINCE, MIKIYA. THERE'S SO MUCH MORE RIDING ON YOU THAN THERE IS FOR YOUICHI.
YOU UNDER-STAND THAT, RIGHT?
MY PARENTS, WHO PUT ALL THEIR STOCK IN THEIR SON BEING A PRINCE, AND ALL THE S.O.B.s OUT THERE WHO BELIEVE IT...
SCREW 'EM.

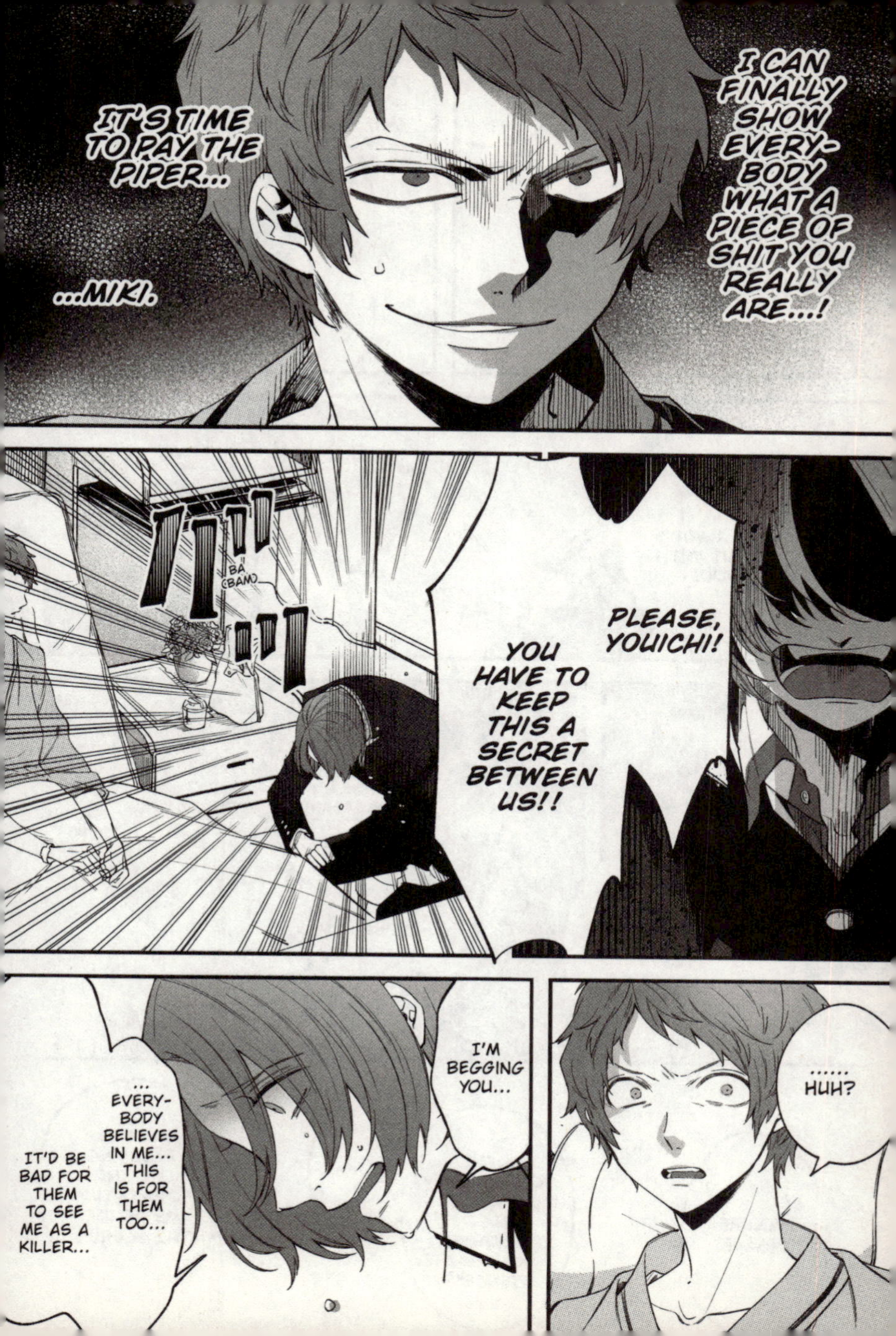
I CAN FINALLY SHOW EVERYBODY WHAT A PIECE OF SHIT YOU REALLY ARE...!
IT'S TIME TO PAY THE PIPER...
...MIKI.
PLEASE, YOUICHI!
YOU HAVE TO KEEP THIS A SECRET BETWEEN US!!
BA BAM
......HUH?
I'M BEGGING YOU...
...EVERYBODY BELIEVES IN ME... THIS IS FOR THEM TOO...
IT'D BE BAD FOR THEM TO SEE ME AS A KILLER...

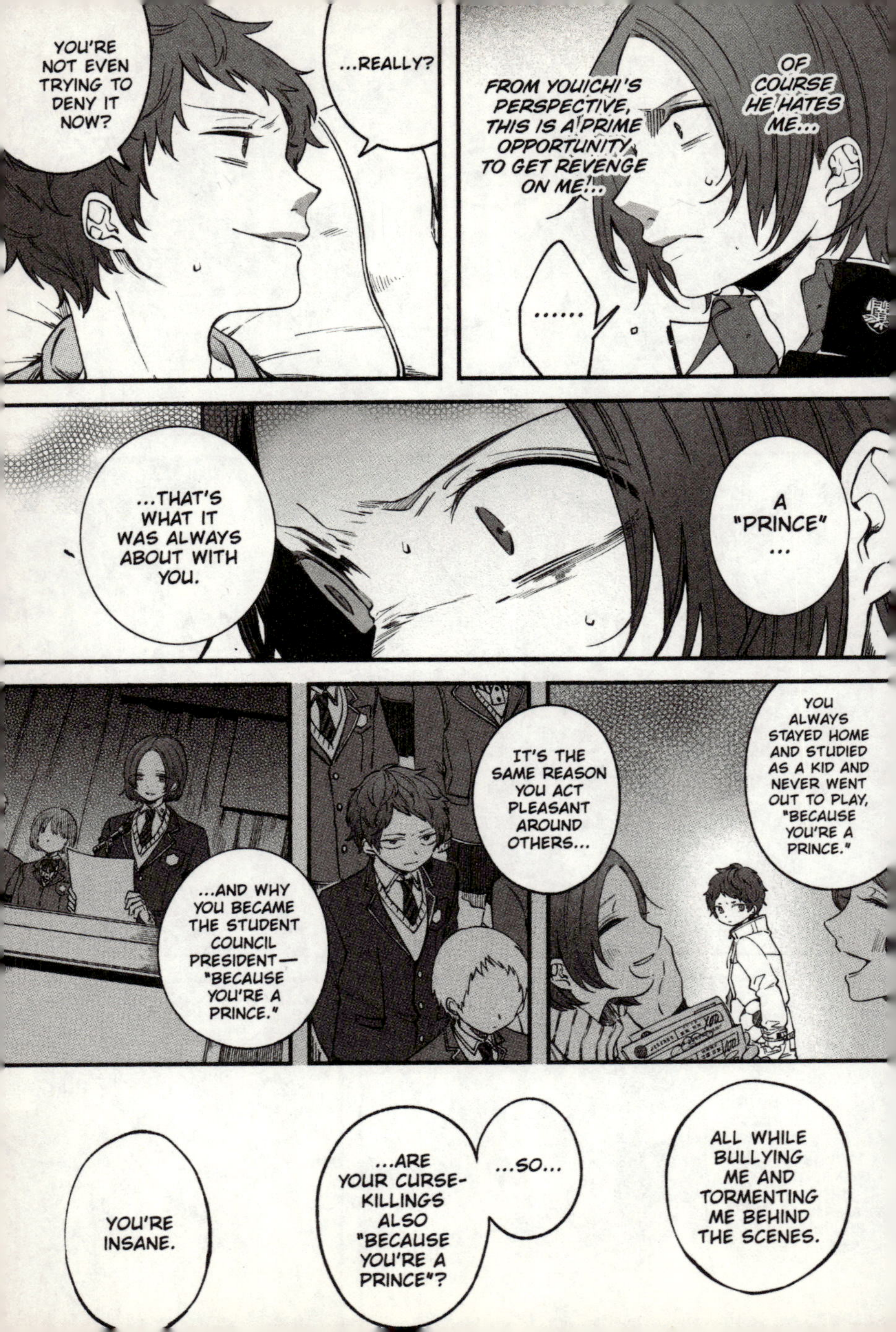
OF COURSE HE HATES ME...
FROM YOUICHI'S PERSPECTIVE, THIS IS A PRIME OPPORTUNITY TO GET REVENGE ON ME!...
......
...REALLY?
YOU'RE NOT EVEN TRYING TO DENY IT NOW?
A "PRINCE"...
...THAT'S WHAT IT WAS ALWAYS ABOUT WITH YOU.
YOU ALWAYS STAYED HOME AND STUDIED AS A KID AND NEVER WENT OUT TO PLAY, "BECAUSE YOU'RE A PRINCE."
IT'S THE SAME REASON YOU ACT PLEASANT AROUND OTHERS...
...AND WHY YOU BECAME THE STUDENT COUNCIL PRESIDENT—"BECAUSE YOU'RE A PRINCE."
ALL WHILE BULLYING ME AND TORMENTING ME BEHIND THE SCENES.
...SO...
...ARE YOUR CURSE-KILLINGS ALSO "BECAUSE YOU'RE A PRINCE"?
YOU'RE INSANE.

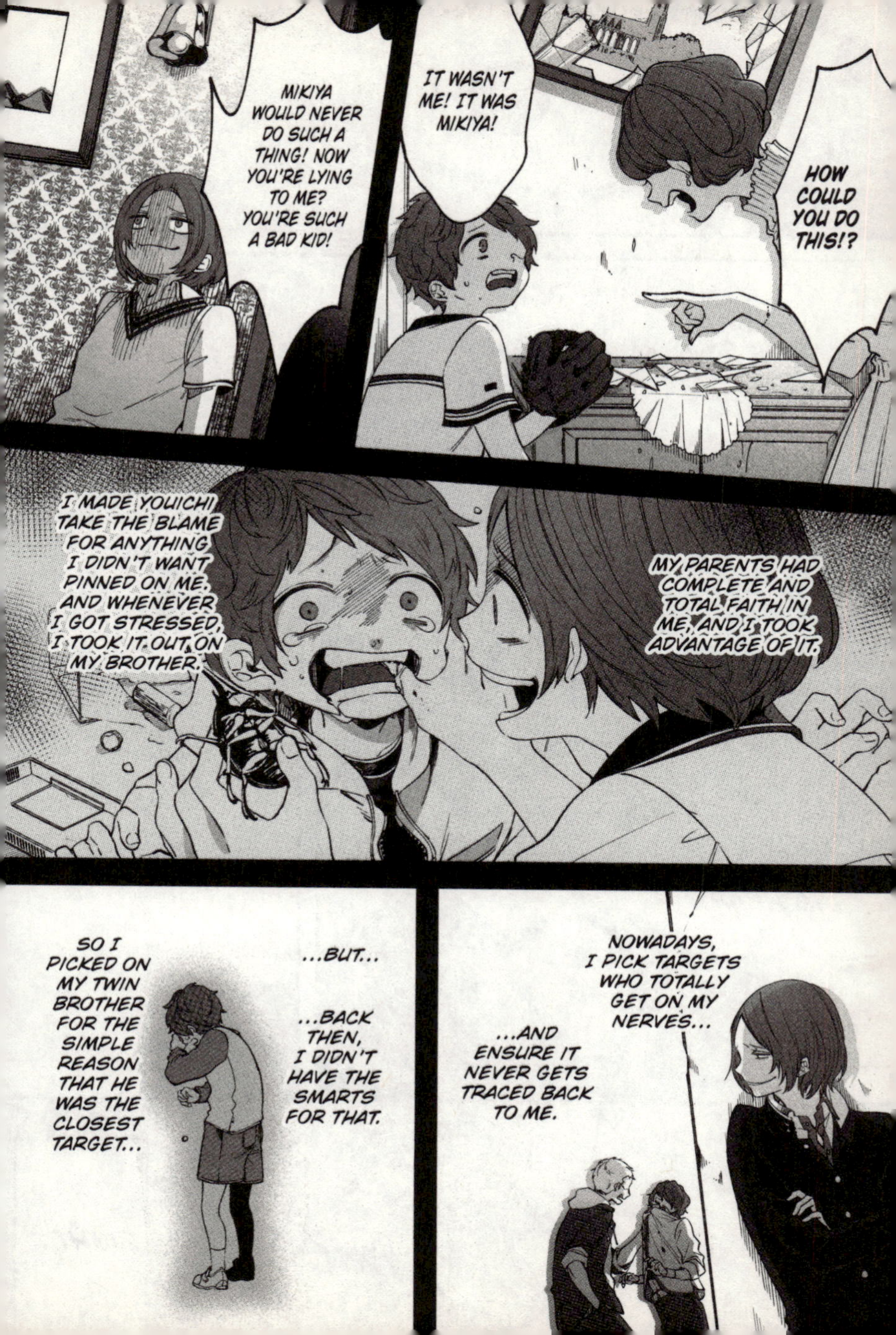
HOW COULD YOU DO THIS!?
IT WASN'T ME! IT WAS MIKIYA!
MIKIYA WOULD NEVER DO SUCH A THING! NOW YOU'RE LYING TO ME? YOU'RE SUCH A BAD KID!
I MADE YOUICHI TAKE THE BLAME FOR ANYTHING I DIDN'T WANT PINNED ON ME. AND WHENEVER I GOT STRESSED, I TOOK IT OUT ON MY BROTHER.
MY PARENTS HAD COMPLETE AND TOTAL FAITH IN ME, AND I TOOK ADVANTAGE OF IT.
NOWADAYS, I PICK TARGETS WHO TOTALLY GET ON MY NERVES...
...AND ENSURE IT NEVER GETS TRACED BACK TO ME.
SO I PICKED ON MY TWIN BROTHER FOR THE SIMPLE REASON THAT HE WAS THE CLOSEST TARGET...
...BUT...
...BACK THEN, I DIDN'T HAVE THE SMARTS FOR THAT.

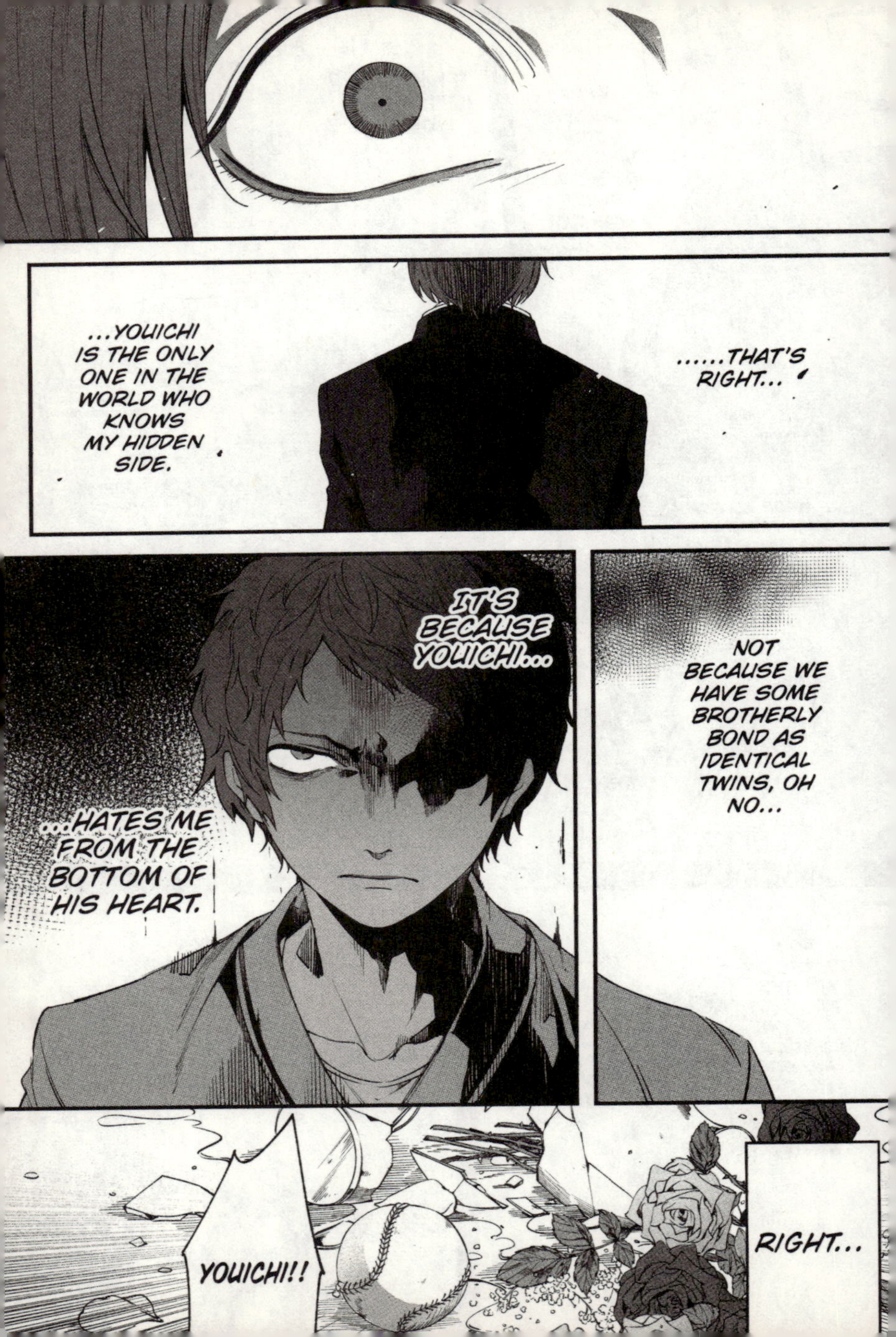
......THAT'S RIGHT...
...YOUICHI IS THE ONLY ONE IN THE WORLD WHO KNOWS MY HIDDEN SIDE.
NOT BECAUSE WE HAVE SOME BROTHERLY BOND AS IDENTICAL TWINS, OH NO...
IT'S BECAUSE YOUICHI...
...HATES ME FROM THE BOTTOM OF HIS HEART.
RIGHT...
YOUICHI!!

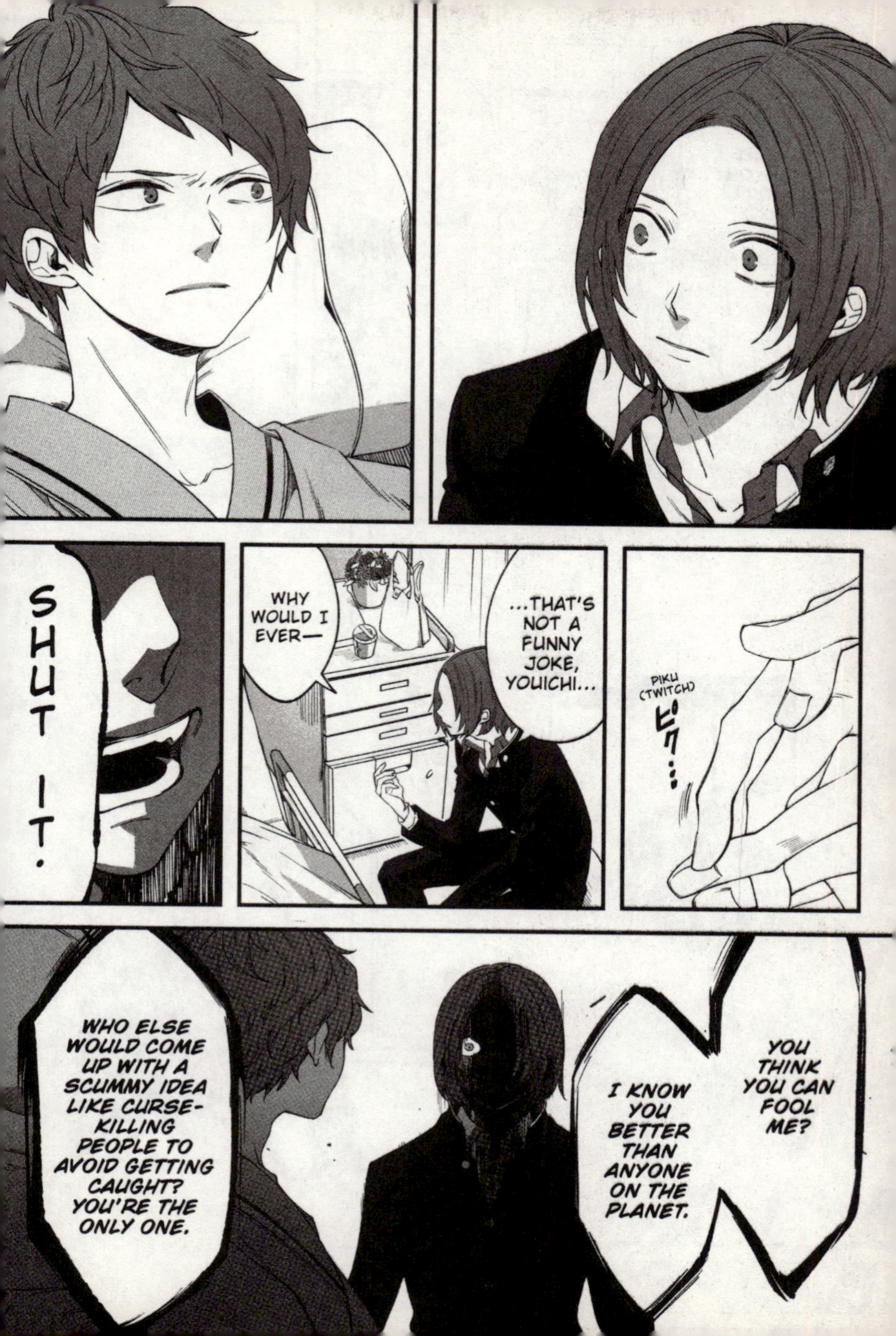
PIKU (TWITCH)
ピク…
...THAT'S NOT A FUNNY JOKE, YOUICHI...
WHY WOULD I EVER—
SHUT IT.
YOU THINK YOU CAN FOOL ME?
I KNOW YOU BETTER THAN ANYONE ON THE PLANET.
WHO ELSE WOULD COME UP WITH A SCUMMY IDEA LIKE CURSE-KILLING PEOPLE TO AVOID GETTING CAUGHT? YOU'RE THE ONLY ONE.

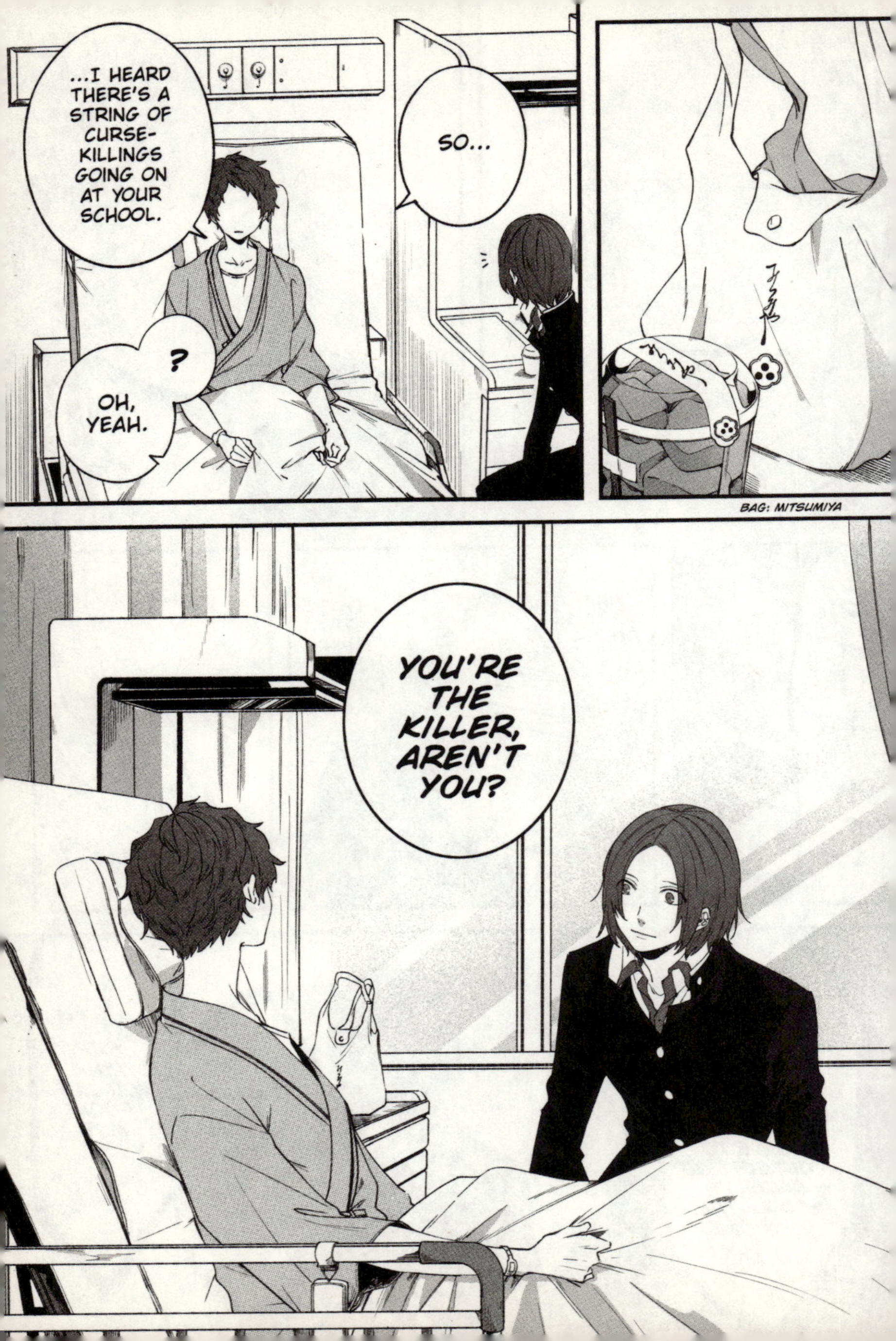
BAG: MITSUMIYA
SO...
...I HEARD THERE'S A STRING OF CURSE-KILLINGS GOING ON AT YOUR SCHOOL.
?
OH, YEAH.
YOU'RE THE KILLER, AREN'T YOU?

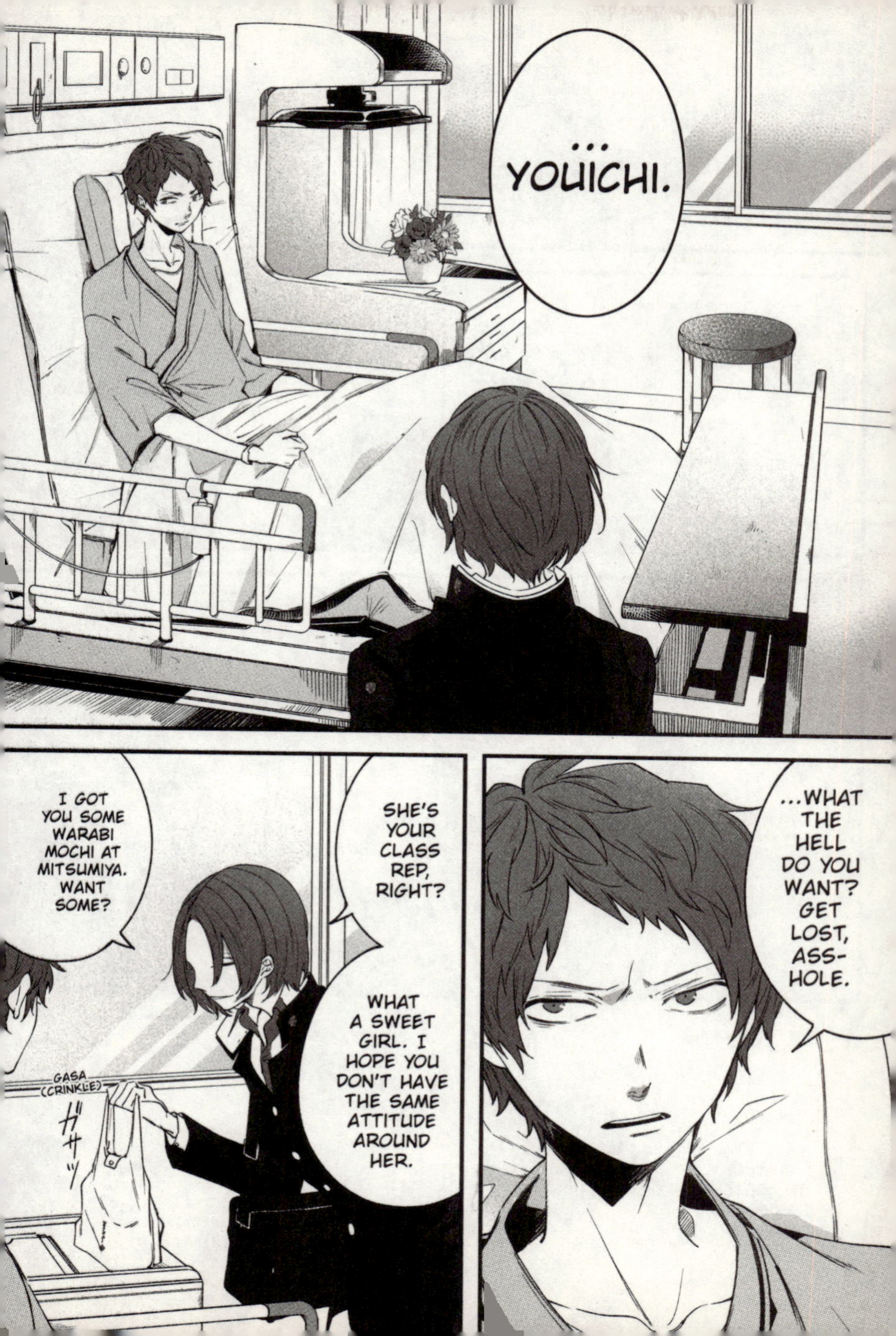
...
YOUÏCHI.
...WHAT THE HELL DO YOU WANT? GET LOST, ASS-HOLE.
SHE'S YOUR CLASS REP, RIGHT?
I GOT YOU SOME WARABI MOCHI AT MITSUMIYA. WANT SOME?
WHAT A SWEET GIRL. I HOPE YOU DON'T HAVE THE SAME ATTITUDE AROUND HER.
GASA (CRINKLE)
ガサッ

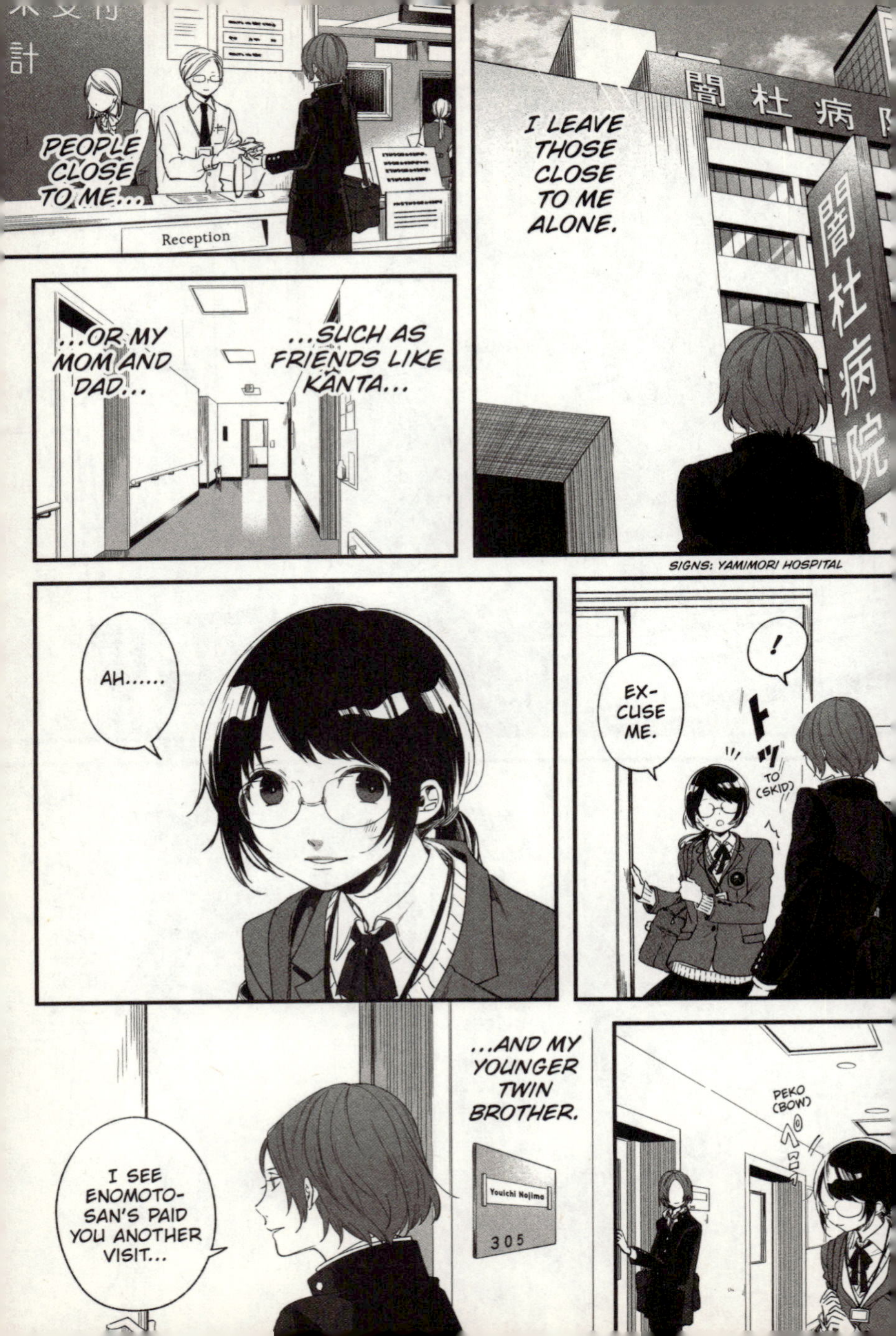
闇杜病院
闇杜病院
I LEAVE THOSE CLOSE TO ME ALONE.
SIGNS: YAMIMORI HOSPITAL
PEOPLE CLOSE TO ME...
Reception
...SUCH AS FRIENDS LIKE KANTA...
...OR MY MOM AND DAD...
!
EX-CUSE ME.
TO (SKID)
AH......
PEKO (BOW)
...AND MY YOUNGER TWIN BROTHER.
Youichi Nojima
305
I SEE ENOMOTO-SAN'S PAID YOU ANOTHER VISIT...

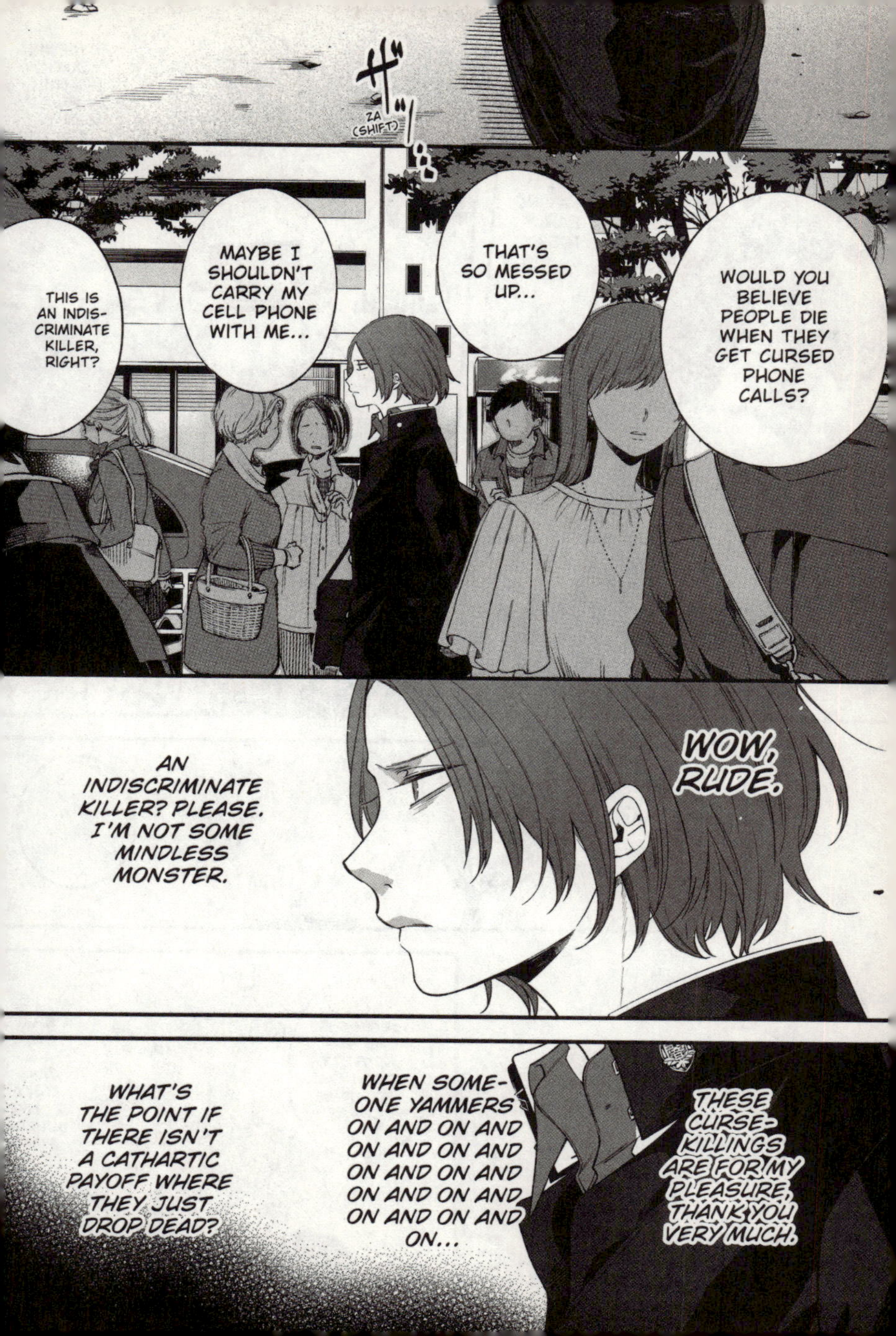
ZA (SHIFT)
WOULD YOU BELIEVE PEOPLE DIE WHEN THEY GET CURSED PHONE CALLS?
THAT'S SO MESSED UP...
MAYBE I SHOULDN'T CARRY MY CELL PHONE WITH ME...
THIS IS AN INDIS-CRIMINATE KILLER, RIGHT?
WOW, RUDE.
AN INDISCRIMINATE KILLER? PLEASE. I'M NOT SOME MINDLESS MONSTER.
THESE CURSE-KILLINGS ARE FOR MY PLEASURE, THANK YOU VERY MUCH.
WHEN SOME-ONE YAMMERS ON AND ON AND ON AND ON AND ON AND ON AND ON AND ON AND ON AND ON AND ON...
WHAT'S THE POINT IF THERE ISN'T A CATHARTIC PAYOFF WHERE THEY JUST DROP DEAD?

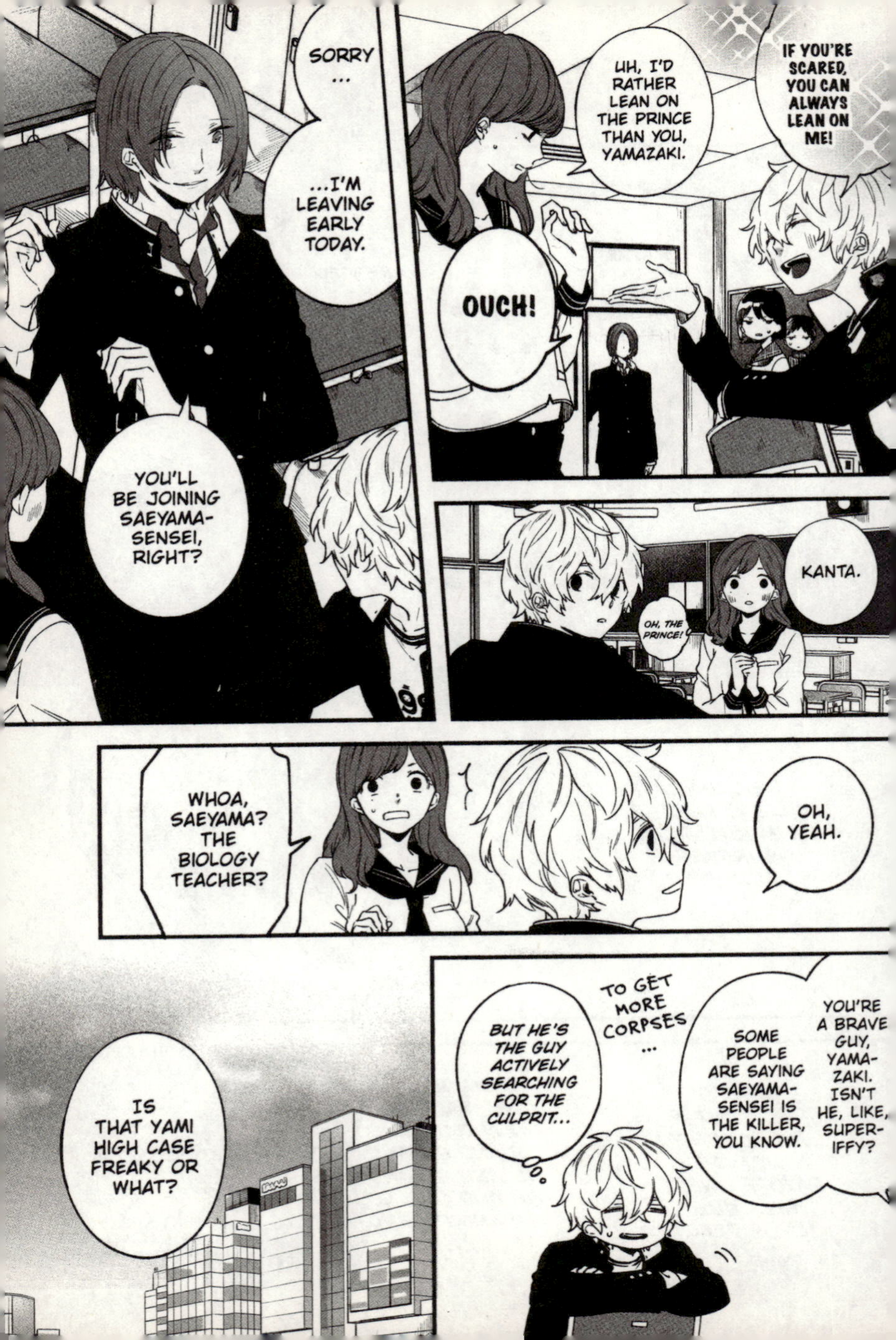
IF YOU'RE SCARED, YOU CAN ALWAYS LEAN ON ME!
UH, I'D RATHER LEAN ON THE PRINCE THAN YOU, YAMAZAKI.
OUCH!
KANTA.
OH, THE PRINCE!
SORRY...
...I'M LEAVING EARLY TODAY.
YOU'LL BE JOINING SAEYAMA-SENSEI, RIGHT?
OH, YEAH.
WHOA, SAEYAMA? THE BIOLOGY TEACHER?
YOU'RE A BRAVE GUY, YAMAZAKI. ISN'T HE, LIKE, SUPER-IFFY?
SOME PEOPLE ARE SAYING SAEYAMA-SENSEI IS THE KILLER, YOU KNOW.
TO GET MORE CORPSES...
BUT HE'S THE GUY ACTIVELY SEARCHING FOR THE CULPRIT...
IS THAT YAMI HIGH CASE FREAKY OR WHAT?

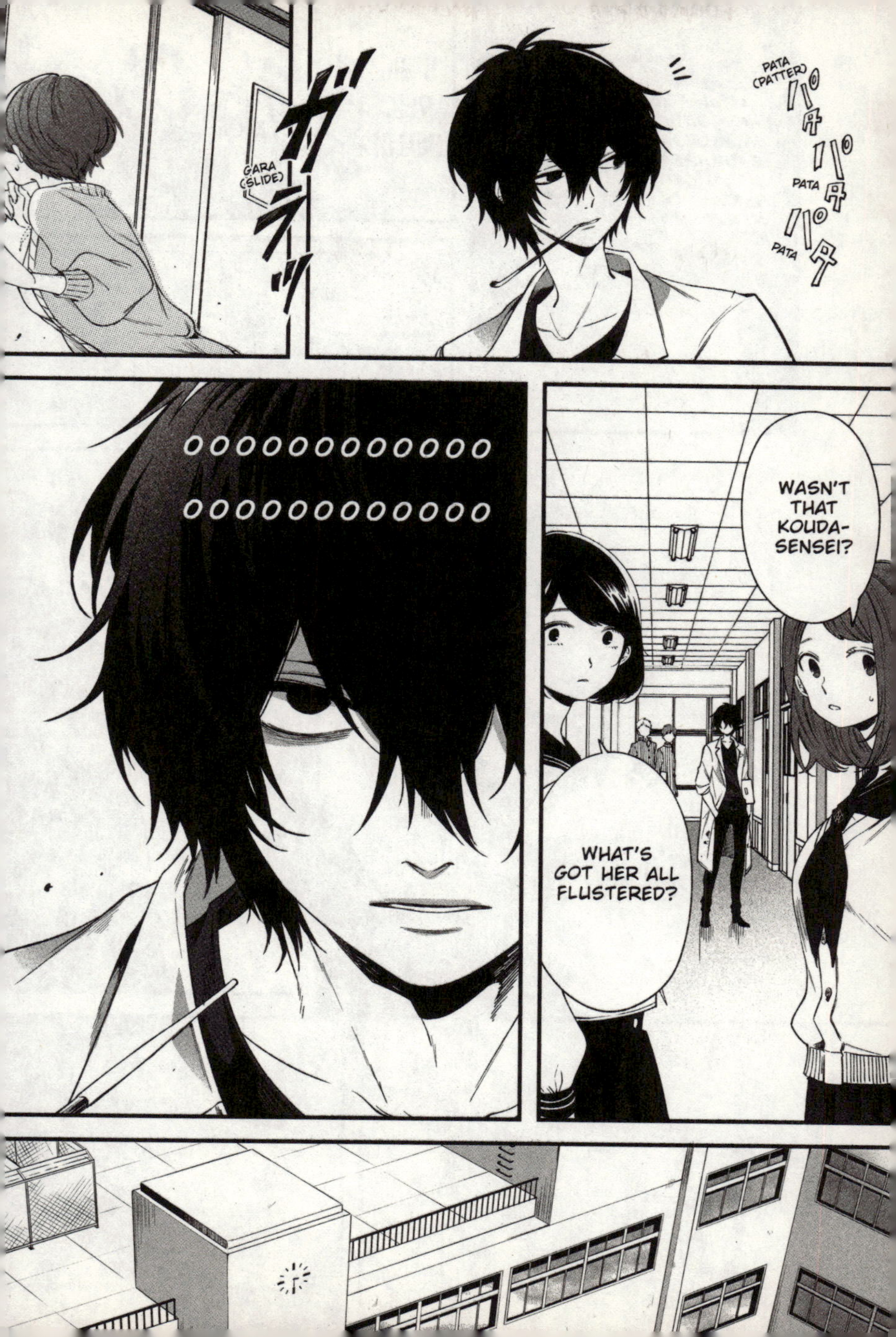
PATA (PATTER)
PATA
PATA
GARA (SLIDE)
WASN'T THAT KOUDA-SENSEI?
WHAT'S GOT HER ALL FLUSTERED?
OOOOOOOOOOOOO
OOOOOOOOOOOOO

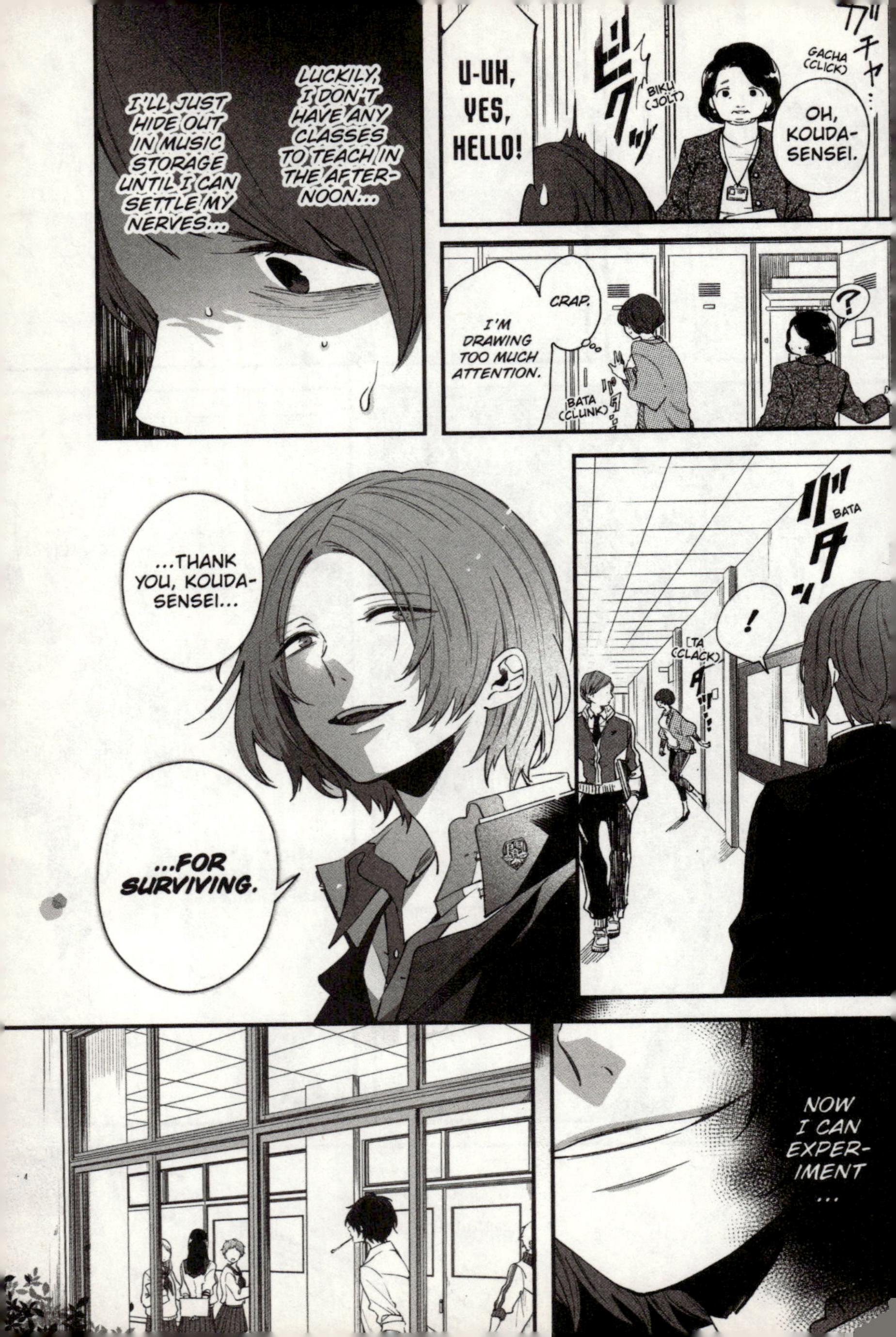

GACHA (CLICK)
OH, KOUDA-SENSEI.
BIKU (JOLT)
U-UH, YES, HELLO!
CRAP.
I'M DRAWING TOO MUCH ATTENTION.
BATA (CLUNK)
?
LUCKILY, I DON'T HAVE ANY CLASSES TO TEACH IN THE AFTER-NOON...
I'LL JUST HIDE OUT IN MUSIC STORAGE UNTIL I CAN SETTLE MY NERVES...
BATA
!
TA (CLACK)
...THANK YOU, KOUDA-SENSEI...
...FOR SURVIVING.
NOW I CAN EXPER-IMENT...

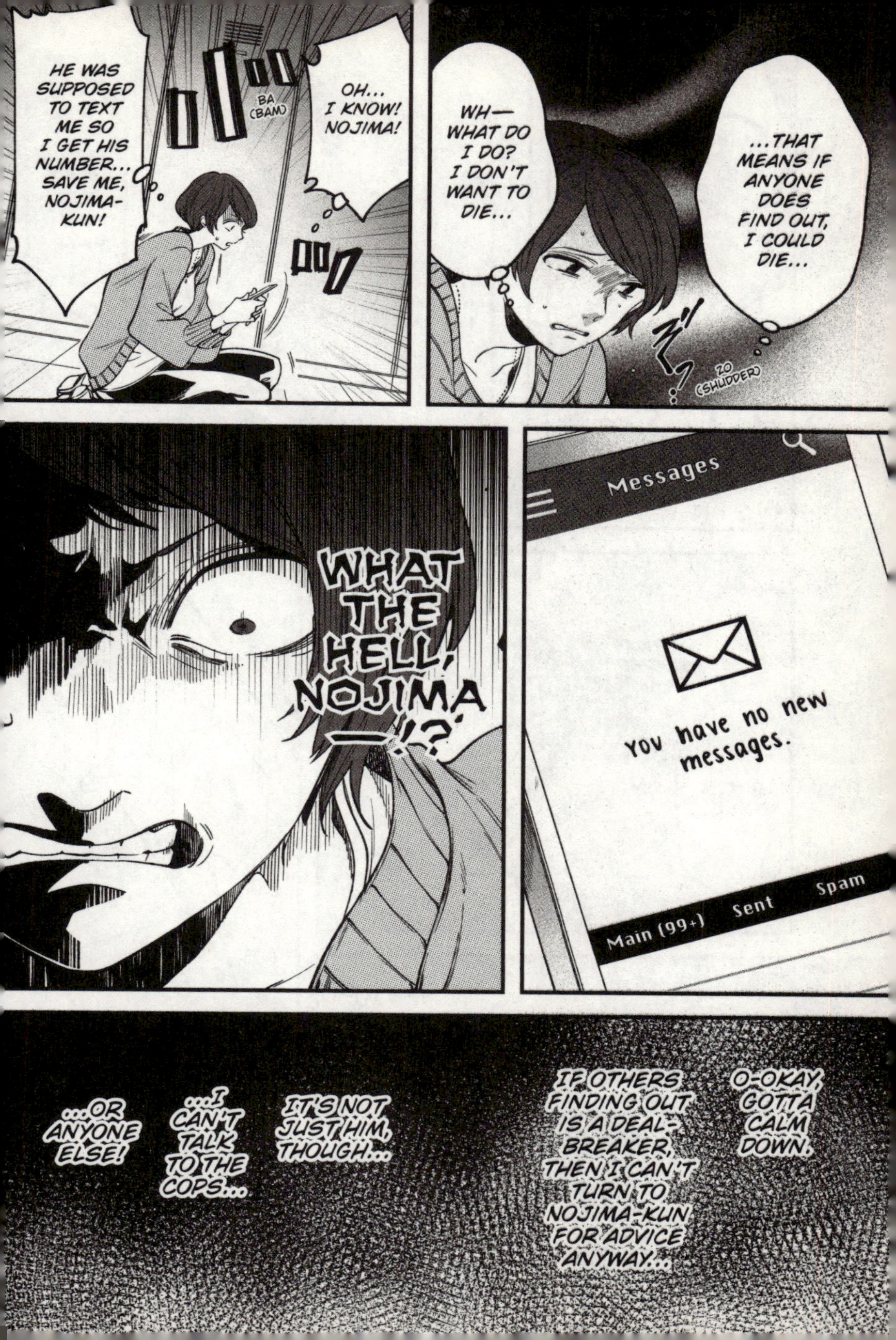
...THAT MEANS IF ANYONE DOES FIND OUT, I COULD DIE...
WH— WHAT DO I DO? I DON'T WANT TO DIE...
ZO (SHUDDER)
OH... I KNOW! NOJIMA!
BA (BAM)
HE WAS SUPPOSED TO TEXT ME SO I GET HIS NUMBER... SAVE ME, NOJIMA-KUN!
Messages
You have no new messages.
Main (99+)
Sent
Spam
WHAT THE HELL, NOJIMA—!?
O-OKAY, GOTTA CALM DOWN.
IF OTHERS FINDING OUT IS A DEAL-BREAKER, THEN I CAN'T TURN TO NOJIMA-KUN FOR ADVICE ANYWAY...
IT'S NOT JUST HIM, THOUGH...
...I CAN'T TALK TO THE COPS...
...OR ANYONE ELSE!

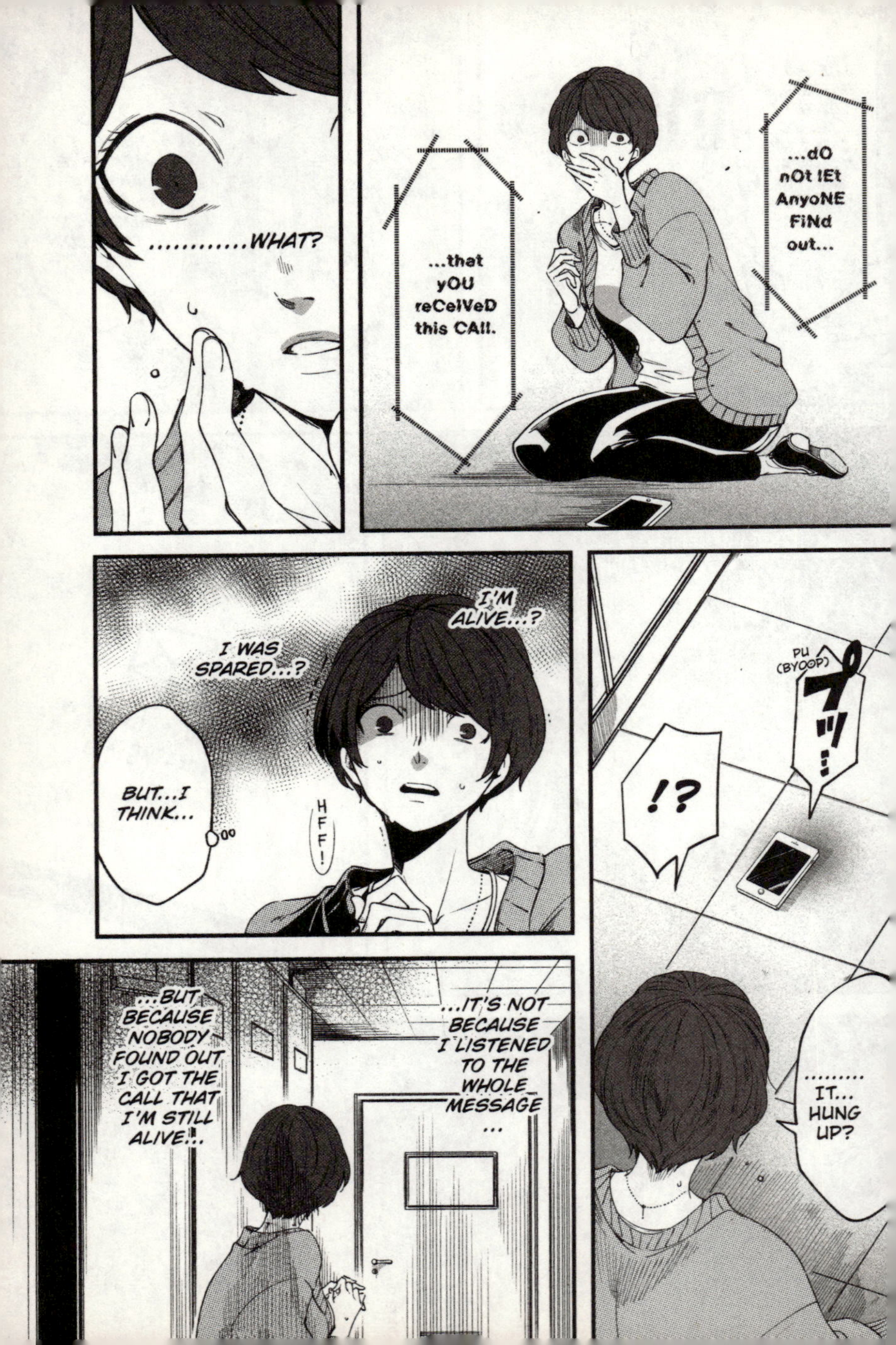
...dO nOt lEt AnyoNE FiNd out...
...that yOU reCeIVeD this CAll.
...........WHAT?
PU (BYOOP)
プッ
!?
.........IT... HUNG UP?
I'M ALIVE...?
I WAS SPARED...?
HFF!
BUT...I THINK...
...IT'S NOT BECAUSE I LISTENED TO THE WHOLE MESSAGE...
...BUT BECAUSE NOBODY FOUND OUT I GOT THE CALL THAT I'M STILL ALIVE...

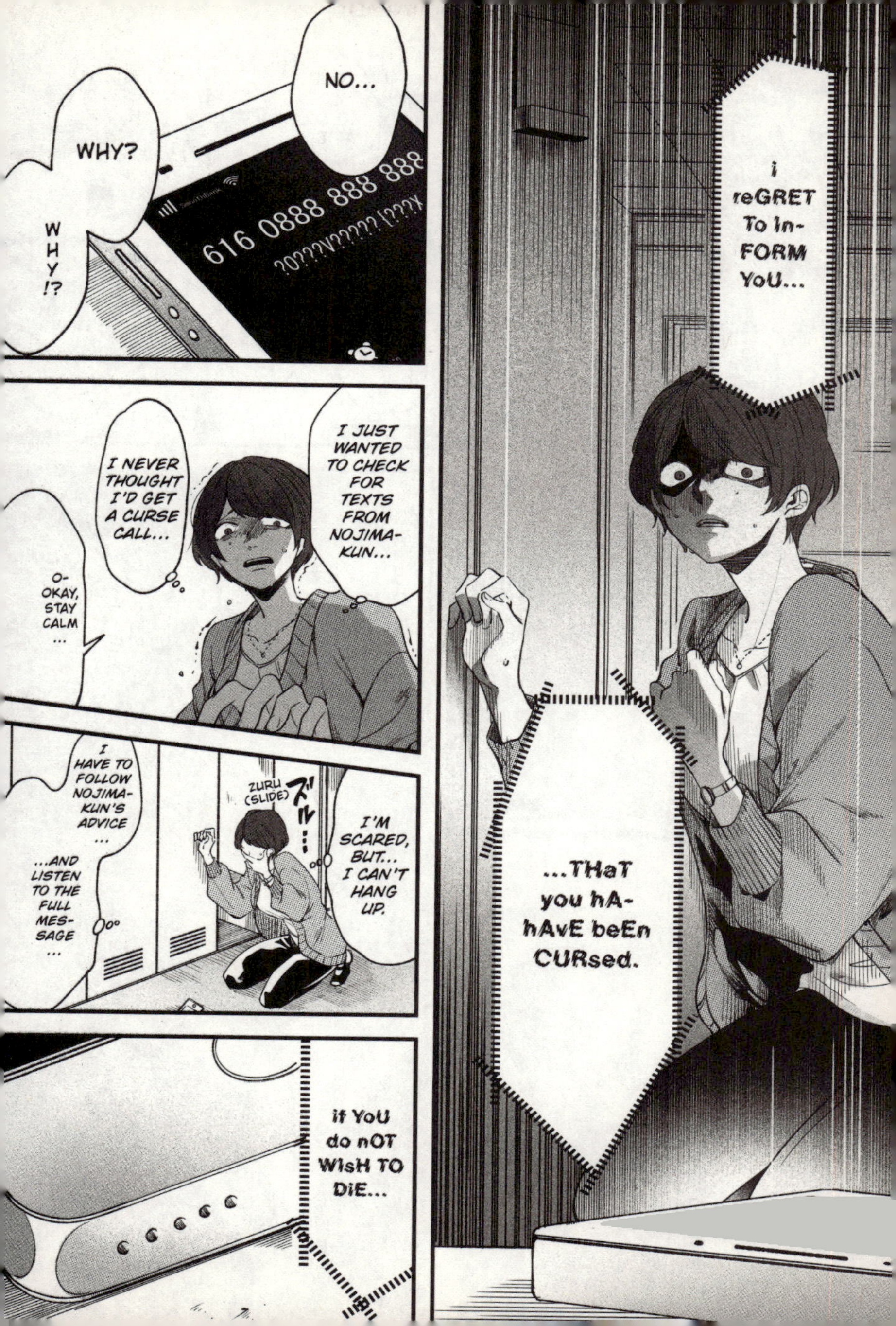
i reGRET To In-FORM YoU...
...THaT you hA-hAvE beEn CURsed.
NO...
616 0888 888 888
WHY?
WHY!?
I JUST WANTED TO CHECK FOR TEXTS FROM NOJIMA-KUN...
I NEVER THOUGHT I'D GET A CURSE CALL...
O-OKAY, STAY CALM...
I'M SCARED, BUT... I CAN'T HANG UP.
ズル…
ZURU (SLIDE)
I HAVE TO FOLLOW NOJIMA-KUN'S ADVICE...
...AND LISTEN TO THE FULL MESSAGE...
if YoU do nOT WIsH TO DiE...

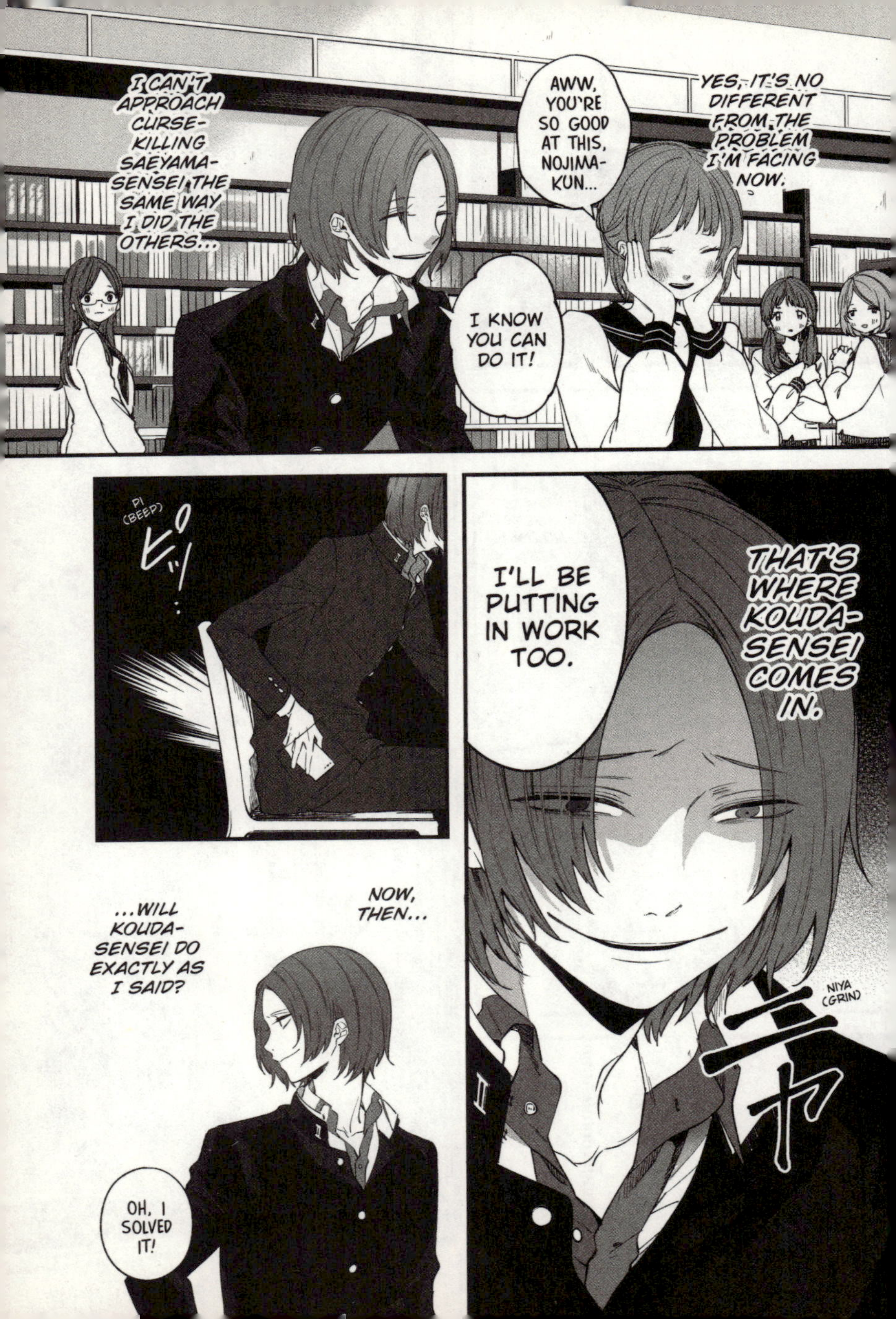
YES, IT'S NO DIFFERENT FROM THE PROBLEM I'M FACING NOW.
AWW, YOU'RE SO GOOD AT THIS, NOJIMA-KUN...
I CAN'T APPROACH CURSE-KILLING SAEYAMA-SENSEI THE SAME WAY I DID THE OTHERS...
I KNOW YOU CAN DO IT!
THAT'S WHERE KOUDA-SENSEI COMES IN.
I'LL BE PUTTING IN WORK TOO.
NIYA (GRIN)
PI (BEEP)
NOW, THEN...
...WILL KOUDA-SENSEI DO EXACTLY AS I SAID?
OH, I SOLVED IT!

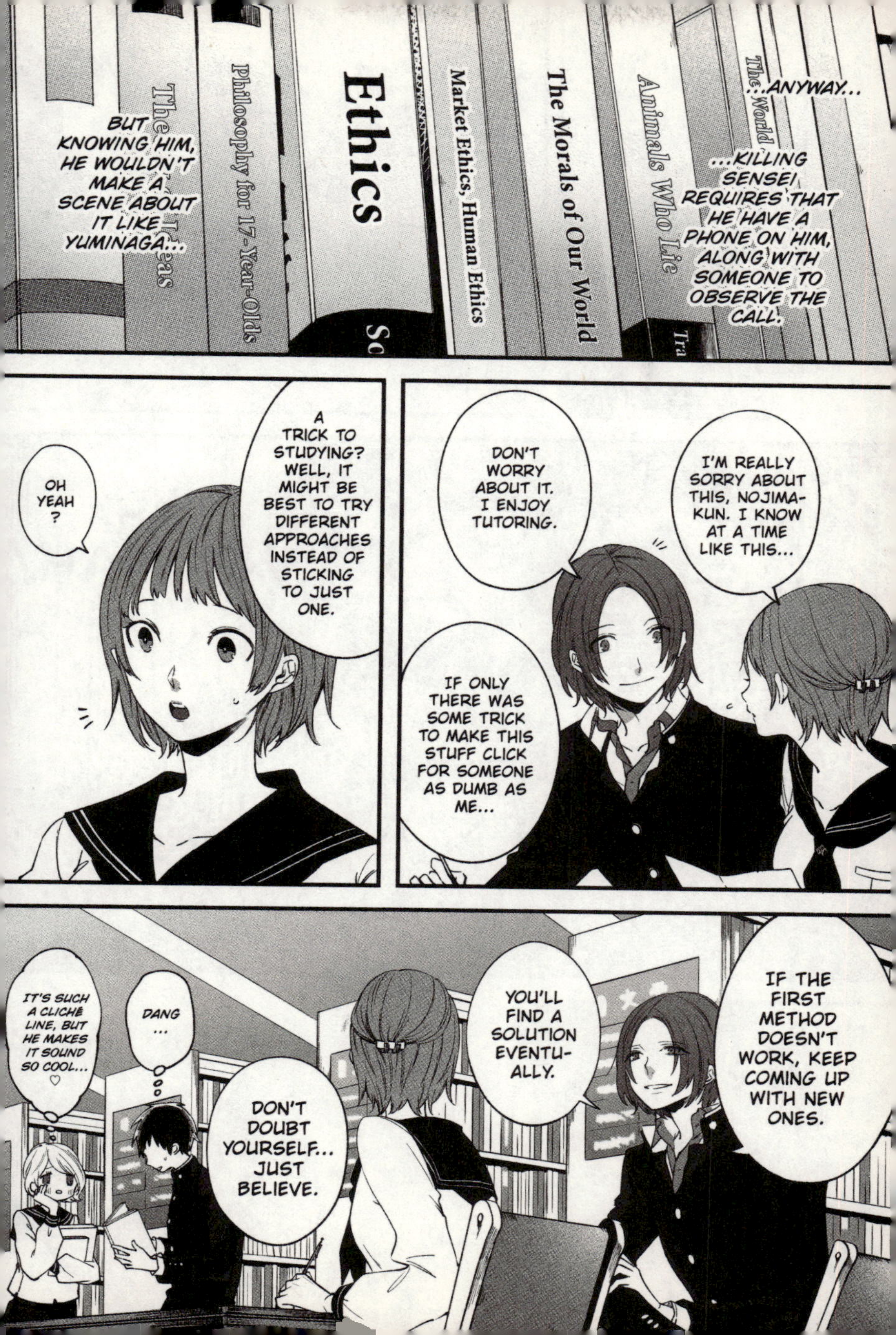
...ANYWAY...
...KILLING SENSEI REQUIRES THAT HE HAVE A PHONE ON HIM, ALONG WITH SOMEONE TO OBSERVE THE CALL.
The World
Animals Who Lie
The Morals of Our World
Market Ethics, Human Ethics
Ethics
Philosophy for 17-Year-Olds
BUT KNOWING HIM, HE WOULDN'T MAKE A SCENE ABOUT IT LIKE YUMINAGA...
I'M REALLY SORRY ABOUT THIS, NOJIMA-KUN. I KNOW AT A TIME LIKE THIS...
DON'T WORRY ABOUT IT. I ENJOY TUTORING.
IF ONLY THERE WAS SOME TRICK TO MAKE THIS STUFF CLICK FOR SOMEONE AS DUMB AS ME...
A TRICK TO STUDYING? WELL, IT MIGHT BE BEST TO TRY DIFFERENT APPROACHES INSTEAD OF STICKING TO JUST ONE.
OH YEAH?
IF THE FIRST METHOD DOESN'T WORK, KEEP COMING UP WITH NEW ONES.
YOU'LL FIND A SOLUTION EVENTU-ALLY.
DON'T DOUBT YOURSELF... JUST BELIEVE.
DANG...
IT'S SUCH A CLICHÉ LINE, BUT HE MAKES IT SOUND SO COOL... ♡

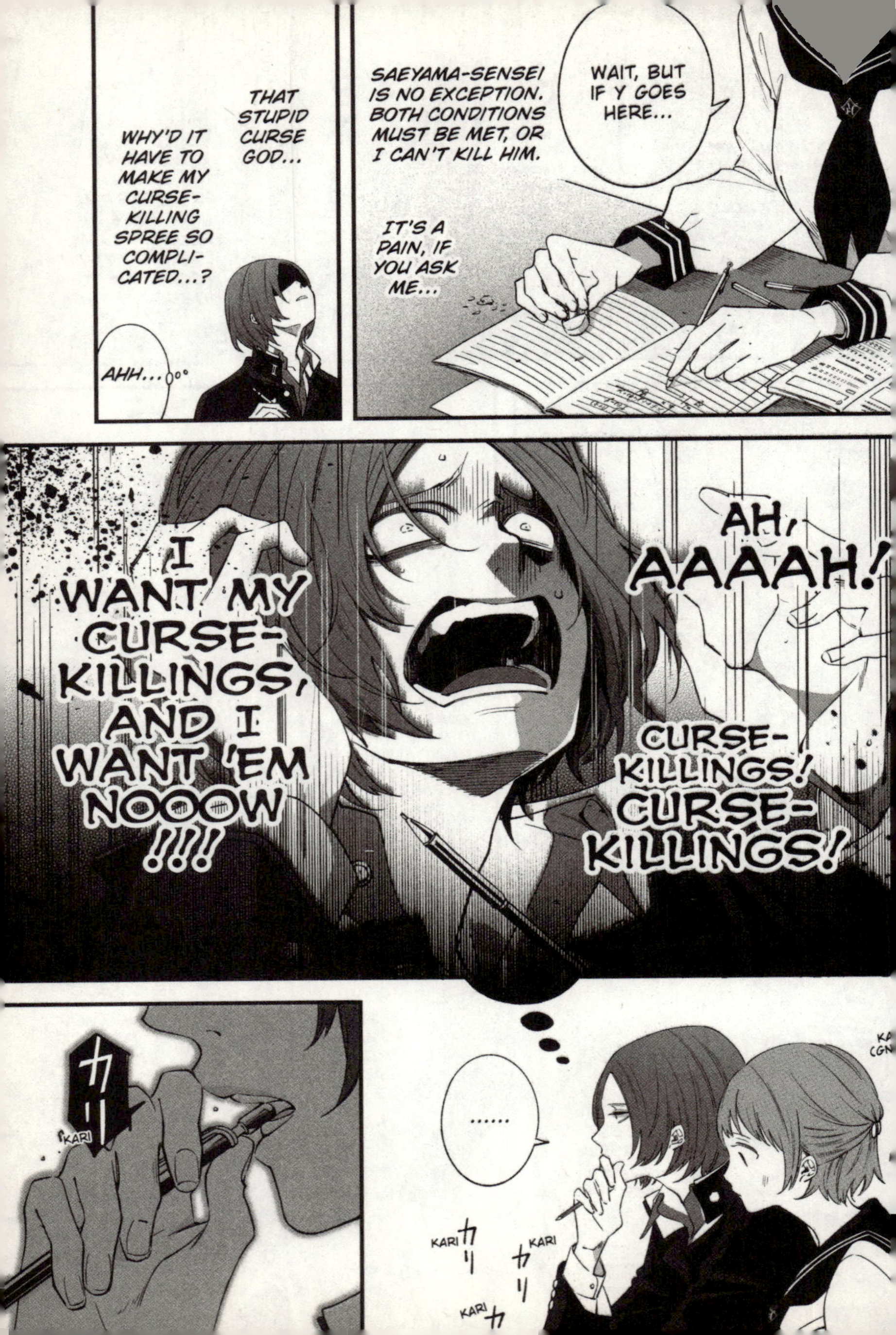
WAIT, BUT IF Y GOES HERE...
SAEYAMA-SENSEI IS NO EXCEPTION. BOTH CONDITIONS MUST BE MET, OR I CAN'T KILL HIM.
IT'S A PAIN, IF YOU ASK ME...
THAT STUPID CURSE GOD...
WHY'D IT HAVE TO MAKE MY CURSE-KILLING SPREE SO COMPLICATED...?
AHH...
AH, AAAAH!
CURSE-KILLINGS! CURSE-KILLINGS!
I WANT MY CURSE-KILLINGS, AND I WANT 'EM NOOOW!!!!
......
KARI
KARI
KARI
KARI

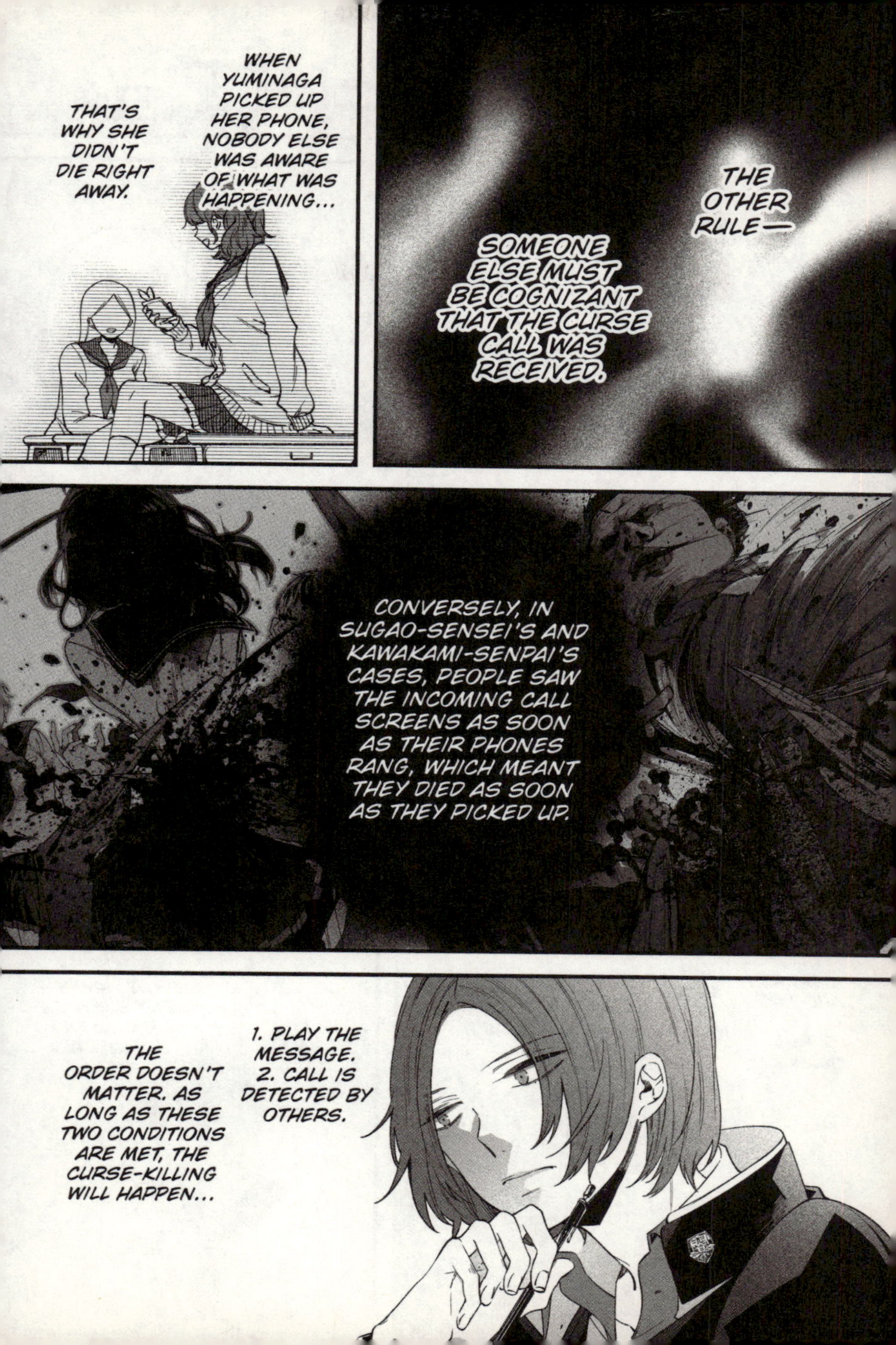
THE OTHER RULE—
SOMEONE ELSE MUST BE COGNIZANT THAT THE CURSE CALL WAS RECEIVED.
WHEN YUMINAGA PICKED UP HER PHONE, NOBODY ELSE WAS AWARE OF WHAT WAS HAPPENING...
THAT'S WHY SHE DIDN'T DIE RIGHT AWAY.
CONVERSELY, IN SUGAO-SENSEI'S AND KAWAKAMI-SENPAI'S CASES, PEOPLE SAW THE INCOMING CALL SCREENS AS SOON AS THEIR PHONES RANG, WHICH MEANT THEY DIED AS SOON AS THEY PICKED UP.
1. PLAY THE MESSAGE. 2. CALL IS DETECTED BY OTHERS.
THE ORDER DOESN'T MATTER. AS LONG AS THESE TWO CONDITIONS ARE MET, THE CURSE-KILLING WILL HAPPEN...

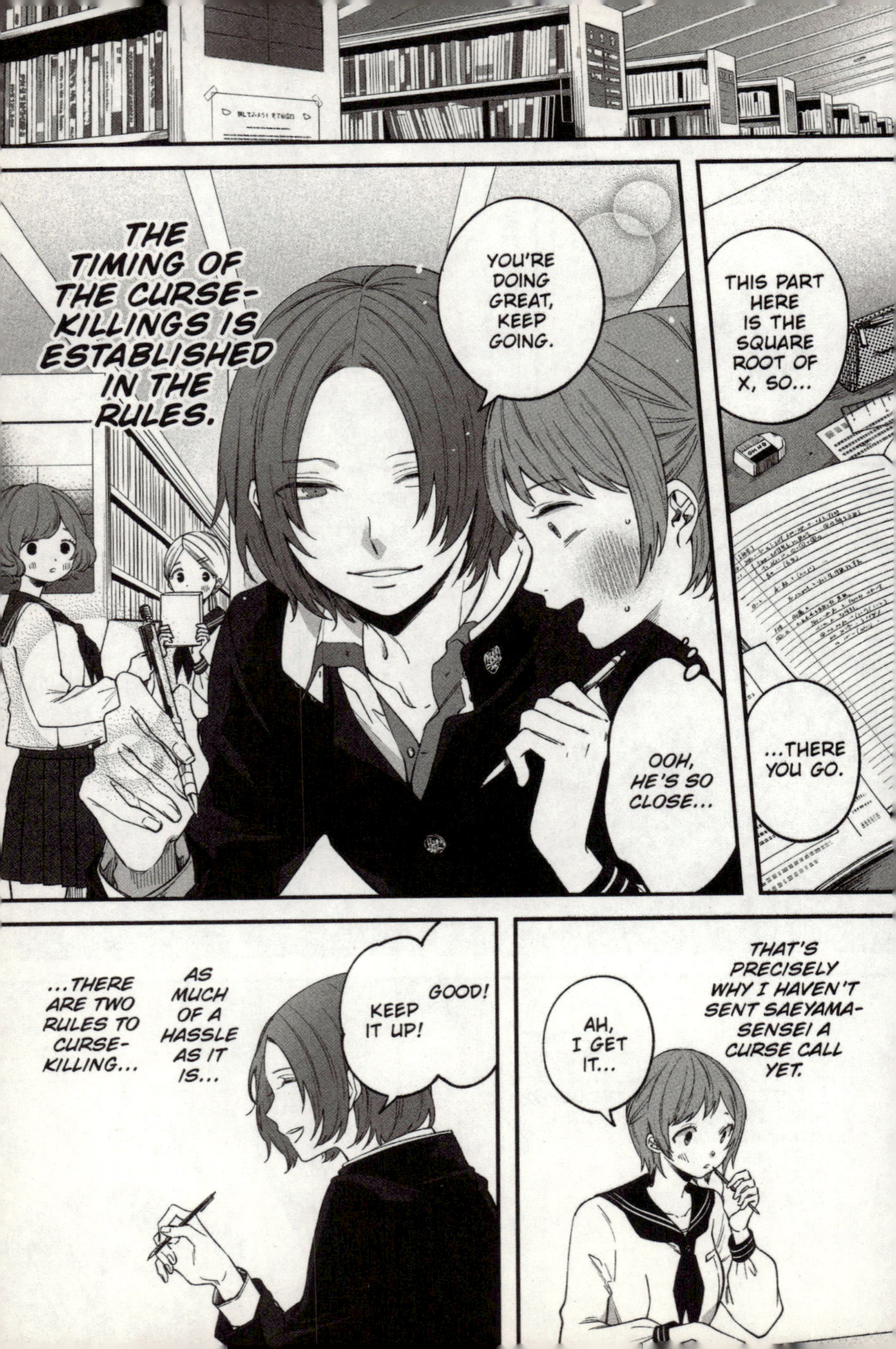
THIS PART HERE IS THE SQUARE ROOT OF X, SO...
...THERE YOU GO.
YOU'RE DOING GREAT, KEEP GOING.
OOH, HE'S SO CLOSE...
THE TIMING OF THE CURSE-KILLINGS IS ESTABLISHED IN THE RULES.
THAT'S PRECISELY WHY I HAVEN'T SENT SAEYAMA-SENSEI A CURSE CALL YET.
AH, I GET IT...
GOOD!
KEEP IT UP!
AS MUCH OF A HASSLE AS IT IS...
...THERE ARE TWO RULES TO CURSE-KILLING...

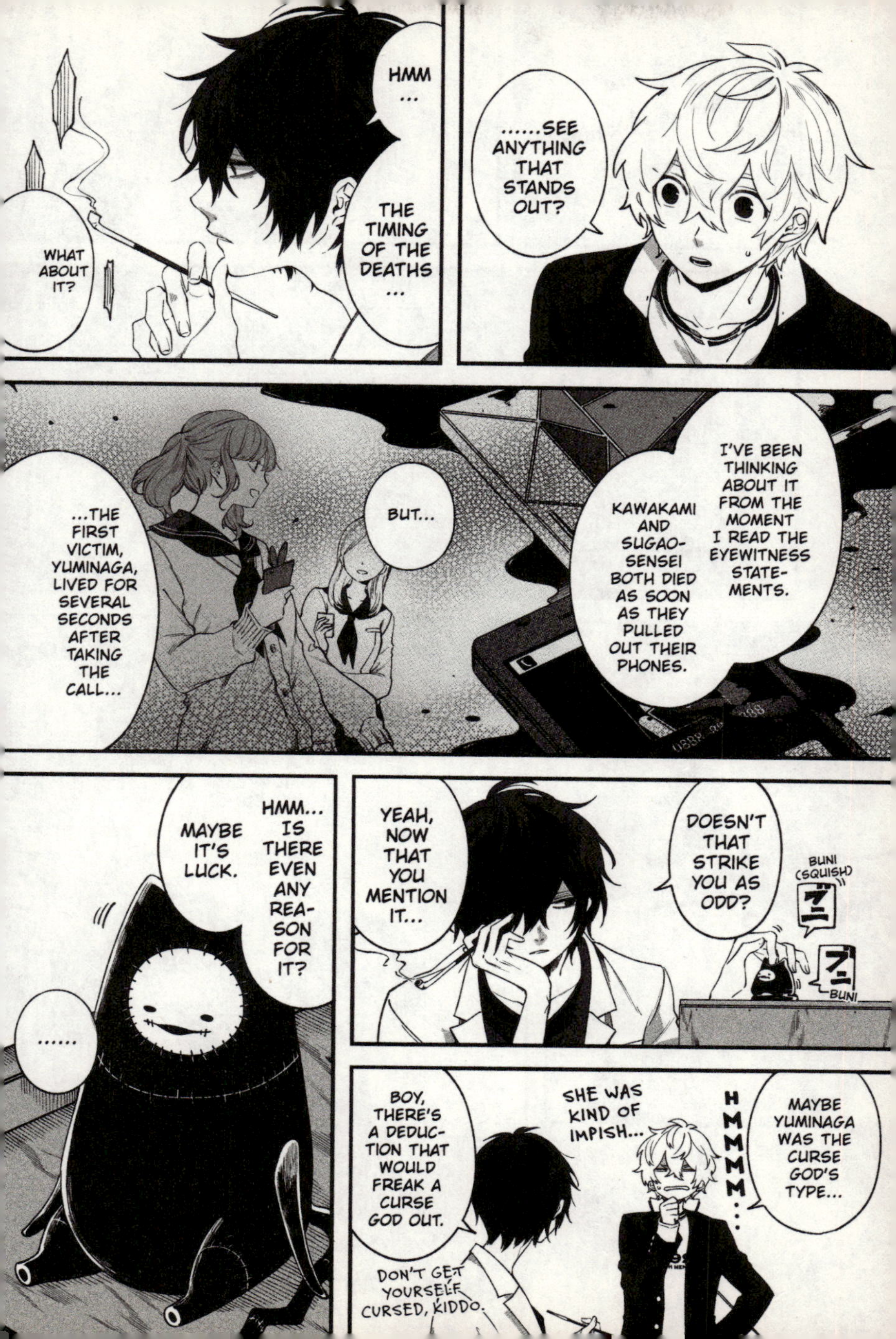
......SEE ANYTHING THAT STANDS OUT?
HMM ...
THE TIMING OF THE DEATHS ...
WHAT ABOUT IT?
I'VE BEEN THINKING ABOUT IT FROM THE MOMENT I READ THE EYEWITNESS STATEMENTS.
KAWAKAMI AND SUGAO-SENSEI BOTH DIED AS SOON AS THEY PULLED OUT THEIR PHONES.
BUT...
...THE FIRST VICTIM, YUMINAGA, LIVED FOR SEVERAL SECONDS AFTER TAKING THE CALL...
DOESN'T THAT STRIKE YOU AS ODD?
ブニ
BUNI (SQUISH)
ブニ
BUNI
YEAH, NOW THAT YOU MENTION IT...
MAYBE YUMINAGA WAS THE CURSE GOD'S TYPE...
HMMMM...
SHE WAS KIND OF IMPISH...
BOY, THERE'S A DEDUCTION THAT WOULD FREAK A CURSE GOD OUT.
DON'T GET YOURSELF CURSED, KIDDO.
HMM... IS THERE EVEN ANY REASON FOR IT?
MAYBE IT'S LUCK.
......

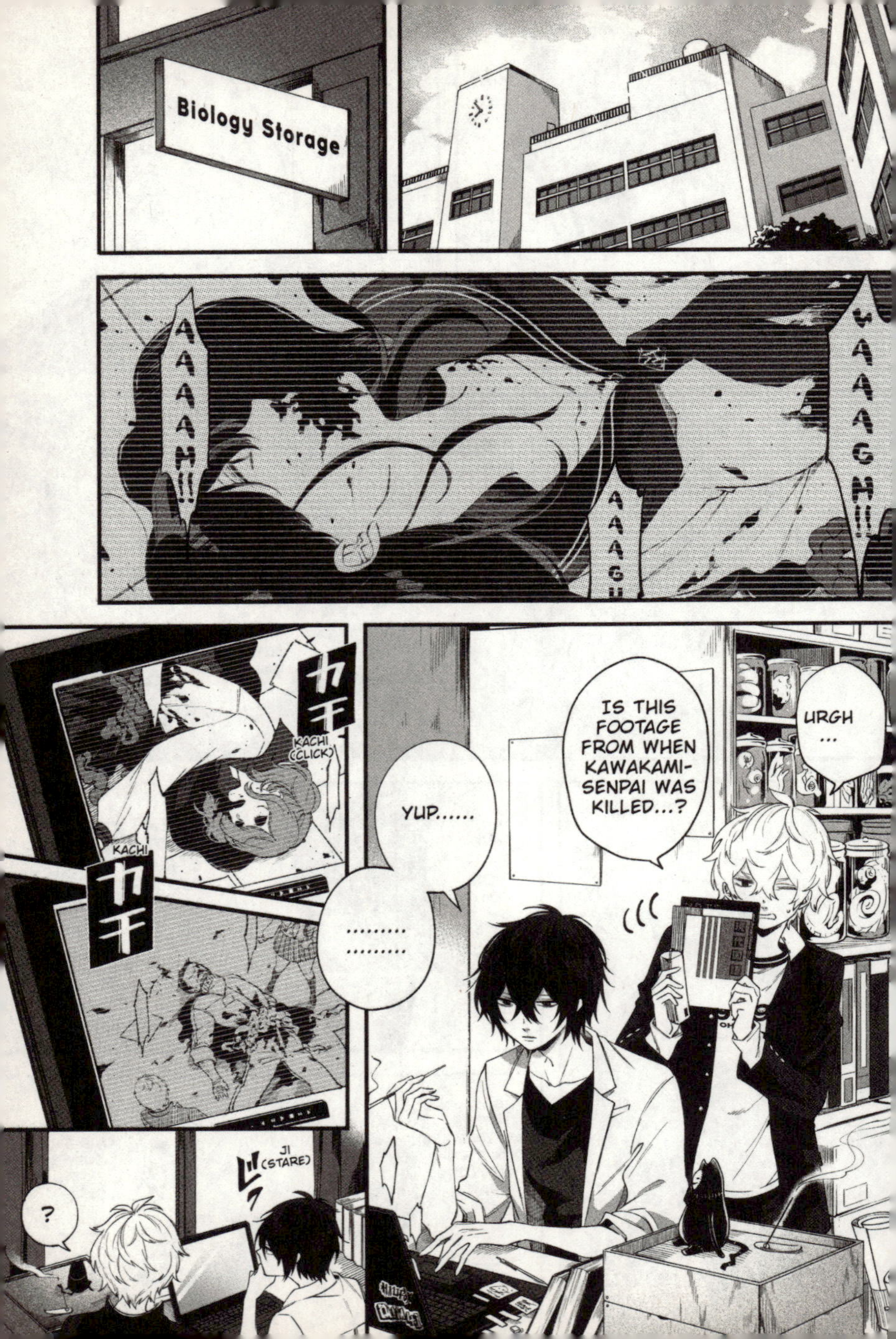
Biology Storage
AAAAAGH!!
AAAAGH
AAAAAH!!
URGH...
IS THIS FOOTAGE FROM WHEN KAWAKAMI-SENPAI WAS KILLED...?
YUP......
....
....
カチ
KACHI (CLICK)
カチ
KACHI
ジッ
JI (STARE)
?

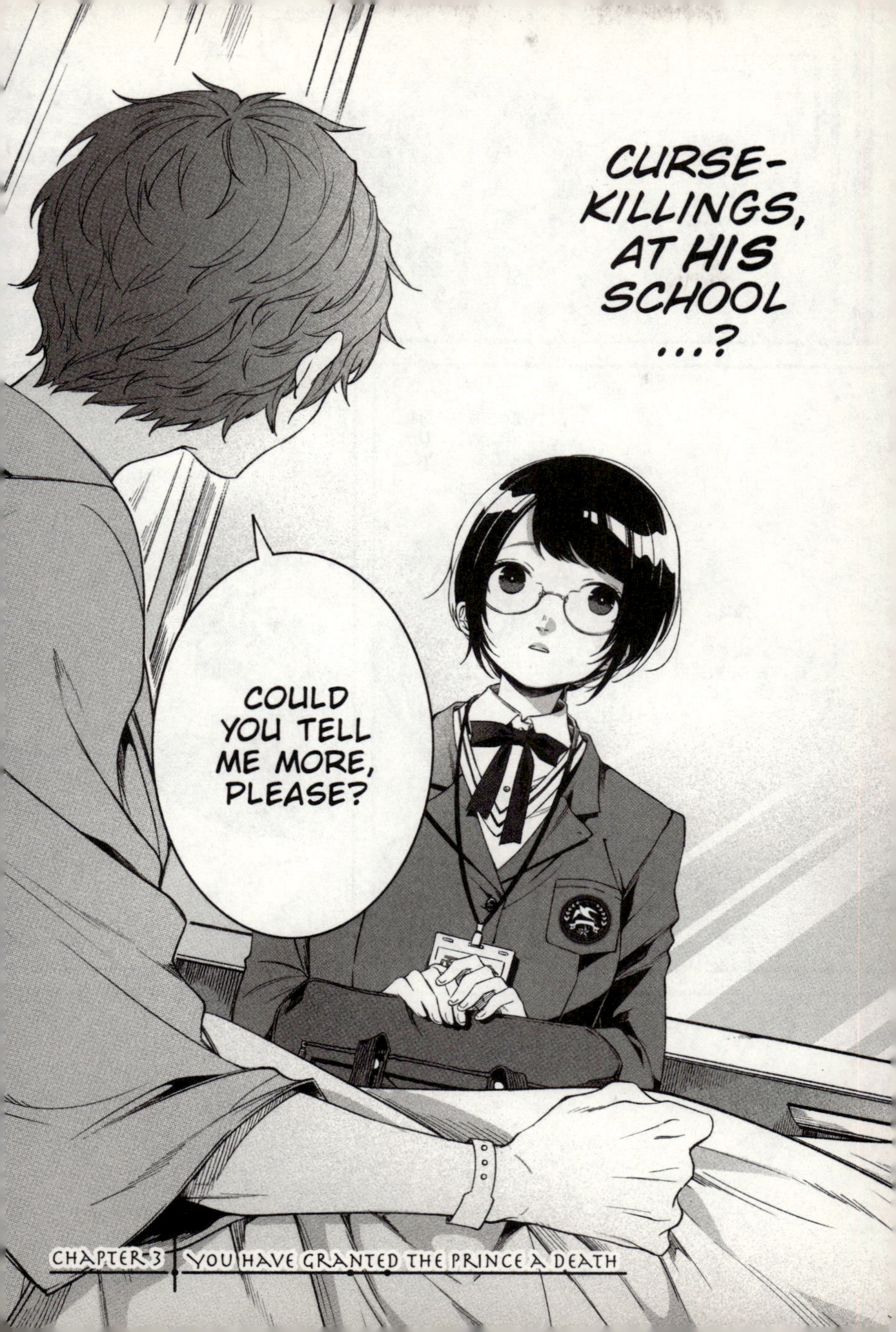
CURSE-KILLINGS, AT HIS SCHOOL ...?
COULD YOU TELL ME MORE, PLEASE?
CHAPTER 3 YOU HAVE GRANTED THE PRINCE A DEATH

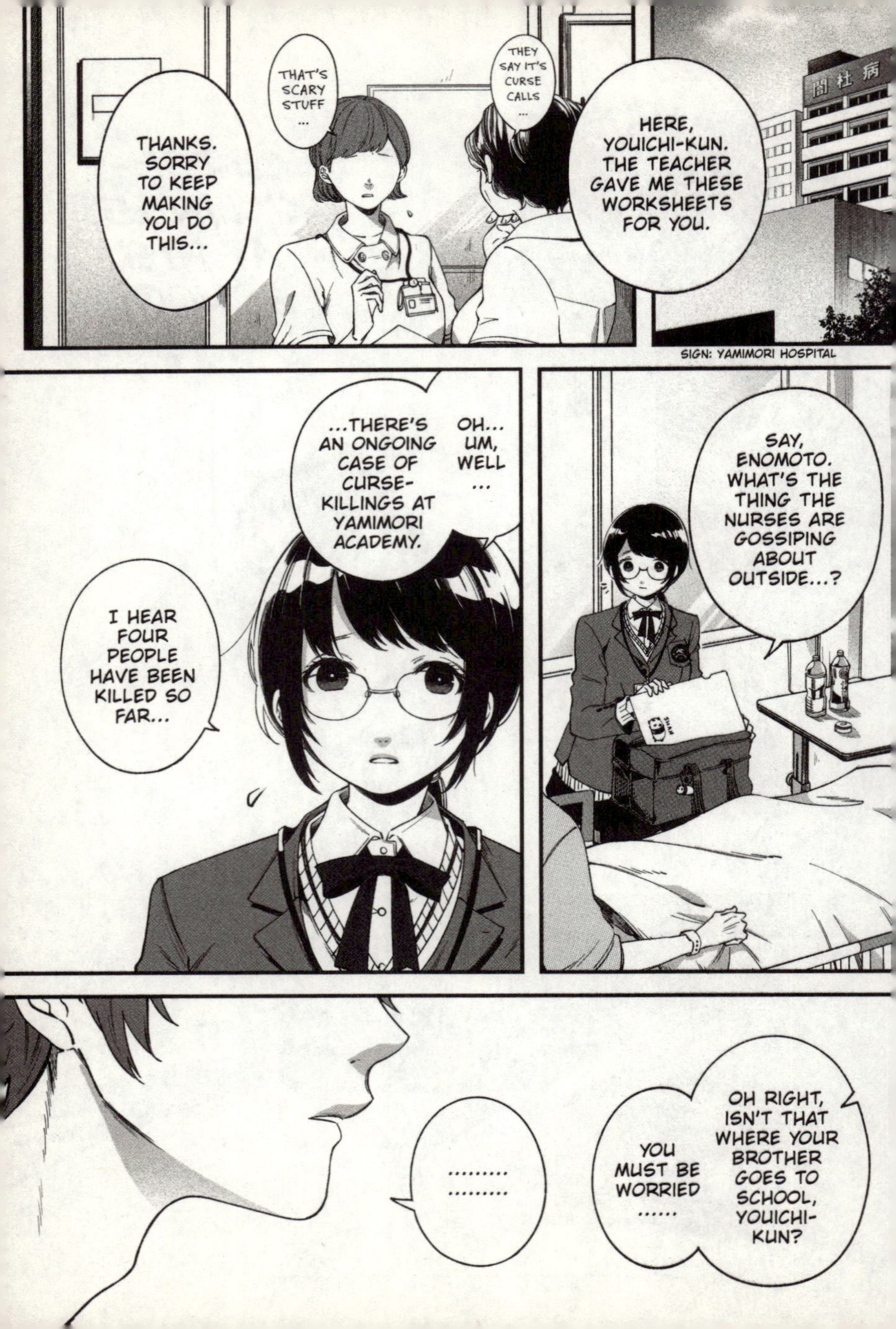
闇杜病
HERE, YOUICHI-KUN. THE TEACHER GAVE ME THESE WORKSHEETS FOR YOU.
THEY SAY IT'S CURSE CALLS ...
THAT'S SCARY STUFF ...
THANKS. SORRY TO KEEP MAKING YOU DO THIS...
SIGN: YAMIMORI HOSPITAL
SAY, ENOMOTO. WHAT'S THE THING THE NURSES ARE GOSSIPING ABOUT OUTSIDE...?
OH... UM, WELL ...
...THERE'S AN ONGOING CASE OF CURSE-KILLINGS AT YAMIMORI ACADEMY.
I HEAR FOUR PEOPLE HAVE BEEN KILLED SO FAR...
OH RIGHT, ISN'T THAT WHERE YOUR BROTHER GOES TO SCHOOL, YOUICHI-KUN?
YOU MUST BE WORRIED ......
....
....

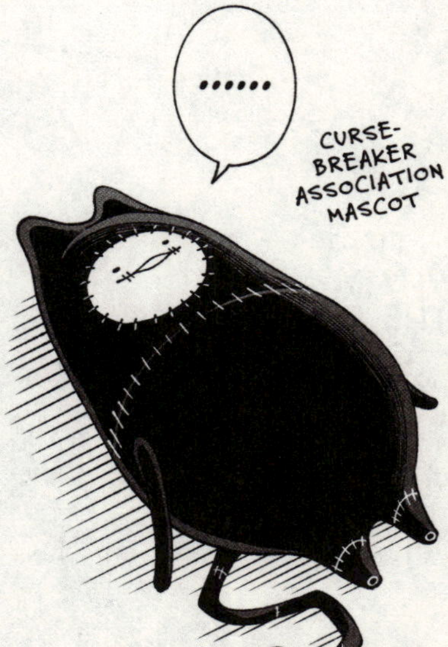
......
CURSE-BREAKER ASSOCIATION MASCOT

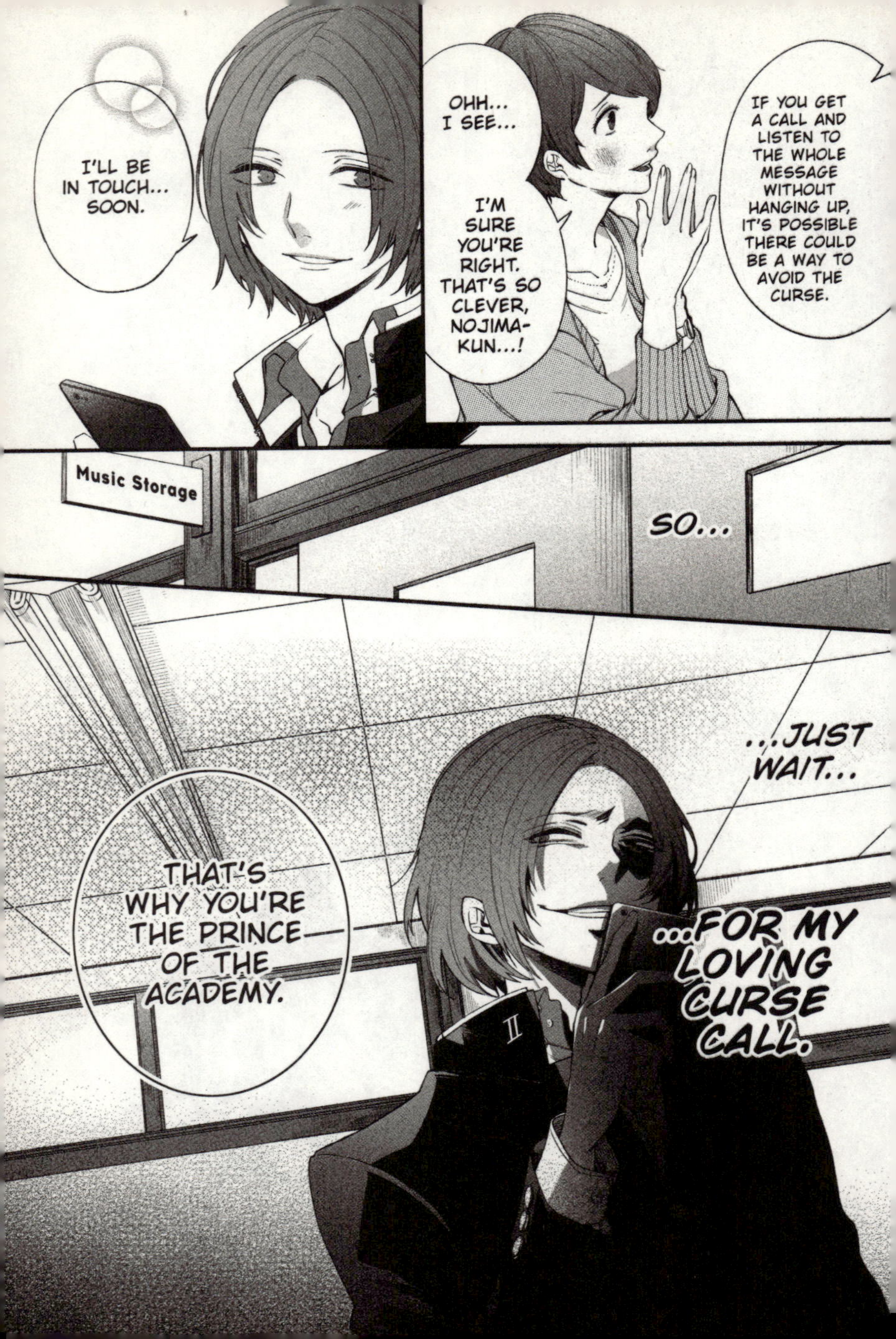
IF YOU GET A CALL AND LISTEN TO THE WHOLE MESSAGE WITHOUT HANGING UP, IT'S POSSIBLE THERE COULD BE A WAY TO AVOID THE CURSE.
OHH... I SEE...
I'M SURE YOU'RE RIGHT. THAT'S SO CLEVER, NOJIMA-KUN...!
I'LL BE IN TOUCH... SOON.
Music Storage
SO...
...JUST WAIT...
...FOR MY LOVING CURSE CALL.
THAT'S WHY YOU'RE THE PRINCE OF THE ACADEMY.

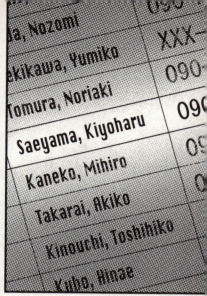

THERE IT IS!!

...da, Nozomi	XXX-
...ekikawa, Yumiko	090
...tomura, Noriaki	090
Saeyama, Kiyoharu	0...
Kaneko, Mihiro	
Takarai, Akiko	
Kinouchi, Toshihiko	
Kubo, Hinae	

SURE...

...JUST DON'T GET SEEN DOING IT, OKAY?

DO YOU MIND IF I TEXT YOU DURING LUNCH BREAK?

...THANKS A LOT.

OH, REALLY? SO IF I GET A CALL...

NONE OF THE CURSE-KILLING VICTIMS ACTUALLY LISTENED TO THE *ENTIRE CURSE MESSAGE.*

...I NOTICED SOMETHING.

BY THE WAY...

ER...YES. TEACHERS AND STUDENTS TRADING CONTACT INFO WOULD BE—

I GUESS ASKING YOU FOR YOUR ADDRESS WOULD BE OUT OF THE QUESTION?

SENSEI...

HOLD ON A SECOND.

....

WOULD IT BE WRONG FOR ME TO COME RUNNING IF YOU'RE SCARED?

......

20XX Teachers - Emergency Contact

	Name	Phone No.
1	Yoshizawa, Masaaki	
2	Iwabuchi, Hisa	
3	Ishikawa, Yuna	
4	Honma, Yuu	
5	Ko...zomi	090-XXXX-XX
6	...kawa, Yumiko	090-XXXX-X
	Tomura, Noriaki	
9	Saeyama, Kiyoh	
10	Kaneko, Mih	
11	Takarai, Ak	
12	Kinouchi, Tos	
13	Kubo, Hinae	
14	Kishi, Souta	

PA CPOINT

Emergency contacts

THIS IS MY CONTACT INFO.

090-XXXX-XXXX

I LEFT MY CELL PHONE IN MY LOCKER, BUT...

...I AM SCARED.

KACHI (CLICK)

KACHI

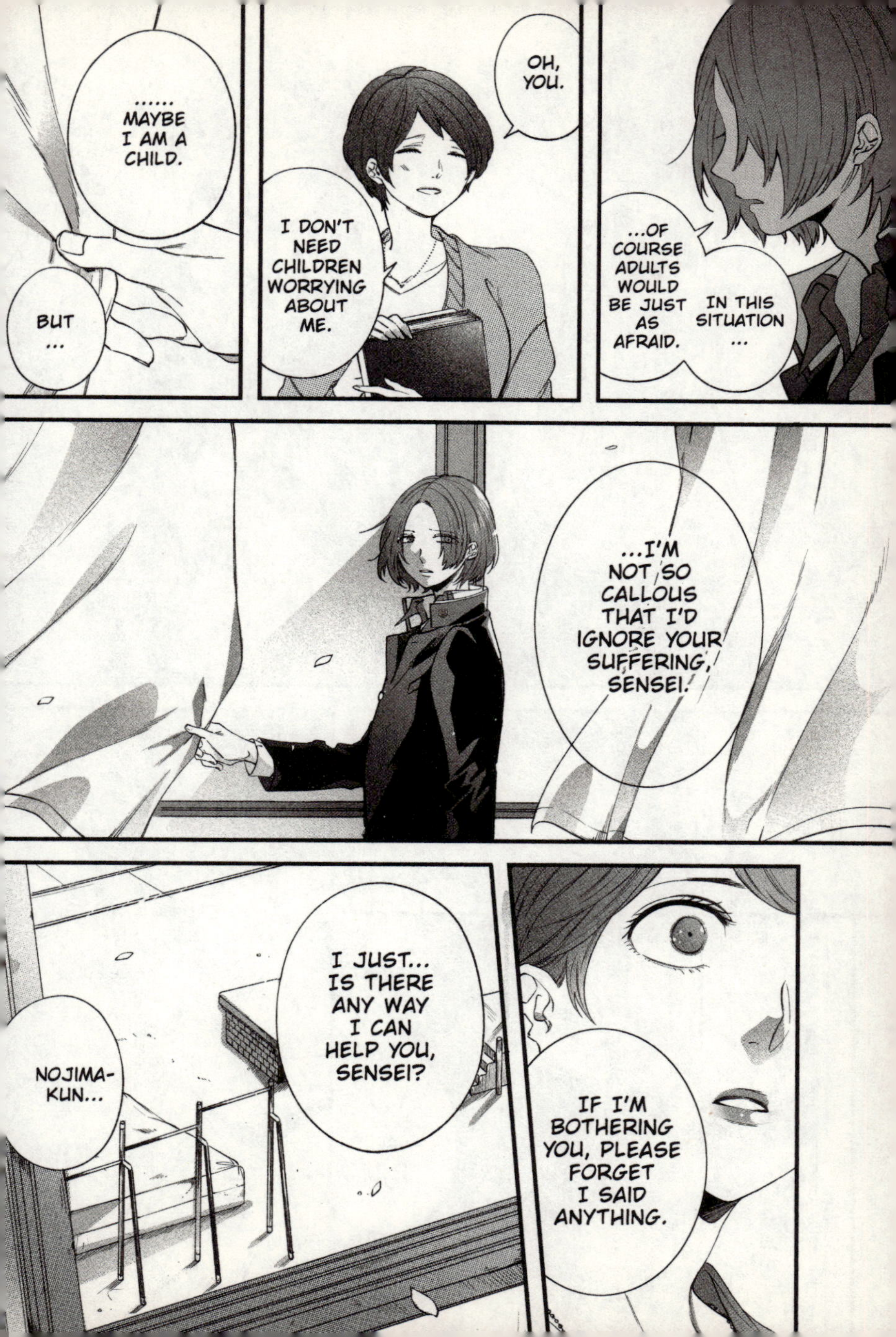
IN THIS SITUATION ...
...OF COURSE ADULTS WOULD BE JUST AS AFRAID.
OH, YOU.
I DON'T NEED CHILDREN WORRYING ABOUT ME.
...... MAYBE I AM A CHILD.
BUT ...
...I'M NOT SO CALLOUS THAT I'D IGNORE YOUR SUFFERING, SENSEI.
IF I'M BOTHERING YOU, PLEASE FORGET I SAID ANYTHING.
I JUST... IS THERE ANY WAY I CAN HELP YOU, SENSEI?
NOJIMA-KUN...

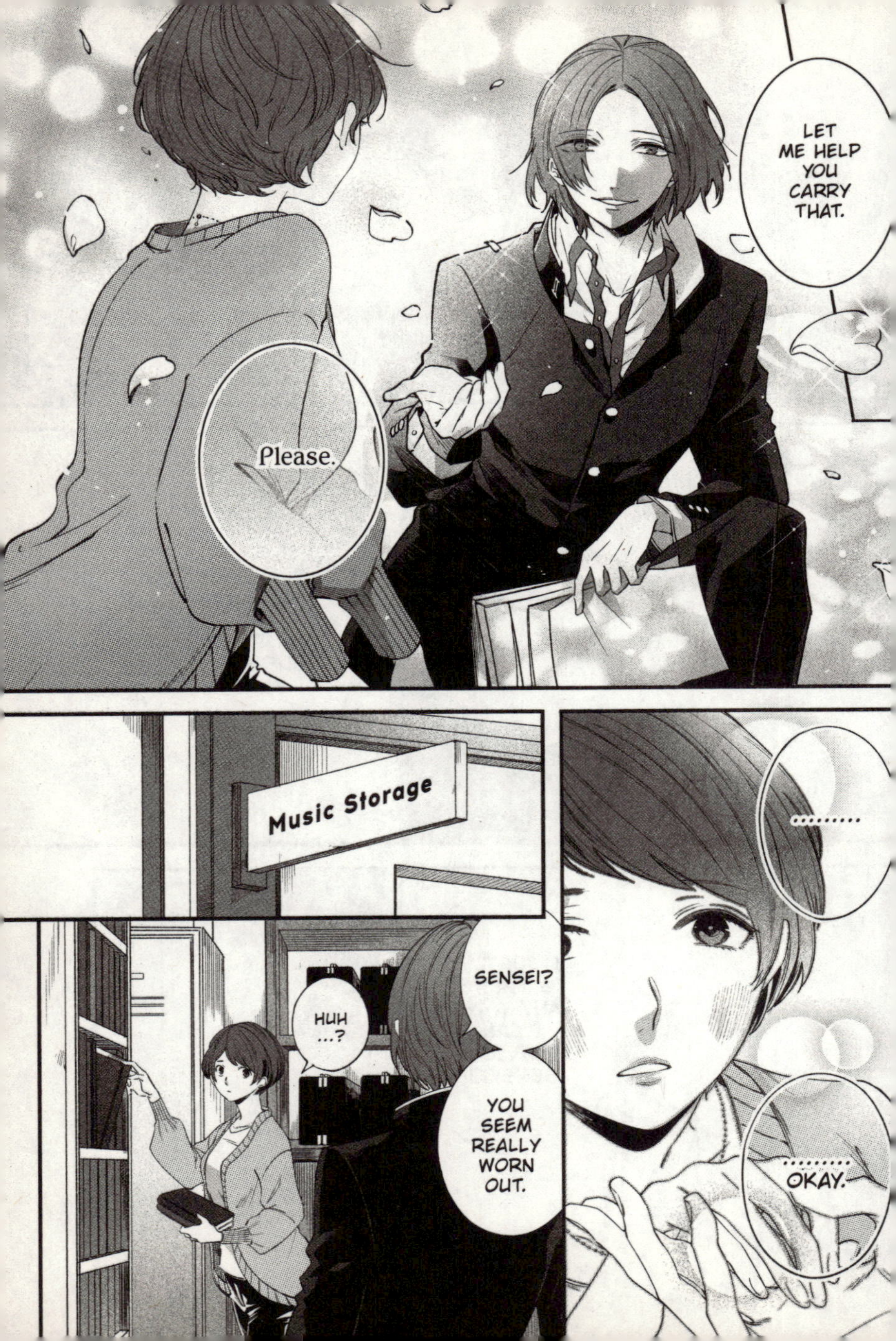
LET ME HELP YOU CARRY THAT.
Please.
....
.... OKAY.
Music Storage
SENSEI?
YOU SEEM REALLY WORN OUT.
HUH ...?

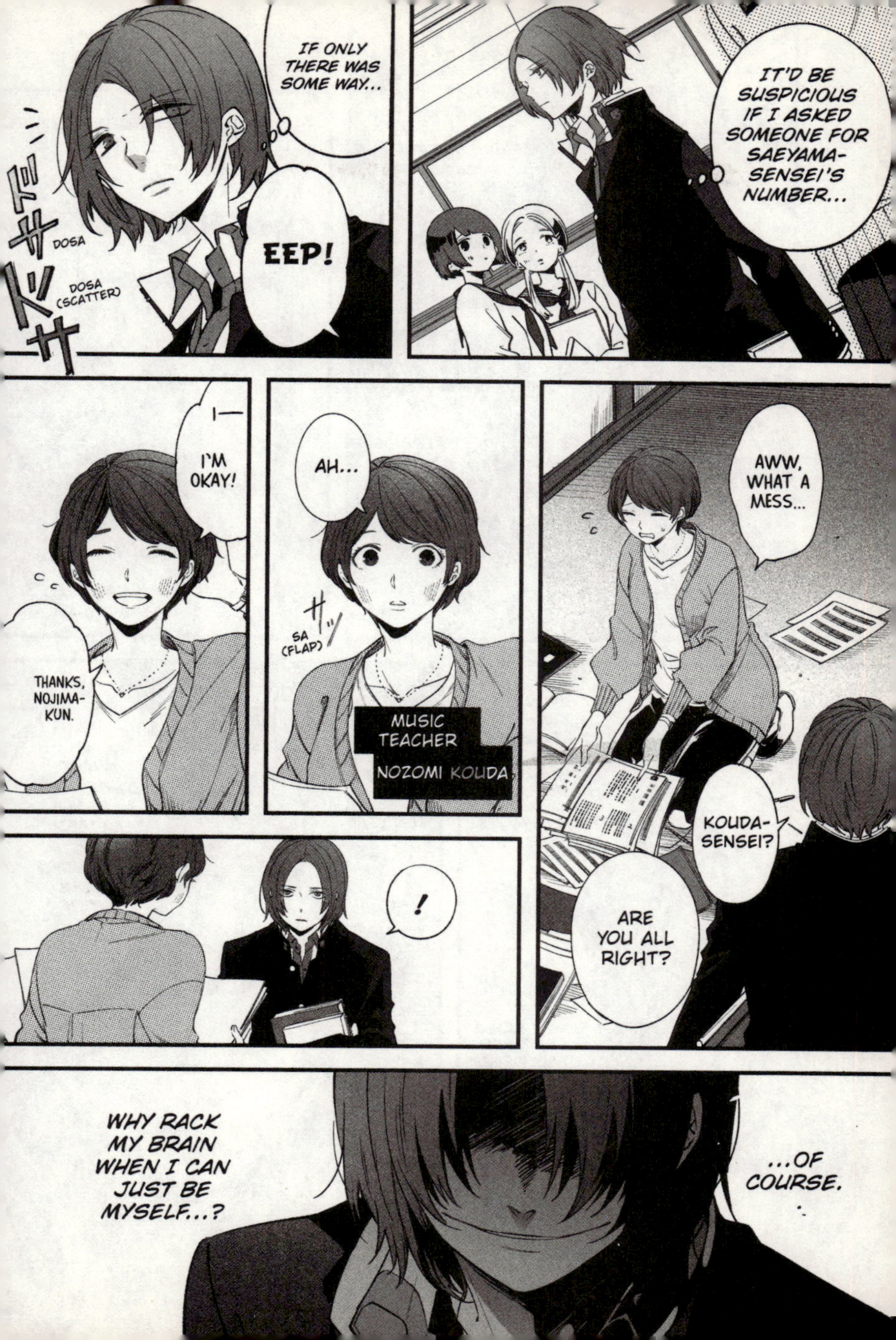
IT'D BE SUSPICIOUS IF I ASKED SOMEONE FOR SAEYAMA-SENSEI'S NUMBER...
IF ONLY THERE WAS SOME WAY...
EEP!
DOSA
DOSA (SCATTER)
AWW, WHAT A MESS...
KOUDA-SENSEI?
ARE YOU ALL RIGHT?
AH...
SA (FLAP)
MUSIC TEACHER
NOZOMI KOUDA
I— I'M OKAY!
THANKS, NOJIMA-KUN.
!
...OF COURSE.
WHY RACK MY BRAIN WHEN I CAN JUST BE MYSELF...?

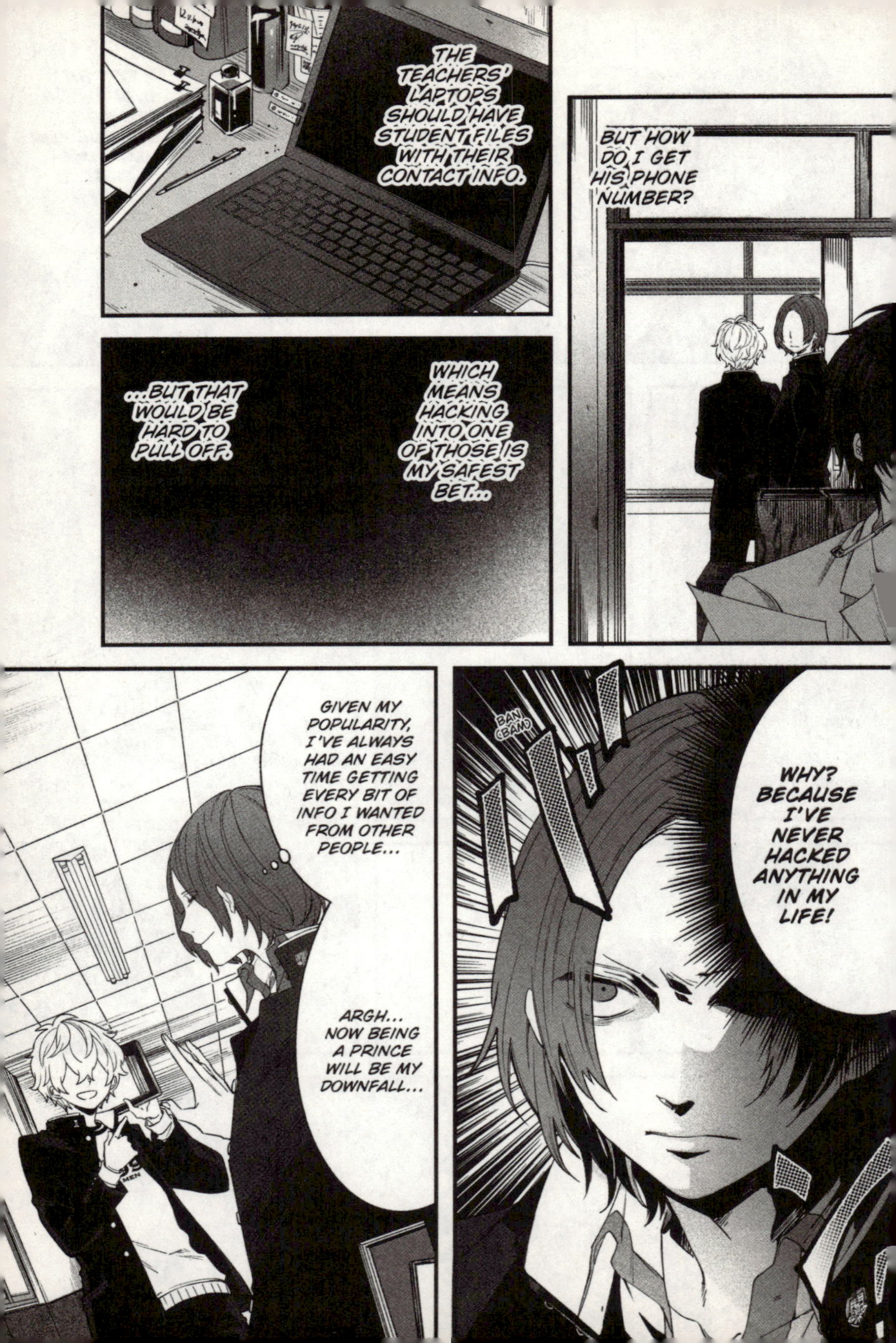

BUT HOW DO I GET HIS PHONE NUMBER?
THE TEACHERS' LAPTOPS SHOULD HAVE STUDENT FILES WITH THEIR CONTACT INFO.
WHICH MEANS HACKING INTO ONE OF THOSE IS MY SAFEST BET...
...BUT THAT WOULD BE HARD TO PULL OFF.
WHY? BECAUSE I'VE NEVER HACKED ANYTHING IN MY LIFE!
BAN BAN
GIVEN MY POPULARITY, I'VE ALWAYS HAD AN EASY TIME GETTING EVERY BIT OF INFO I WANTED FROM OTHER PEOPLE...
ARGH... NOW BEING A PRINCE WILL BE MY DOWNFALL...

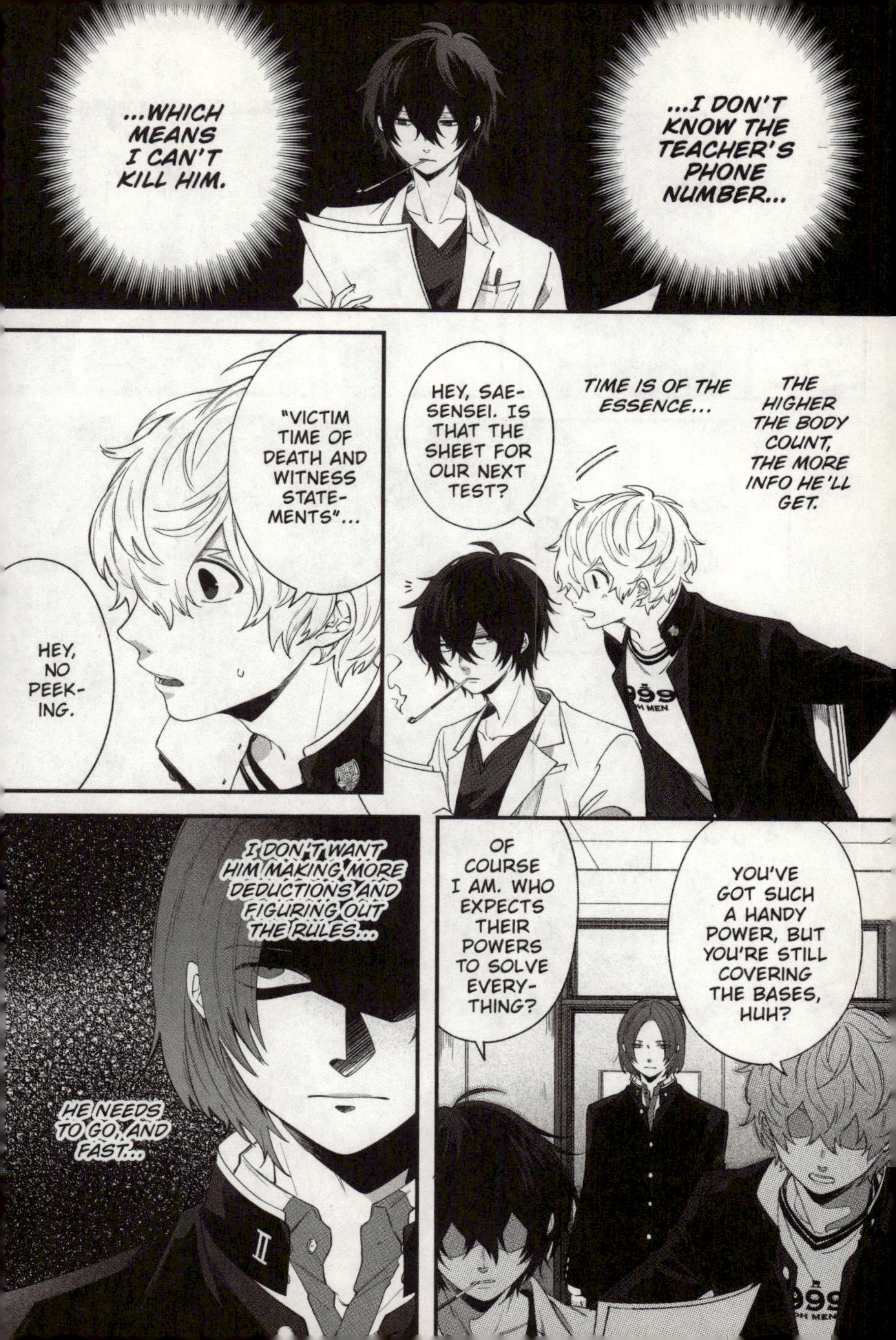
...I DON'T KNOW THE TEACHER'S PHONE NUMBER...
...WHICH MEANS I CAN'T KILL HIM.
THE HIGHER THE BODY COUNT, THE MORE INFO HE'LL GET.
TIME IS OF THE ESSENCE...
HEY, SAE-SENSEI. IS THAT THE SHEET FOR OUR NEXT TEST?
"VICTIM TIME OF DEATH AND WITNESS STATEMENTS"...
HEY, NO PEEKING.
YOU'VE GOT SUCH A HANDY POWER, BUT YOU'RE STILL COVERING THE BASES, HUH?
OF COURSE I AM. WHO EXPECTS THEIR POWERS TO SOLVE EVERYTHING?
I DON'T WANT HIM MAKING MORE DEDUCTIONS AND FIGURING OUT THE RULES...
HE NEEDS TO GO, AND FAST...

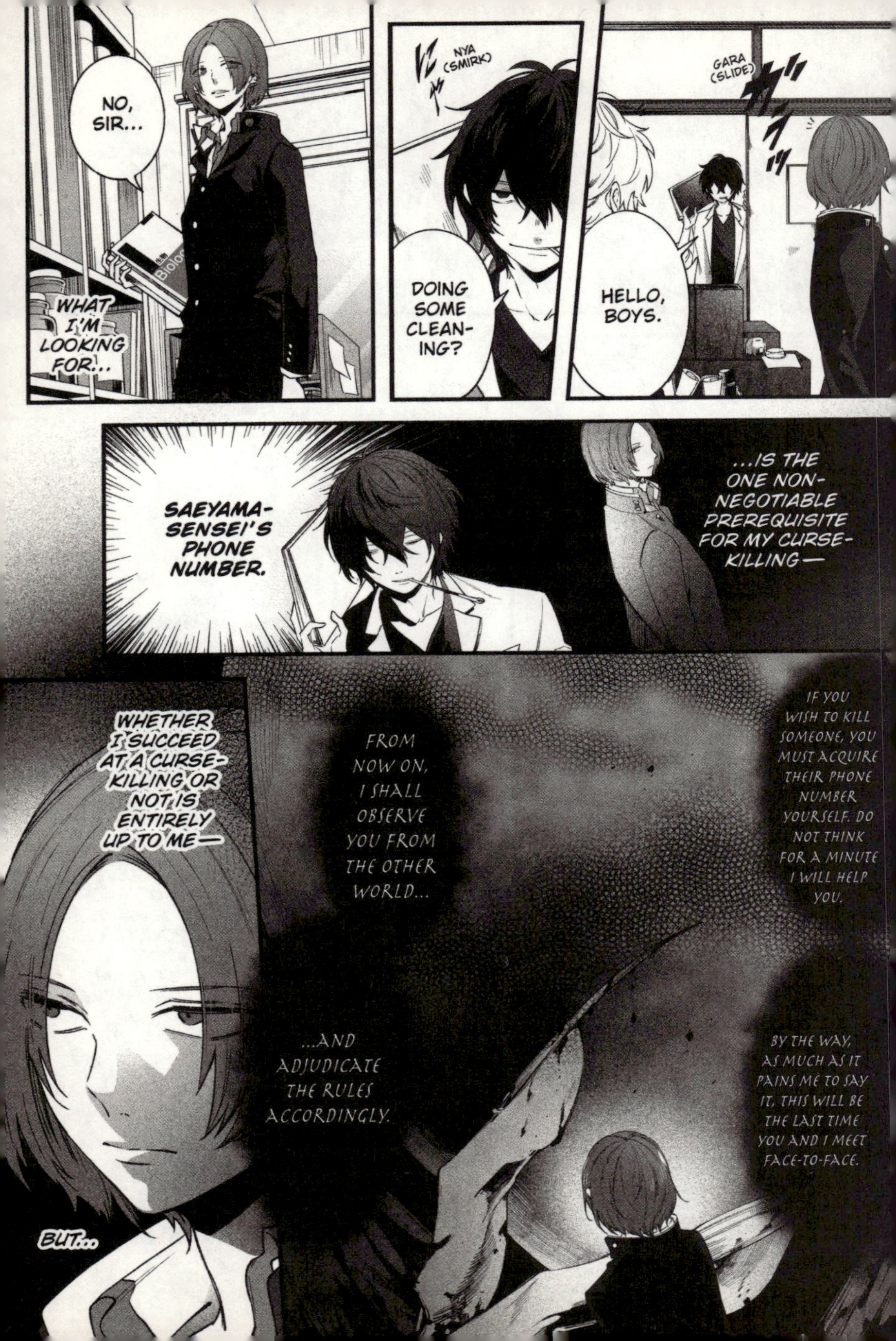

GARA (SLIDE)
HELLO, BOYS.
NYA (SMIRK)
DOING SOME CLEAN-ING?
NO, SIR...
WHAT I'M LOOKING FOR...
...IS THE ONE NON-NEGOTIABLE PREREQUISITE FOR MY CURSE-KILLING—
SAEYAMA-SENSEI'S PHONE NUMBER.
IF YOU WISH TO KILL SOMEONE, YOU MUST ACQUIRE THEIR PHONE NUMBER YOURSELF. DO NOT THINK FOR A MINUTE I WILL HELP YOU.
FROM NOW ON, I SHALL OBSERVE YOU FROM THE OTHER WORLD...
WHETHER I SUCCEED AT A CURSE-KILLING OR NOT IS ENTIRELY UP TO ME—
BY THE WAY, AS MUCH AS IT PAINS ME TO SAY IT, THIS WILL BE THE LAST TIME YOU AND I MEET FACE-TO-FACE.
...AND ADJUDICATE THE RULES ACCORDINGLY.
BUT...

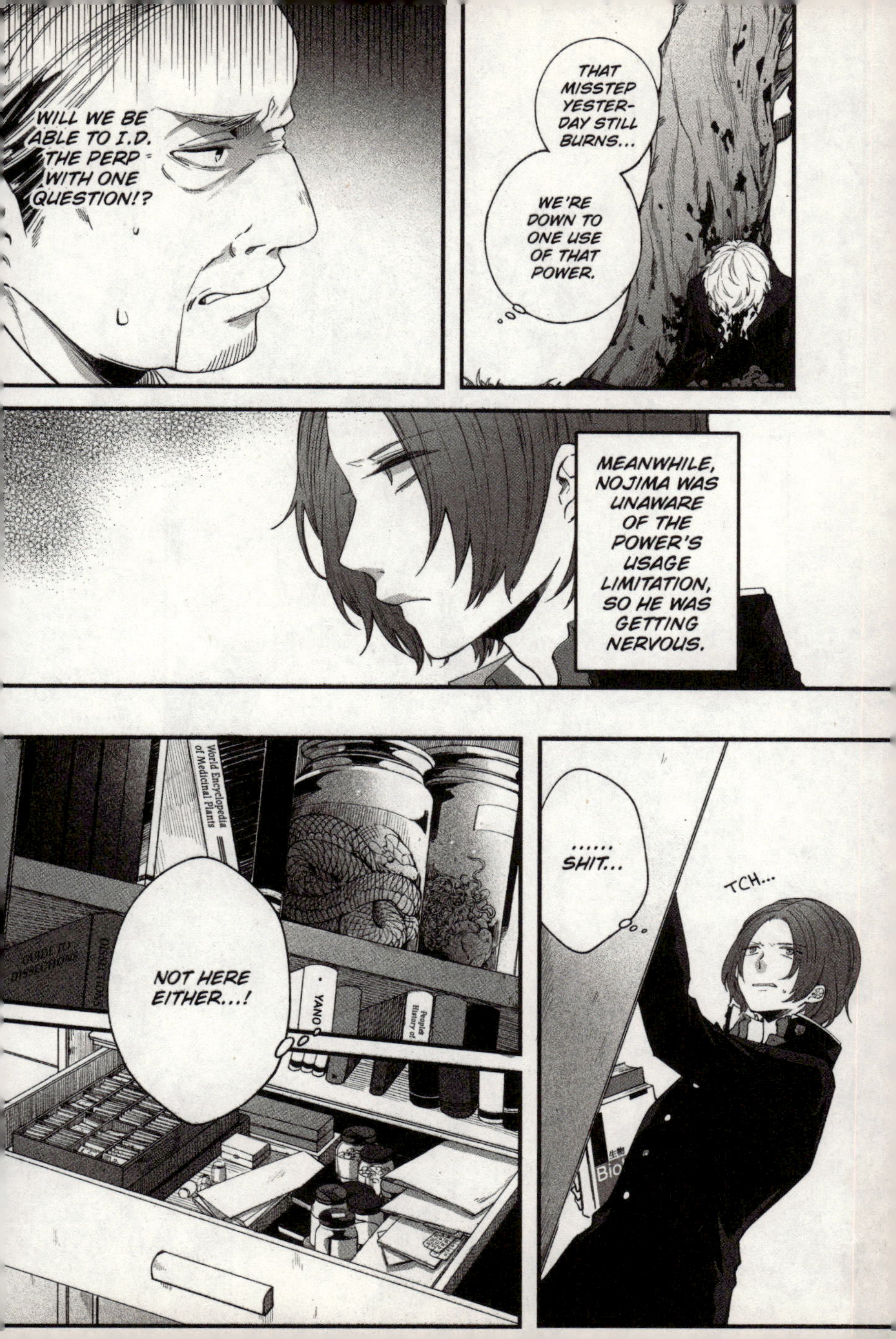
THAT MISSTEP YESTERDAY STILL BURNS...
WE'RE DOWN TO ONE USE OF THAT POWER.
WILL WE BE ABLE TO I.D. THE PERP WITH ONE QUESTION!?
MEANWHILE, NOJIMA WAS UNAWARE OF THE POWER'S USAGE LIMITATION, SO HE WAS GETTING NERVOUS.
...... SHIT...
TCH...
World Encyclopedia of Medicinal Plants
YANO
NOT HERE EITHER...!

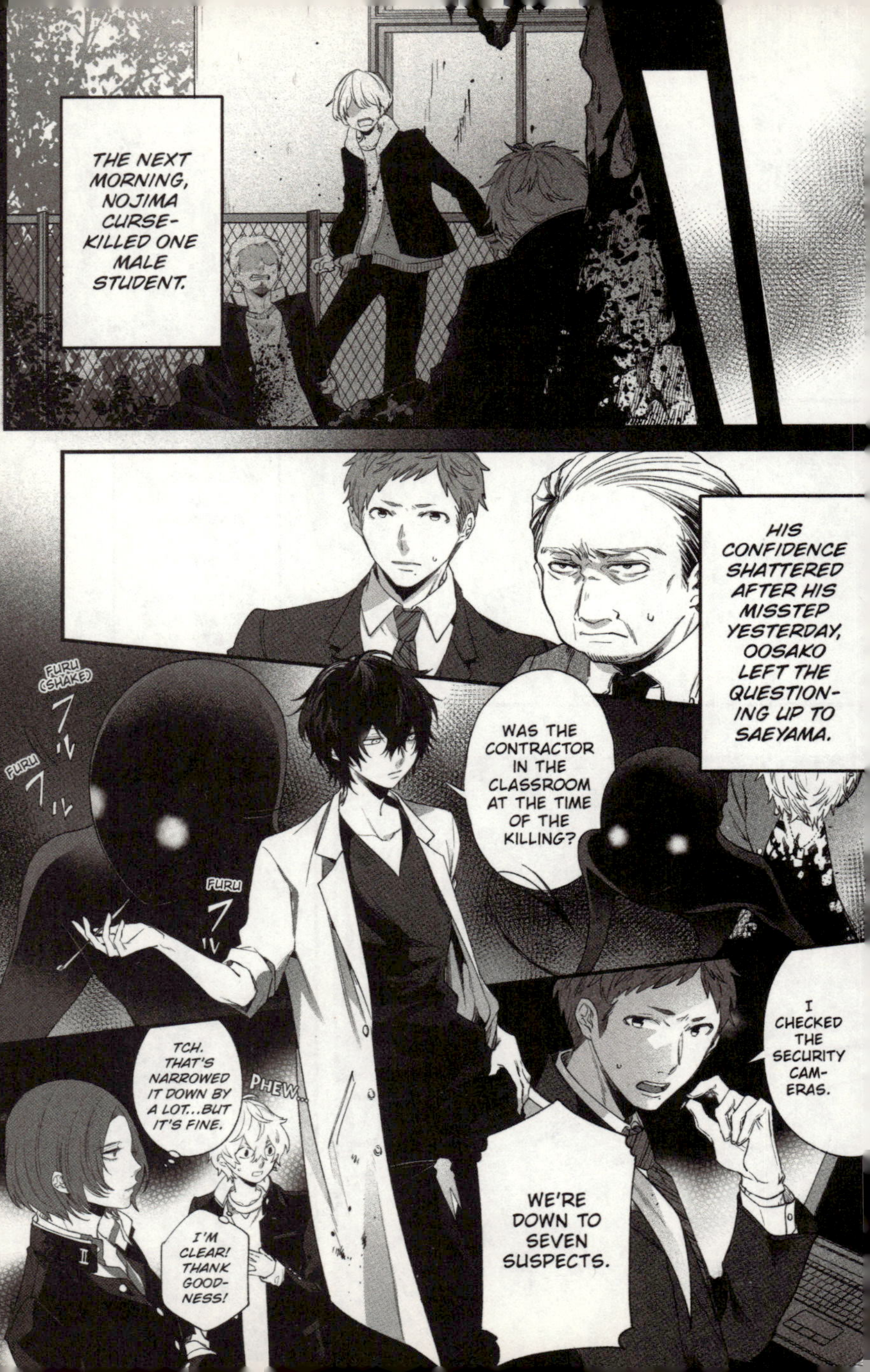
THE NEXT MORNING, NOJIMA CURSE-KILLED ONE MALE STUDENT.
HIS CONFIDENCE SHATTERED AFTER HIS MISSTEP YESTERDAY, OOSAKO LEFT THE QUESTIONING UP TO SAEYAMA.
WAS THE CONTRACTOR IN THE CLASSROOM AT THE TIME OF THE KILLING?
FURU (SHAKE)
FURU
FURU
I CHECKED THE SECURITY CAMERAS.
WE'RE DOWN TO SEVEN SUSPECTS.
PHEW...
TCH. THAT'S NARROWED IT DOWN BY A LOT...BUT IT'S FINE.
I'M CLEAR! THANK GOODNESS!

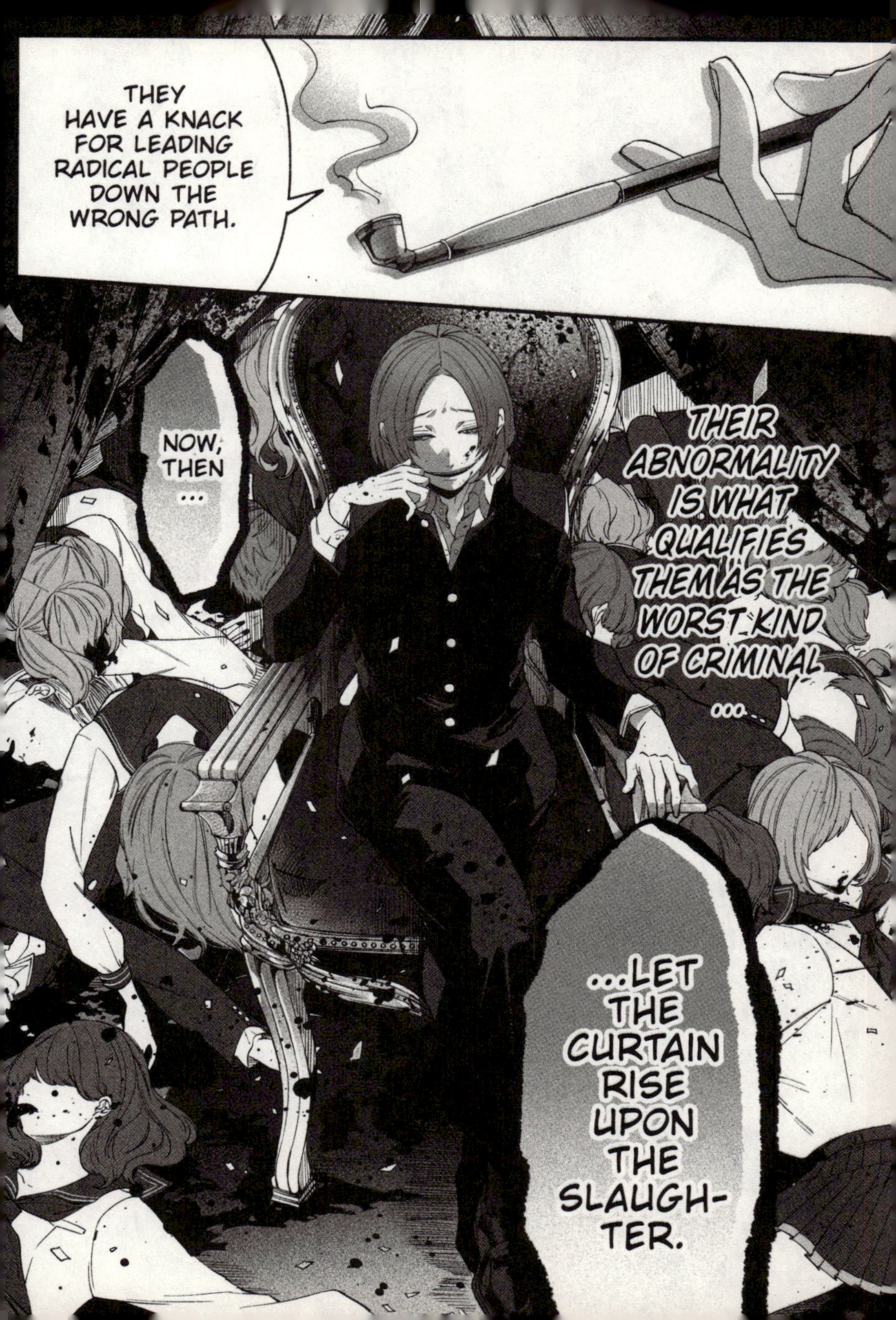
THEY HAVE A KNACK FOR LEADING RADICAL PEOPLE DOWN THE WRONG PATH.
THEIR ABNORMALITY IS WHAT QUALIFIES THEM AS THE WORST KIND OF CRIMINAL...
NOW, THEN...
...LET THE CURTAIN RISE UPON THE SLAUGH-TER.

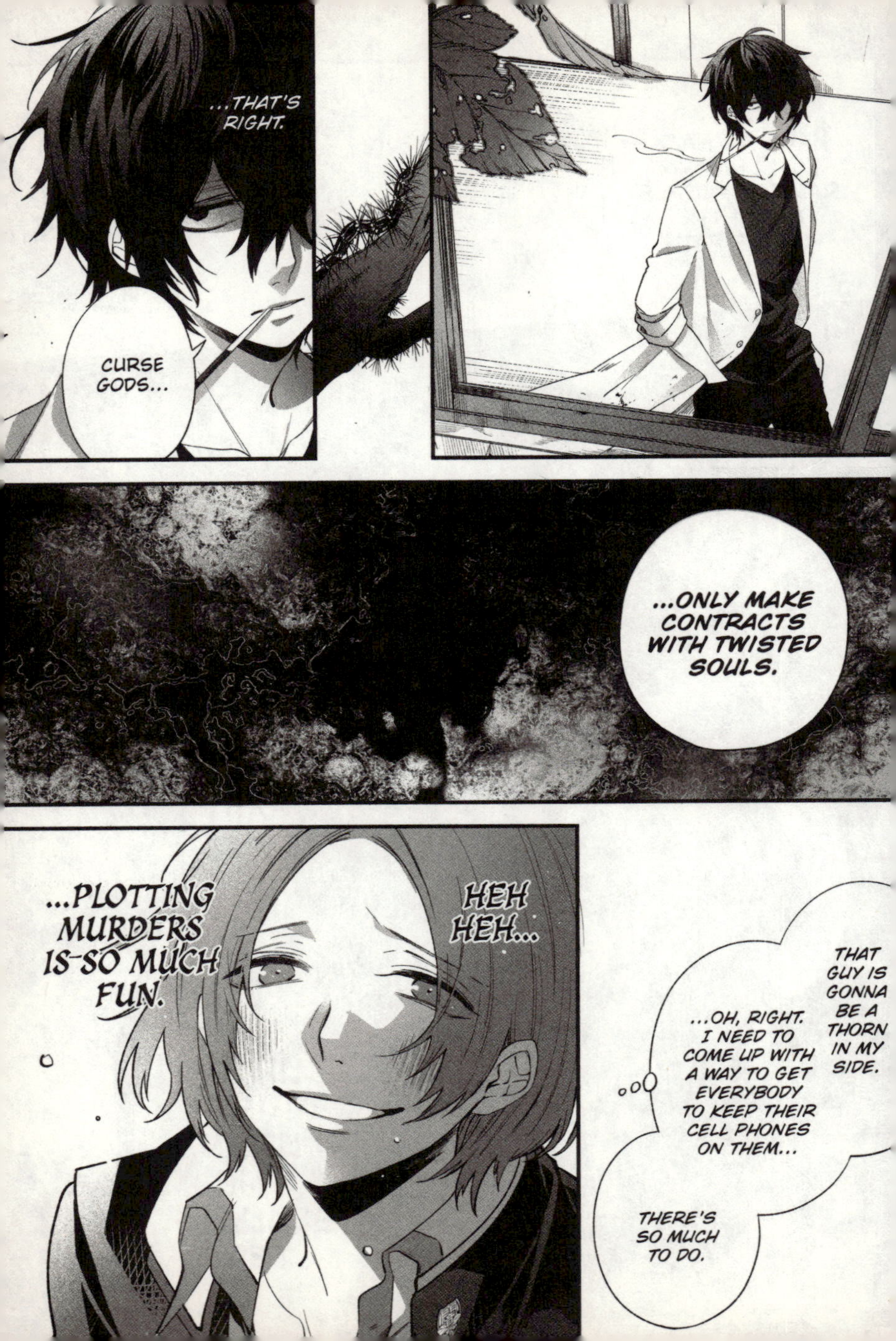
...THAT'S RIGHT.
CURSE GODS...
...ONLY MAKE CONTRACTS WITH TWISTED SOULS.
THAT GUY IS GONNA BE A THORN IN MY SIDE.
...OH, RIGHT. I NEED TO COME UP WITH A WAY TO GET EVERYBODY TO KEEP THEIR CELL PHONES ON THEM...
THERE'S SO MUCH TO DO.
HEH HEH...
...PLOTTING MURDERS IS SO MUCH FUN.

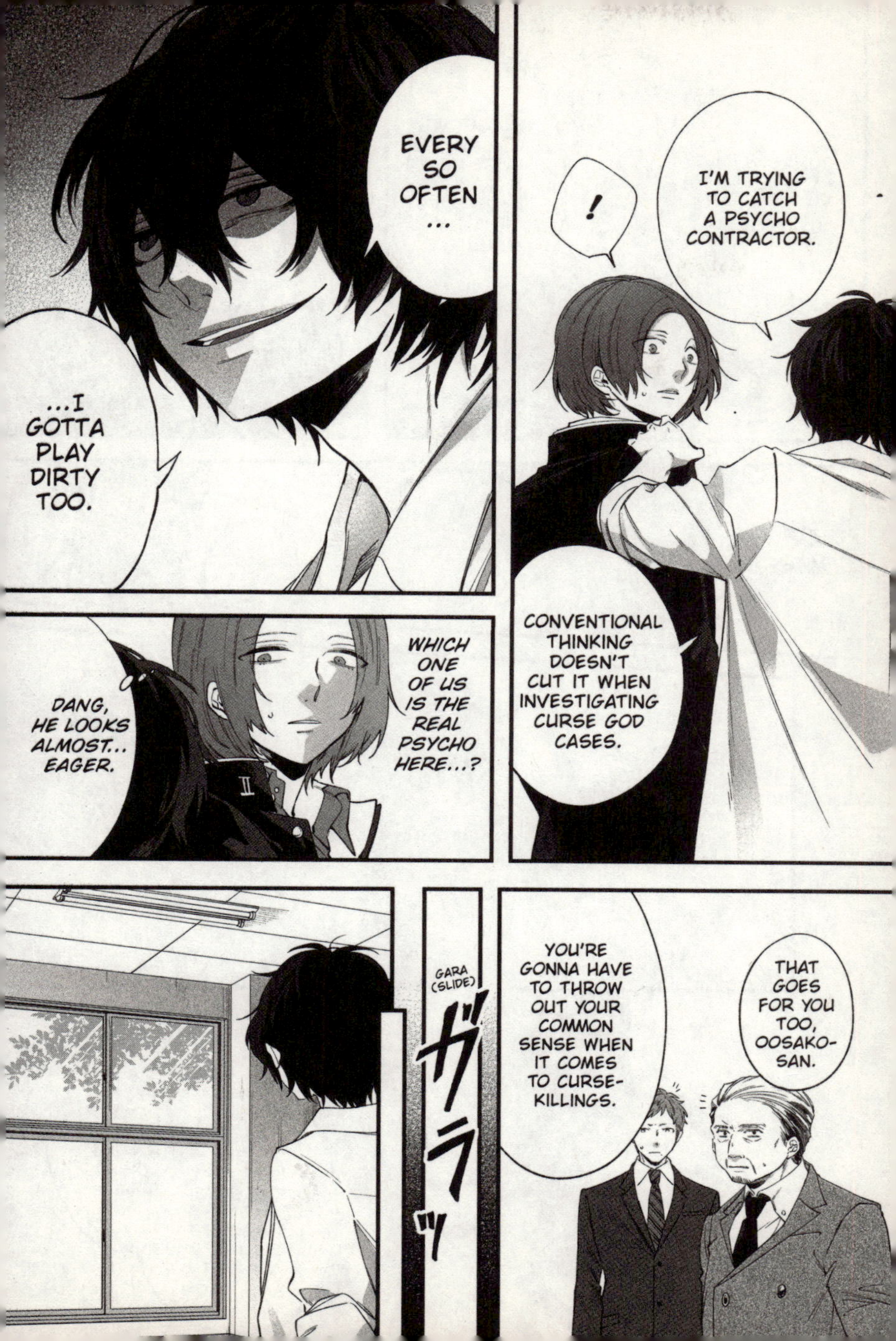
!
I'M TRYING TO CATCH A PSYCHO CONTRACTOR.
CONVENTIONAL THINKING DOESN'T CUT IT WHEN INVESTIGATING CURSE GOD CASES.
EVERY SO OFTEN...
...I GOTTA PLAY DIRTY TOO.
WHICH ONE OF US IS THE REAL PSYCHO HERE...?
DANG, HE LOOKS ALMOST... EAGER.
YOU'RE GONNA HAVE TO THROW OUT YOUR COMMON SENSE WHEN IT COMES TO CURSE-KILLINGS.
THAT GOES FOR YOU TOO, OOSAKO-SAN.
GARA (SLIDE)

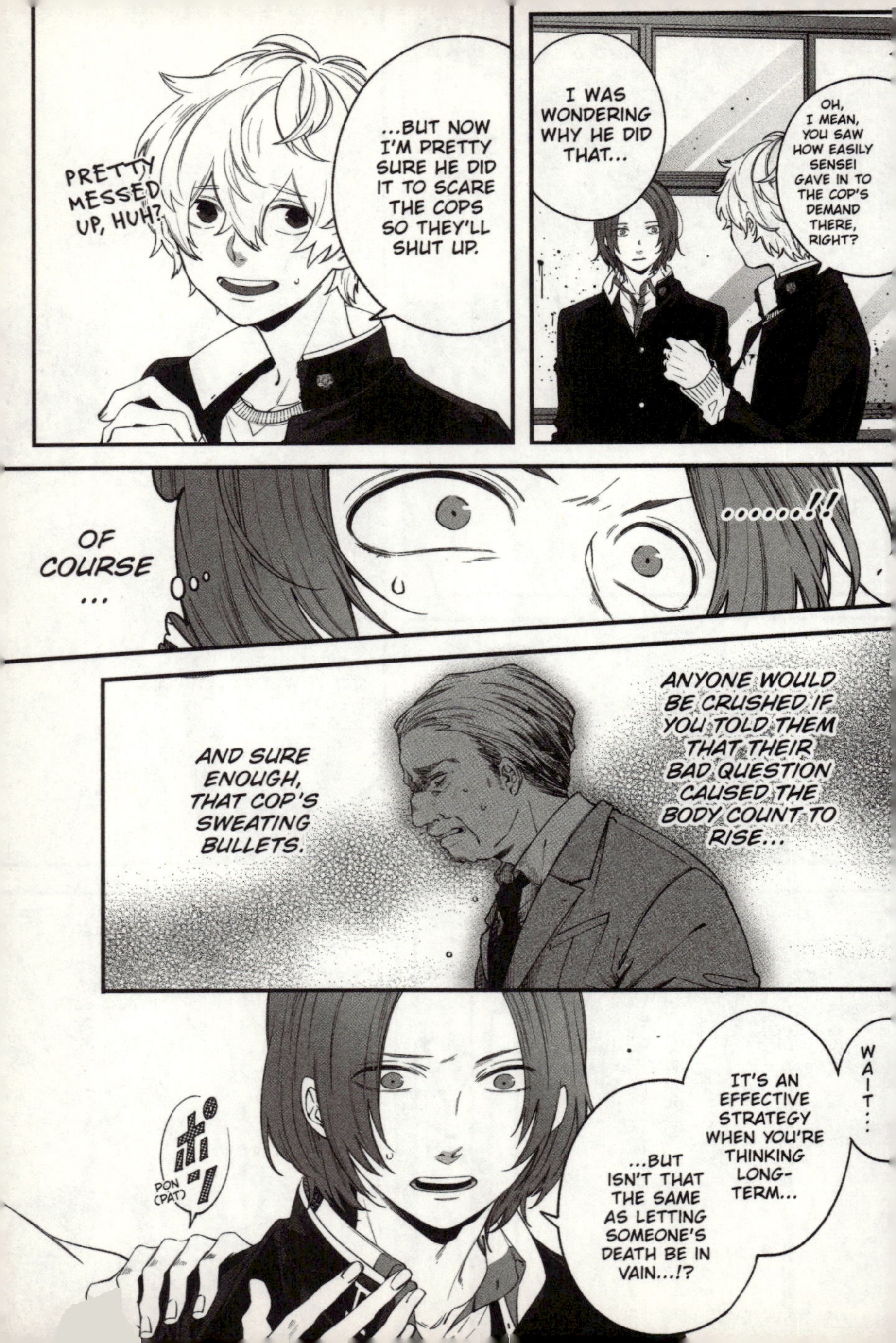
OH, I MEAN, YOU SAW HOW EASILY SENSEI GAVE IN TO THE COP'S DEMAND THERE, RIGHT?
I WAS WONDERING WHY HE DID THAT...
...BUT NOW I'M PRETTY SURE HE DID IT TO SCARE THE COPS SO THEY'LL SHUT UP.
PRETTY MESSED UP, HUH?
oooooo!!
OF COURSE...
ANYONE WOULD BE CRUSHED IF YOU TOLD THEM THAT THEIR BAD QUESTION CAUSED THE BODY COUNT TO RISE...
AND SURE ENOUGH, THAT COP'S SWEATING BULLETS.
WAIT...
IT'S AN EFFECTIVE STRATEGY WHEN YOU'RE THINKING LONG-TERM...
...BUT ISN'T THAT THE SAME AS LETTING SOMEONE'S DEATH BE IN VAIN...!?
PON (PAT)

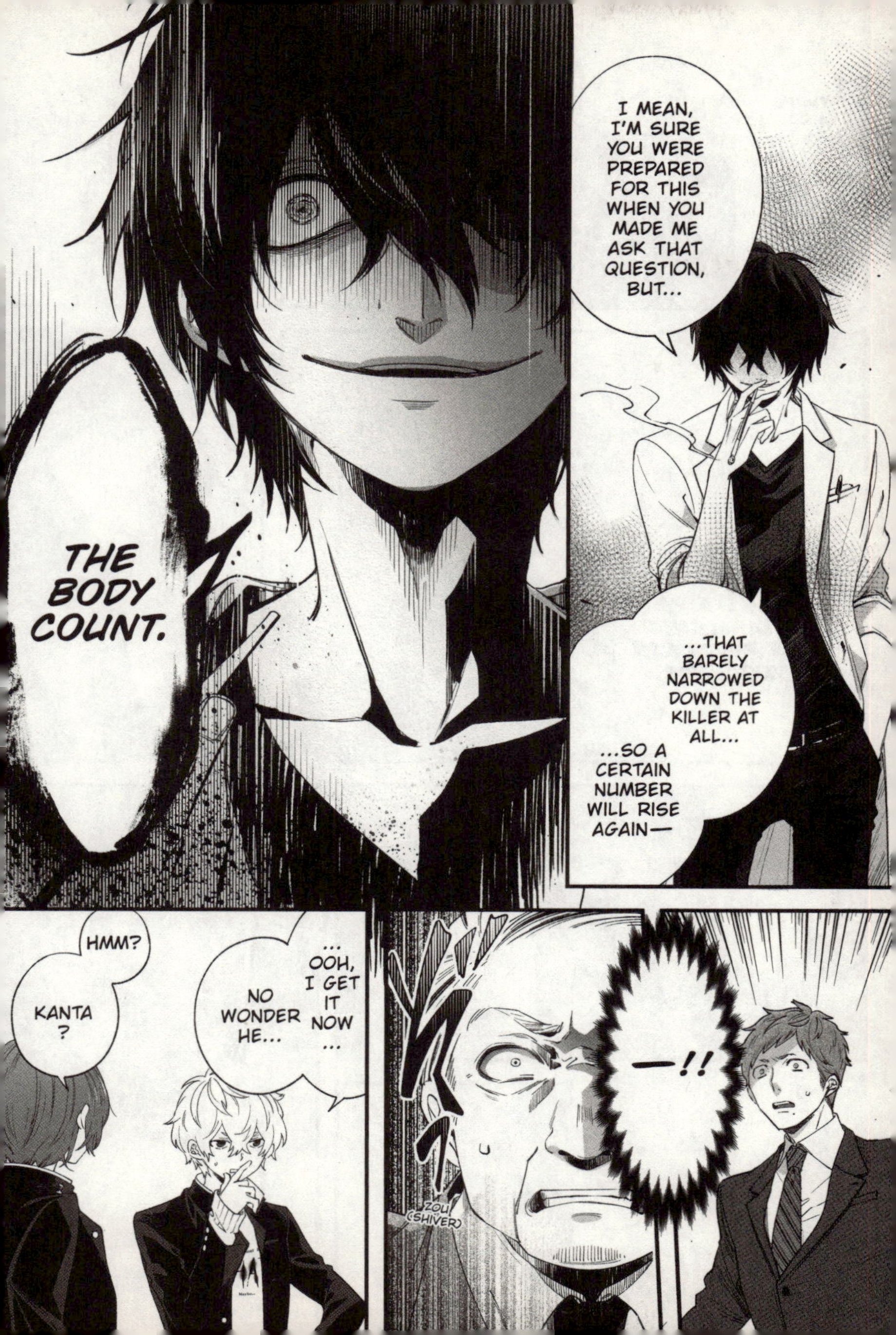
I MEAN, I'M SURE YOU WERE PREPARED FOR THIS WHEN YOU MADE ME ASK THAT QUESTION, BUT...
...THAT BARELY NARROWED DOWN THE KILLER AT ALL...
...SO A CERTAIN NUMBER WILL RISE AGAIN—
THE BODY COUNT.
—!!
ZOU (SHIVER)
...OOH, I GET IT NOW...
NO WONDER HE...
HMM?
KANTA?

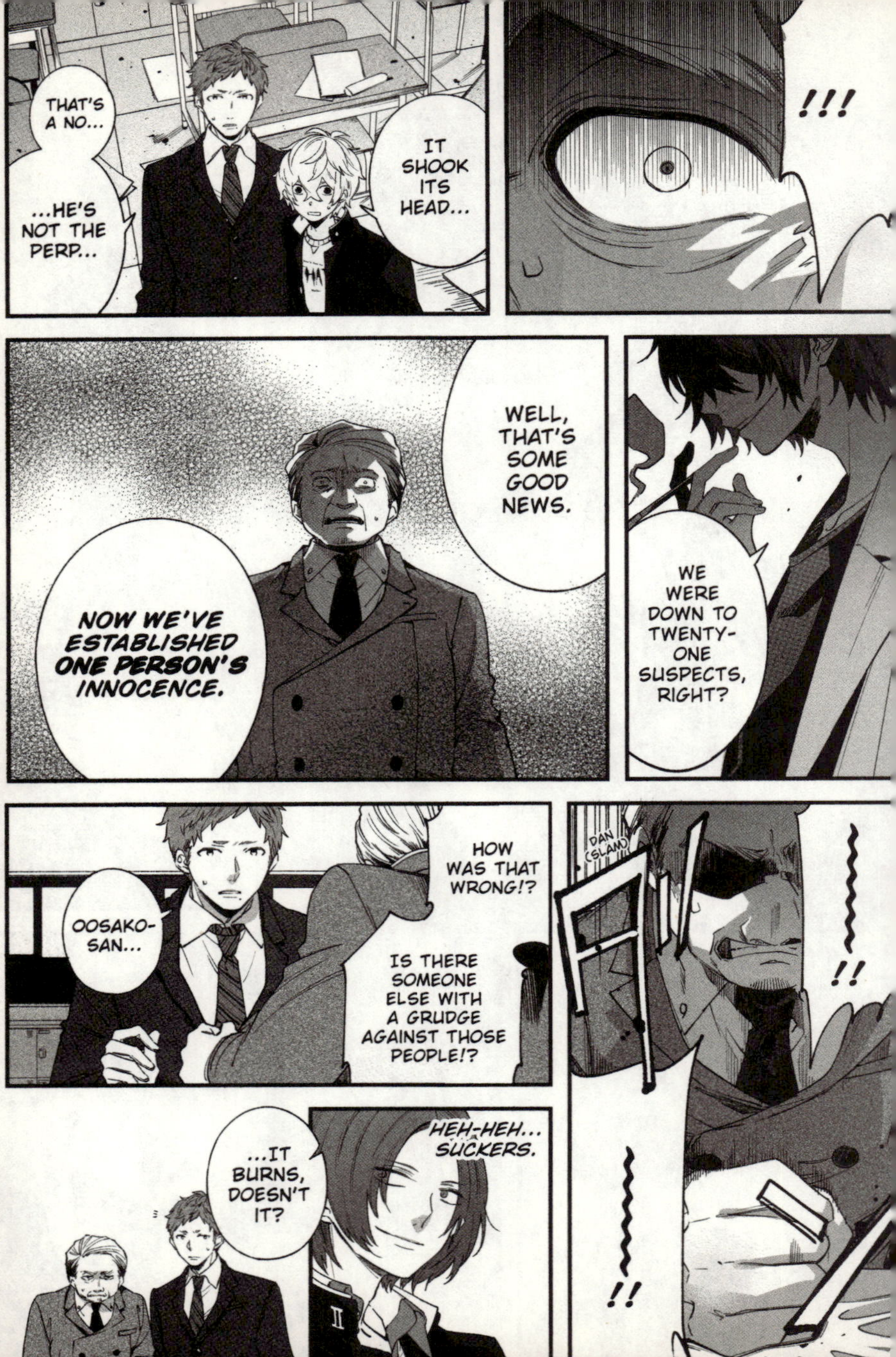
!!!
IT SHOOK ITS HEAD...
THAT'S A NO...
...HE'S NOT THE PERP...
WE WERE DOWN TO TWENTY-ONE SUSPECTS, RIGHT?
WELL, THAT'S SOME GOOD NEWS.
NOW WE'VE ESTABLISHED ONE PERSON'S INNOCENCE.
!!
DAN (SLAM)
!!
HOW WAS THAT WRONG!?
IS THERE SOMEONE ELSE WITH A GRUDGE AGAINST THOSE PEOPLE!?
OOSAKO-SAN...
HEH-HEH... SUCKERS.
...IT BURNS, DOESN'T IT?

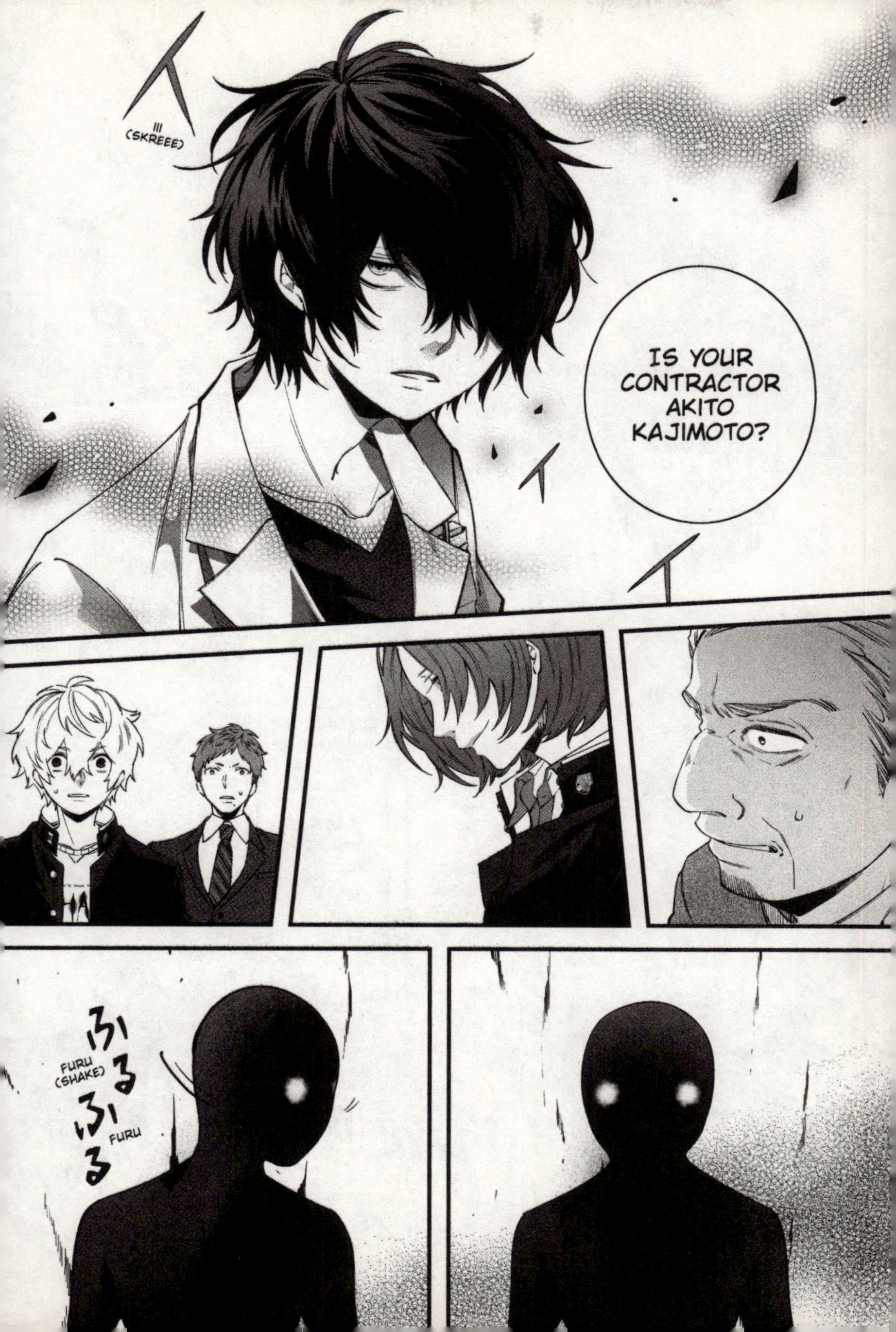
III
(SKREEE)
IS YOUR CONTRACTOR AKITO KAJIMOTO?
ふるふる
FURU (SHAKE)
FURU

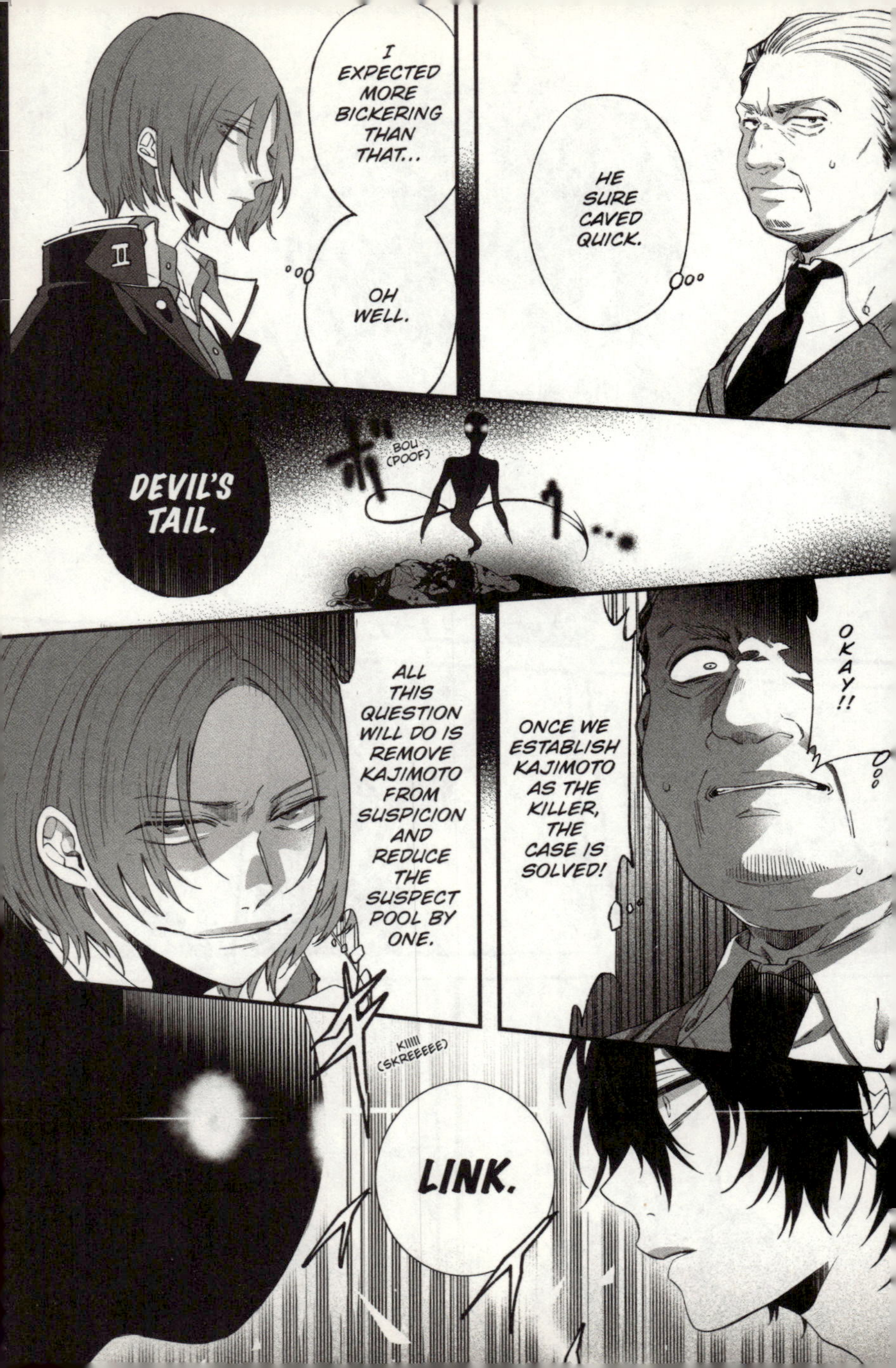
HE SURE CAVED QUICK.
I EXPECTED MORE BICKERING THAN THAT...
OH WELL.
BOU (POOF)
DEVIL'S TAIL.
OKAY!!
ONCE WE ESTABLISH KAJIMOTO AS THE KILLER, THE CASE IS SOLVED!
ALL THIS QUESTION WILL DO IS REMOVE KAJIMOTO FROM SUSPICION AND REDUCE THE SUSPECT POOL BY ONE.
KIIIII (SKREEEEEE)
LINK.

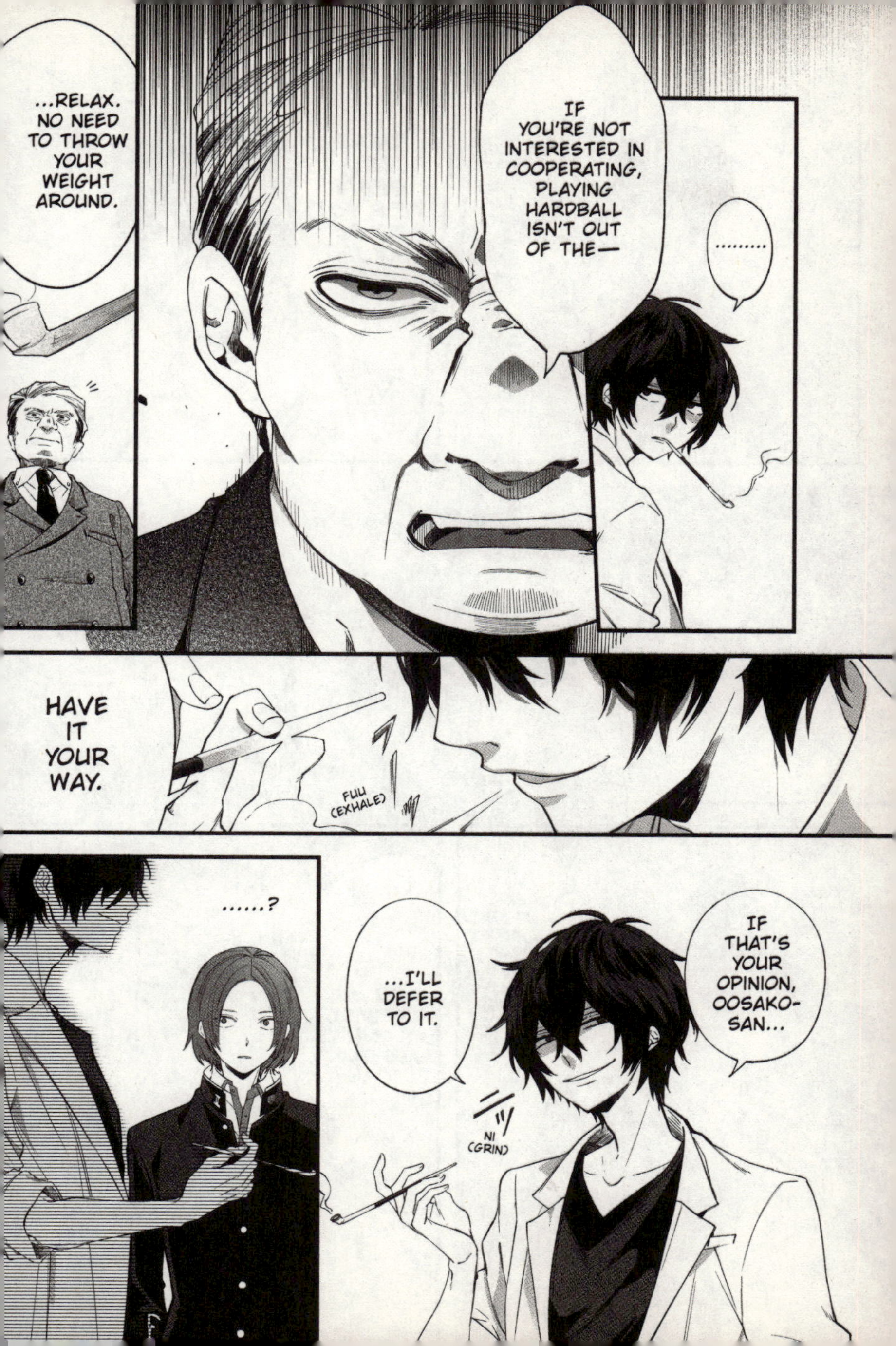
IF YOU'RE NOT INTERESTED IN COOPERATING, PLAYING HARDBALL ISN'T OUT OF THE—
....
...RELAX. NO NEED TO THROW YOUR WEIGHT AROUND.
FUU (EXHALE)
HAVE IT YOUR WAY.
IF THAT'S YOUR OPINION, OOSAKO-SAN...
...I'LL DEFER TO IT.
NI (GRIN)
......?

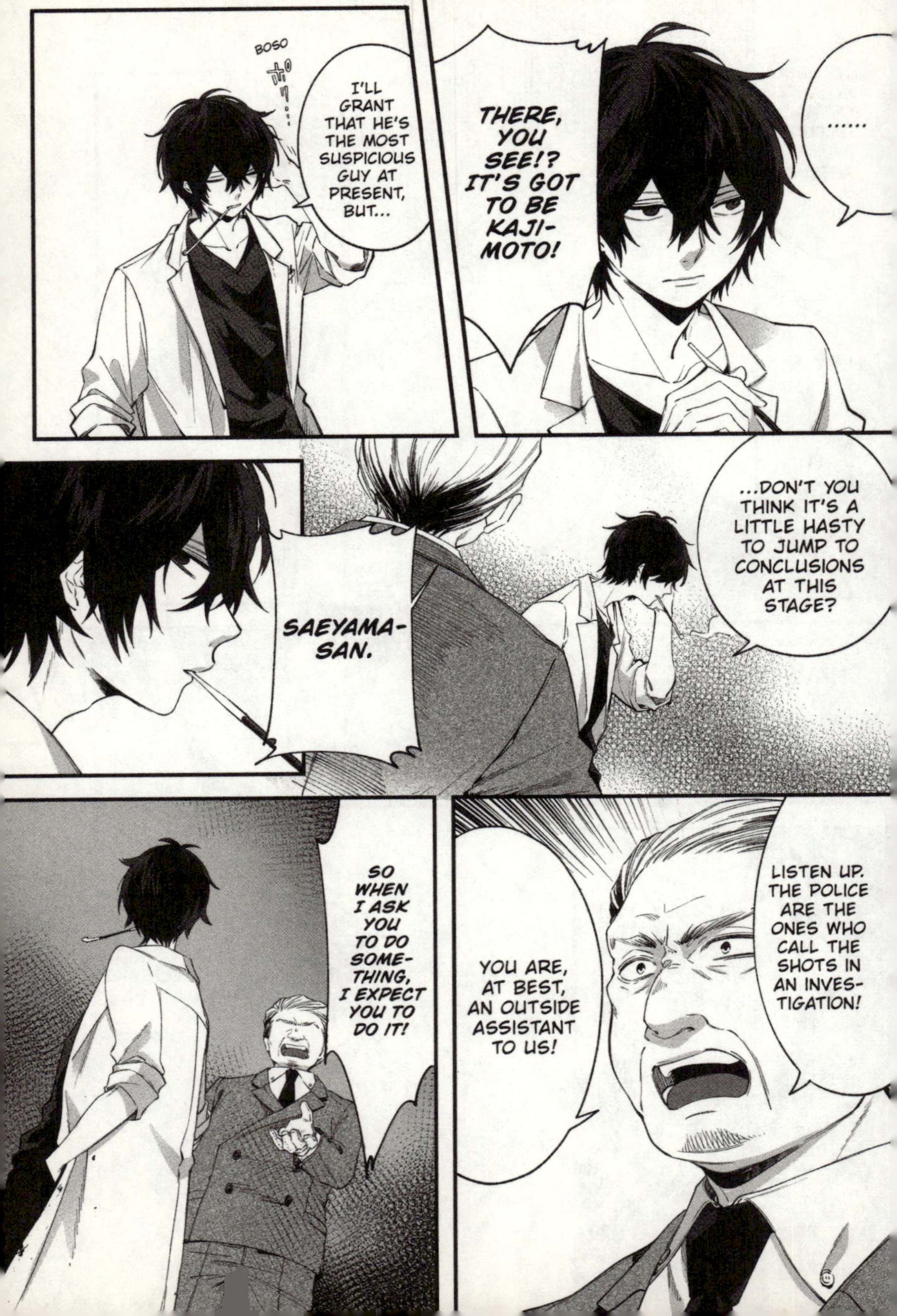
THERE, YOU SEE!? IT'S GOT TO BE KAJIMOTO!
......
BOSO
I'LL GRANT THAT HE'S THE MOST SUSPICIOUS GUY AT PRESENT, BUT...
...DON'T YOU THINK IT'S A LITTLE HASTY TO JUMP TO CONCLUSIONS AT THIS STAGE?
SAEYAMA-SAN.
LISTEN UP. THE POLICE ARE THE ONES WHO CALL THE SHOTS IN AN INVESTIGATION!
YOU ARE, AT BEST, AN OUTSIDE ASSISTANT TO US!
SO WHEN I ASK YOU TO DO SOMETHING, I EXPECT YOU TO DO IT!

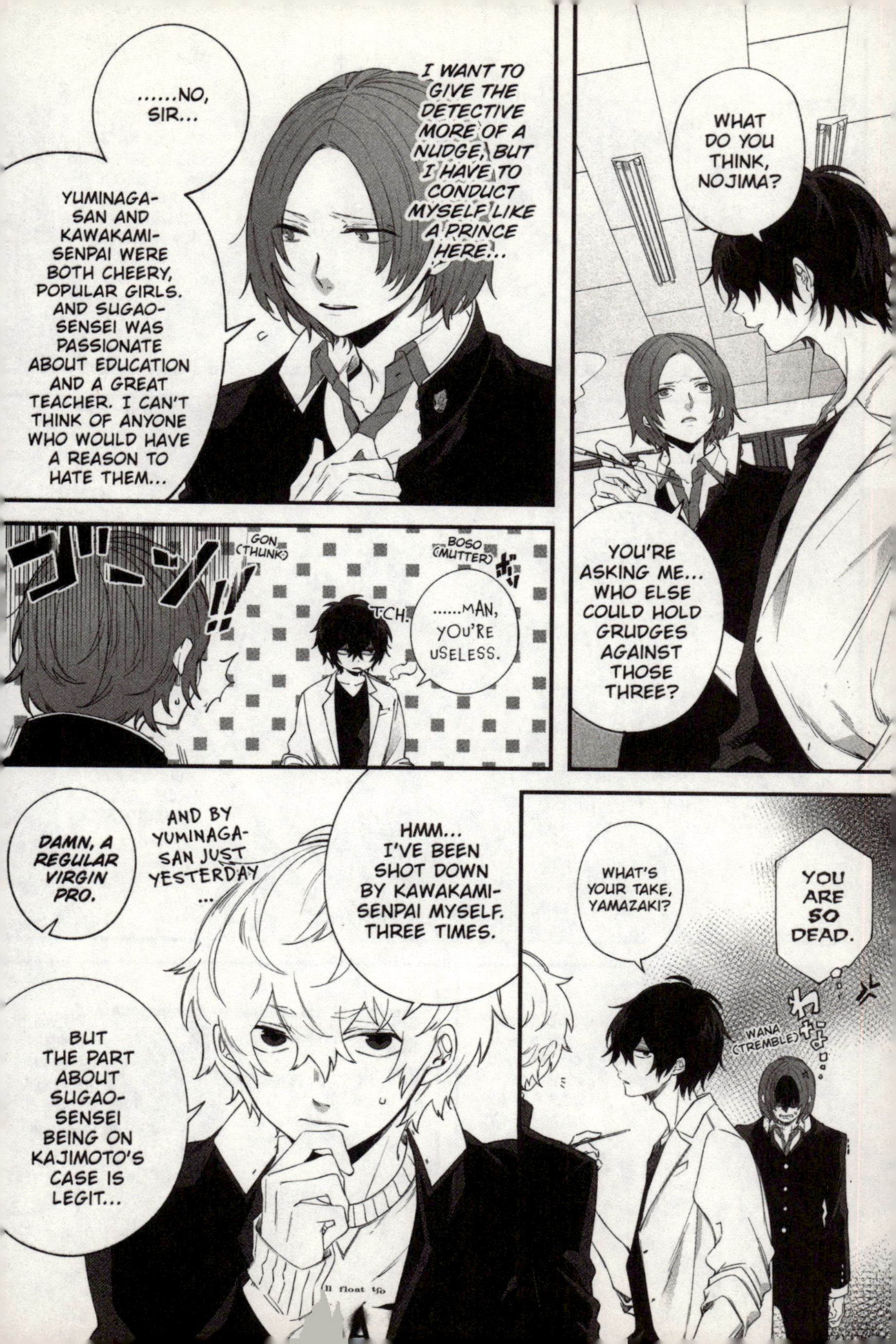
WHAT DO YOU THINK, NOJIMA?
YOU'RE ASKING ME... WHO ELSE COULD HOLD GRUDGES AGAINST THOSE THREE?
I WANT TO GIVE THE DETECTIVE MORE OF A NUDGE, BUT I HAVE TO CONDUCT MYSELF LIKE A PRINCE HERE...
......NO, SIR...
YUMINAGA-SAN AND KAWAKAMI-SENPAI WERE BOTH CHEERY, POPULAR GIRLS. AND SUGAO-SENSEI WAS PASSIONATE ABOUT EDUCATION AND A GREAT TEACHER. I CAN'T THINK OF ANYONE WHO WOULD HAVE A REASON TO HATE THEM...
BOSO (MUTTER)
......MAN, YOU'RE USELESS.
TCH.
GON (THUNK)
YOU ARE SO DEAD.
WHAT'S YOUR TAKE, YAMAZAKI?
WANA (TREMBLE)
HMM... I'VE BEEN SHOT DOWN BY KAWAKAMI-SENPAI MYSELF. THREE TIMES.
AND BY YUMINAGA-SAN JUST YESTERDAY ...
DAMN, A REGULAR VIRGIN PRO.
BUT THE PART ABOUT SUGAO-SENSEI BEING ON KAJIMOTO'S CASE IS LEGIT...

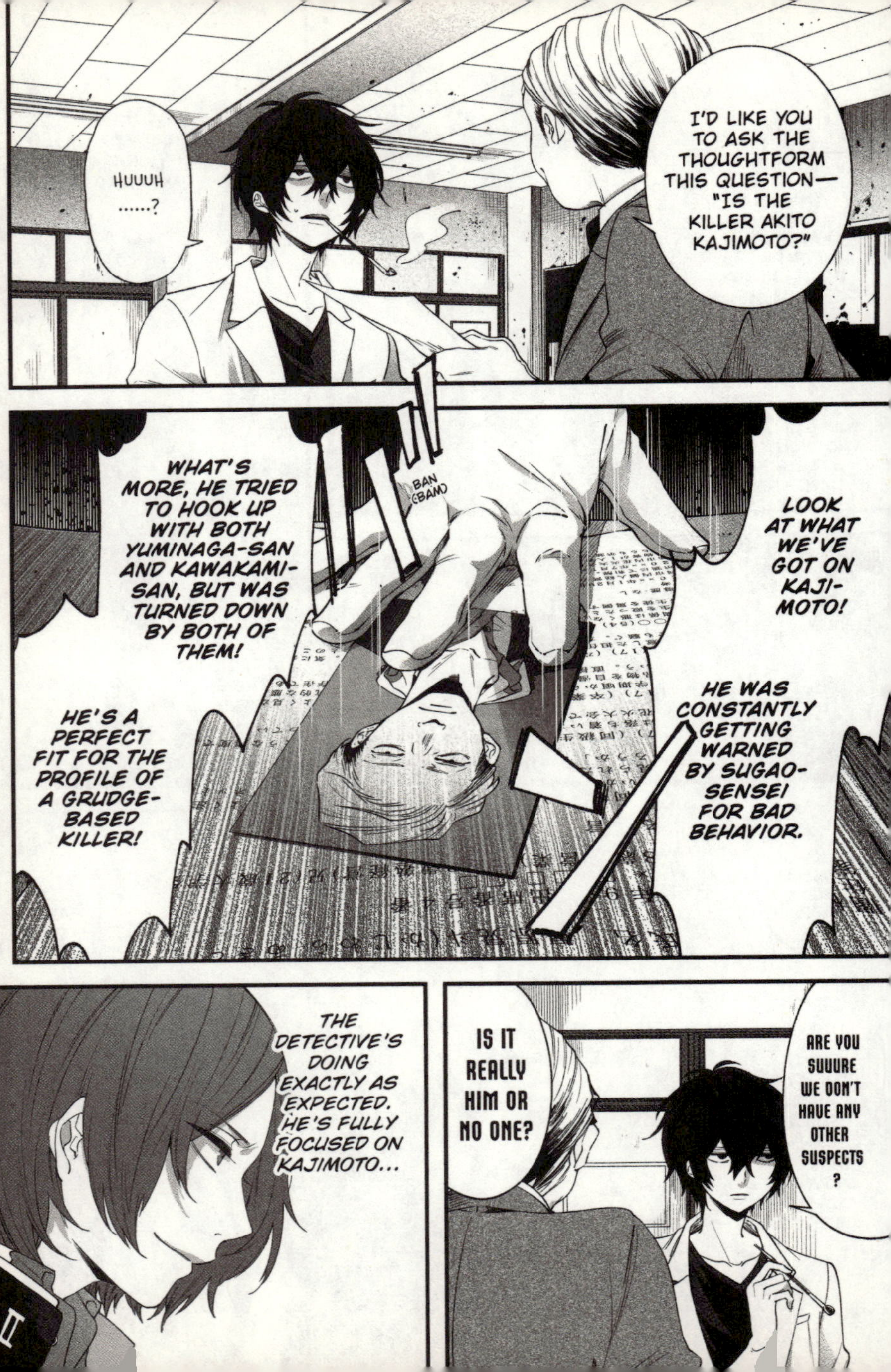
I'D LIKE YOU TO ASK THE THOUGHTFORM THIS QUESTION—"IS THE KILLER AKITO KAJIMOTO?"
HUUUH ......?
LOOK AT WHAT WE'VE GOT ON KAJI-MOTO!
HE WAS CONSTANTLY GETTING WARNED BY SUGAO-SENSEI FOR BAD BEHAVIOR.
BAN (BAM)
WHAT'S MORE, HE TRIED TO HOOK UP WITH BOTH YUMINAGA-SAN AND KAWAKAMI-SAN, BUT WAS TURNED DOWN BY BOTH OF THEM!
HE'S A PERFECT FIT FOR THE PROFILE OF A GRUDGE-BASED KILLER!
ARE YOU SUUURE WE DON'T HAVE ANY OTHER SUSPECTS?
IS IT REALLY HIM OR NO ONE?
THE DETECTIVE'S DOING EXACTLY AS EXPECTED. HE'S FULLY FOCUSED ON KAJIMOTO...

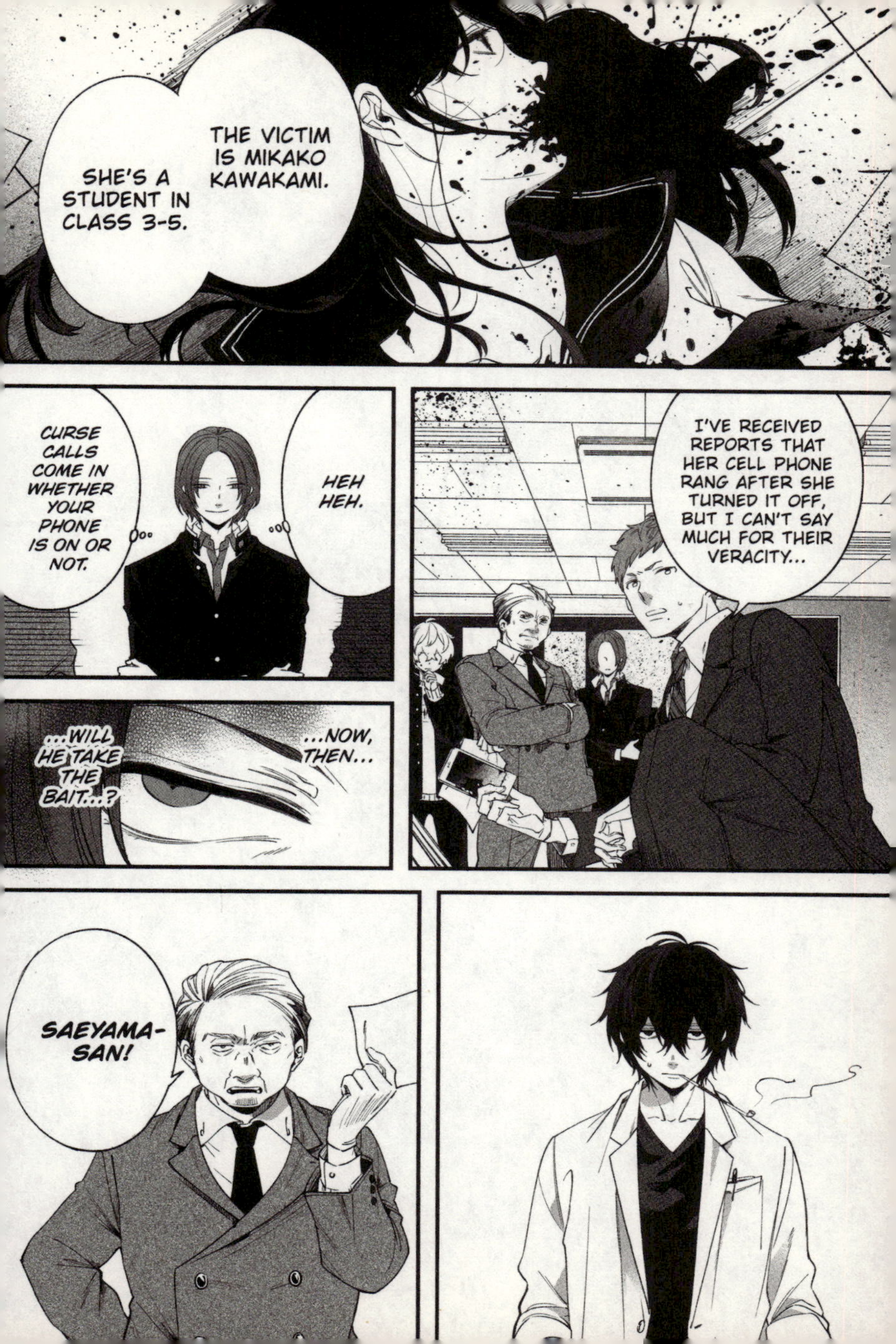
THE VICTIM IS MIKAKO KAWAKAMI.
SHE'S A STUDENT IN CLASS 3-5.
I'VE RECEIVED REPORTS THAT HER CELL PHONE RANG AFTER SHE TURNED IT OFF, BUT I CAN'T SAY MUCH FOR THEIR VERACITY...
HEH HEH.
CURSE CALLS COME IN WHETHER YOUR PHONE IS ON OR NOT.
...NOW, THEN...
...WILL HE TAKE THE BAIT...?
SAEYAMA-SAN!

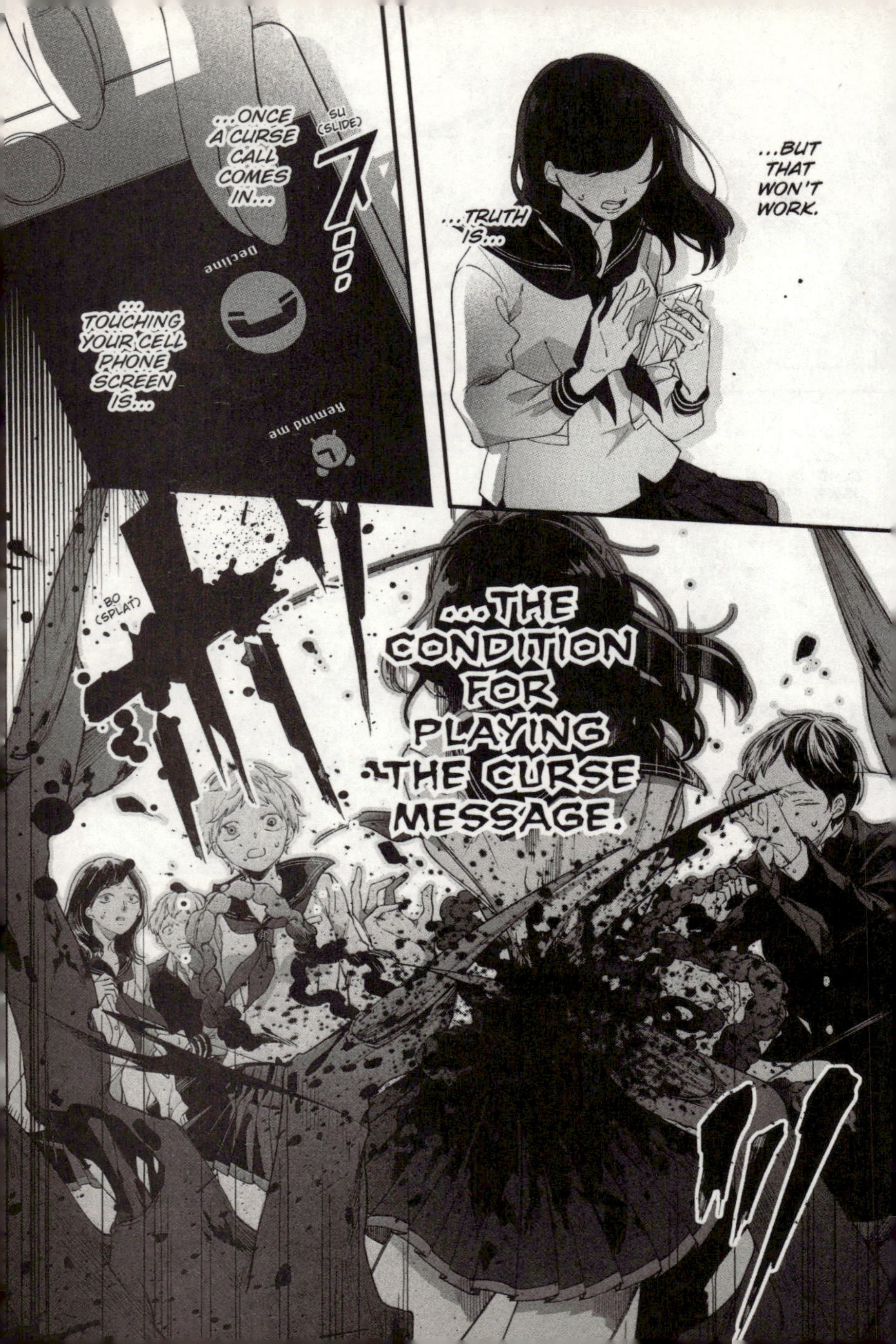
...BUT THAT WON'T WORK.
...TRUTH IS...
SU (SLIDE)
...ONCE A CURSE CALL COMES IN...
Decline
...TOUCHING YOUR CELL PHONE SCREEN IS...
Remind me
...THE CONDITION FOR PLAYING THE CURSE MESSAGE.
BO (SPLAT)

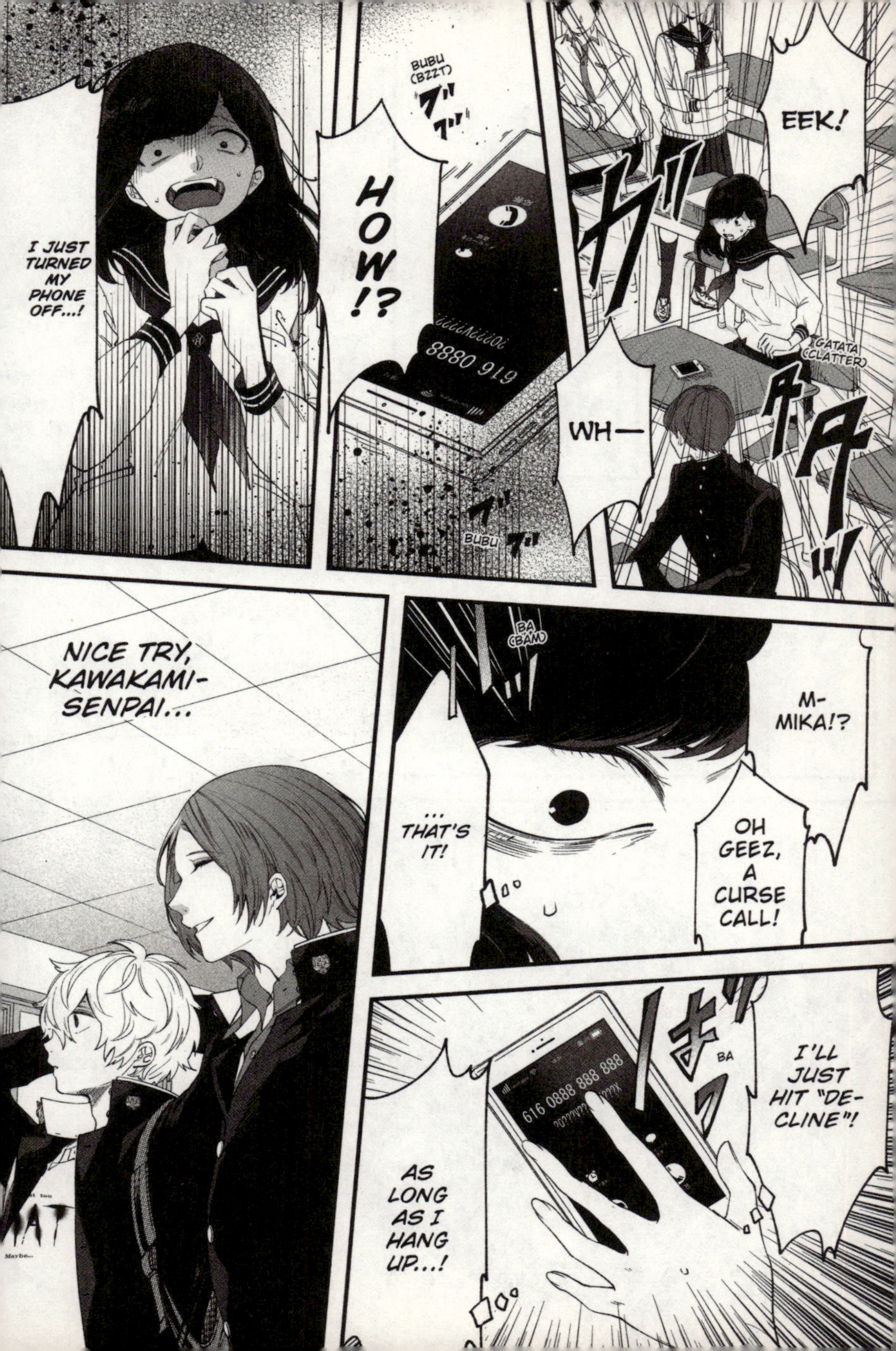
EEK!
GATATA (CLATTER)
WH—
BUBU (BZZT)
HOW!?
616 0888
BUBU
I JUST TURNED MY PHONE OFF...!
BA (BAM)
M-MIKA!?
OH GEEZ, A CURSE CALL!
...THAT'S IT!
BA
I'LL JUST HIT "DECLINE"!
616 0888 888 888
AS LONG AS I HANG UP...!
NICE TRY, KAWAKAMI-SENPAI...

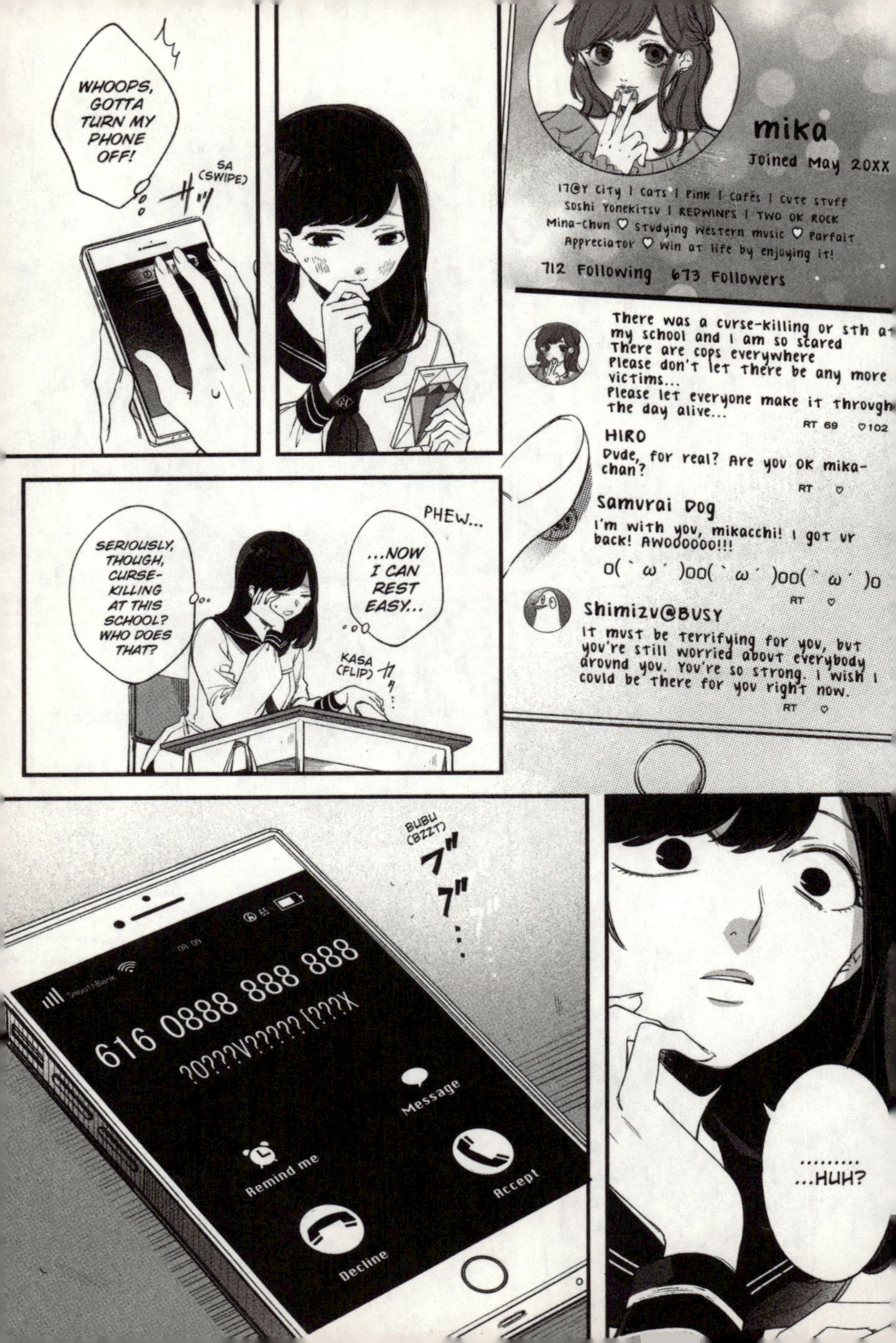
mika
Joined May 20XX
17@Y City | Cats | Pink | Cafés | Cute stuff
Soshi Yonekitsu | REDWINPS | TWO OK ROCK
Mina-Chun ♡ Studying Western music ♡ Parfait
Appreciator ♡ Win at life by enjoying it!
712 Following 673 Followers
There was a curse-killing or sth at my school and I am so scared
There are cops everywhere
Please don't let there be any more victims...
Please let everyone make it through the day alive...
RT 69 ♡102
HIRO
Dude, for real? Are you OK mika-chan?
RT ♡
Samurai Dog
I'm with you, mikacchi! I got ur back! AWOOOOOO!!!
o(ˋωˊ)oo(ˋωˊ)oo(ˋωˊ)o
RT ♡
Shimizu@BUSY
It must be terrifying for you, but you're still worried about everybody around you. You're so strong. I wish I could be there for you right now.
RT ♡
WHOOPS, GOTTA TURN MY PHONE OFF!
SA (SWIPE)
PHEW...
...NOW I CAN REST EASY...
SERIOUSLY, THOUGH, CURSE-KILLING AT THIS SCHOOL? WHO DOES THAT?
KASA (FLIP)
....
...HUH?
BUBU (BZZT)
616 0888 888 888
?0???V?????{???X
Message
Remind me
Accept
Decline

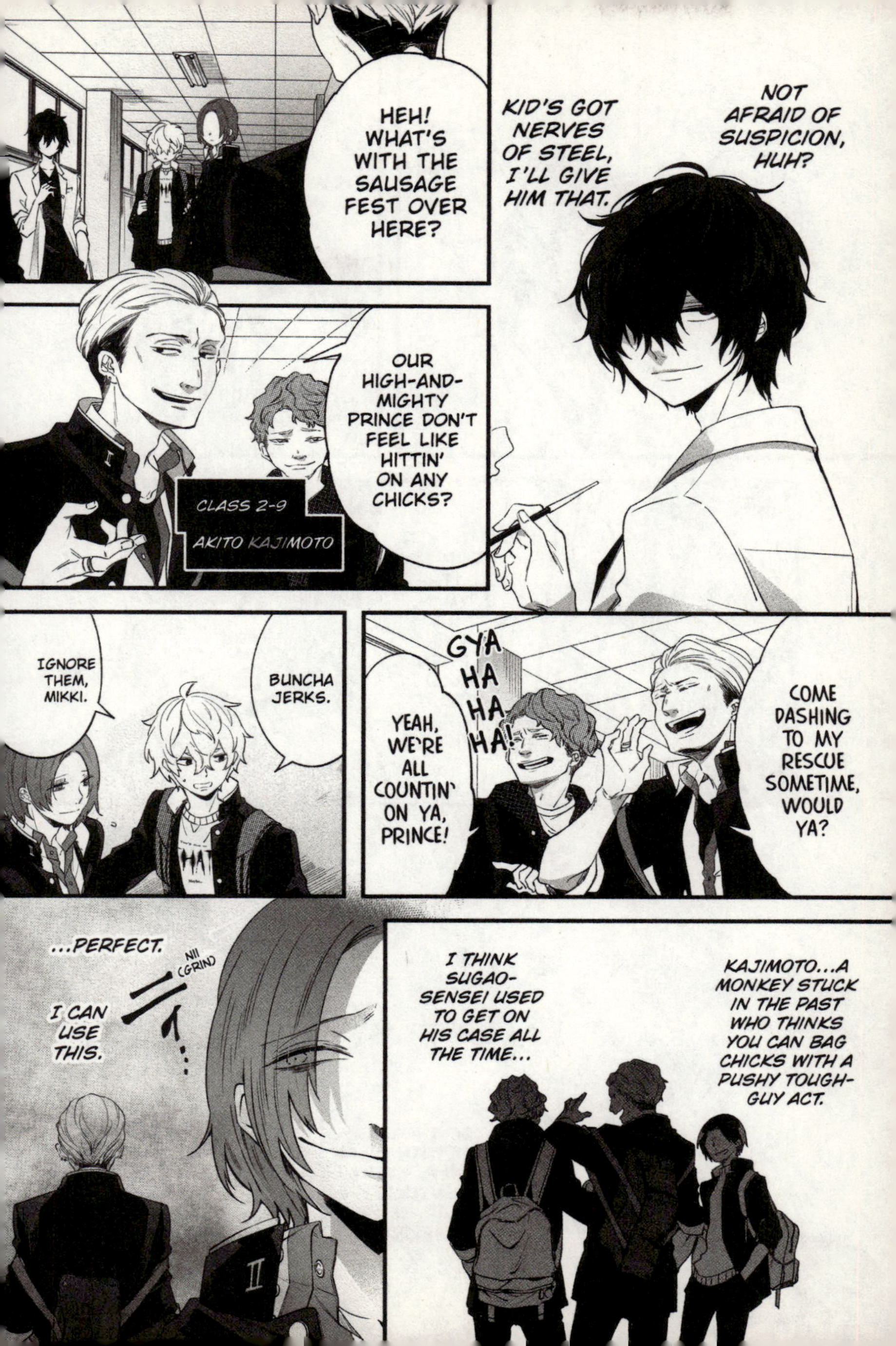
NOT AFRAID OF SUSPICION, HUH?
KID'S GOT NERVES OF STEEL, I'LL GIVE HIM THAT.
HEH! WHAT'S WITH THE SAUSAGE FEST OVER HERE?
OUR HIGH-AND-MIGHTY PRINCE DON'T FEEL LIKE HITTIN' ON ANY CHICKS?
CLASS 2-9
AKITO KAJIMOTO
COME DASHING TO MY RESCUE SOMETIME, WOULD YA?
GYA HA HA HA!
YEAH, WE'RE ALL COUNTIN' ON YA, PRINCE!
BUNCHA JERKS.
IGNORE THEM, MIKKI.
KAJIMOTO...A MONKEY STUCK IN THE PAST WHO THINKS YOU CAN BAG CHICKS WITH A PUSHY TOUGH-GUY ACT.
I THINK SUGAO-SENSEI USED TO GET ON HIS CASE ALL THE TIME...
...PERFECT.
NII (GRIN)
I CAN USE THIS.

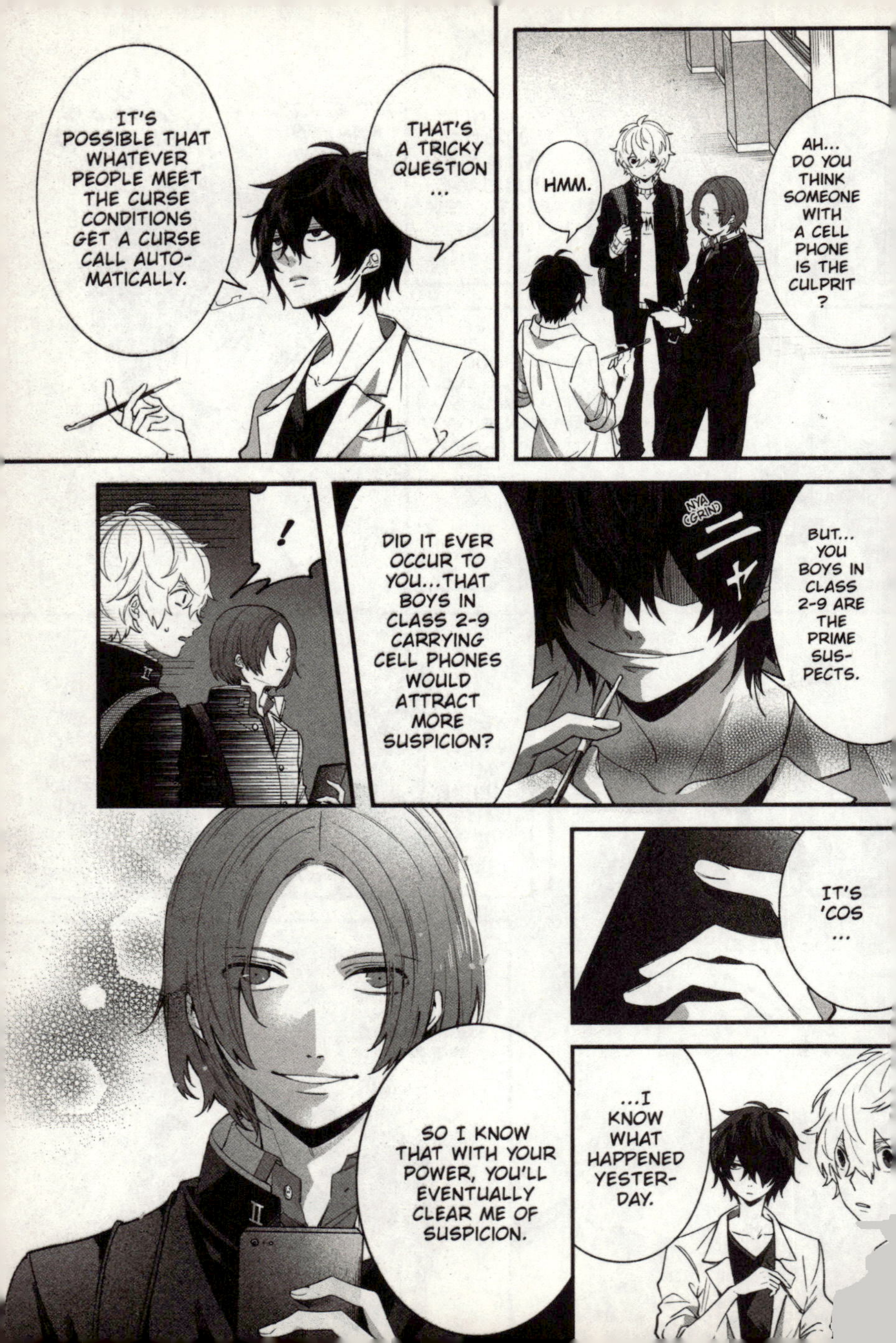
AH... DO YOU THINK SOMEONE WITH A CELL PHONE IS THE CULPRIT?
HMM.
THAT'S A TRICKY QUESTION...
IT'S POSSIBLE THAT WHATEVER PEOPLE MEET THE CURSE CONDITIONS GET A CURSE CALL AUTO-MATICALLY.
BUT... YOU BOYS IN CLASS 2-9 ARE THE PRIME SUS-PECTS.
NYA (GRIN)
DID IT EVER OCCUR TO YOU...THAT BOYS IN CLASS 2-9 CARRYING CELL PHONES WOULD ATTRACT MORE SUSPICION?
!
IT'S 'COS...
...I KNOW WHAT HAPPENED YESTER-DAY.
SO I KNOW THAT WITH YOUR POWER, YOU'LL EVENTUALLY CLEAR ME OF SUSPICION.

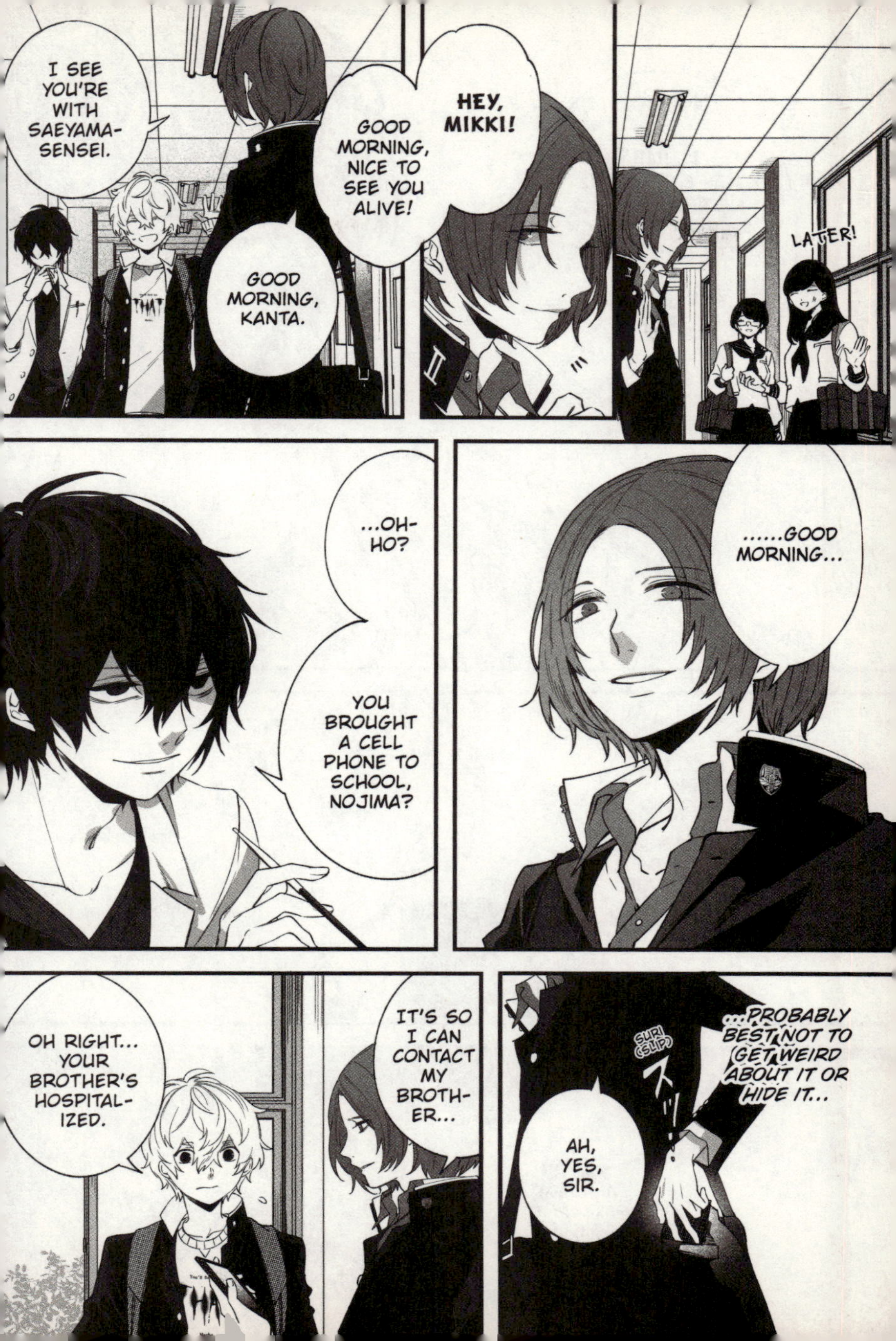
LATER!
HEY, MIKKI!
GOOD MORNING, NICE TO SEE YOU ALIVE!
GOOD MORNING, KANTA.
I SEE YOU'RE WITH SAEYAMA-SENSEI.
......GOOD MORNING...
...OH-HO?
YOU BROUGHT A CELL PHONE TO SCHOOL, NOJIMA?
...PROBABLY BEST NOT TO GET WEIRD ABOUT IT OR HIDE IT...
SURI (SLIP)
AH, YES, SIR.
IT'S SO I CAN CONTACT MY BROTHER...
OH RIGHT... YOUR BROTHER'S HOSPITALIZED.

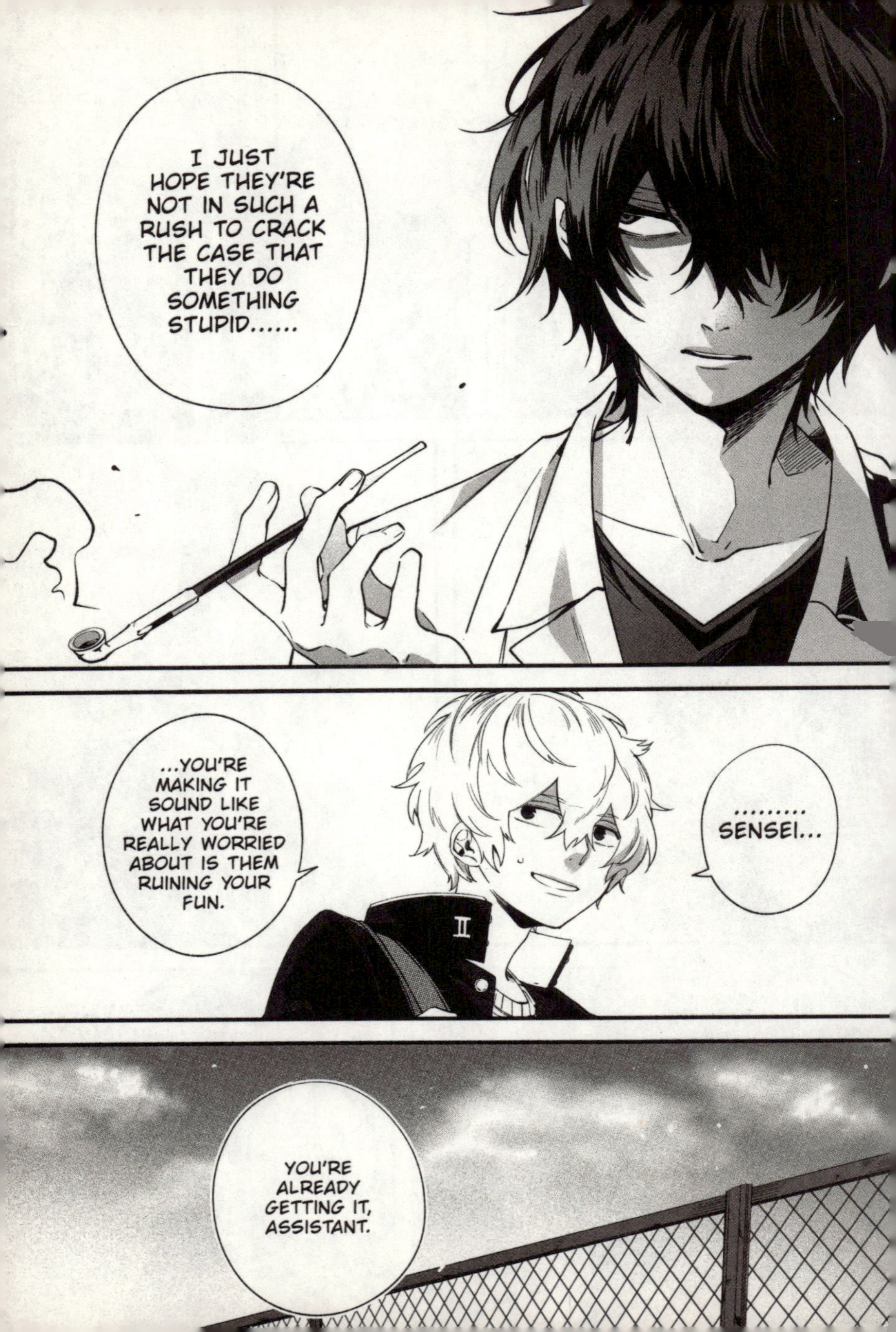
I JUST HOPE THEY'RE NOT IN SUCH A RUSH TO CRACK THE CASE THAT THEY DO SOMETHING STUPID......
.... SENSEI...
...YOU'RE MAKING IT SOUND LIKE WHAT YOU'RE REALLY WORRIED ABOUT IS THEM RUINING YOUR FUN.
YOU'RE ALREADY GETTING IT, ASSISTANT.

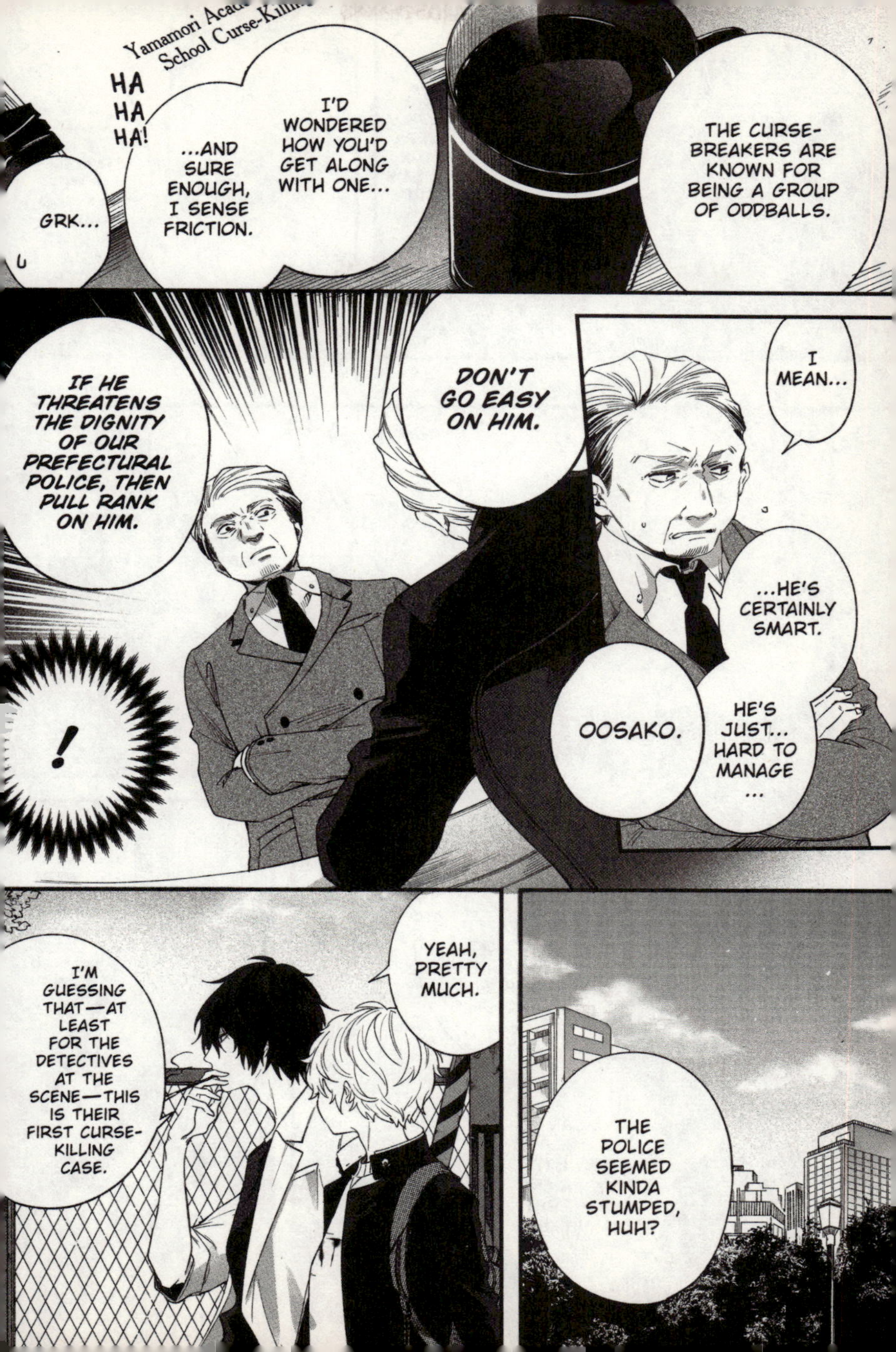
THE CURSE-BREAKERS ARE KNOWN FOR BEING A GROUP OF ODDBALLS.
I'D WONDERED HOW YOU'D GET ALONG WITH ONE...
...AND SURE ENOUGH, I SENSE FRICTION.
HA HA HA!
GRK...
I MEAN...
...HE'S CERTAINLY SMART.
HE'S JUST... HARD TO MANAGE...
OOSAKO.
DON'T GO EASY ON HIM.
IF HE THREATENS THE DIGNITY OF OUR PREFECTURAL POLICE, THEN PULL RANK ON HIM.
!
THE POLICE SEEMED KINDA STUMPED, HUH?
YEAH, PRETTY MUCH.
I'M GUESSING THAT—AT LEAST FOR THE DETECTIVES AT THE SCENE—THIS IS THEIR FIRST CURSE-KILLING CASE.

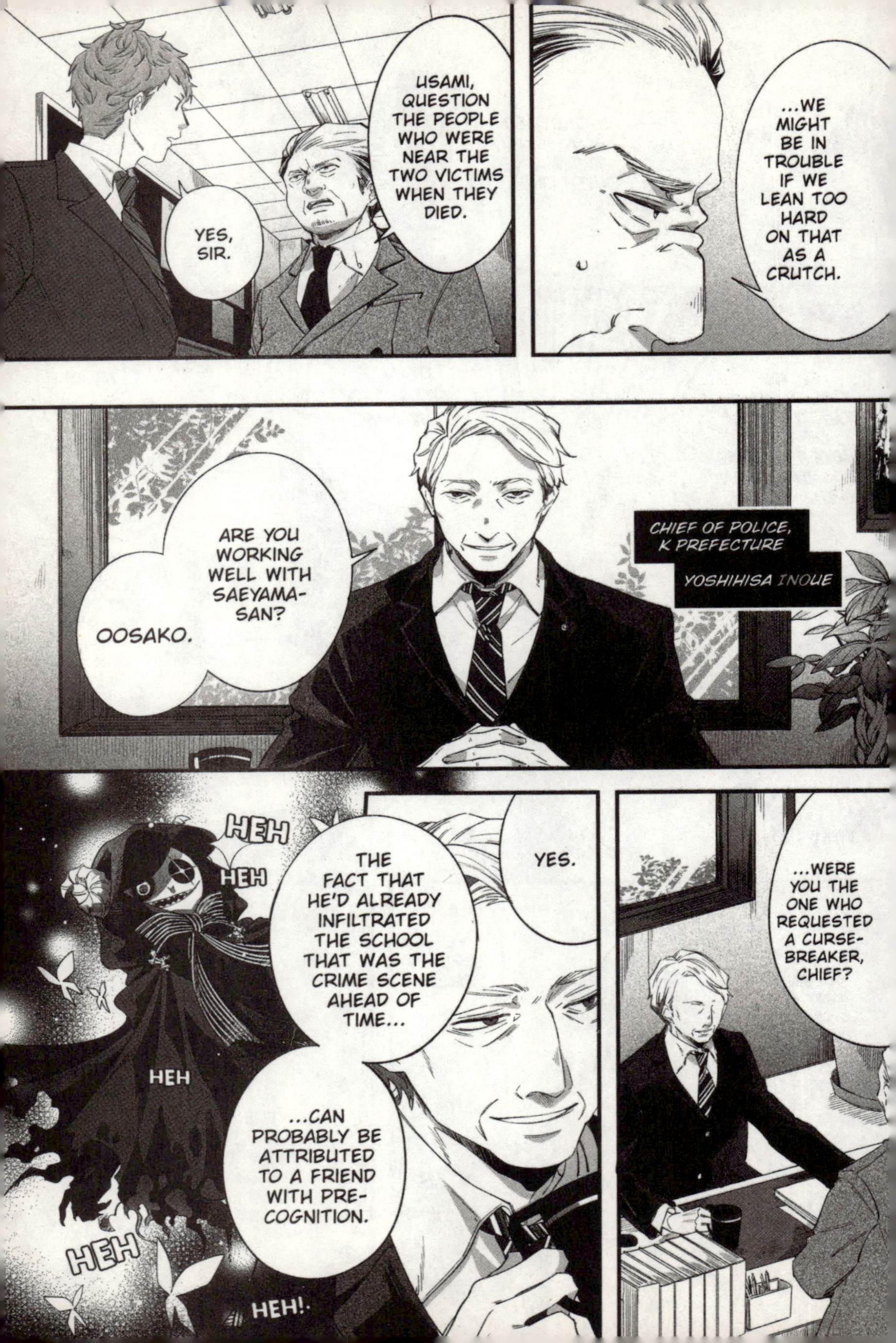
...WE MIGHT BE IN TROUBLE IF WE LEAN TOO HARD ON THAT AS A CRUTCH.
USAMI, QUESTION THE PEOPLE WHO WERE NEAR THE TWO VICTIMS WHEN THEY DIED.
YES, SIR.
CHIEF OF POLICE, K PREFECTURE
YOSHIHISA INOUE
ARE YOU WORKING WELL WITH SAEYAMA-SAN?
OOSAKO.
...WERE YOU THE ONE WHO REQUESTED A CURSE-BREAKER, CHIEF?
YES.
THE FACT THAT HE'D ALREADY INFILTRATED THE SCHOOL THAT WAS THE CRIME SCENE AHEAD OF TIME...
...CAN PROBABLY BE ATTRIBUTED TO A FRIEND WITH PRE-COGNITION.
HEH
HEH
HEH
HEH
HEH!

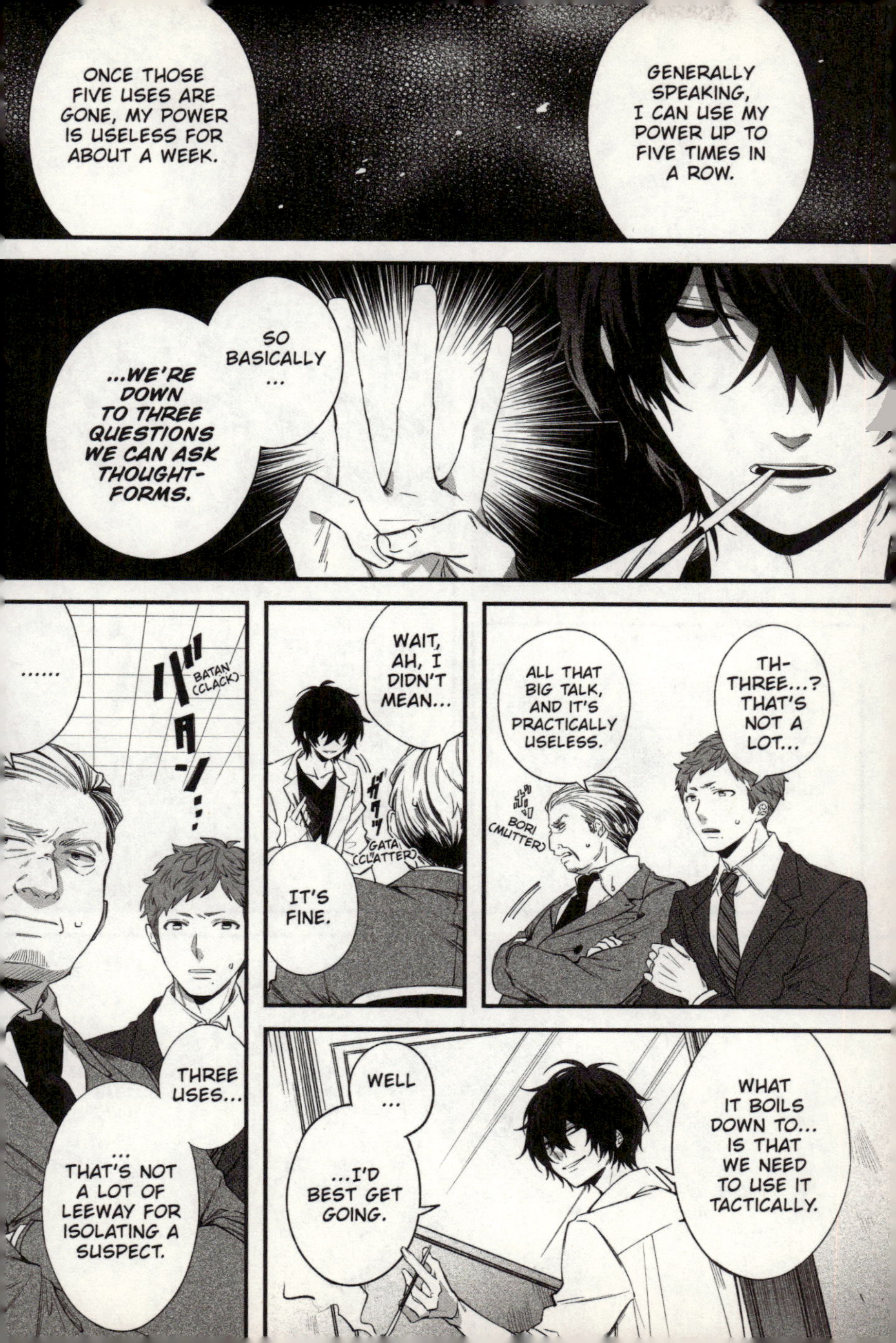
GENERALLY SPEAKING, I CAN USE MY POWER UP TO FIVE TIMES IN A ROW.
ONCE THOSE FIVE USES ARE GONE, MY POWER IS USELESS FOR ABOUT A WEEK.
SO BASICALLY ...
...WE'RE DOWN TO THREE QUESTIONS WE CAN ASK THOUGHT-FORMS.
TH- THREE...? THAT'S NOT A LOT...
ALL THAT BIG TALK, AND IT'S PRACTICALLY USELESS.
BORI (MUTTER)
WAIT, AH, I DIDN'T MEAN...
GATA (CLATTER)
IT'S FINE.
WHAT IT BOILS DOWN TO... IS THAT WE NEED TO USE IT TACTICALLY.
WELL ...
...I'D BEST GET GOING.
......
BATAN (CLACK)
THREE USES...
... THAT'S NOT A LOT OF LEEWAY FOR ISOLATING A SUSPECT.

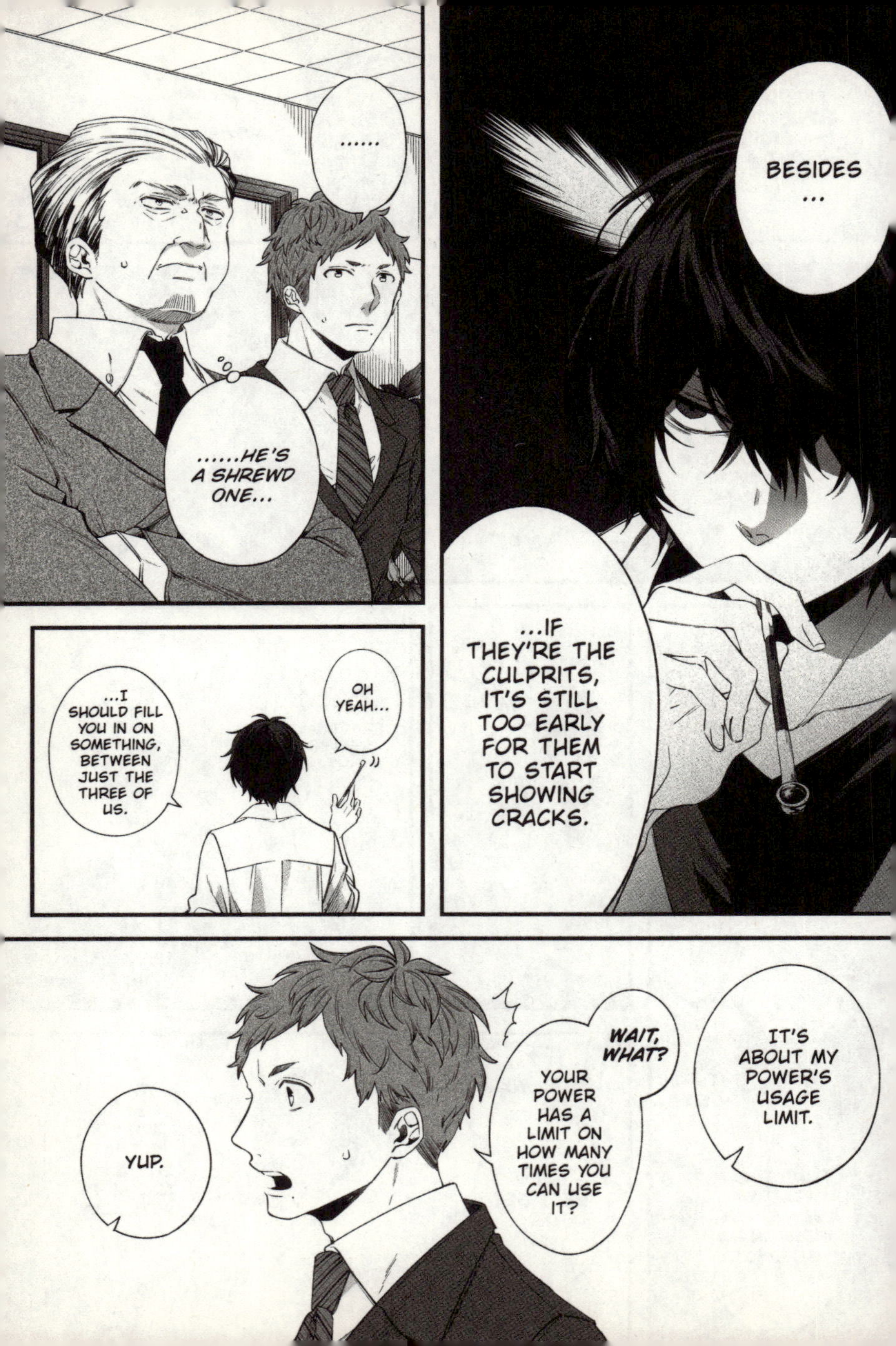
BESIDES...
...IF THEY'RE THE CULPRITS, IT'S STILL TOO EARLY FOR THEM TO START SHOWING CRACKS.
......
......HE'S A SHREWD ONE...
OH YEAH...
...I SHOULD FILL YOU IN ON SOMETHING, BETWEEN JUST THE THREE OF US.
IT'S ABOUT MY POWER'S USAGE LIMIT.
WAIT, WHAT?
YOUR POWER HAS A LIMIT ON HOW MANY TIMES YOU CAN USE IT?
YUP.

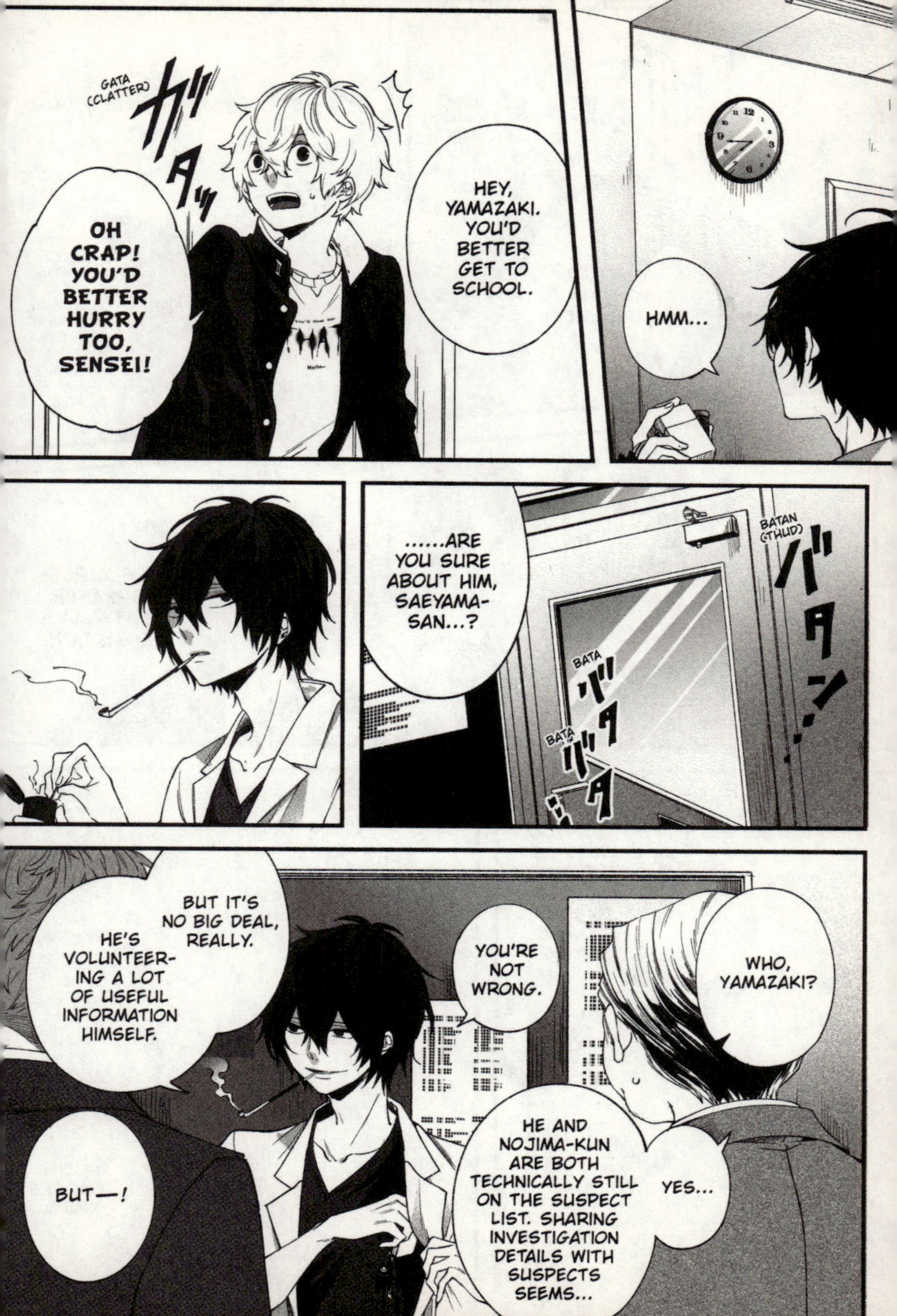
HMM...
HEY, YAMAZAKI. YOU'D BETTER GET TO SCHOOL.
GATA (CLATTER)
OH CRAP! YOU'D BETTER HURRY TOO, SENSEI!
BATAN (THUD)
......ARE YOU SURE ABOUT HIM, SAEYAMA-SAN...?
BATA
BATA
WHO, YAMAZAKI?
YES...
HE AND NOJIMA-KUN ARE BOTH TECHNICALLY STILL ON THE SUSPECT LIST. SHARING INVESTIGATION DETAILS WITH SUSPECTS SEEMS...
BUT—!
YOU'RE NOT WRONG.
BUT IT'S NO BIG DEAL, REALLY.
HE'S VOLUNTEERING A LOT OF USEFUL INFORMATION HIMSELF.

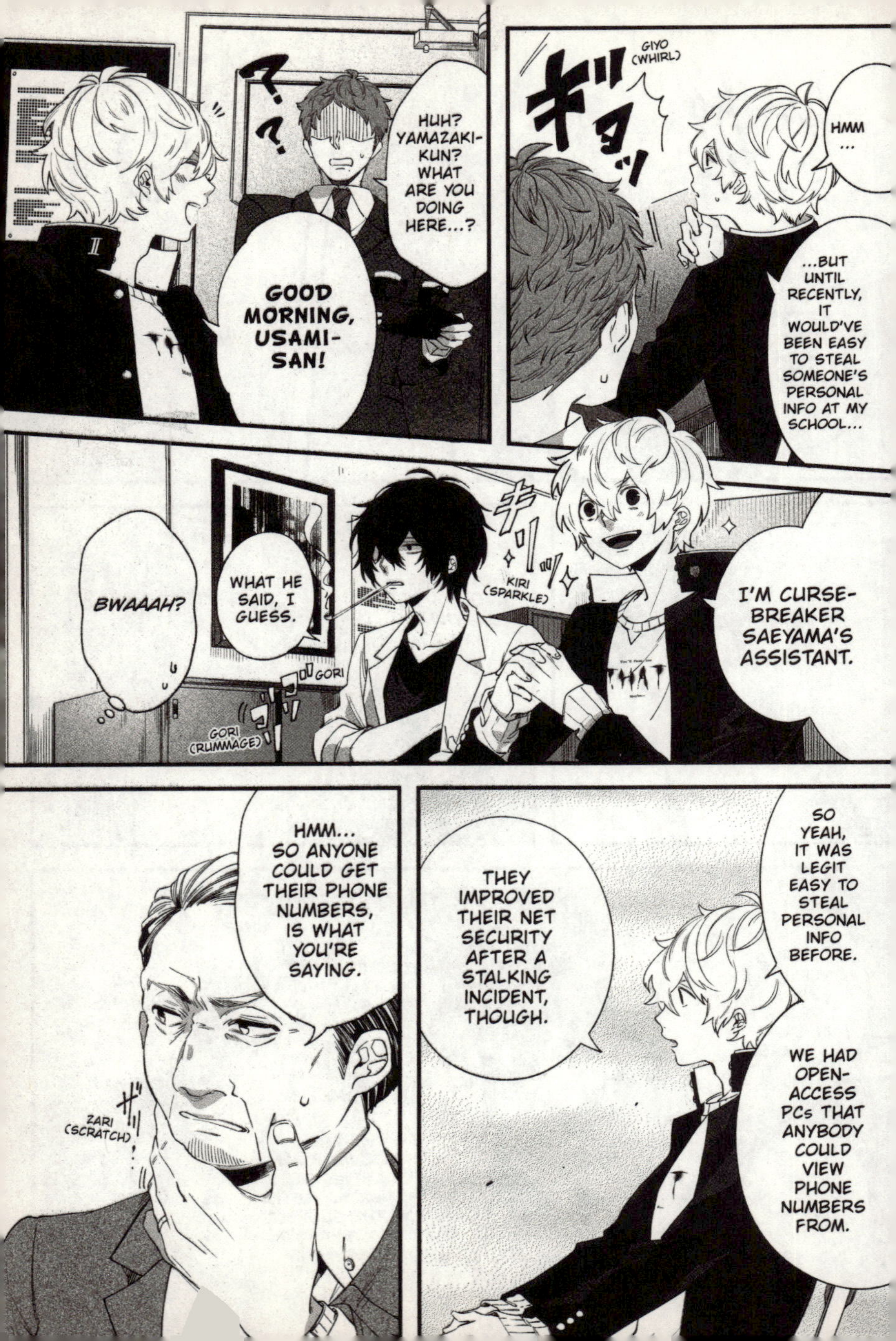
HMM …
GIYO (WHIRL)
…BUT UNTIL RECENTLY, IT WOULD'VE BEEN EASY TO STEAL SOMEONE'S PERSONAL INFO AT MY SCHOOL…
HUH? YAMAZAKI-KUN? WHAT ARE YOU DOING HERE…?
??
GOOD MORNING, USAMI-SAN!
I'M CURSE-BREAKER SAEYAMA'S ASSISTANT.
KIRI (SPARKLE)
WHAT HE SAID, I GUESS.
GORI
GORI (RUMMAGE)
BWAAAH?
SO YEAH, IT WAS LEGIT EASY TO STEAL PERSONAL INFO BEFORE.
WE HAD OPEN-ACCESS PCs THAT ANYBODY COULD VIEW PHONE NUMBERS FROM.
THEY IMPROVED THEIR NET SECURITY AFTER A STALKING INCIDENT, THOUGH.
HMM… SO ANYONE COULD GET THEIR PHONE NUMBERS, IS WHAT YOU'RE SAYING.
ZARI (SCRATCH)

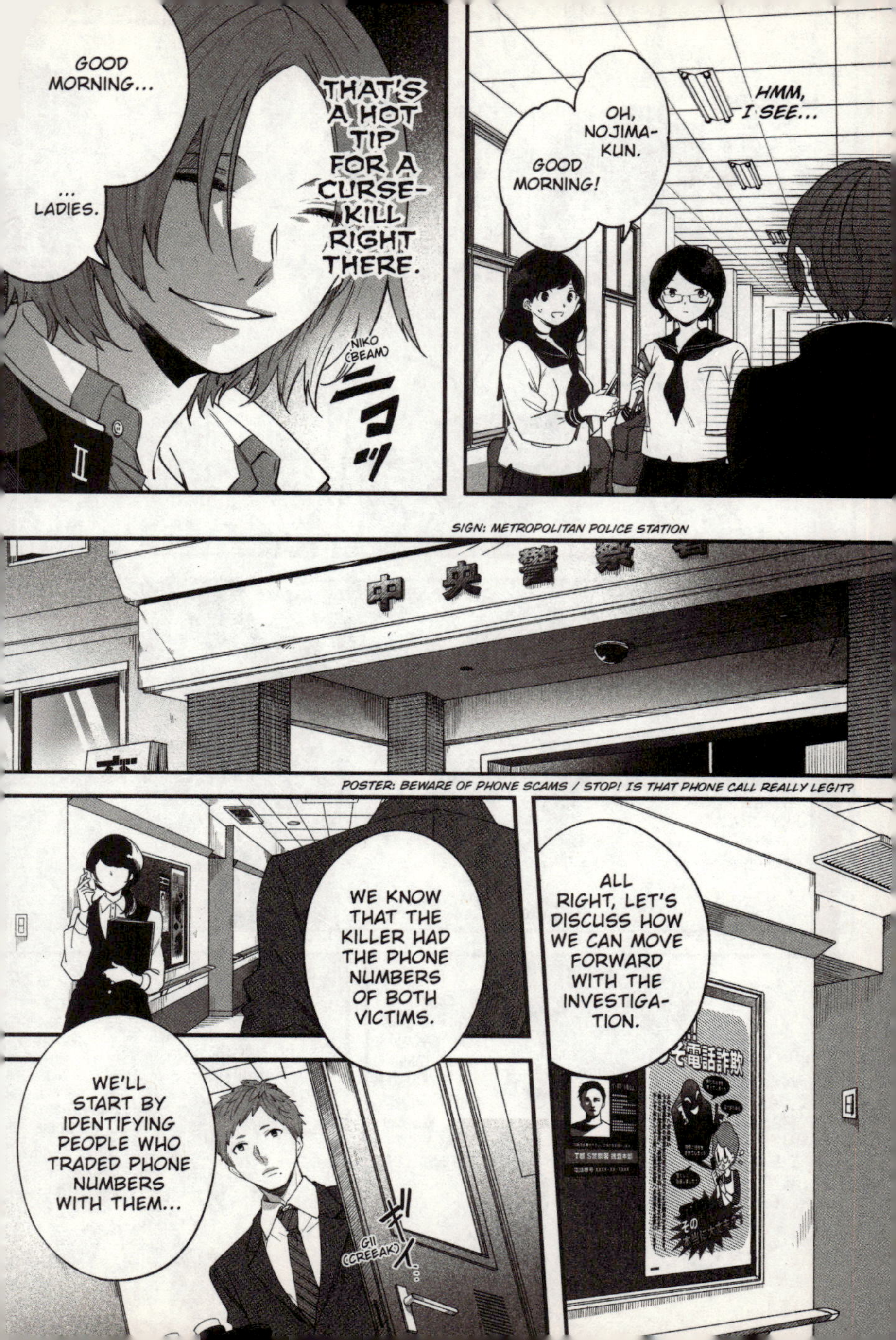
HMM, I SEE...
OH, NOJIMA-KUN. GOOD MORNING!
THAT'S A HOT TIP FOR A CURSE-KILL RIGHT THERE.
GOOD MORNING...
... LADIES.
NIKO (BEAM)
SIGN: METROPOLITAN POLICE STATION
POSTER: BEWARE OF PHONE SCAMS / STOP! IS THAT PHONE CALL REALLY LEGIT?
ALL RIGHT, LET'S DISCUSS HOW WE CAN MOVE FORWARD WITH THE INVESTIGA-TION.
WE KNOW THAT THE KILLER HAD THE PHONE NUMBERS OF BOTH VICTIMS.
WE'LL START BY IDENTIFYING PEOPLE WHO TRADED PHONE NUMBERS WITH THEM...
GII (CREEAK)

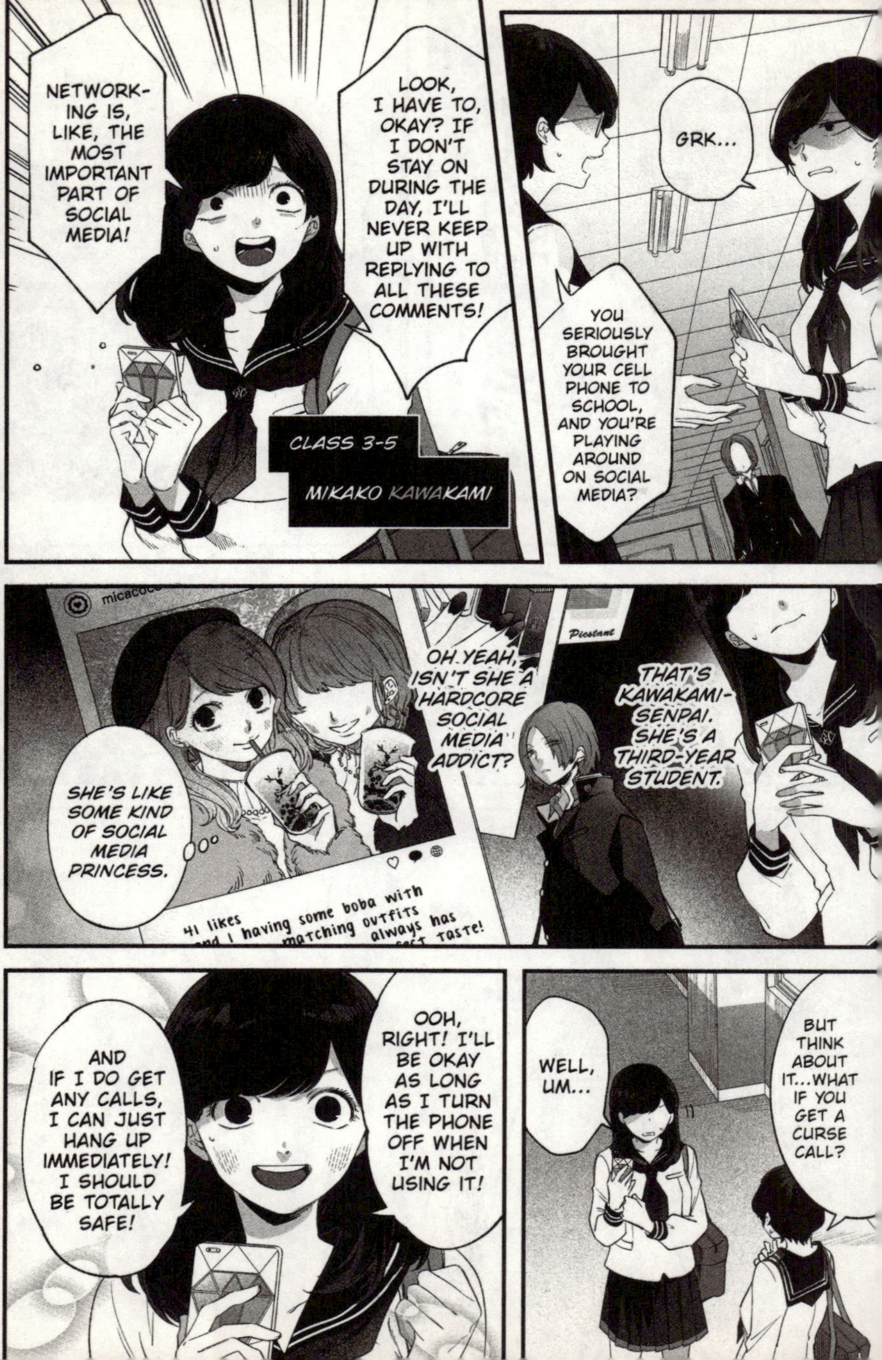
GRK...
YOU SERIOUSLY BROUGHT YOUR CELL PHONE TO SCHOOL, AND YOU'RE PLAYING AROUND ON SOCIAL MEDIA?
LOOK, I HAVE TO, OKAY? IF I DON'T STAY ON DURING THE DAY, I'LL NEVER KEEP UP WITH REPLYING TO ALL THESE COMMENTS!
NETWORKING IS, LIKE, THE MOST IMPORTANT PART OF SOCIAL MEDIA!
CLASS 3-5
MIKAKO KAWAKAMI
THAT'S KAWAKAMI-SENPAI. SHE'S A THIRD-YEAR STUDENT.
OH YEAH, ISN'T SHE A HARDCORE SOCIAL MEDIA ADDICT?
Picstant
SHE'S LIKE SOME KIND OF SOCIAL MEDIA PRINCESS.
41 likes
BUT THINK ABOUT IT...WHAT IF YOU GET A CURSE CALL?
WELL, UM...
OOH, RIGHT! I'LL BE OKAY AS LONG AS I TURN THE PHONE OFF WHEN I'M NOT USING IT!
AND IF I DO GET ANY CALLS, I CAN JUST HANG UP IMMEDIATELY! I SHOULD BE TOTALLY SAFE!

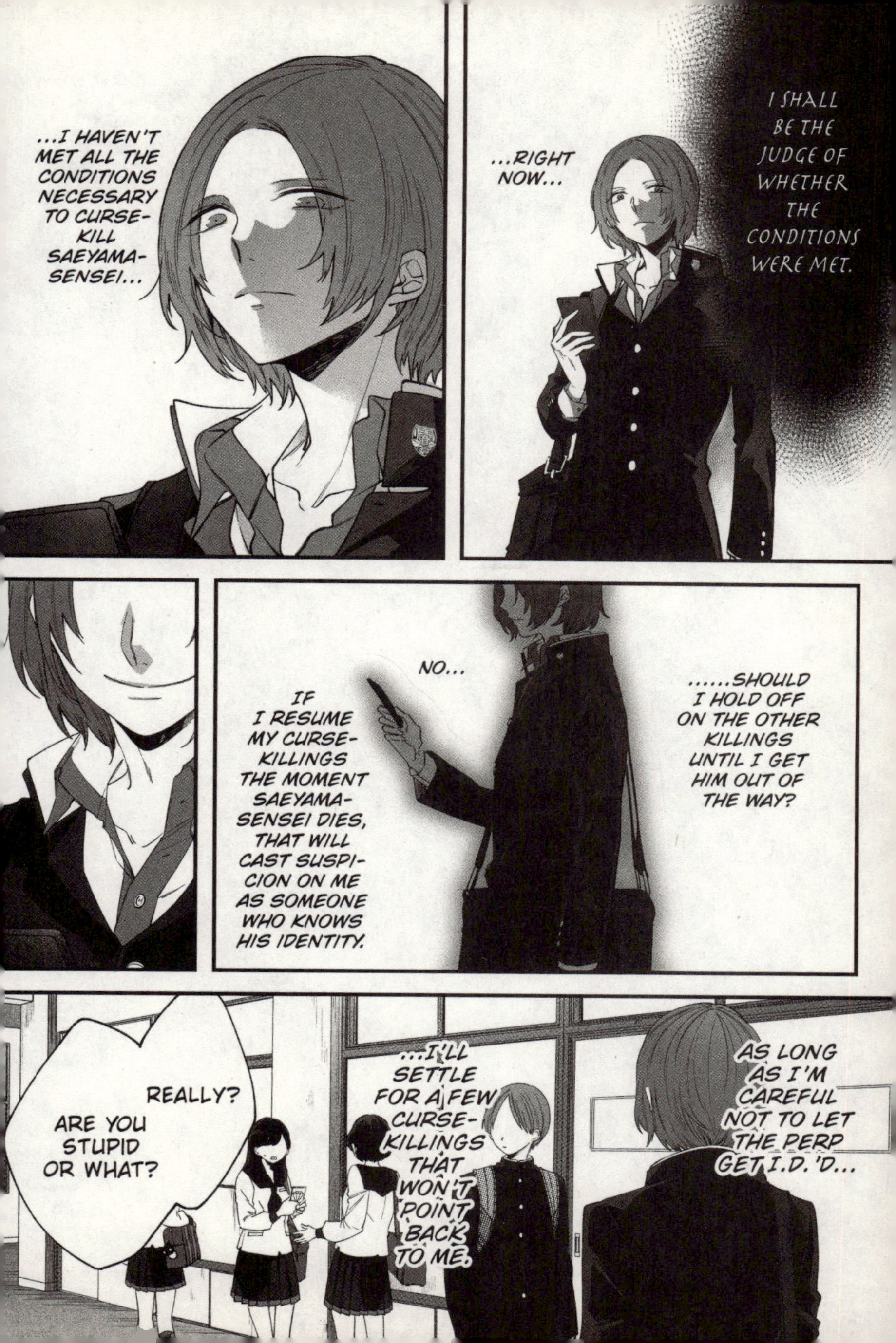
I SHALL BE THE JUDGE OF WHETHER THE CONDITIONS WERE MET.
...RIGHT NOW...
...I HAVEN'T MET ALL THE CONDITIONS NECESSARY TO CURSE-KILL SAEYAMA-SENSEI...
......SHOULD I HOLD OFF ON THE OTHER KILLINGS UNTIL I GET HIM OUT OF THE WAY?
NO...
IF I RESUME MY CURSE-KILLINGS THE MOMENT SAEYAMA-SENSEI DIES, THAT WILL CAST SUSPICION ON ME AS SOMEONE WHO KNOWS HIS IDENTITY.
AS LONG AS I'M CAREFUL NOT TO LET THE PERP GET I.D.'D...
...I'LL SETTLE FOR A FEW CURSE-KILLINGS THAT WON'T POINT BACK TO ME.
REALLY? ARE YOU STUPID OR WHAT?

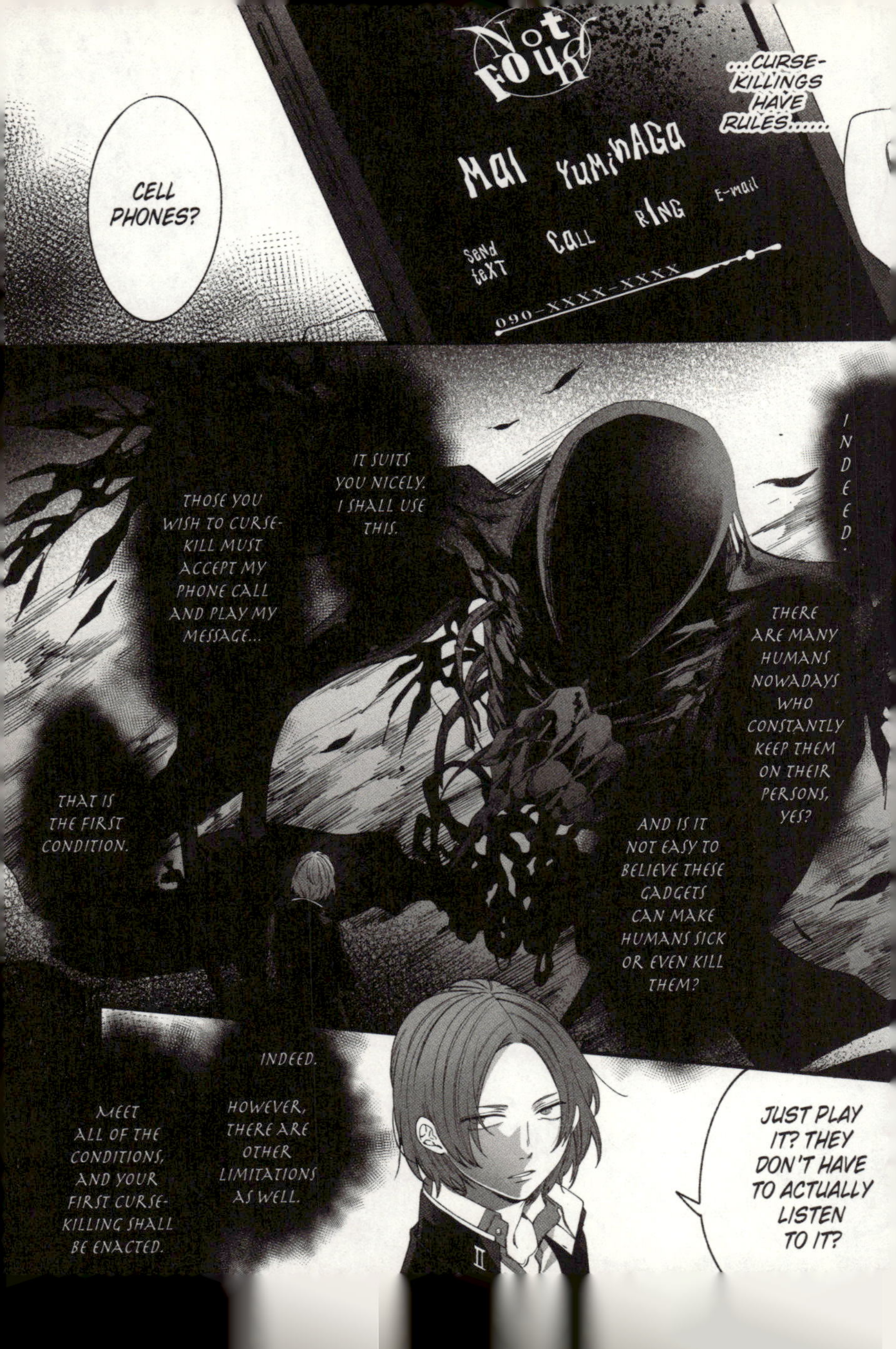
...CURSE-KILLINGS HAVE RULES......
Not Found
Mai Yuminaga
Send text
Call
Ring
E-mail
090-XXXX-XXXX
CELL PHONES?
INDEED.
THERE ARE MANY HUMANS NOWADAYS WHO CONSTANTLY KEEP THEM ON THEIR PERSONS, YES?
AND IS IT NOT EASY TO BELIEVE THESE GADGETS CAN MAKE HUMANS SICK OR EVEN KILL THEM?
IT SUITS YOU NICELY. I SHALL USE THIS.
THOSE YOU WISH TO CURSE-KILL MUST ACCEPT MY PHONE CALL AND PLAY MY MESSAGE...
THAT IS THE FIRST CONDITION.
JUST PLAY IT? THEY DON'T HAVE TO ACTUALLY LISTEN TO IT?
INDEED.
HOWEVER, THERE ARE OTHER LIMITATIONS AS WELL.
MEET ALL OF THE CONDITIONS, AND YOUR FIRST CURSE-KILLING SHALL BE ENACTED.

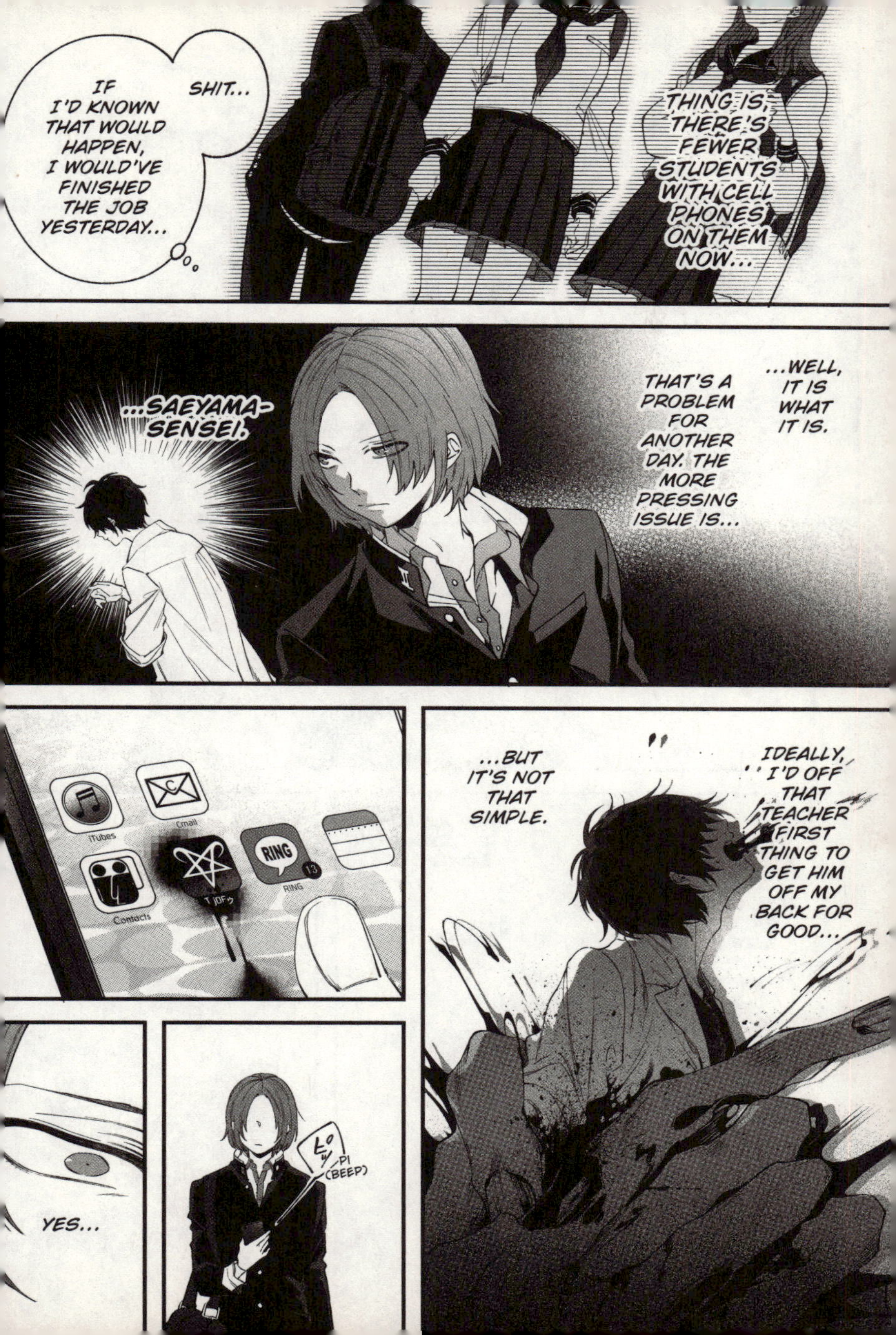
THING IS, THERE'S FEWER STUDENTS WITH CELL PHONES ON THEM NOW...
SHIT...
IF I'D KNOWN THAT WOULD HAPPEN, I WOULD'VE FINISHED THE JOB YESTERDAY...
...WELL, IT IS WHAT IT IS.
THAT'S A PROBLEM FOR ANOTHER DAY. THE MORE PRESSING ISSUE IS...
...SAEYAMA-SENSEI.
IDEALLY, I'D OFF THAT TEACHER FIRST THING TO GET HIM OFF MY BACK FOR GOOD...
...BUT IT'S NOT THAT SIMPLE.
iTunes
Cmail
RING
Contacts
ピ PI (BEEP)
YES...

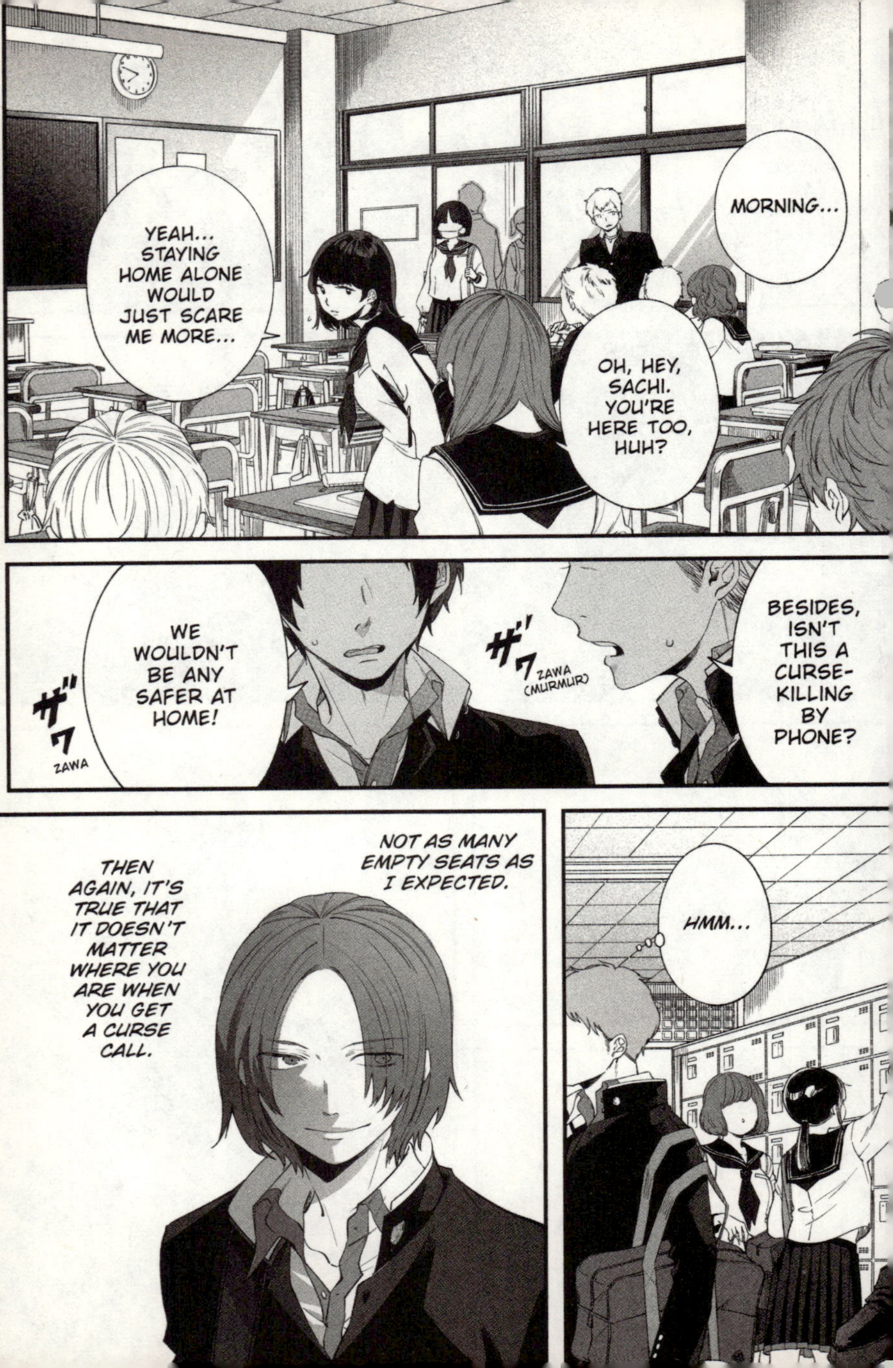
MORNING...
OH, HEY, SACHI. YOU'RE HERE TOO, HUH?
YEAH... STAYING HOME ALONE WOULD JUST SCARE ME MORE...
BESIDES, ISN'T THIS A CURSE-KILLING BY PHONE?
ザワ
ZAWA (MURMUR)
WE WOULDN'T BE ANY SAFER AT HOME!
ザワ
ZAWA
HMM...
NOT AS MANY EMPTY SEATS AS I EXPECTED.
THEN AGAIN, IT'S TRUE THAT IT DOESN'T MATTER WHERE YOU ARE WHEN YOU GET A CURSE CALL.

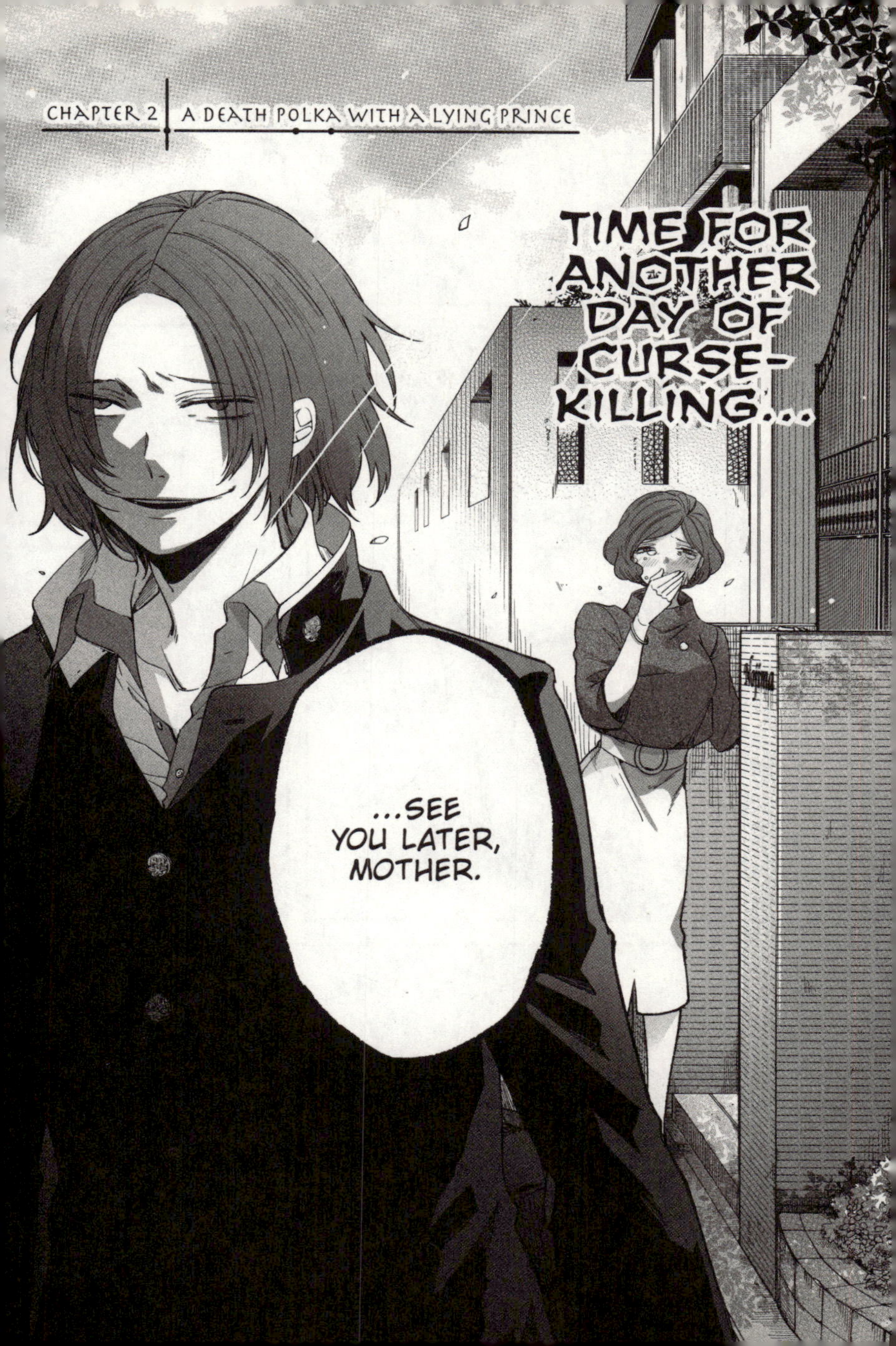
CHAPTER 2 A DEATH POLKA WITH A LYING PRINCE
TIME FOR ANOTHER DAY OF CURSE-KILLING...
...SEE YOU LATER, MOTHER.

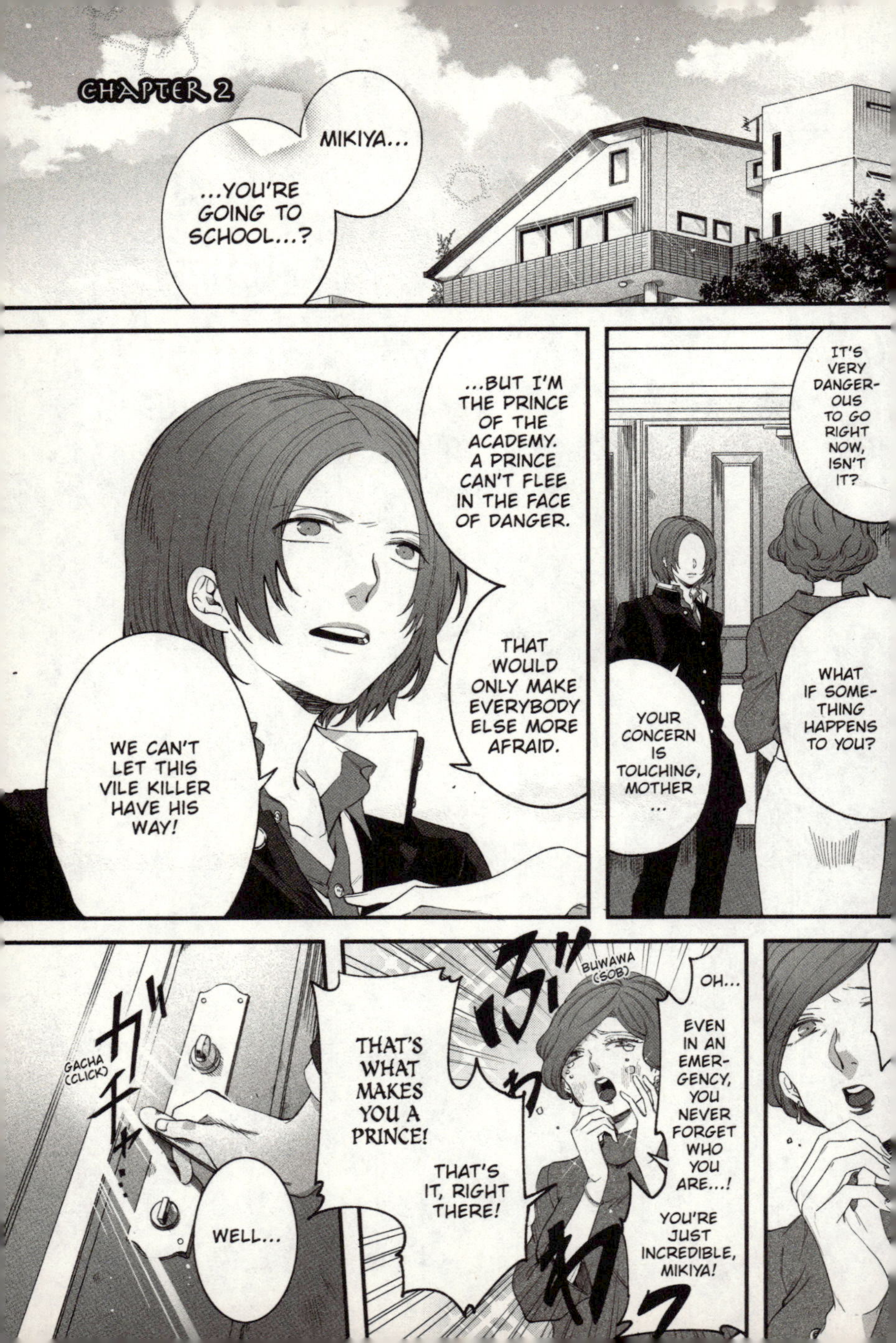
CHAPTER 2
MIKIYA...
...YOU'RE GOING TO SCHOOL...?
IT'S VERY DANGER-OUS TO GO RIGHT NOW, ISN'T IT?
WHAT IF SOME-THING HAPPENS TO YOU?
YOUR CONCERN IS TOUCHING, MOTHER ...
...BUT I'M THE PRINCE OF THE ACADEMY. A PRINCE CAN'T FLEE IN THE FACE OF DANGER.
THAT WOULD ONLY MAKE EVERYBODY ELSE MORE AFRAID.
WE CAN'T LET THIS VILE KILLER HAVE HIS WAY!
BUWAWA (SOB)
OH...
EVEN IN AN EMER-GENCY, YOU NEVER FORGET WHO YOU ARE...!
YOU'RE JUST INCREDIBLE, MIKIYA!
THAT'S WHAT MAKES YOU A PRINCE!
THAT'S IT, RIGHT THERE!
GACHA (CLICK)
WELL...

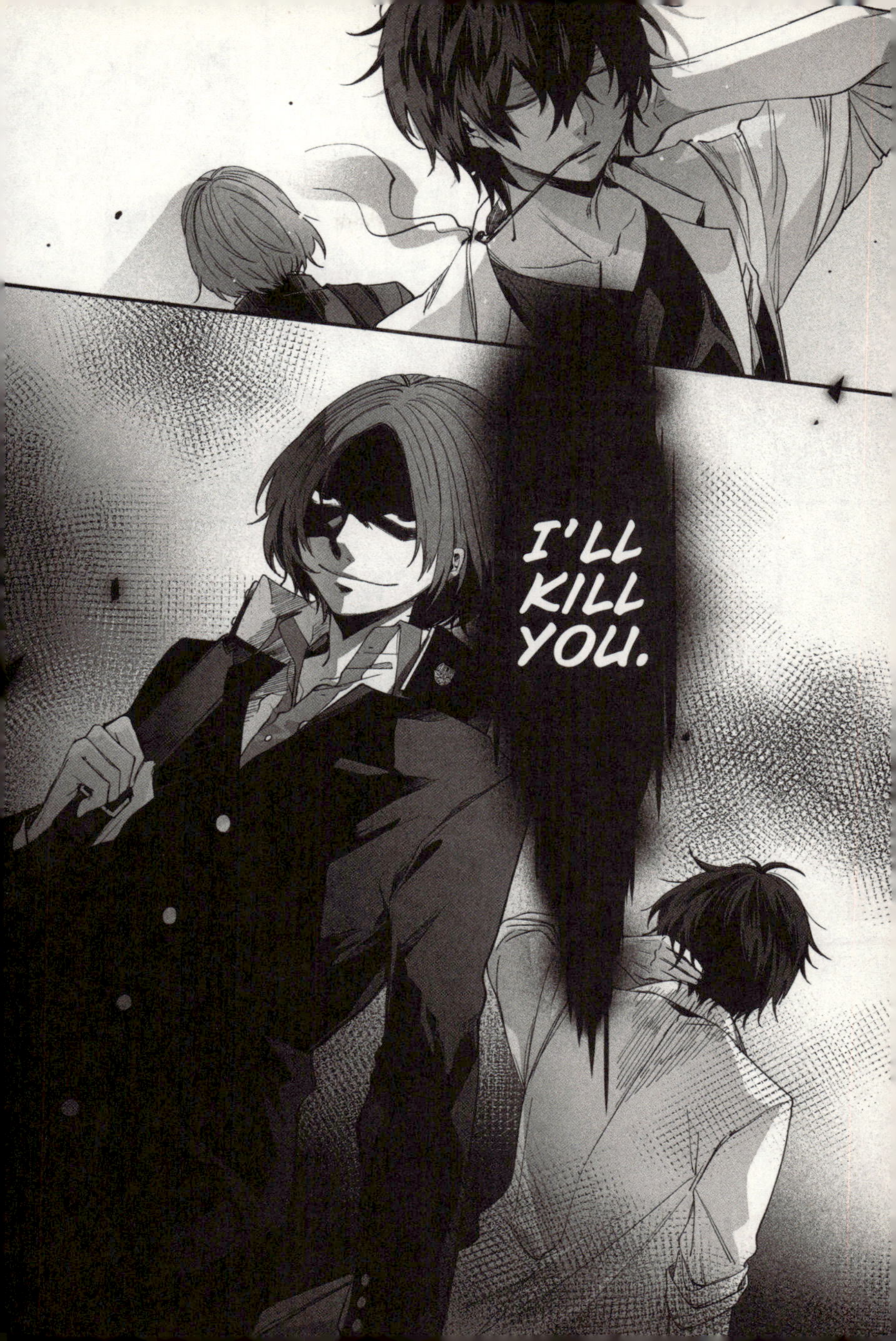
I'LL KILL YOU.

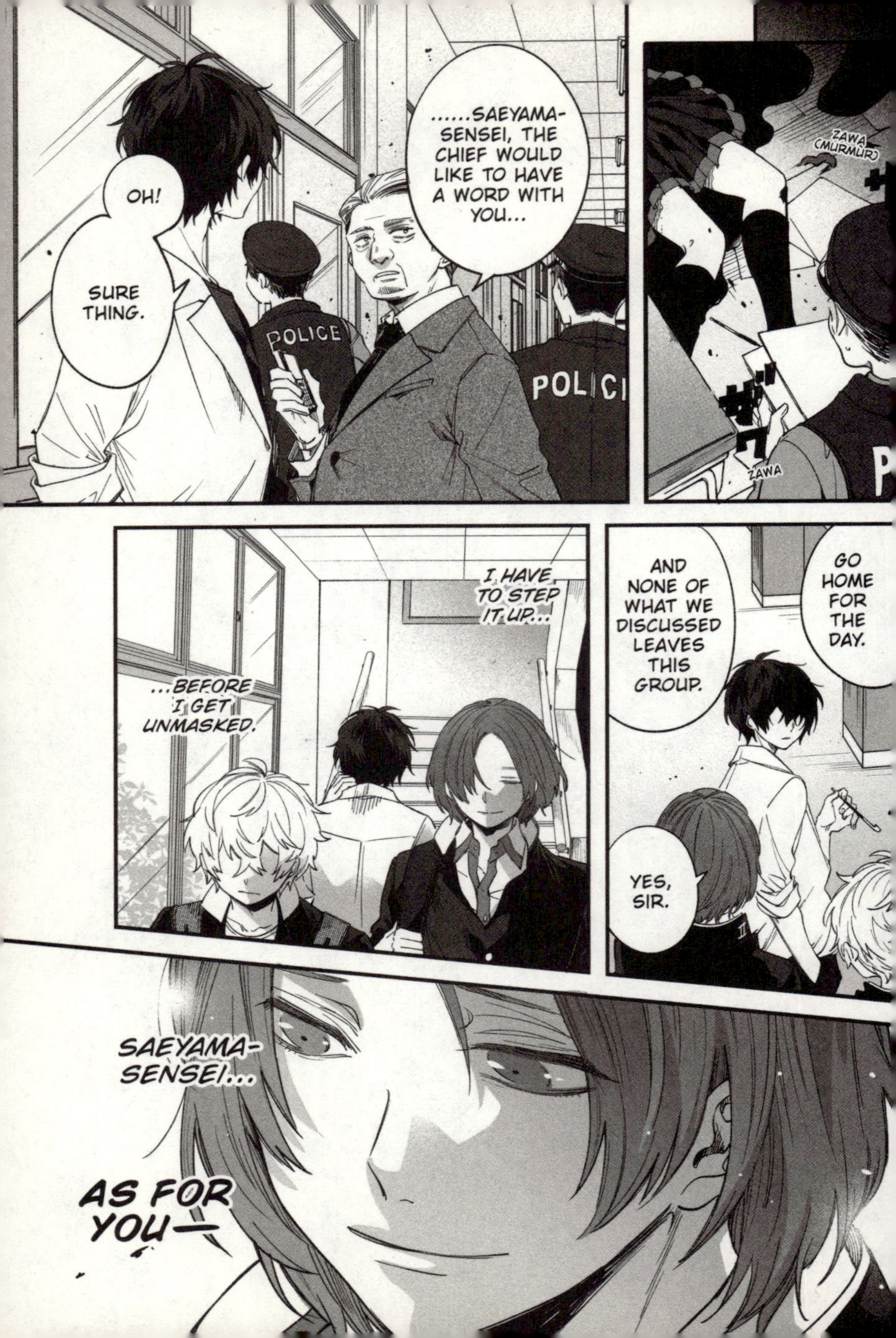
ZAWA (MURMUR)
ZAWA
......SAEYAMA-SENSEI, THE CHIEF WOULD LIKE TO HAVE A WORD WITH YOU...
OH!
SURE THING.
POLICE
POLICE
GO HOME FOR THE DAY.
AND NONE OF WHAT WE DISCUSSED LEAVES THIS GROUP.
YES, SIR.
I HAVE TO STEP IT UP...
...BEFORE I GET UNMASKED.
SAEYAMA-SENSEI...
AS FOR YOU—

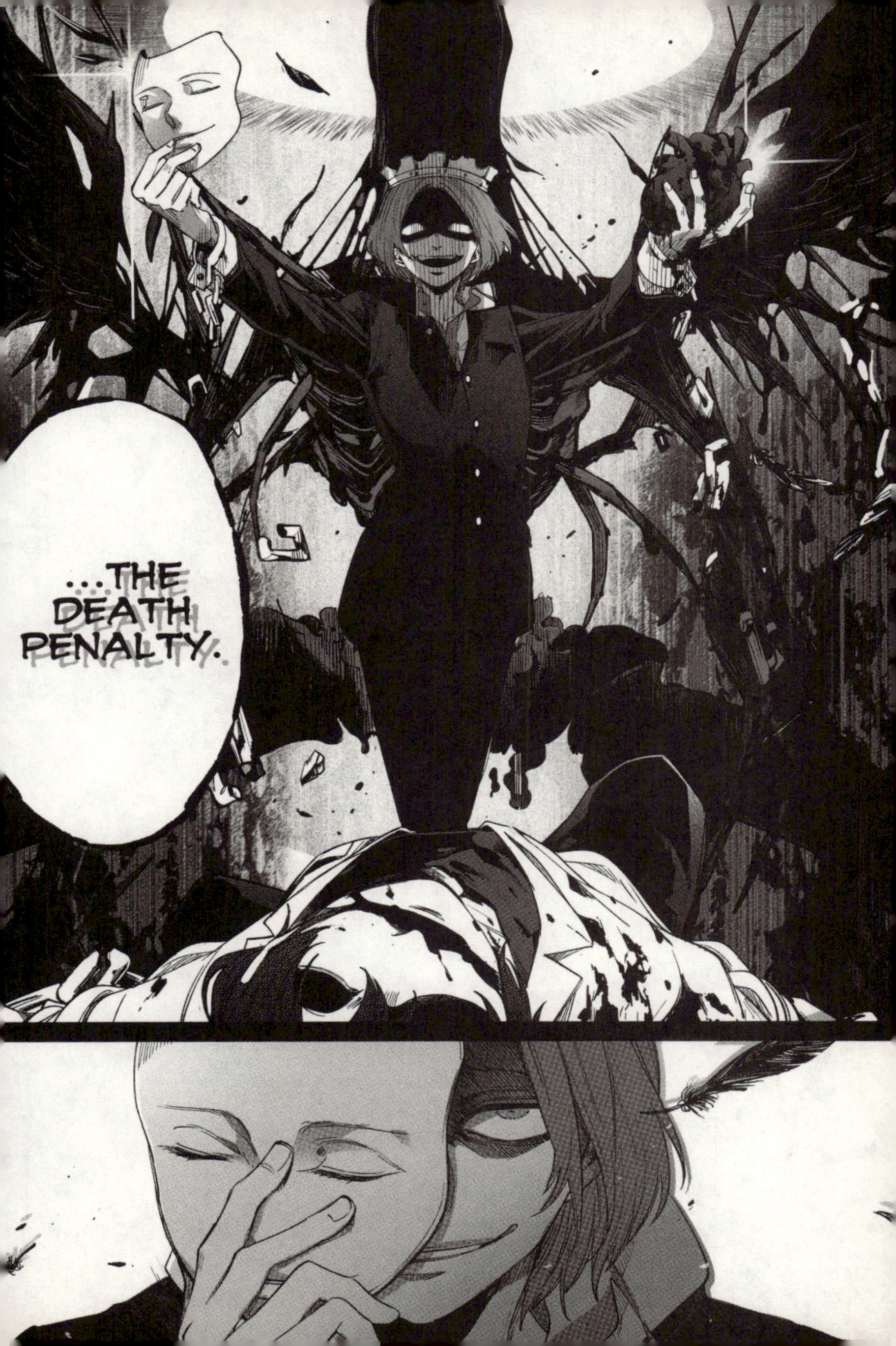
...THE DEATH PENALTY.

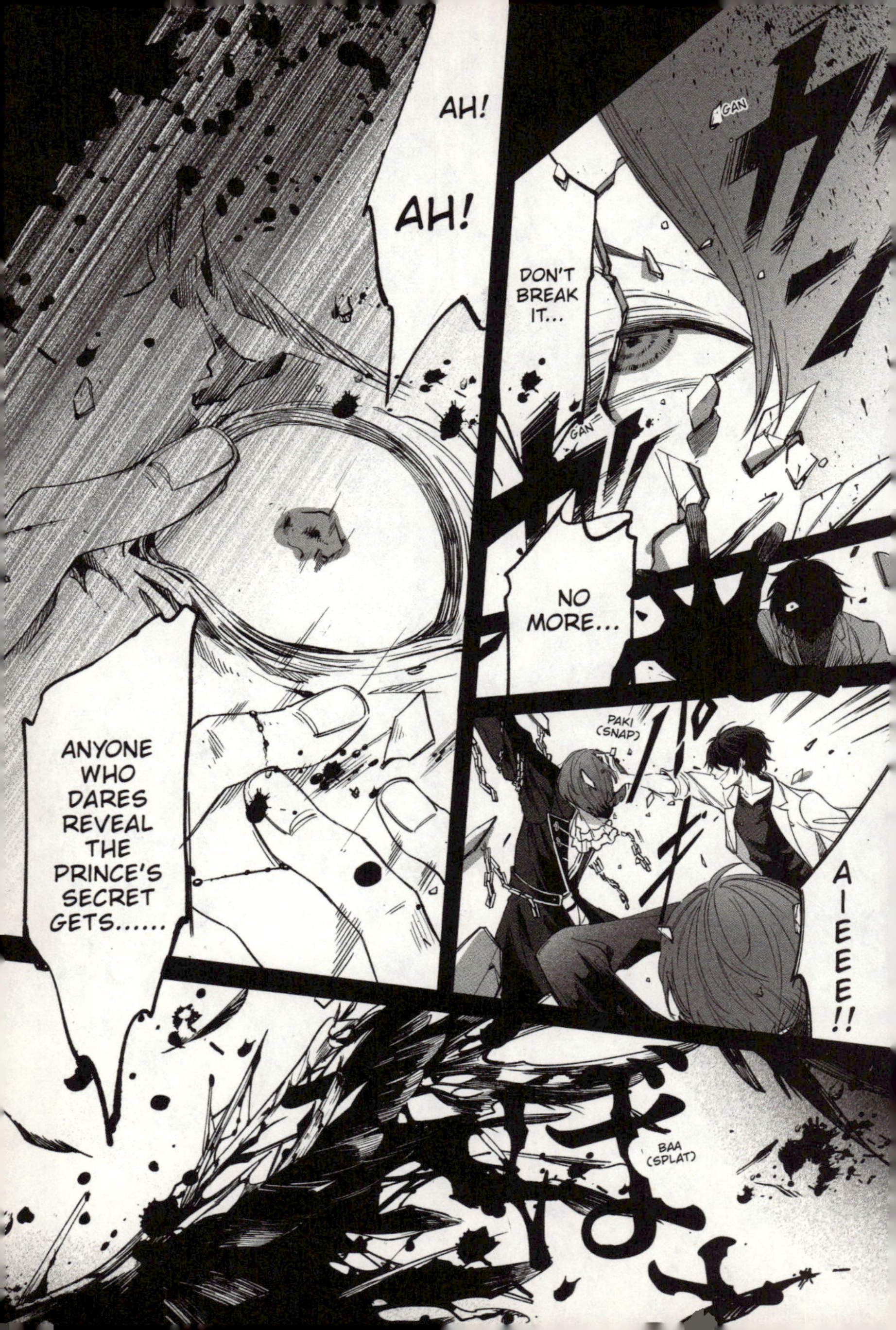
GAN
DON'T BREAK IT...
GAN
NO MORE...
PAKI (SNAP)
AIEEE!!
AH!
AH!
ANYONE WHO DARES REVEAL THE PRINCE'S SECRET GETS......
BAA (SPLAT)

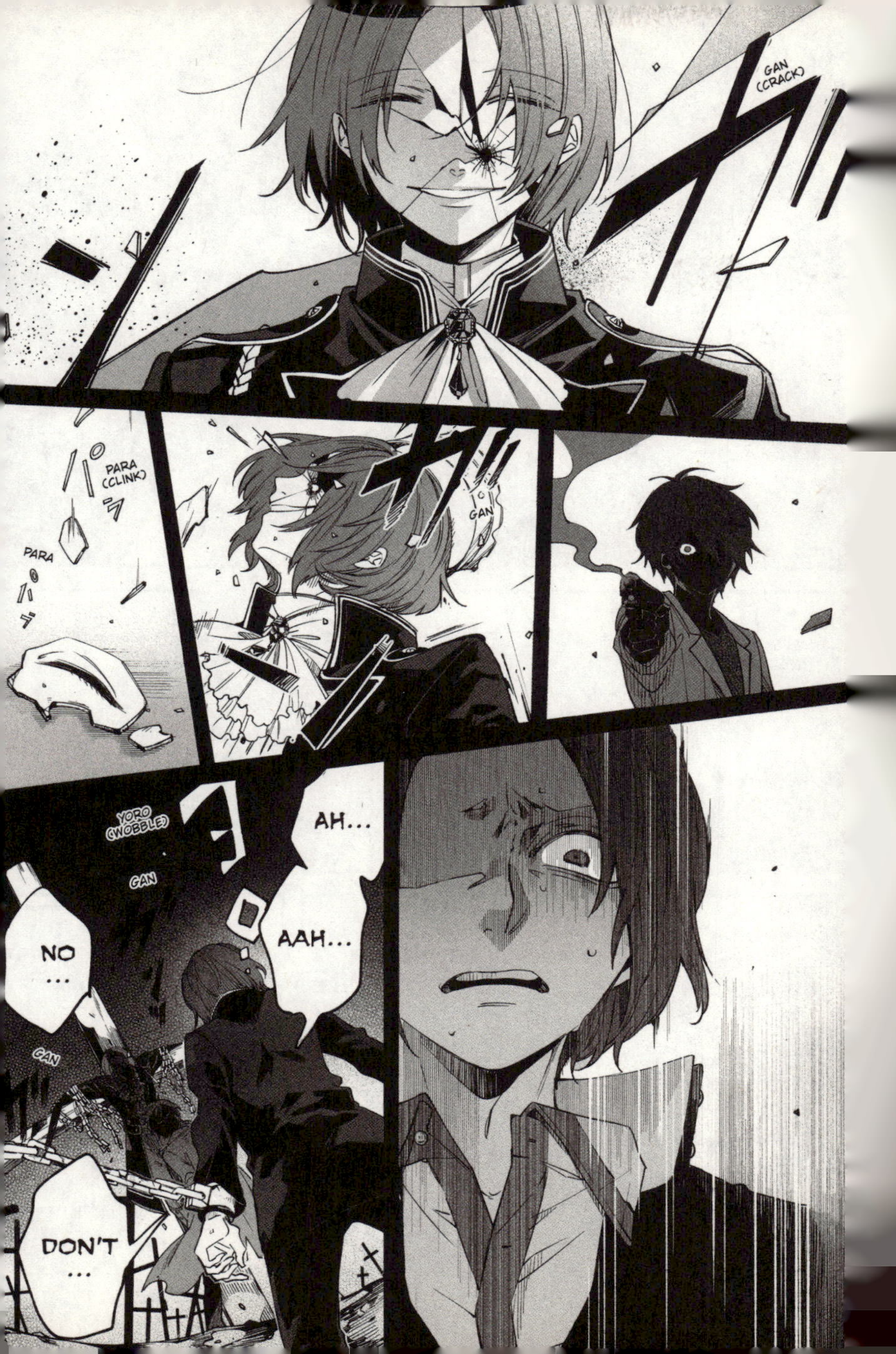
GAN (CRACK)
GAN
PARA (CLINK)
PARA
AH...
YORO (WOBBLE)
GAN
AAH...
NO...
GAN
DON'T...

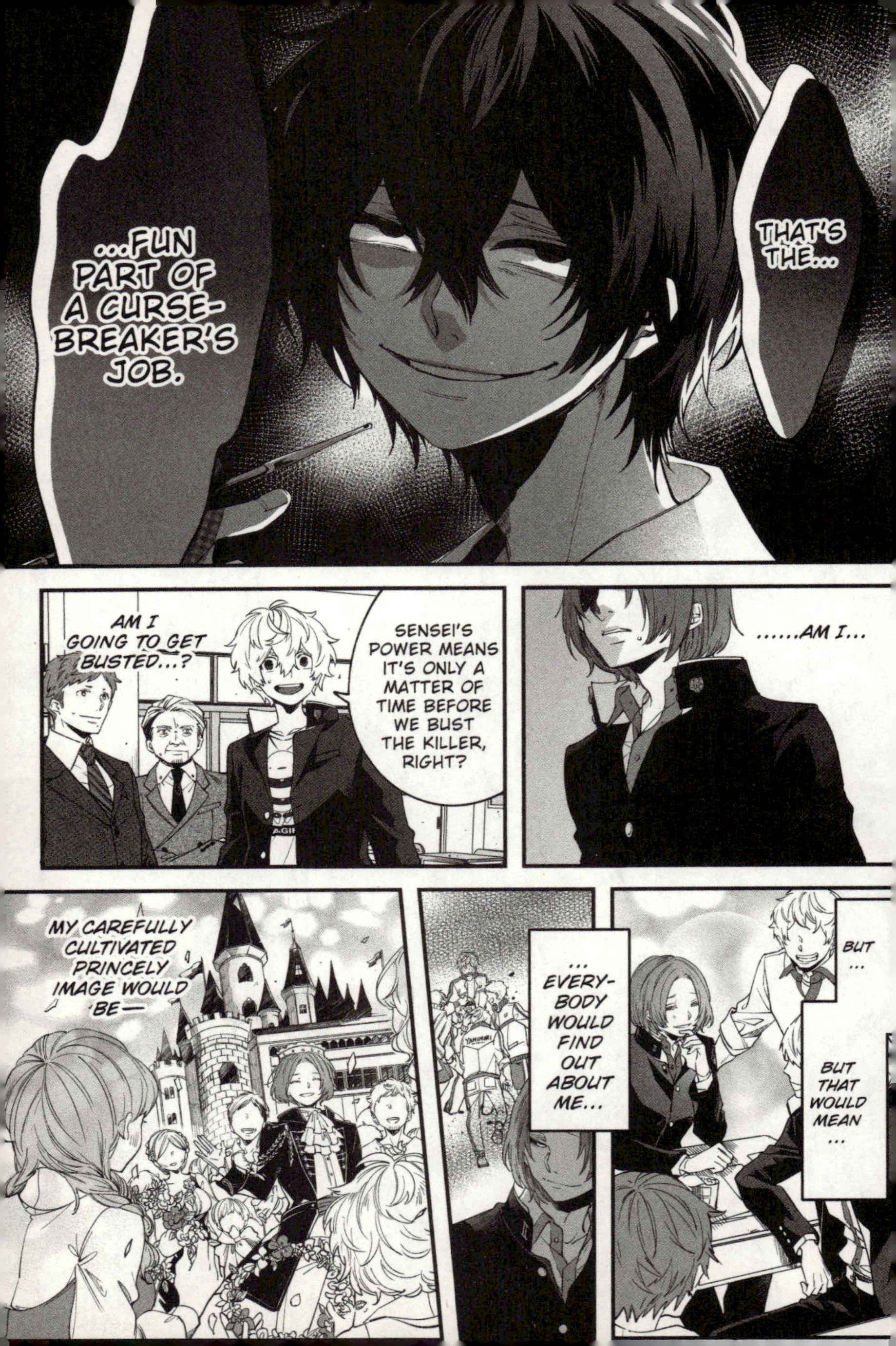
THAT'S THE...
...FUN PART OF A CURSE-BREAKER'S JOB.
......AM I...
SENSEI'S POWER MEANS IT'S ONLY A MATTER OF TIME BEFORE WE BUST THE KILLER, RIGHT?
AM I GOING TO GET BUSTED...?
BUT ...
BUT THAT WOULD MEAN ...
... EVERYBODY WOULD FIND OUT ABOUT ME...
MY CAREFULLY CULTIVATED PRINCELY IMAGE WOULD BE—

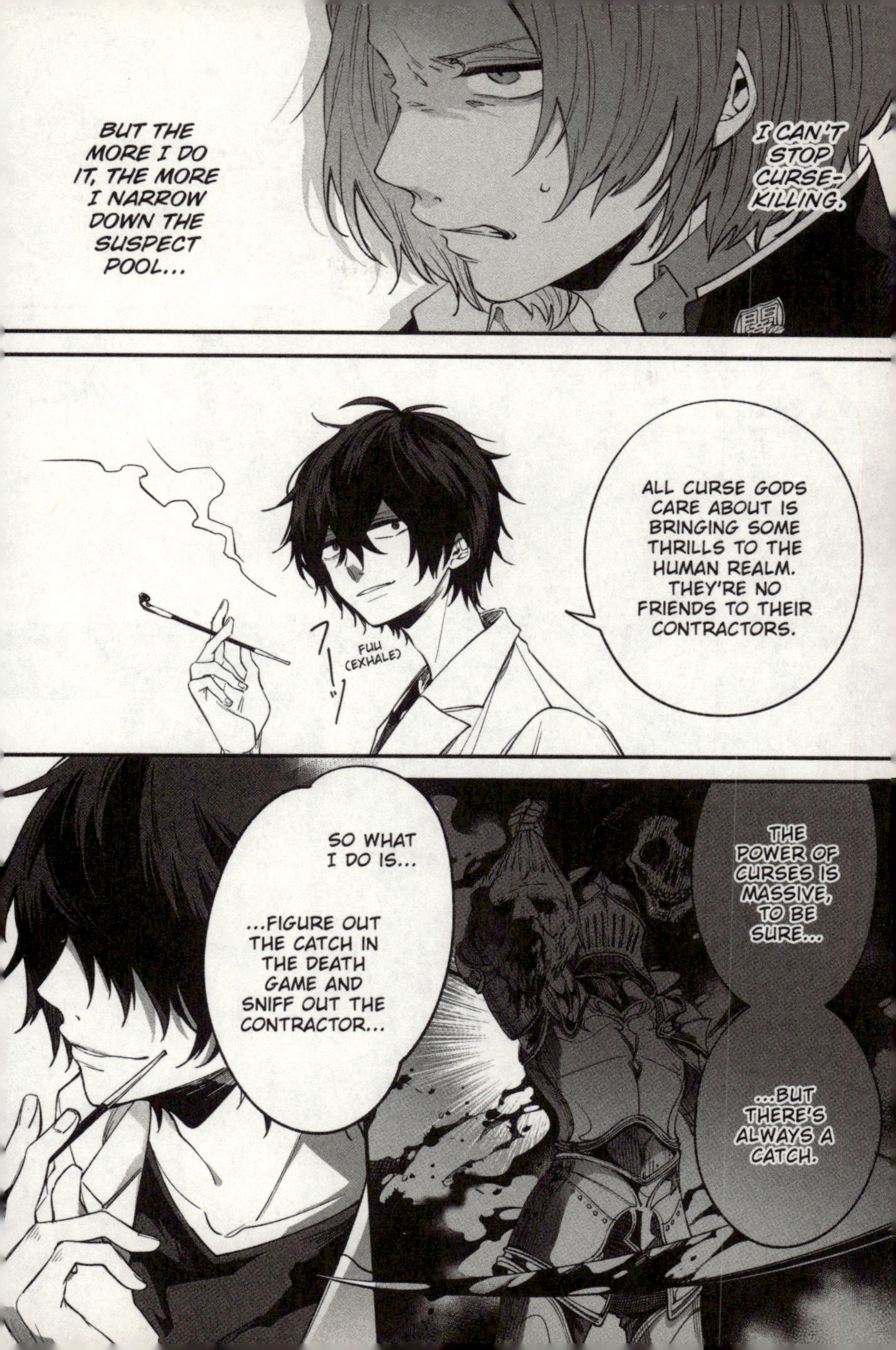
I CAN'T STOP CURSE-KILLING.
BUT THE MORE I DO IT, THE MORE I NARROW DOWN THE SUSPECT POOL...
ALL CURSE GODS CARE ABOUT IS BRINGING SOME THRILLS TO THE HUMAN REALM. THEY'RE NO FRIENDS TO THEIR CONTRACTORS.
FUU (EXHALE)
THE POWER OF CURSES IS MASSIVE, TO BE SURE...
...BUT THERE'S ALWAYS A CATCH.
SO WHAT I DO IS...
...FIGURE OUT THE CATCH IN THE DEATH GAME AND SNIFF OUT THE CONTRACTOR...

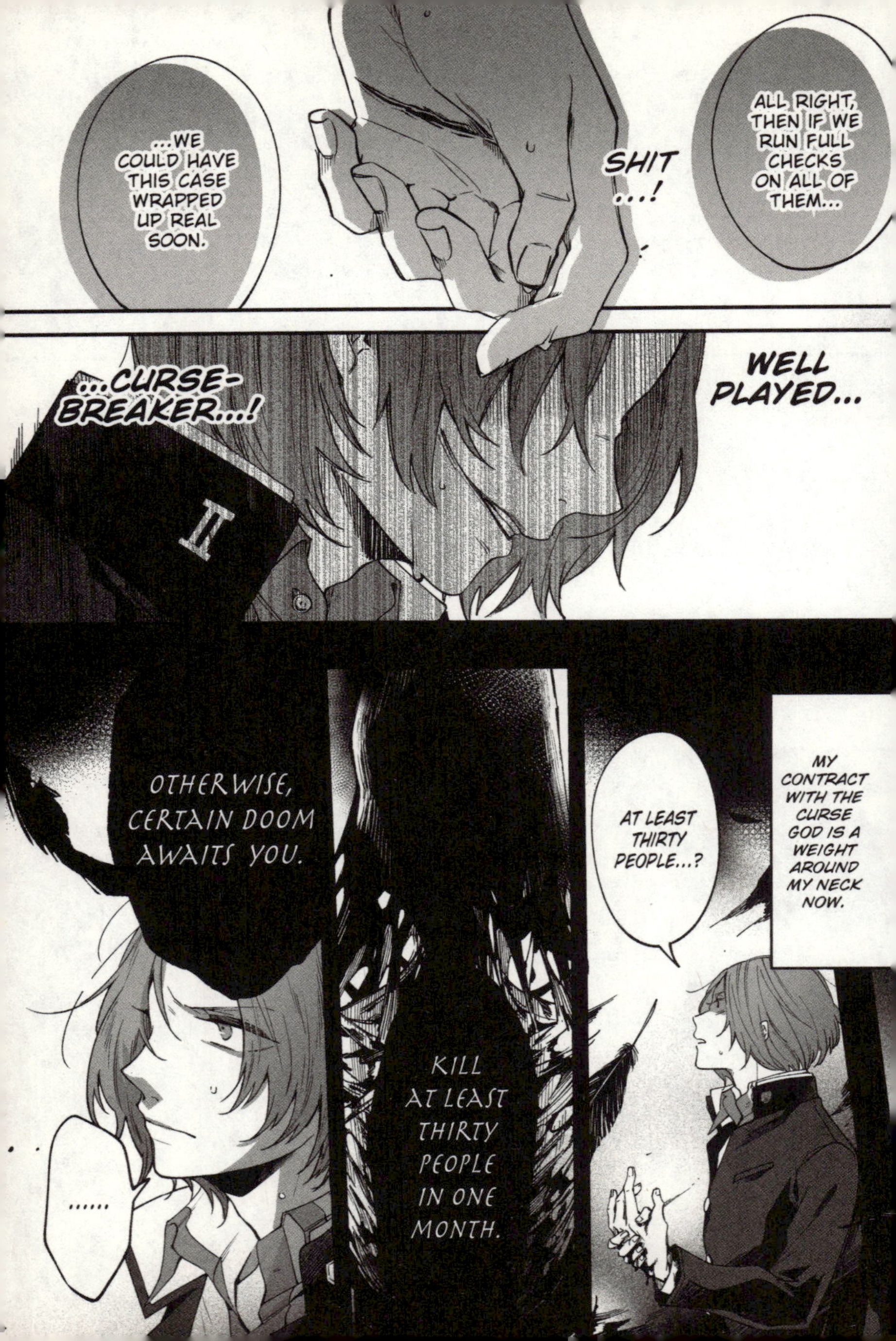
ALL RIGHT, THEN IF WE RUN FULL CHECKS ON ALL OF THEM...
SHIT ...!
...WE COULD HAVE THIS CASE WRAPPED UP REAL SOON.
WELL PLAYED...
...CURSE-BREAKER...!
MY CONTRACT WITH THE CURSE GOD IS A WEIGHT AROUND MY NECK NOW.
AT LEAST THIRTY PEOPLE...?
KILL AT LEAST THIRTY PEOPLE IN ONE MONTH.
OTHERWISE, CERTAIN DOOM AWAITS YOU.
......

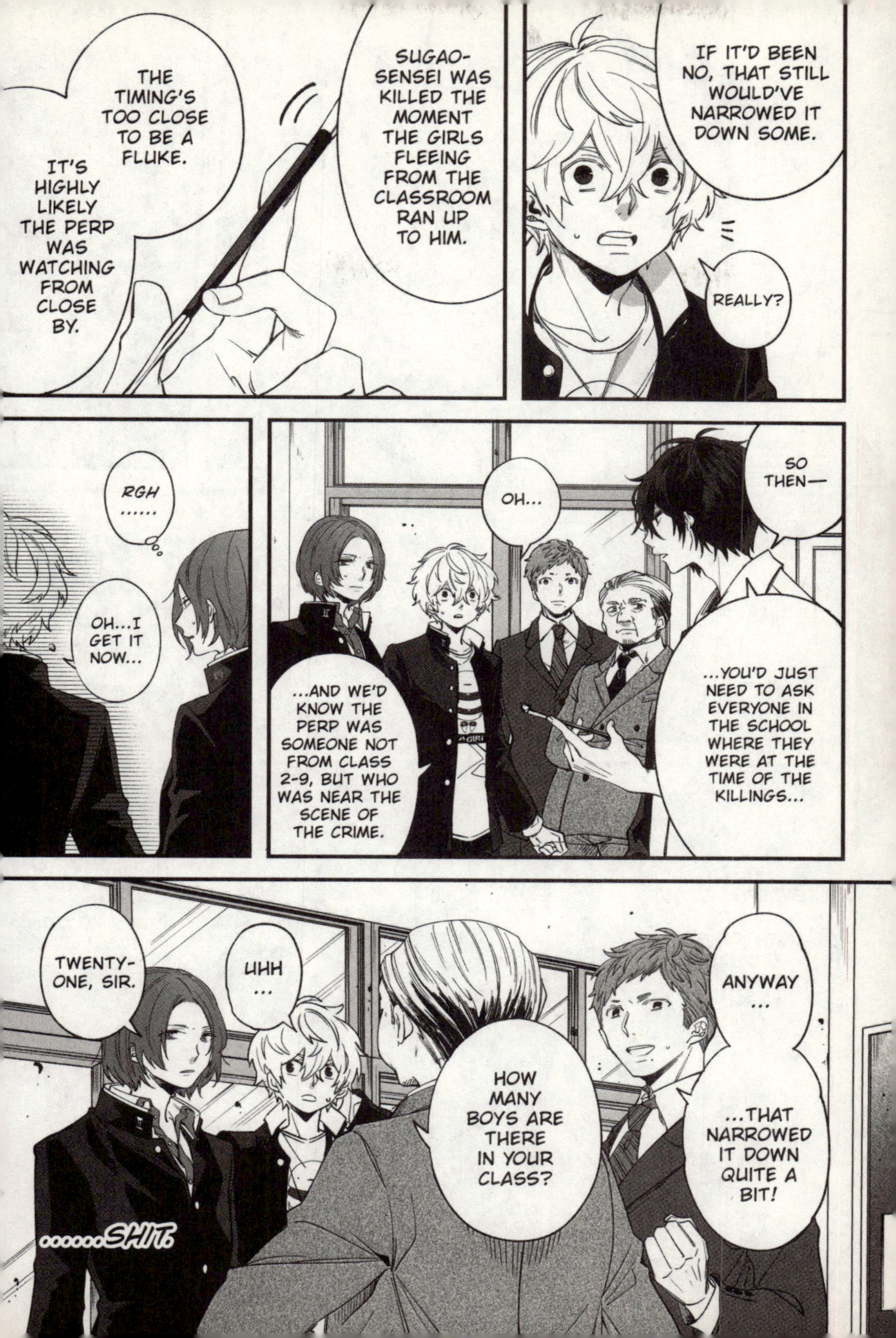
IF IT'D BEEN NO, THAT STILL WOULD'VE NARROWED IT DOWN SOME.
REALLY?
SUGAO-SENSEI WAS KILLED THE MOMENT THE GIRLS FLEEING FROM THE CLASSROOM RAN UP TO HIM.
THE TIMING'S TOO CLOSE TO BE A FLUKE.
IT'S HIGHLY LIKELY THE PERP WAS WATCHING FROM CLOSE BY.
SO THEN—
OH...
...YOU'D JUST NEED TO ASK EVERYONE IN THE SCHOOL WHERE THEY WERE AT THE TIME OF THE KILLINGS...
...AND WE'D KNOW THE PERP WAS SOMEONE NOT FROM CLASS 2-9, BUT WHO WAS NEAR THE SCENE OF THE CRIME.
RGH......
OH...I GET IT NOW...
ANYWAY...
...THAT NARROWED IT DOWN QUITE A BIT!
HOW MANY BOYS ARE THERE IN YOUR CLASS?
UHH...
TWENTY-ONE, SIR.
......SHIT.

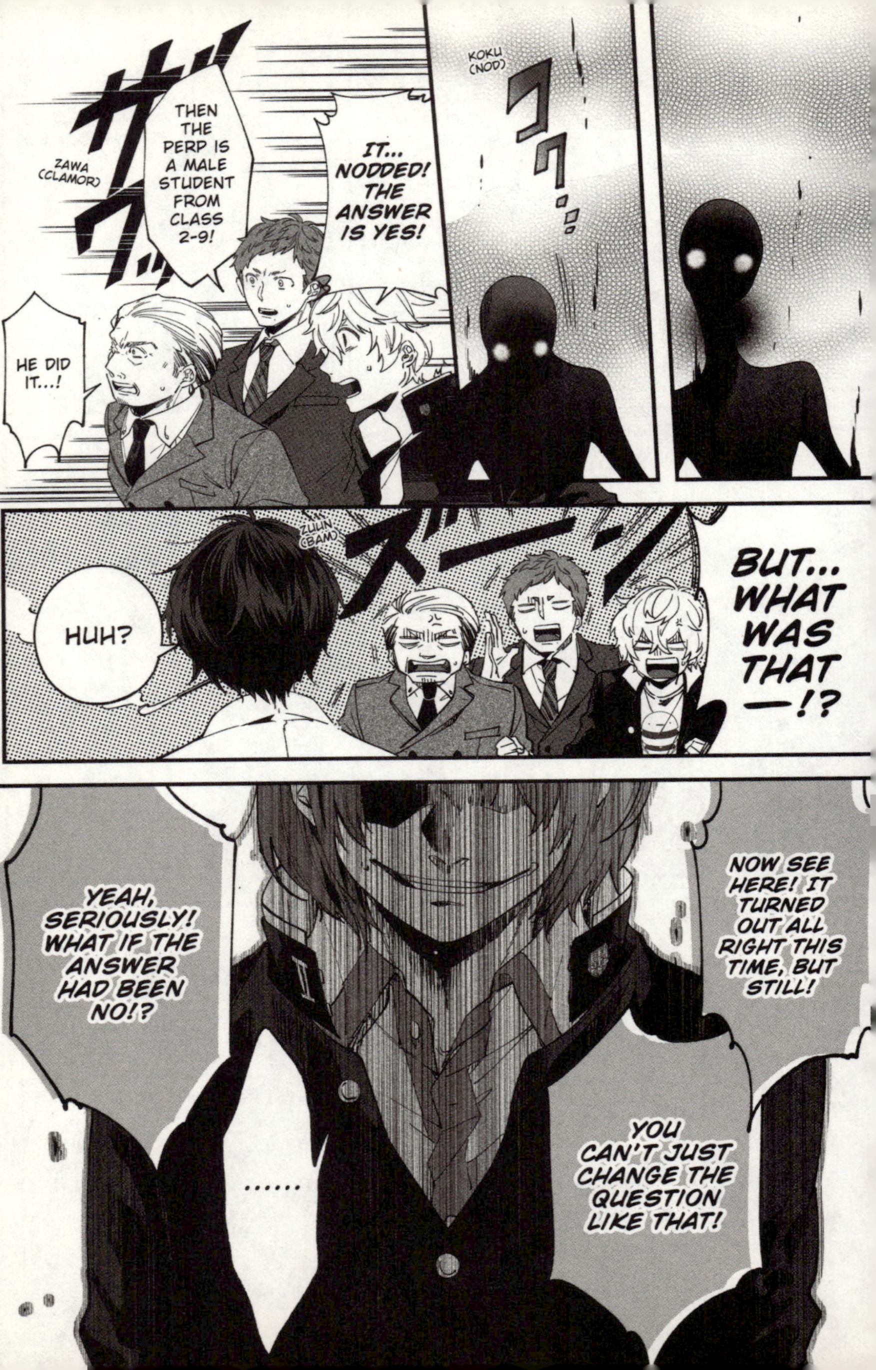
KOKU (NOD)
IT... NODDED! THE ANSWER IS YES!
THEN THE PERP IS A MALE STUDENT FROM CLASS 2-9!
ZAWA (CLAMOR)
HE DID IT...!
BUT... WHAT WAS THAT—!?
ZUUN (BAM)
HUH?
NOW SEE HERE! IT TURNED OUT ALL RIGHT THIS TIME, BUT STILL!
YEAH, SERIOUSLY! WHAT IF THE ANSWER HAD BEEN NO!?
YOU CAN'T JUST CHANGE THE QUESTION LIKE THAT!
......

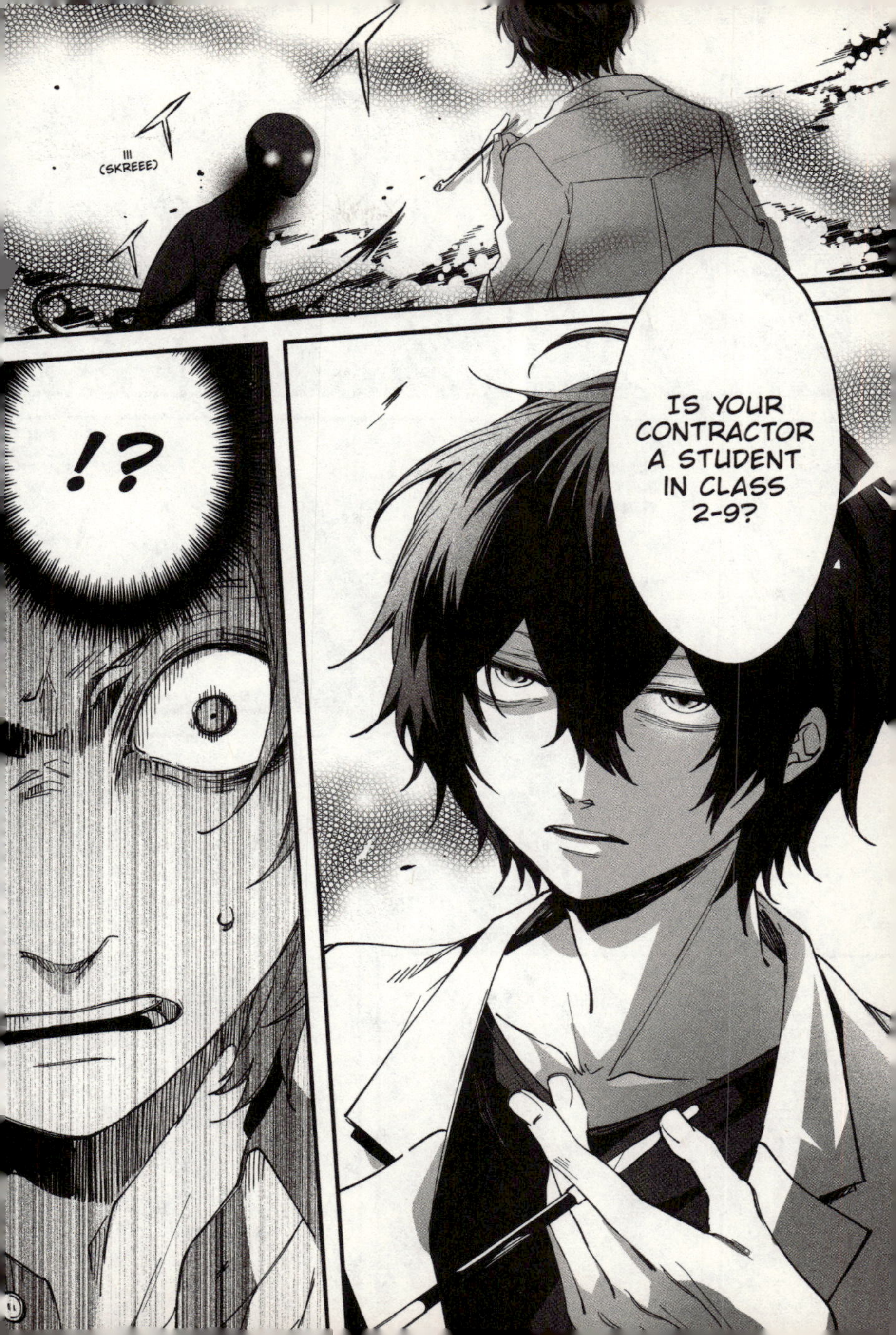
(SKREEE)
IS YOUR CONTRACTOR A STUDENT IN CLASS 2-9?
!?

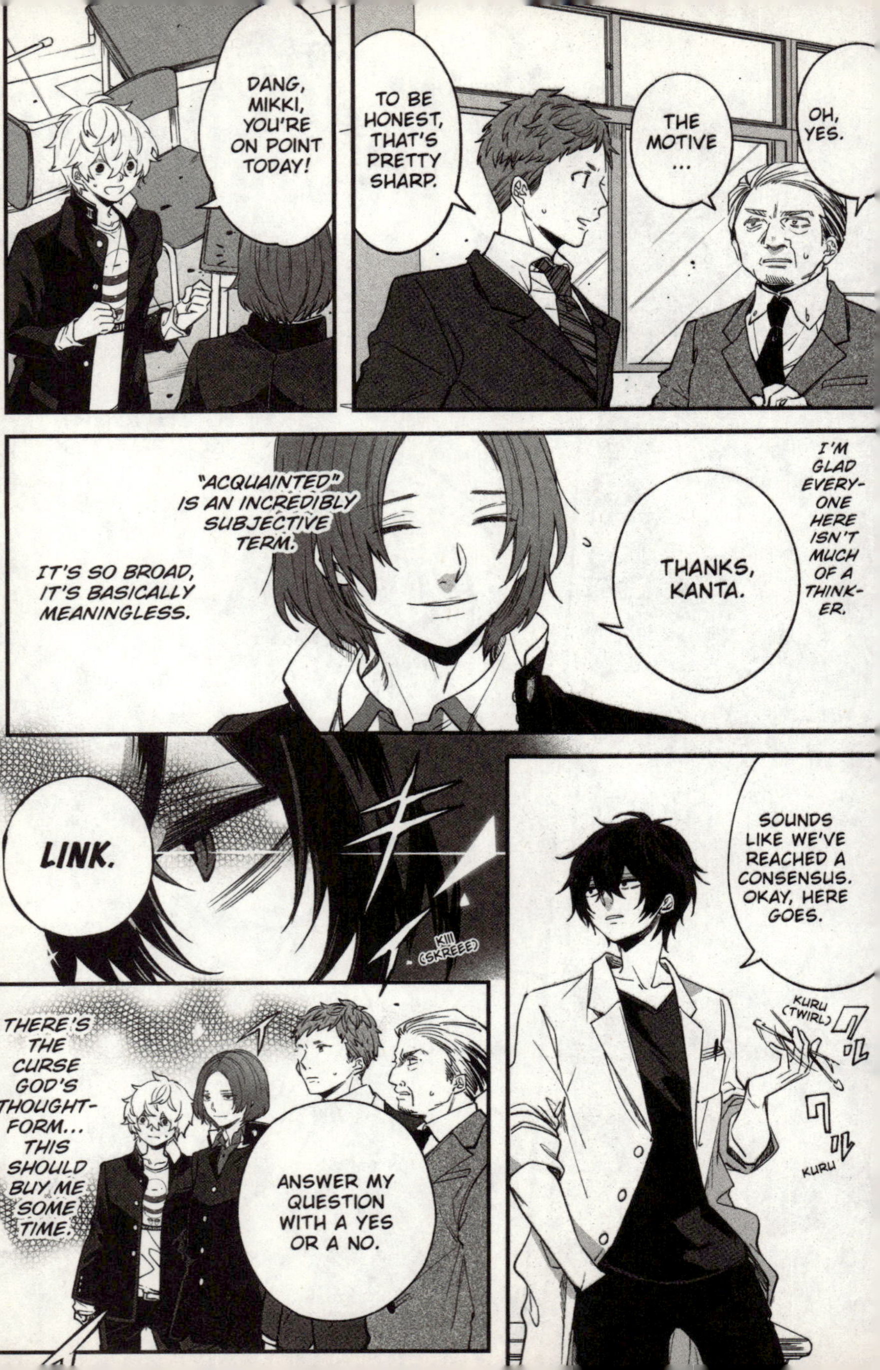
OH, YES.
THE MOTIVE ...
TO BE HONEST, THAT'S PRETTY SHARP.
DANG, MIKKI, YOU'RE ON POINT TODAY!
I'M GLAD EVERYONE HERE ISN'T MUCH OF A THINKER.
THANKS, KANTA.
"ACQUAINTED" IS AN INCREDIBLY SUBJECTIVE TERM.
IT'S SO BROAD, IT'S BASICALLY MEANINGLESS.
SOUNDS LIKE WE'VE REACHED A CONSENSUS. OKAY, HERE GOES.
KURU (TWIRL)
KURU
KIII (SKREEE)
LINK.
ANSWER MY QUESTION WITH A YES OR A NO.
THERE'S THE CURSE GOD'S THOUGHT-FORM... THIS SHOULD BUY ME SOME TIME.

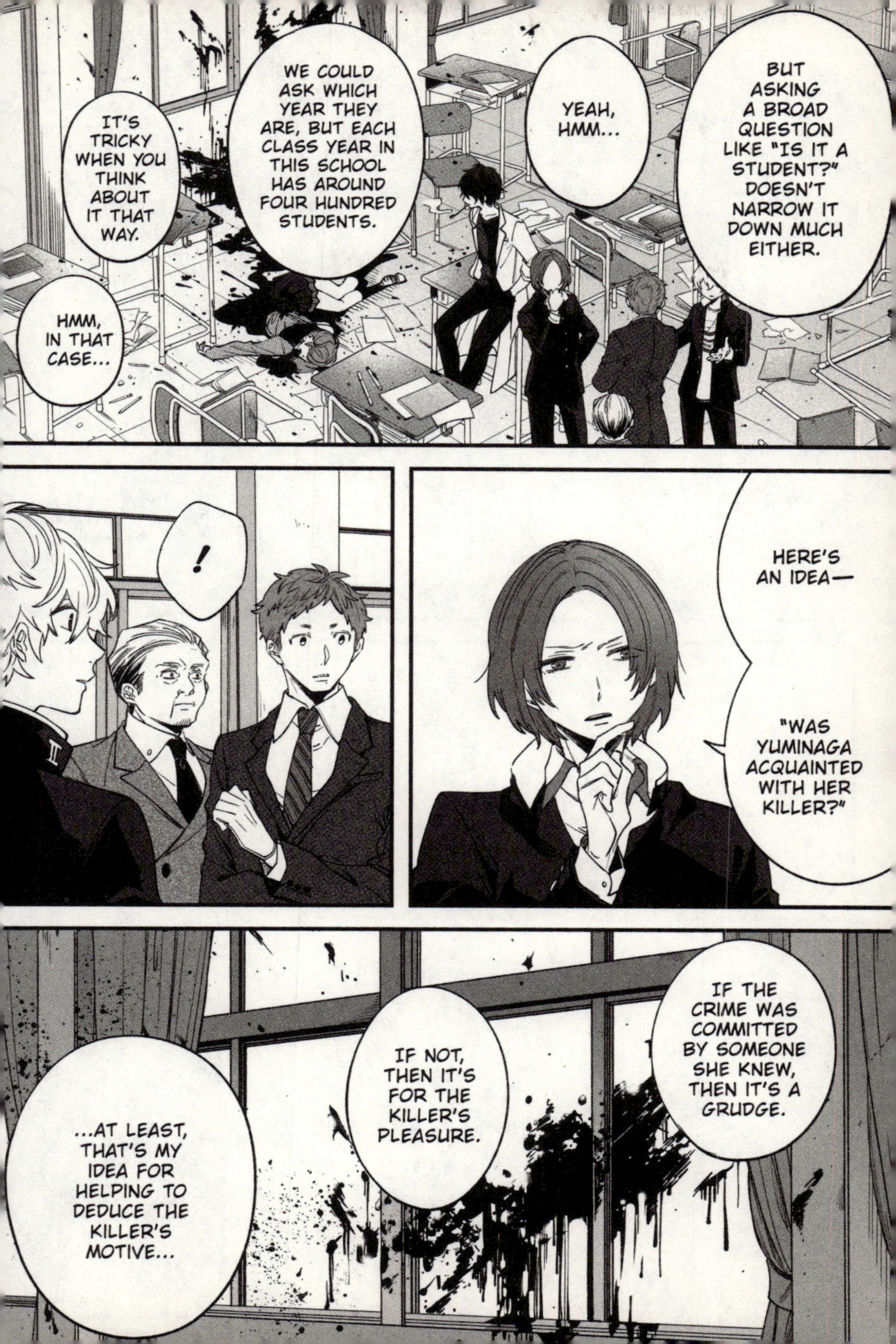
BUT ASKING A BROAD QUESTION LIKE "IS IT A STUDENT?" DOESN'T NARROW IT DOWN MUCH EITHER.
YEAH, HMM...
WE COULD ASK WHICH YEAR THEY ARE, BUT EACH CLASS YEAR IN THIS SCHOOL HAS AROUND FOUR HUNDRED STUDENTS.
IT'S TRICKY WHEN YOU THINK ABOUT IT THAT WAY.
HMM, IN THAT CASE...
HERE'S AN IDEA—
"WAS YUMINAGA ACQUAINTED WITH HER KILLER?"
!
IF THE CRIME WAS COMMITTED BY SOMEONE SHE KNEW, THEN IT'S A GRUDGE.
IF NOT, THEN IT'S FOR THE KILLER'S PLEASURE.
...AT LEAST, THAT'S MY IDEA FOR HELPING TO DEDUCE THE KILLER'S MOTIVE...

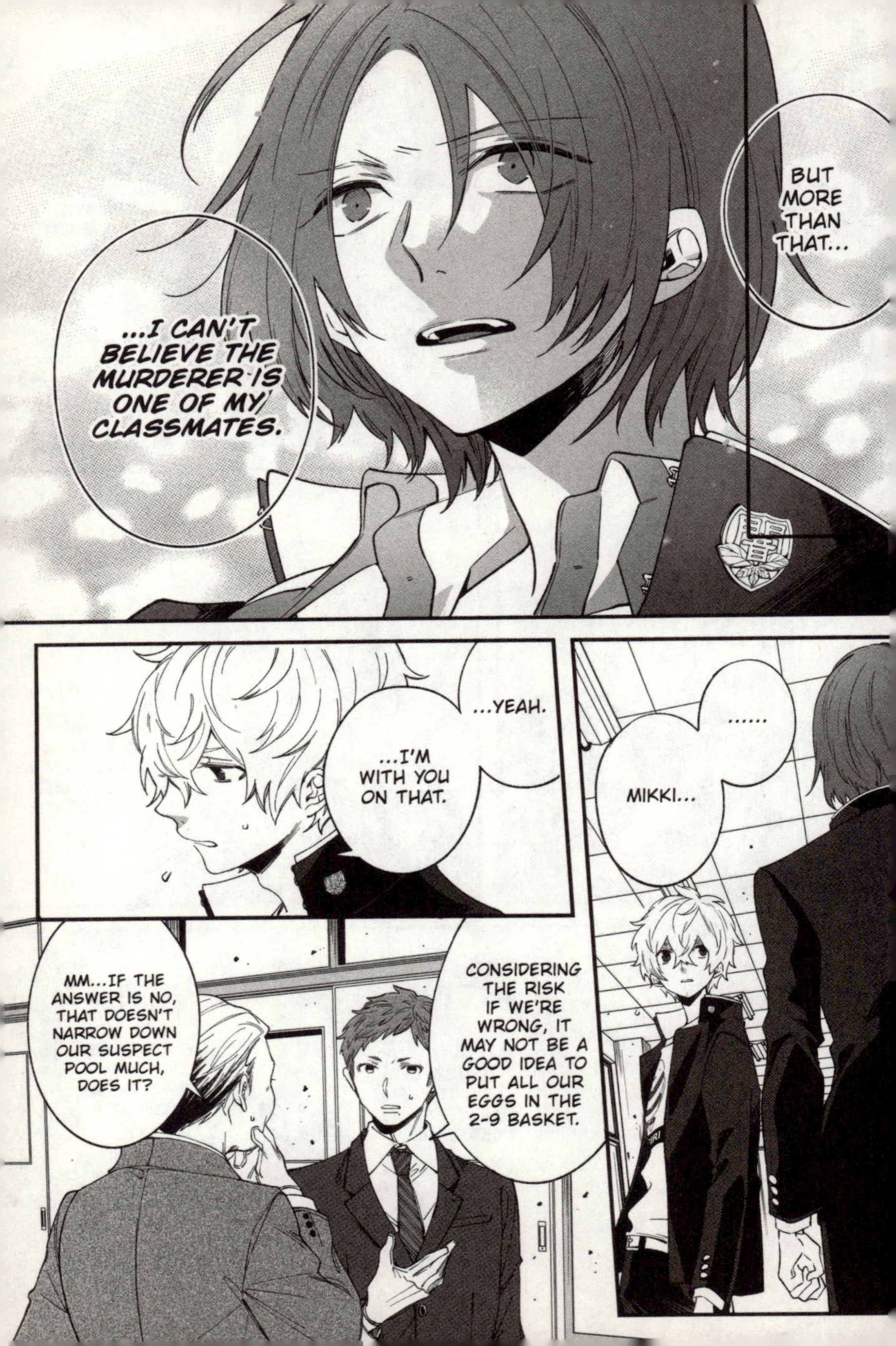
BUT MORE THAN THAT...
...I CAN'T BELIEVE THE MURDERER IS ONE OF MY CLASSMATES.
......
MIKKI...
...YEAH.
...I'M WITH YOU ON THAT.
CONSIDERING THE RISK IF WE'RE WRONG, IT MAY NOT BE A GOOD IDEA TO PUT ALL OUR EGGS IN THE 2-9 BASKET.
MM...IF THE ANSWER IS NO, THAT DOESN'T NARROW DOWN OUR SUSPECT POOL MUCH, DOES IT?

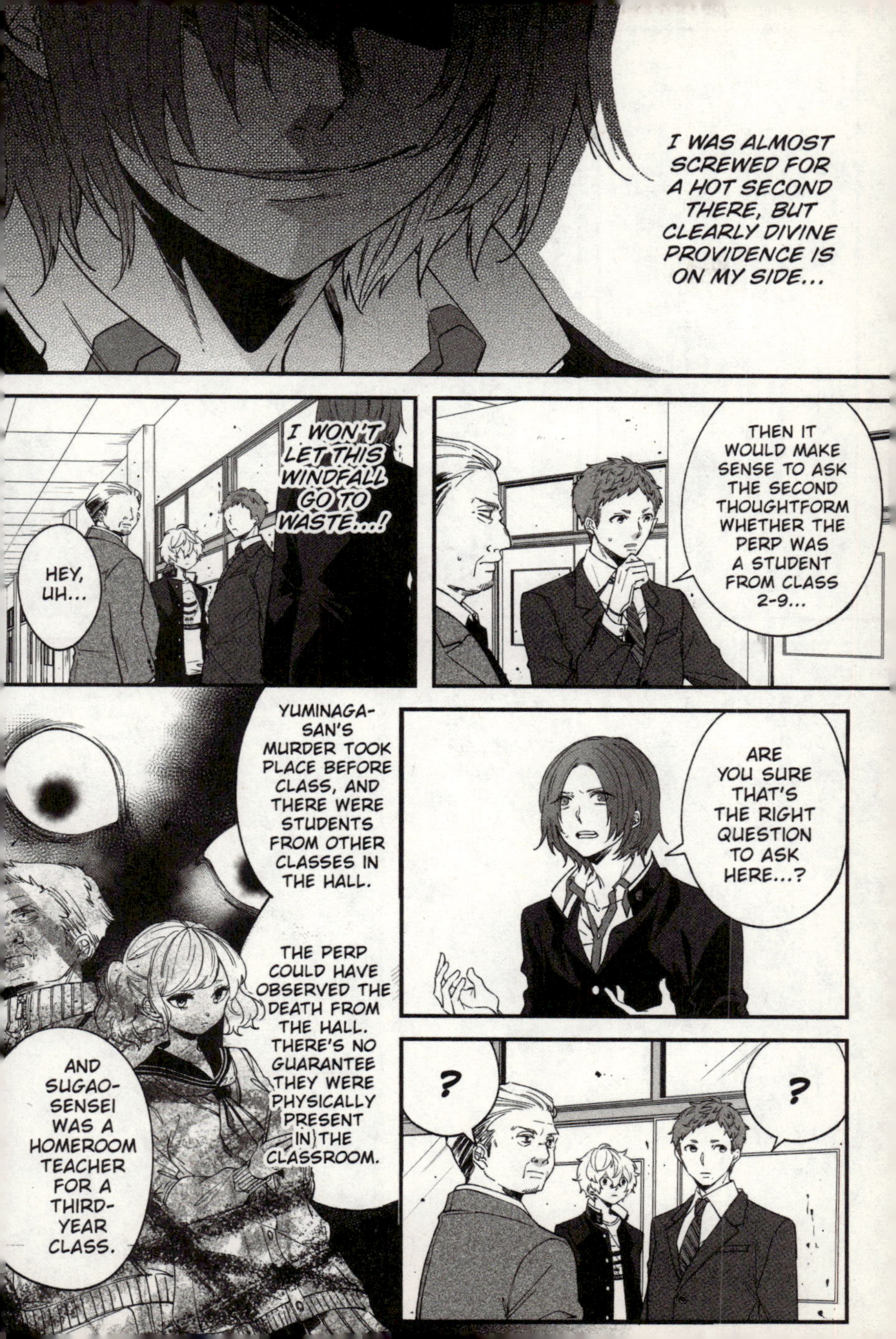
I WAS ALMOST SCREWED FOR A HOT SECOND THERE, BUT CLEARLY DIVINE PROVIDENCE IS ON MY SIDE...
THEN IT WOULD MAKE SENSE TO ASK THE SECOND THOUGHTFORM WHETHER THE PERP WAS A STUDENT FROM CLASS 2-9...
I WON'T LET THIS WINDFALL GO TO WASTE...!
HEY, UH...
ARE YOU SURE THAT'S THE RIGHT QUESTION TO ASK HERE...?
?
?
YUMINAGA-SAN'S MURDER TOOK PLACE BEFORE CLASS, AND THERE WERE STUDENTS FROM OTHER CLASSES IN THE HALL.
THE PERP COULD HAVE OBSERVED THE DEATH FROM THE HALL. THERE'S NO GUARANTEE THEY WERE PHYSICALLY PRESENT IN THE CLASSROOM.
AND SUGAO-SENSEI WAS A HOMEROOM TEACHER FOR A THIRD-YEAR CLASS.

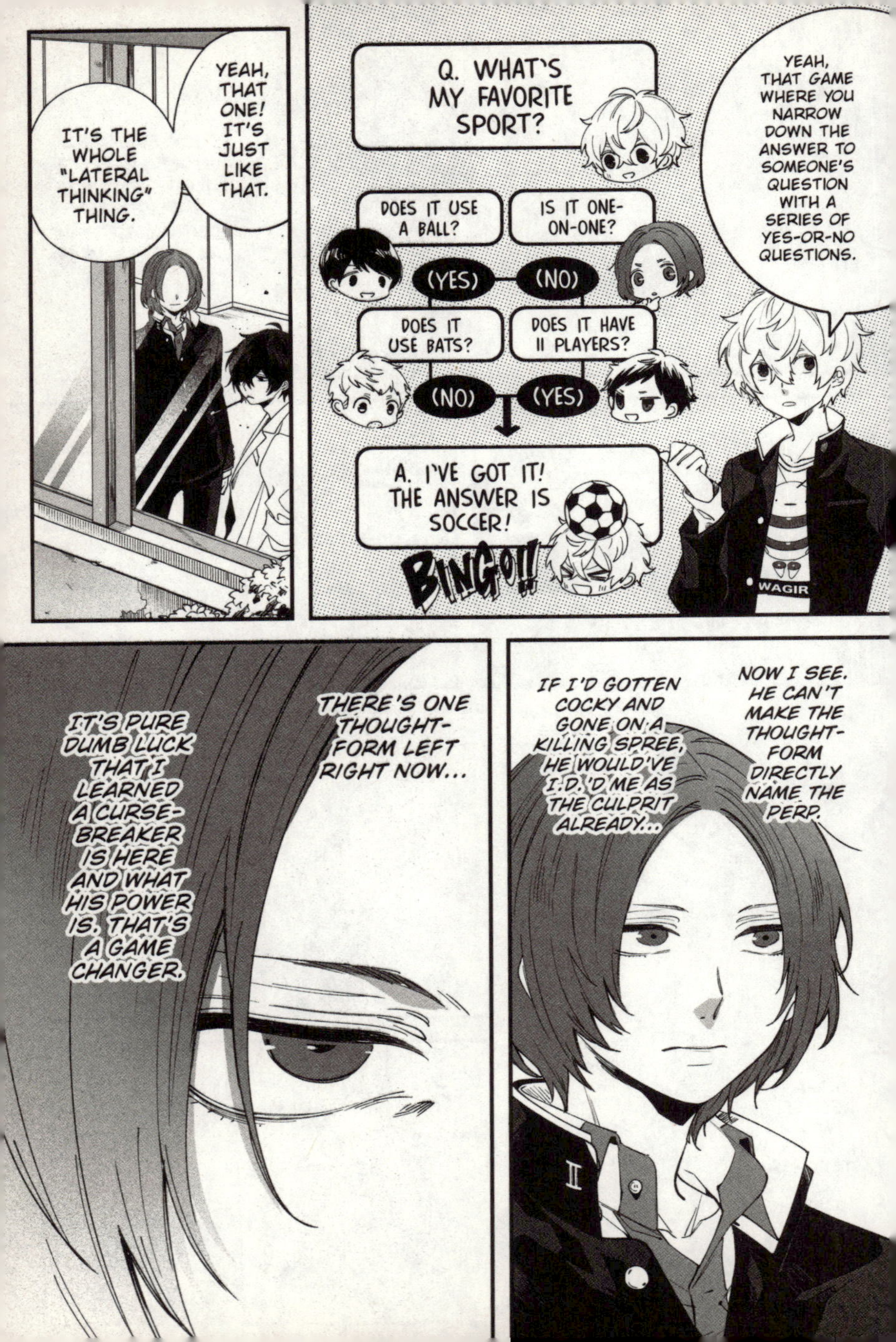
YEAH, THAT GAME WHERE YOU NARROW DOWN THE ANSWER TO SOMEONE'S QUESTION WITH A SERIES OF YES-OR-NO QUESTIONS.
Q. WHAT'S MY FAVORITE SPORT?
IS IT ONE-ON-ONE?
DOES IT USE A BALL?
(YES)
(NO)
DOES IT HAVE 11 PLAYERS?
DOES IT USE BATS?
(NO)
(YES)
A. I'VE GOT IT! THE ANSWER IS SOCCER!
BINGO!!
WAGIR
YEAH, THAT ONE! IT'S JUST LIKE THAT.
IT'S THE WHOLE "LATERAL THINKING" THING.
NOW I SEE. HE CAN'T MAKE THE THOUGHT-FORM DIRECTLY NAME THE PERP.
IF I'D GOTTEN COCKY AND GONE ON A KILLING SPREE, HE WOULD'VE I.D.'D ME AS THE CULPRIT ALREADY...
THERE'S ONE THOUGHT-FORM LEFT RIGHT NOW...
IT'S PURE DUMB LUCK THAT I LEARNED A CURSE-BREAKER IS HERE AND WHAT HIS POWER IS. THAT'S A GAME CHANGER.

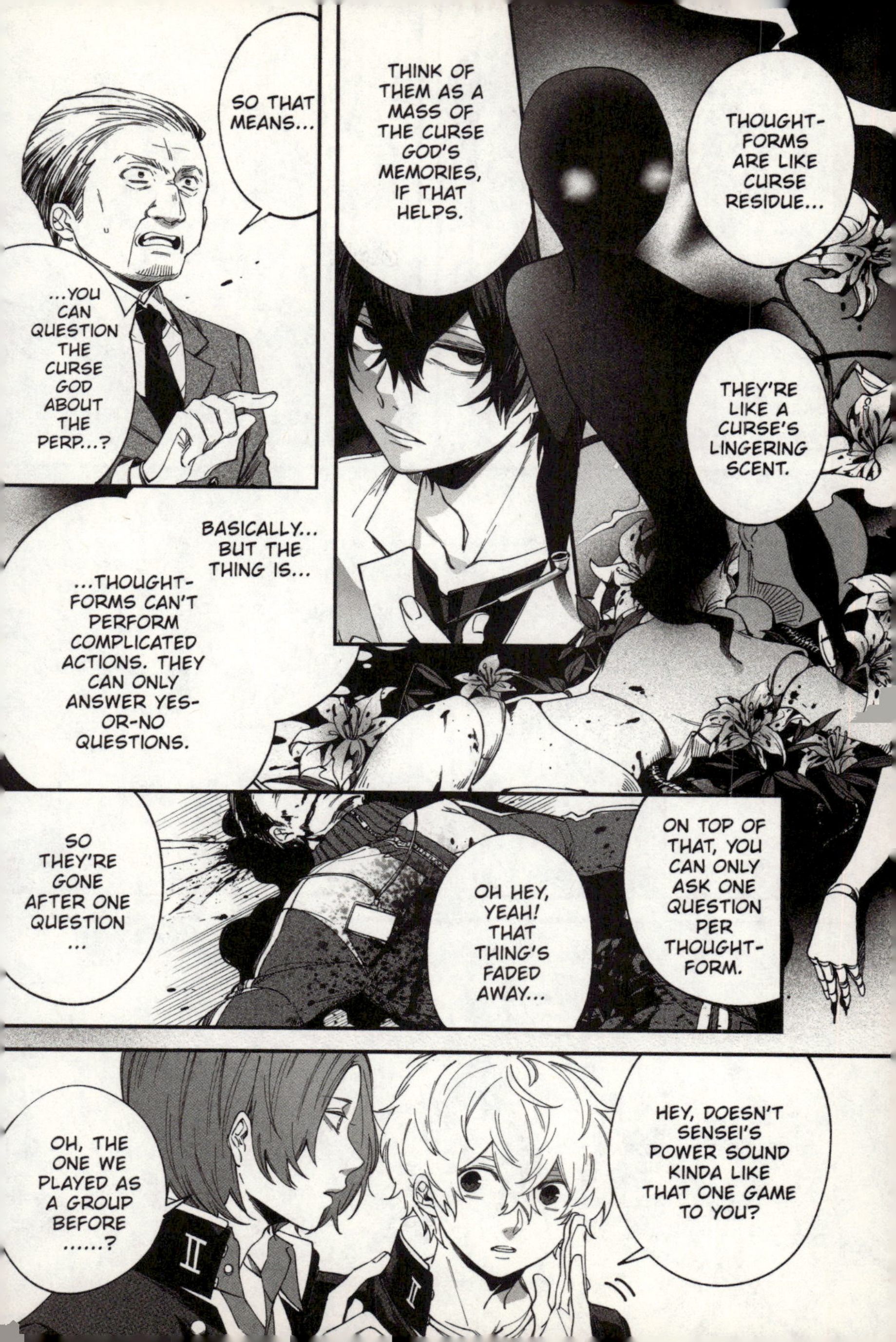
THOUGHT-FORMS ARE LIKE CURSE RESIDUE...
THEY'RE LIKE A CURSE'S LINGERING SCENT.
THINK OF THEM AS A MASS OF THE CURSE GOD'S MEMORIES, IF THAT HELPS.
SO THAT MEANS...
...YOU CAN QUESTION THE CURSE GOD ABOUT THE PERP...?
BASICALLY... BUT THE THING IS...
...THOUGHT-FORMS CAN'T PERFORM COMPLICATED ACTIONS. THEY CAN ONLY ANSWER YES-OR-NO QUESTIONS.
ON TOP OF THAT, YOU CAN ONLY ASK ONE QUESTION PER THOUGHT-FORM.
OH HEY, YEAH! THAT THING'S FADED AWAY...
SO THEY'RE GONE AFTER ONE QUESTION ...
HEY, DOESN'T SENSEI'S POWER SOUND KINDA LIKE THAT ONE GAME TO YOU?
OH, THE ONE WE PLAYED AS A GROUP BEFORE ......?

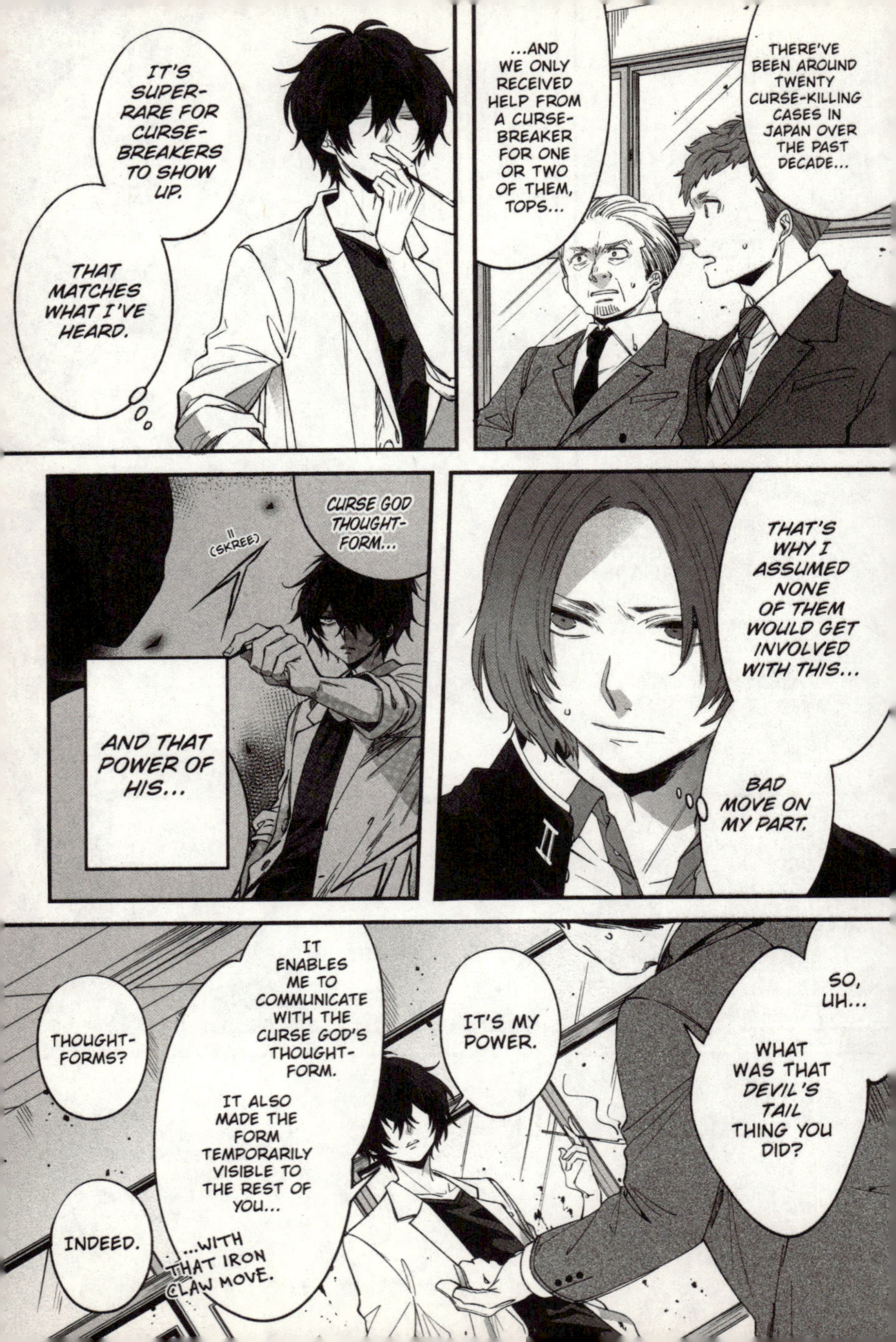
THERE'VE BEEN AROUND TWENTY CURSE-KILLING CASES IN JAPAN OVER THE PAST DECADE...
...AND WE ONLY RECEIVED HELP FROM A CURSE-BREAKER FOR ONE OR TWO OF THEM, TOPS...
IT'S SUPER-RARE FOR CURSE-BREAKERS TO SHOW UP.
THAT MATCHES WHAT I'VE HEARD.
THAT'S WHY I ASSUMED NONE OF THEM WOULD GET INVOLVED WITH THIS...
BAD MOVE ON MY PART.
CURSE GOD THOUGHT-FORM...
(SKREE)
AND THAT POWER OF HIS...
SO, UH...
WHAT WAS THAT DEVIL'S TAIL THING YOU DID?
IT'S MY POWER.
IT ENABLES ME TO COMMUNICATE WITH THE CURSE GOD'S THOUGHT-FORM.
IT ALSO MADE THE FORM TEMPORARILY VISIBLE TO THE REST OF YOU...
...WITH THAT IRON CLAW MOVE.
THOUGHT-FORMS?
INDEED.

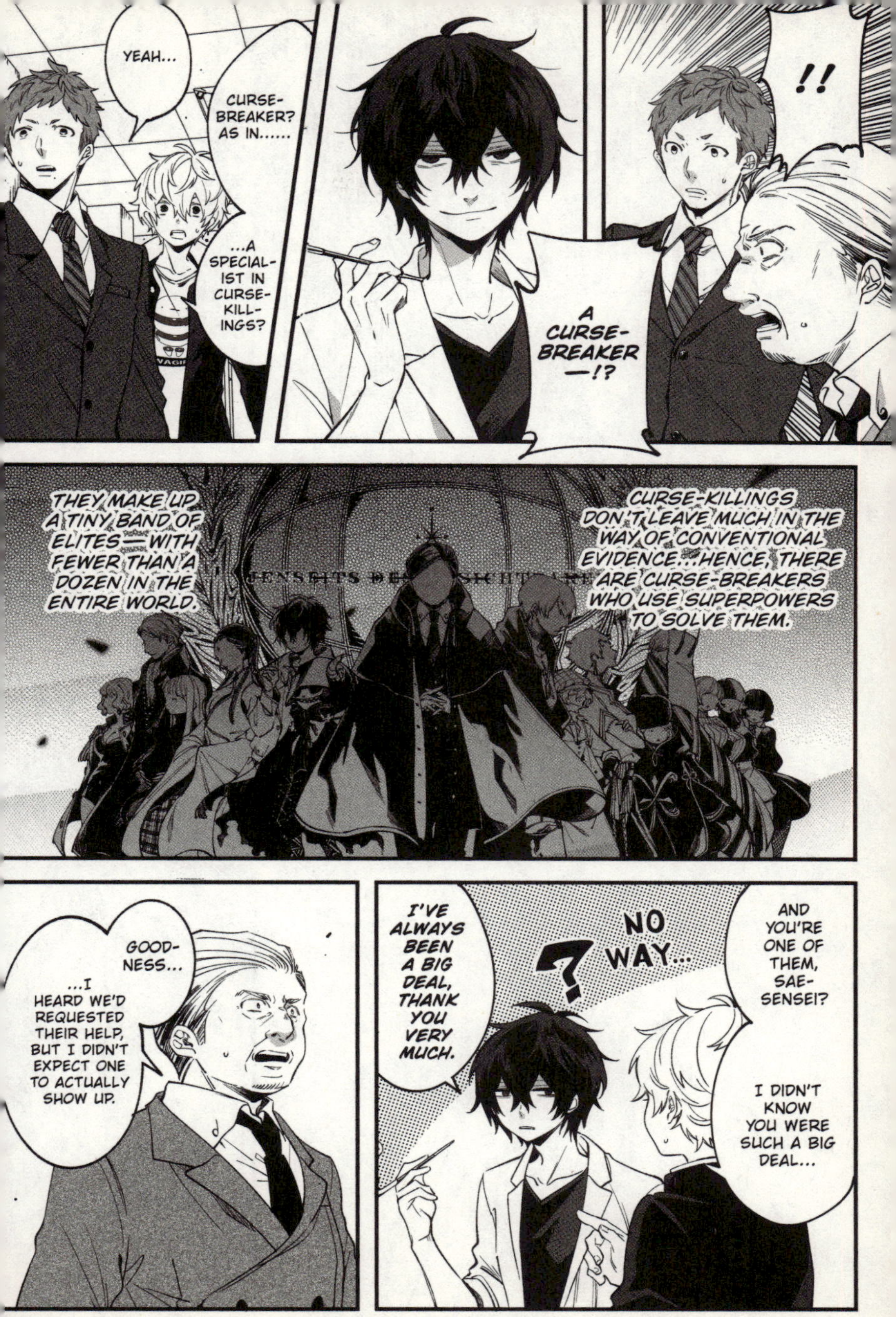
!!
A CURSE-BREAKER—!?
CURSE-BREAKER? AS IN......
YEAH...
...A SPECIALIST IN CURSE-KILLINGS?
CURSE-KILLINGS DON'T LEAVE MUCH IN THE WAY OF CONVENTIONAL EVIDENCE...HENCE, THERE ARE CURSE-BREAKERS WHO USE SUPERPOWERS TO SOLVE THEM.
THEY MAKE UP A TINY BAND OF ELITES—WITH FEWER THAN A DOZEN IN THE ENTIRE WORLD.
AND YOU'RE ONE OF THEM, SAE-SENSEI?
NO WAY...
I DIDN'T KNOW YOU WERE SUCH A BIG DEAL...
?
I'VE ALWAYS BEEN A BIG DEAL, THANK YOU VERY MUCH.
GOODNESS...
...I HEARD WE'D REQUESTED THEIR HELP, BUT I DIDN'T EXPECT ONE TO ACTUALLY SHOW UP.

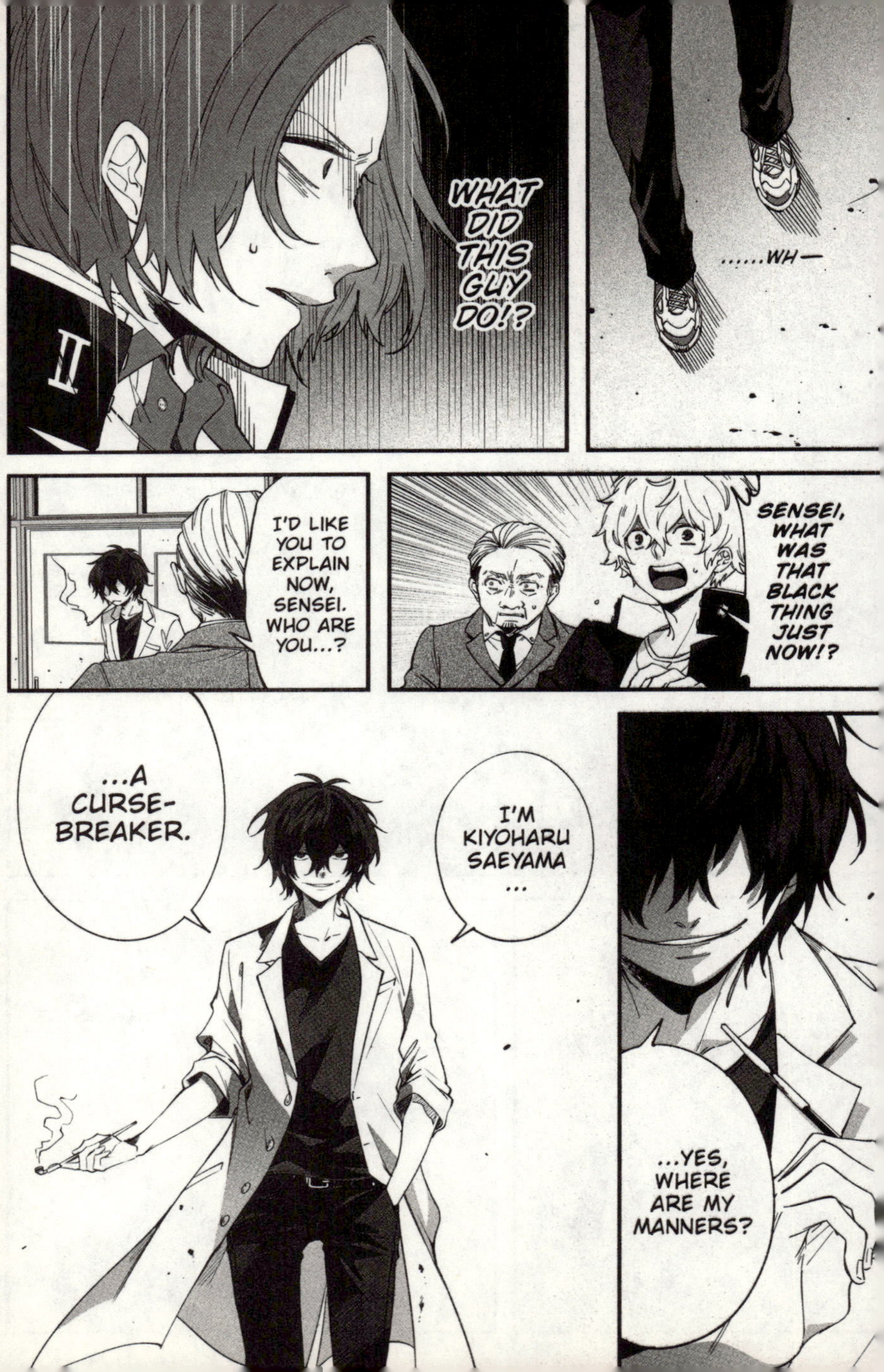
......WH—
WHAT DID THIS GUY DO!?
SENSEI, WHAT WAS THAT BLACK THING JUST NOW!?
I'D LIKE YOU TO EXPLAIN NOW, SENSEI. WHO ARE YOU...?
...YES, WHERE ARE MY MANNERS?
I'M KIYOHARU SAEYAMA ...
...A CURSE-BREAKER.

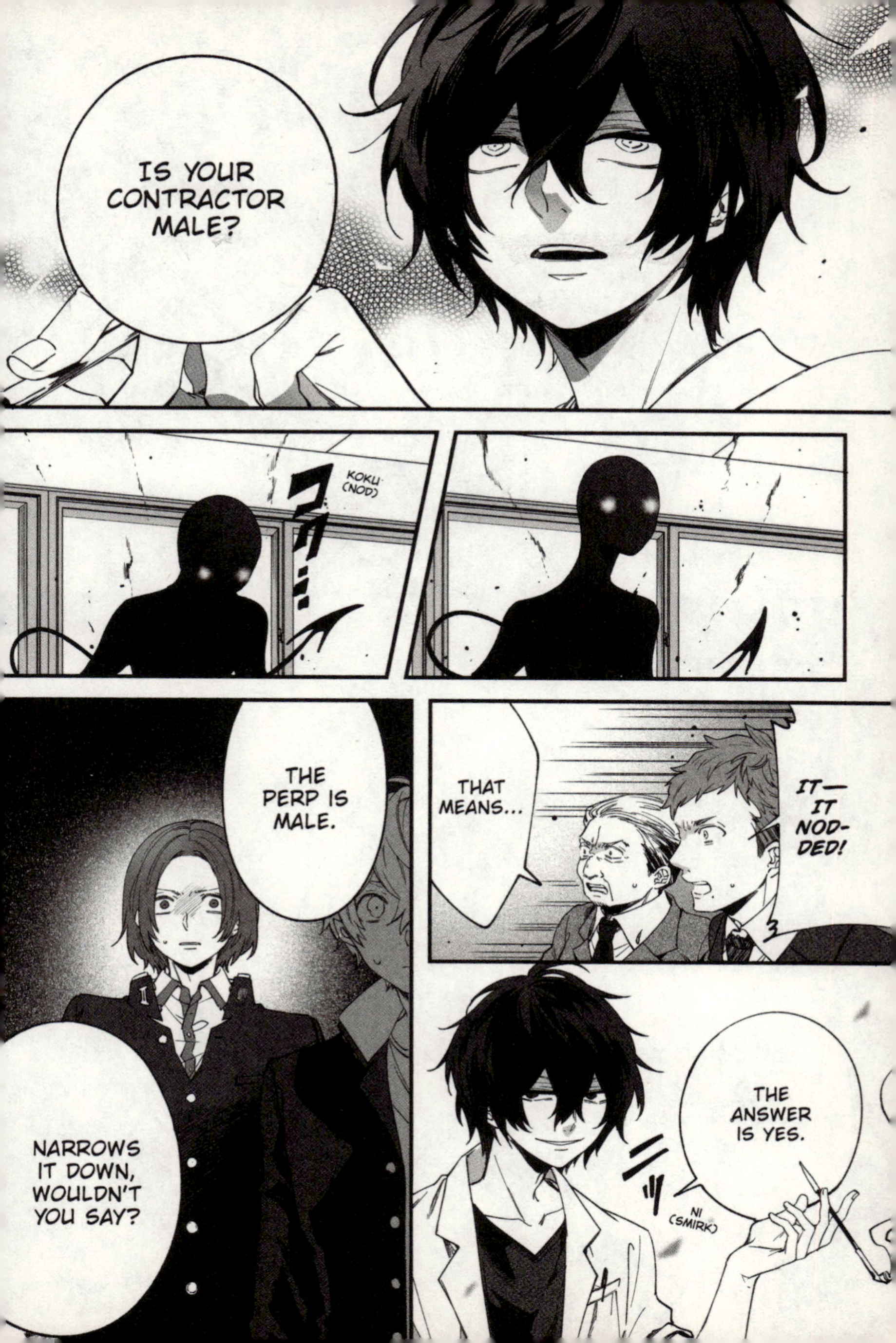
IS YOUR CONTRACTOR MALE?
KOKU (NOD)
IT— IT NOD-DED!
THAT MEANS...
THE ANSWER IS YES.
NI (SMIRK)
THE PERP IS MALE.
NARROWS IT DOWN, WOULDN'T YOU SAY?

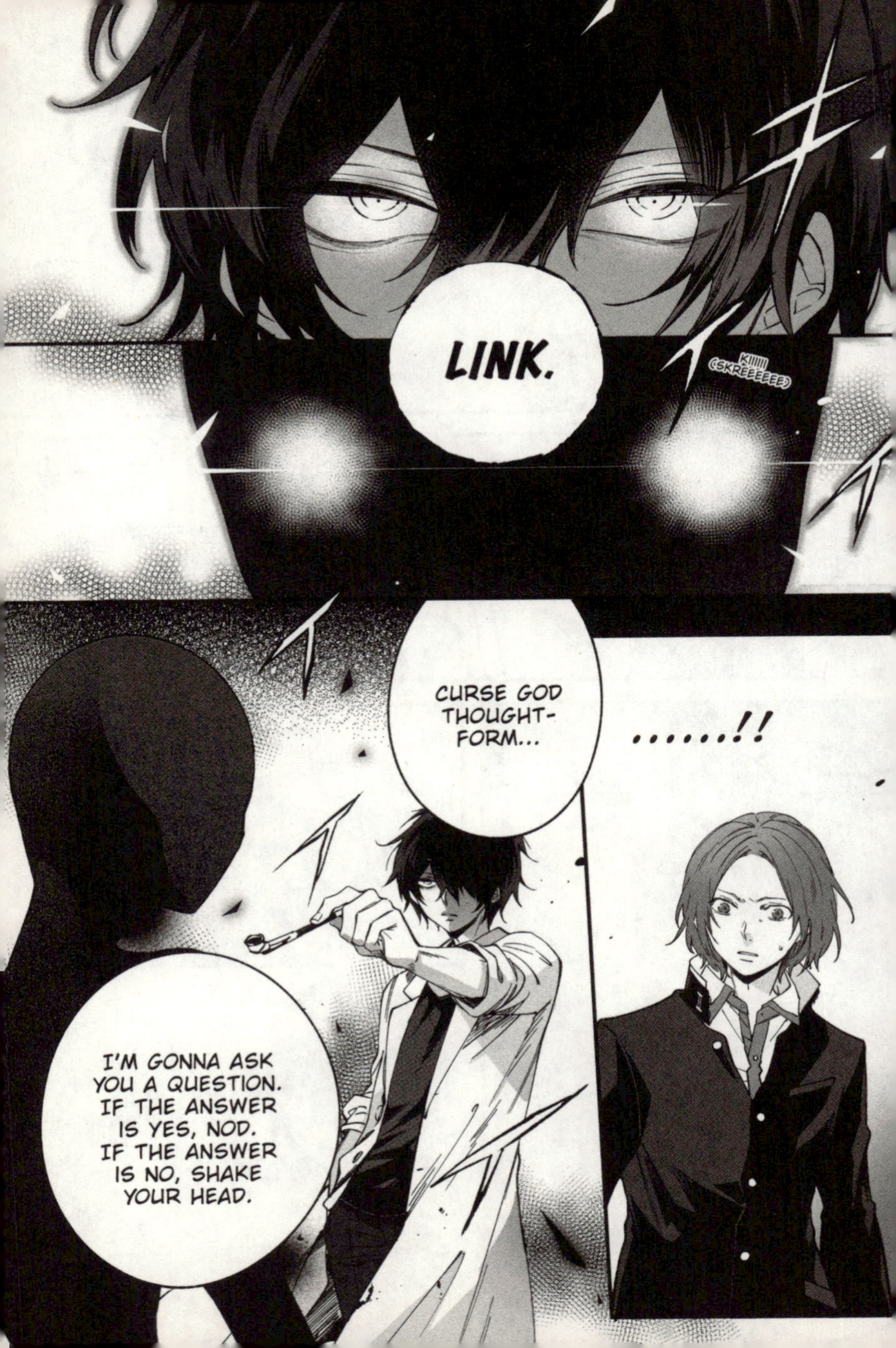
LINK.
KIIIIII (SKREEEEEEE)
......!!
CURSE GOD THOUGHT-FORM...
I'M GONNA ASK YOU A QUESTION. IF THE ANSWER IS YES, NOD. IF THE ANSWER IS NO, SHAKE YOUR HEAD.

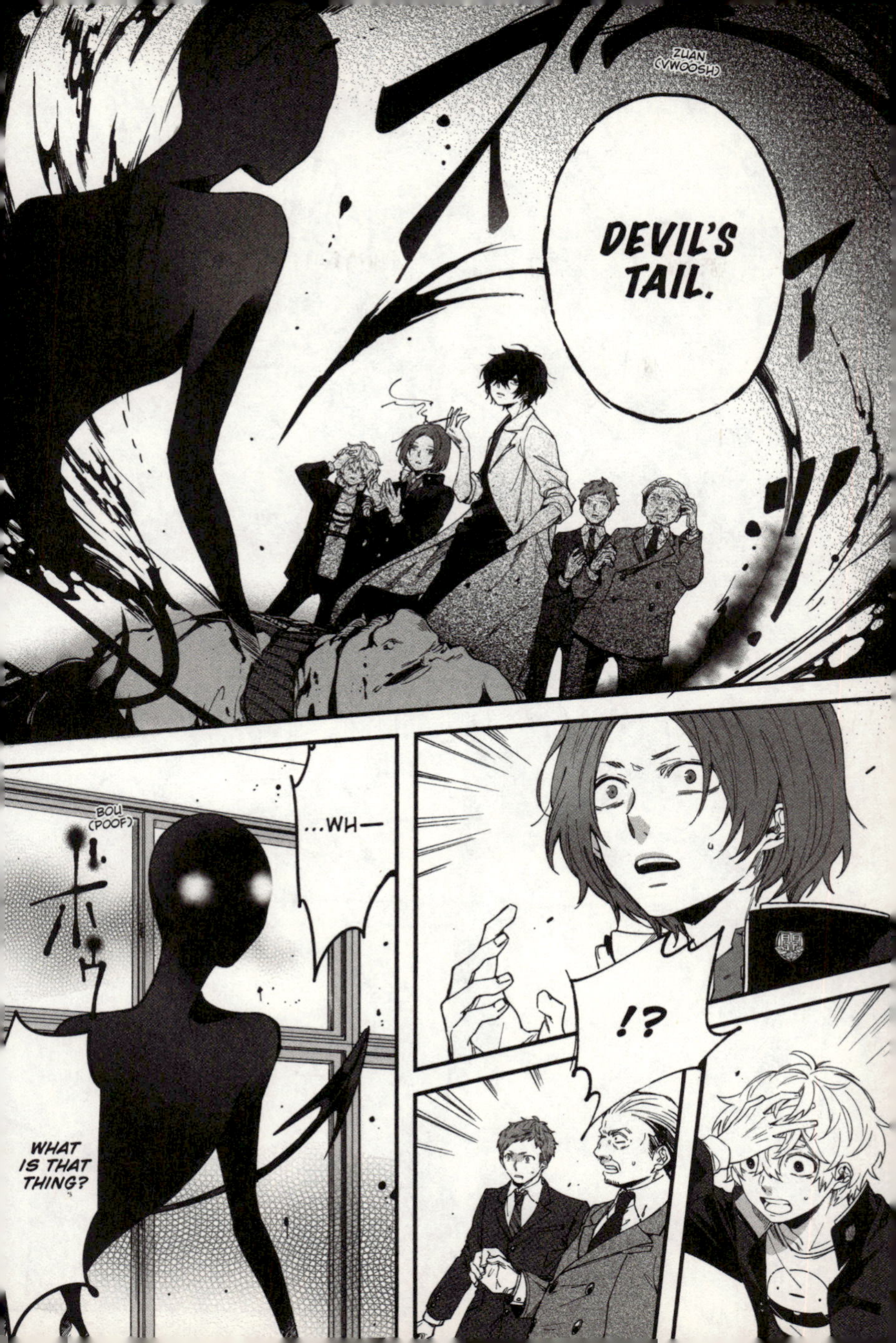
ZUAN
(VWOOSH)
DEVIL'S TAIL.
!?
...WH—
BOU
(POOF)
WHAT IS THAT THING?

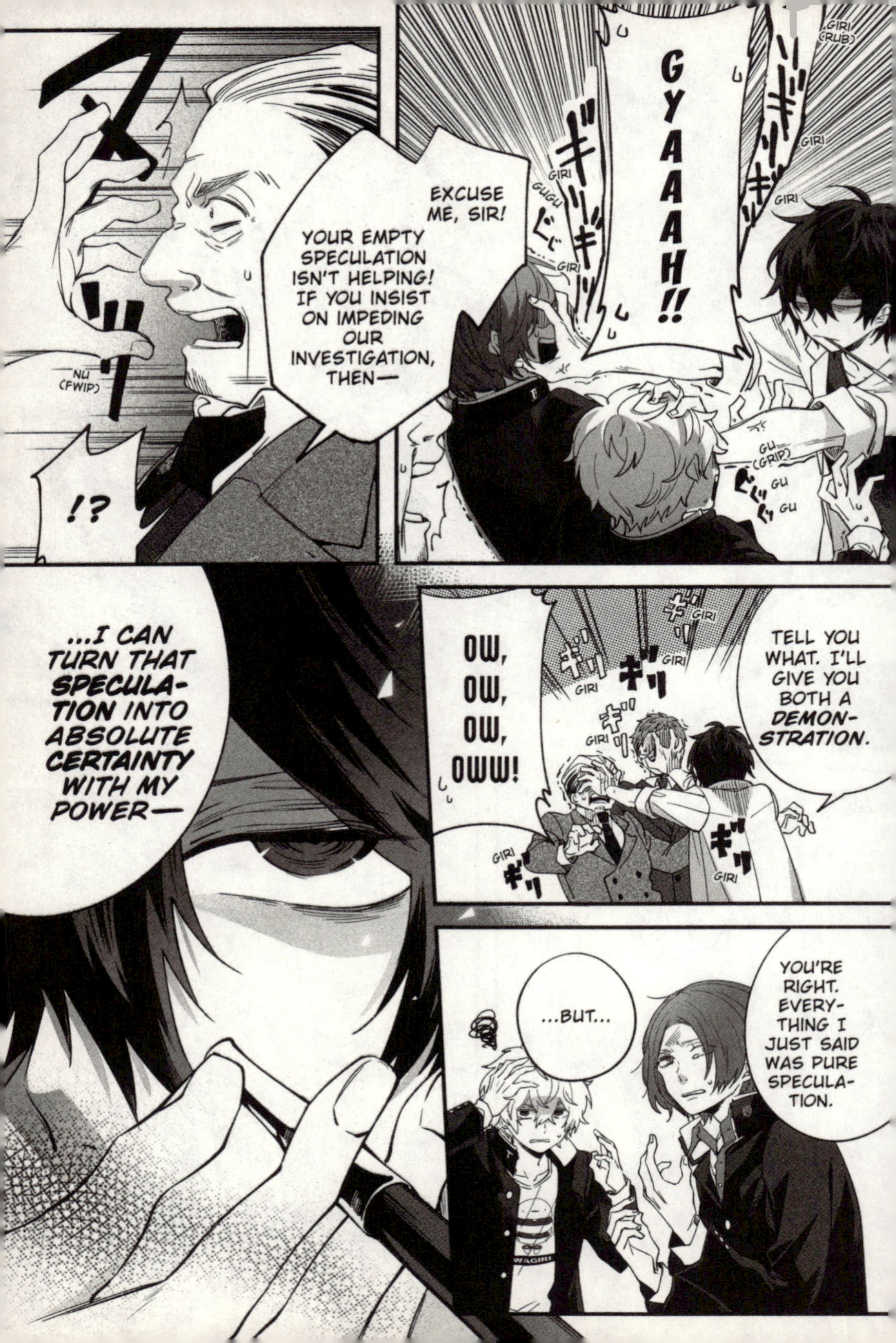

GIRI (RUB)
GYAAAH!!
GIRI
GIRI
GUGU
GIRI
GU (GRIP)
GU
GU
EXCUSE ME, SIR!
YOUR EMPTY SPECULATION ISN'T HELPING! IF YOU INSIST ON IMPEDING OUR INVESTIGATION, THEN—
NU (FWIP)
!?
TELL YOU WHAT. I'LL GIVE YOU BOTH A DEMONSTRATION.
GIRI
GIRI
GIRI
GIRI
OW, OW, OW, OWW!
GIRI
GIRI
YOU'RE RIGHT. EVERYTHING I JUST SAID WAS PURE SPECULATION.
...BUT...
...I CAN TURN THAT SPECULATION INTO ABSOLUTE CERTAINTY WITH MY POWER—

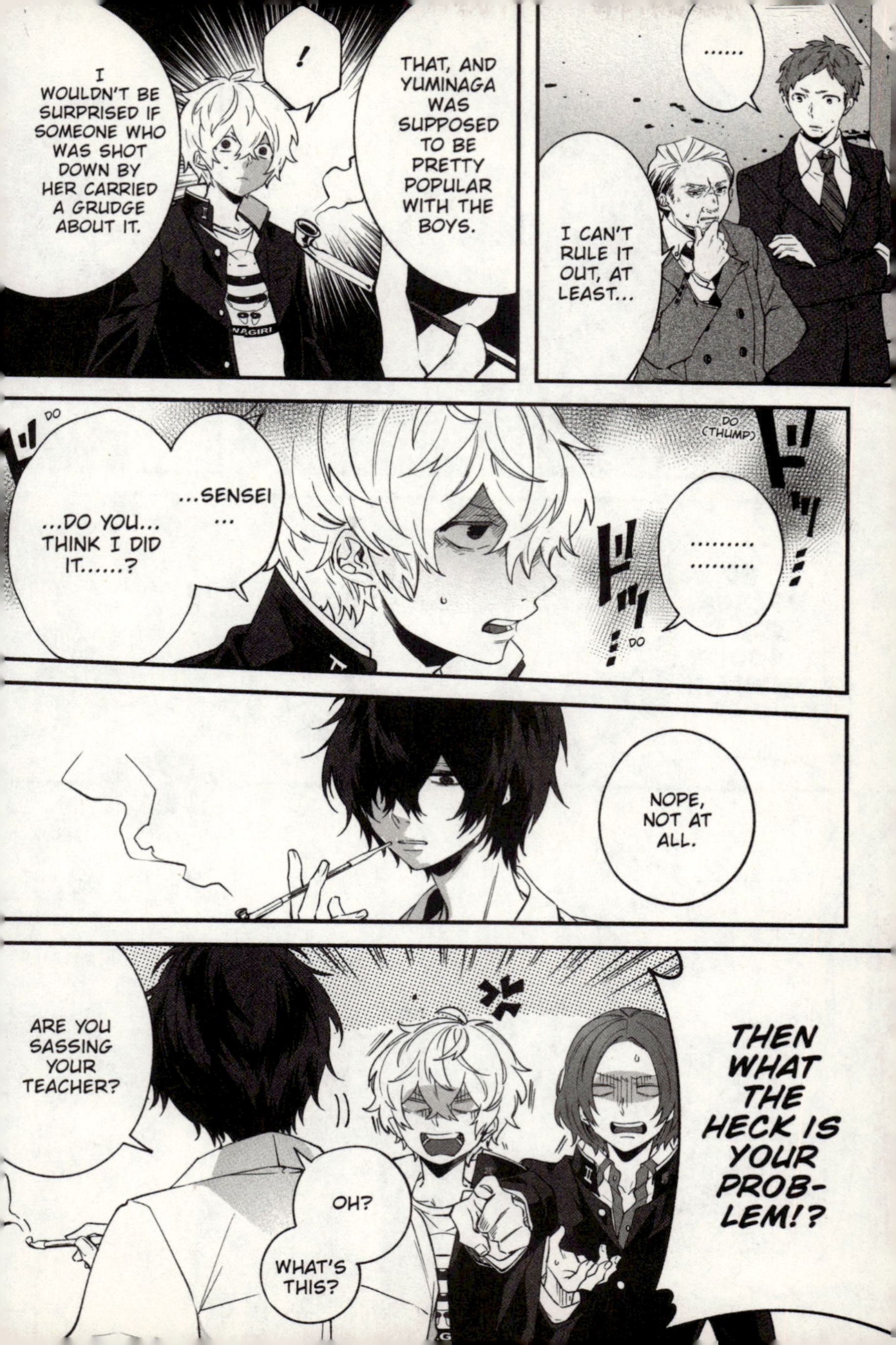
......
I CAN'T RULE IT OUT, AT LEAST...
THAT, AND YUMINAGA WAS SUPPOSED TO BE PRETTY POPULAR WITH THE BOYS.
!
I WOULDN'T BE SURPRISED IF SOMEONE WHO WAS SHOT DOWN BY HER CARRIED A GRUDGE ABOUT IT.
DO (THUMP)
....
....
DO
...SENSEI ...
...DO YOU... THINK I DID IT......?
DO
NOPE, NOT AT ALL.
THEN WHAT THE HECK IS YOUR PROB-LEM!?
OH?
WHAT'S THIS?
ARE YOU SASSING YOUR TEACHER?

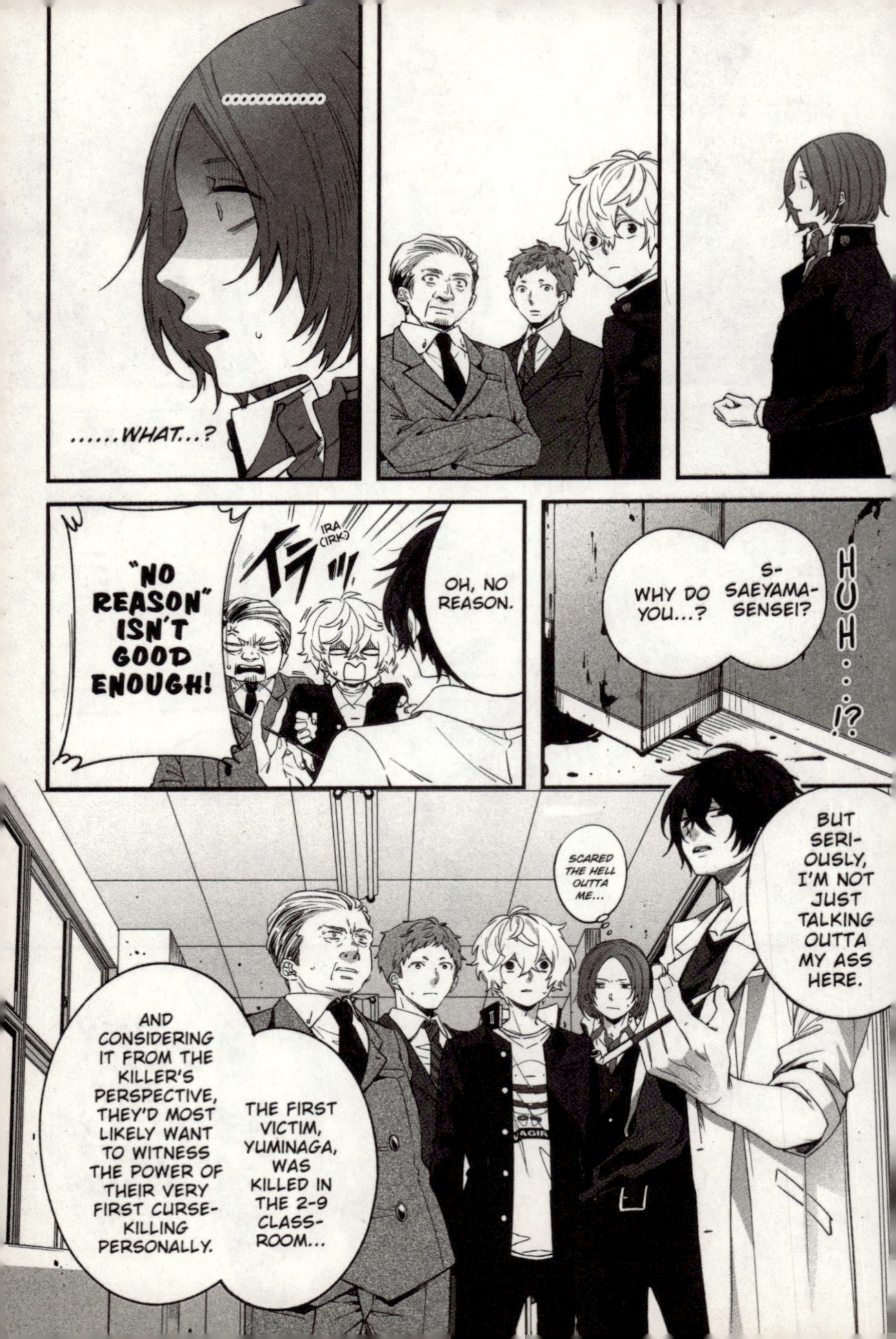
......WHAT...?
HUH...!?
S-SAEYAMA-SENSEI?
WHY DO YOU...?
OH, NO REASON.
IRA (IRK)
"NO REASON" ISN'T GOOD ENOUGH!
BUT SERIOUSLY, I'M NOT JUST TALKING OUTTA MY ASS HERE.
SCARED THE HELL OUTTA ME...
THE FIRST VICTIM, YUMINAGA, WAS KILLED IN THE 2-9 CLASSROOM...
AND CONSIDERING IT FROM THE KILLER'S PERSPECTIVE, THEY'D MOST LIKELY WANT TO WITNESS THE POWER OF THEIR VERY FIRST CURSE-KILLING PERSONALLY.

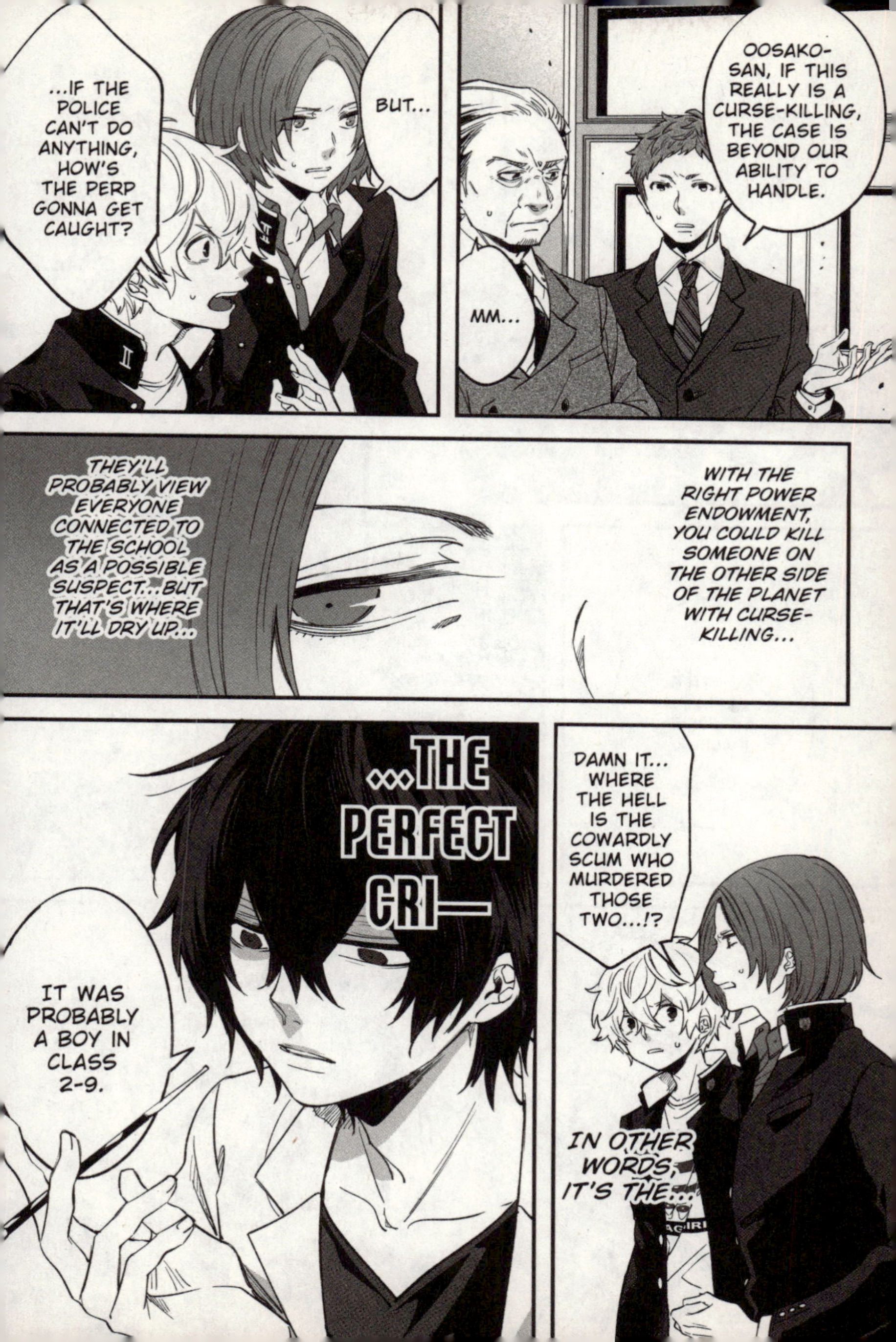
OOSAKO-SAN, IF THIS REALLY IS A CURSE-KILLING, THE CASE IS BEYOND OUR ABILITY TO HANDLE.
MM...
BUT...
...IF THE POLICE CAN'T DO ANYTHING, HOW'S THE PERP GONNA GET CAUGHT?
WITH THE RIGHT POWER ENDOWMENT, YOU COULD KILL SOMEONE ON THE OTHER SIDE OF THE PLANET WITH CURSE-KILLING...
THEY'LL PROBABLY VIEW EVERYONE CONNECTED TO THE SCHOOL AS A POSSIBLE SUSPECT...BUT THAT'S WHERE IT'LL DRY UP...
DAMN IT... WHERE THE HELL IS THE COWARDLY SCUM WHO MURDERED THOSE TWO...!?
IN OTHER WORDS, IT'S THE...
...THE PERFECT CRI—
IT WAS PROBABLY A BOY IN CLASS 2-9.

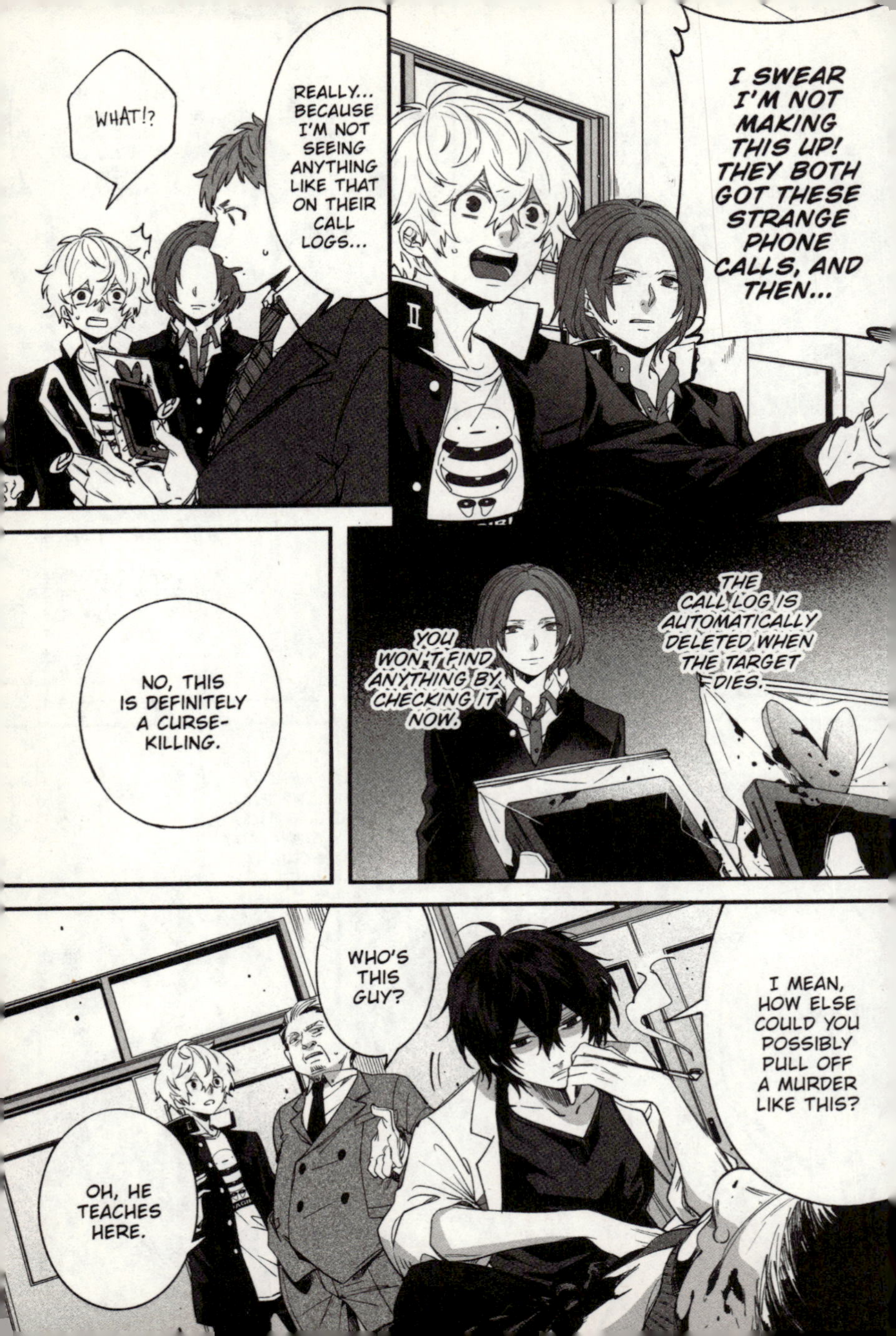
I SWEAR I'M NOT MAKING THIS UP! THEY BOTH GOT THESE STRANGE PHONE CALLS, AND THEN...
REALLY... BECAUSE I'M NOT SEEING ANYTHING LIKE THAT ON THEIR CALL LOGS...
WHAT!?
THE CALL LOG IS AUTOMATICALLY DELETED WHEN THE TARGET DIES.
YOU WON'T FIND ANYTHING BY CHECKING IT NOW.
NO, THIS IS DEFINITELY A CURSE-KILLING.
I MEAN, HOW ELSE COULD YOU POSSIBLY PULL OFF A MURDER LIKE THIS?
WHO'S THIS GUY?
OH, HE TEACHES HERE.

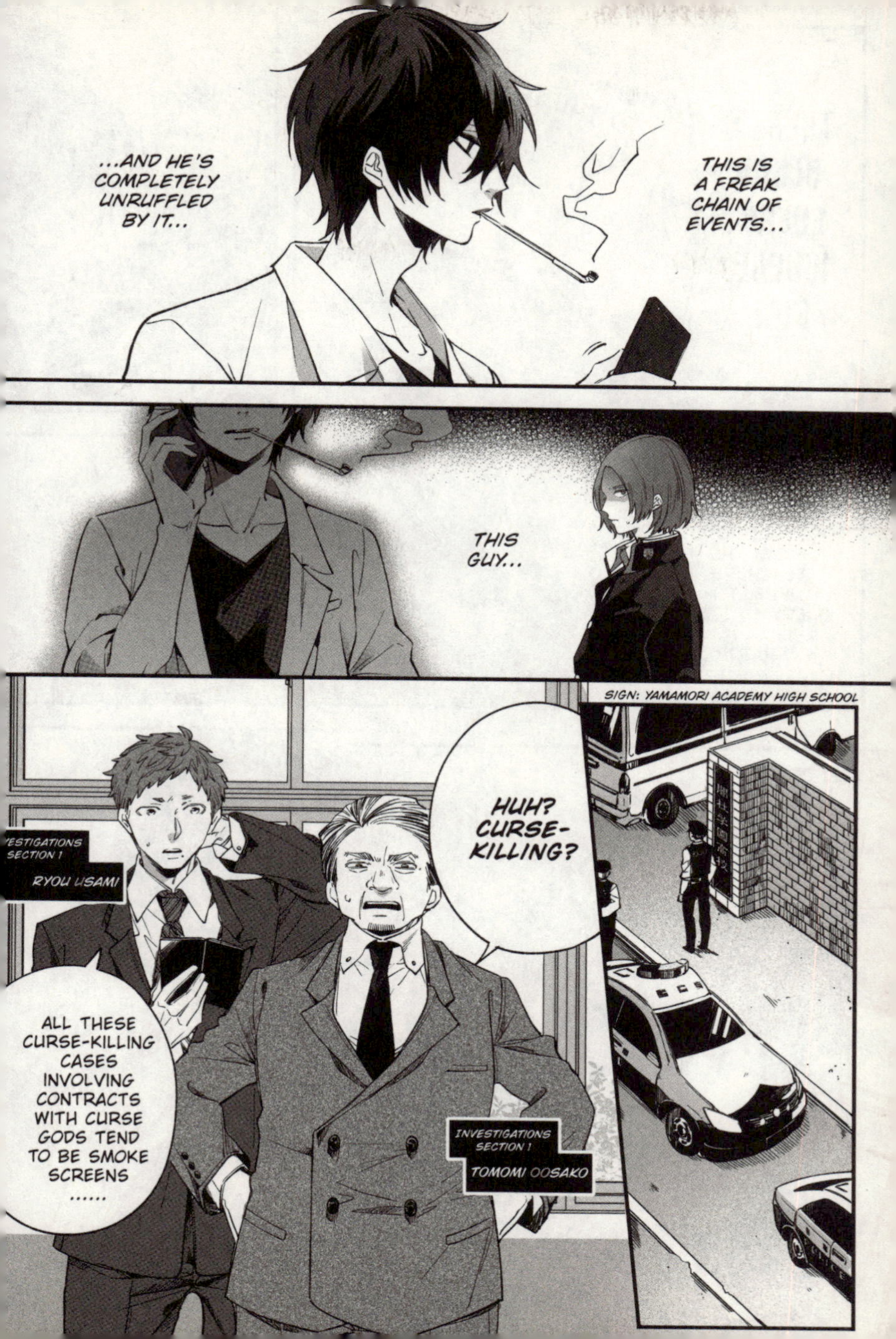
THIS IS A FREAK CHAIN OF EVENTS...
...AND HE'S COMPLETELY UNRUFFLED BY IT...
THIS GUY...
SIGN: YAMAMORI ACADEMY HIGH SCHOOL
HUH? CURSE-KILLING?
VESTIGATIONS SECTION 1
RYOU USAMI
INVESTIGATIONS SECTION 1
TOMOMI OOSAKO
ALL THESE CURSE-KILLING CASES INVOLVING CONTRACTS WITH CURSE GODS TEND TO BE SMOKE SCREENS ......

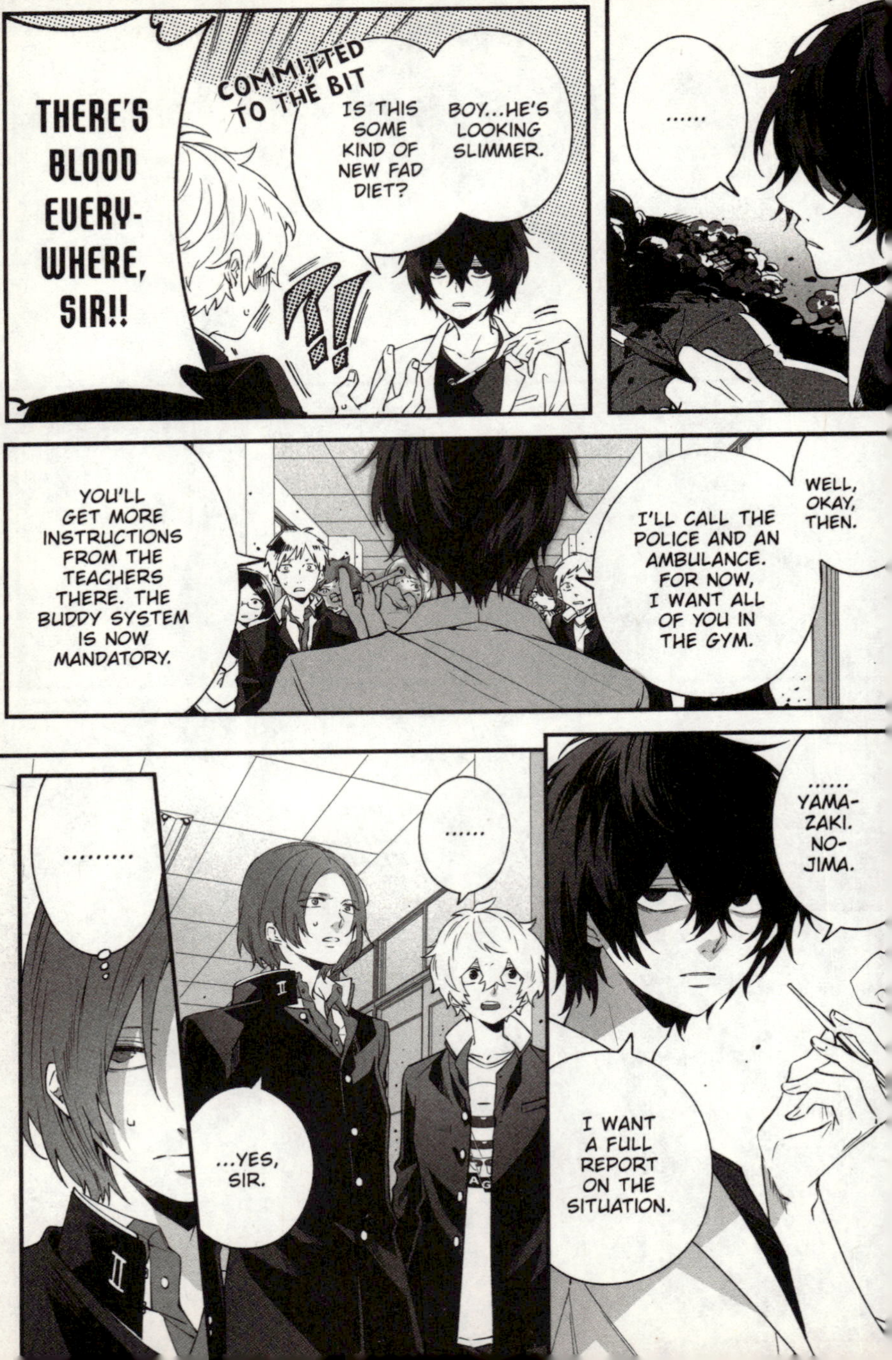
......
BOY...HE'S LOOKING SLIMMER.
IS THIS SOME KIND OF NEW FAD DIET?
COMMITTED TO THE BIT
?!
THERE'S BLOOD EVERYWHERE, SIR!!
WELL, OKAY, THEN.
I'LL CALL THE POLICE AND AN AMBULANCE. FOR NOW, I WANT ALL OF YOU IN THE GYM.
YOU'LL GET MORE INSTRUCTIONS FROM THE TEACHERS THERE. THE BUDDY SYSTEM IS NOW MANDATORY.
......YAMAZAKI. NOJIMA.
I WANT A FULL REPORT ON THE SITUATION.
......
....
...YES, SIR.

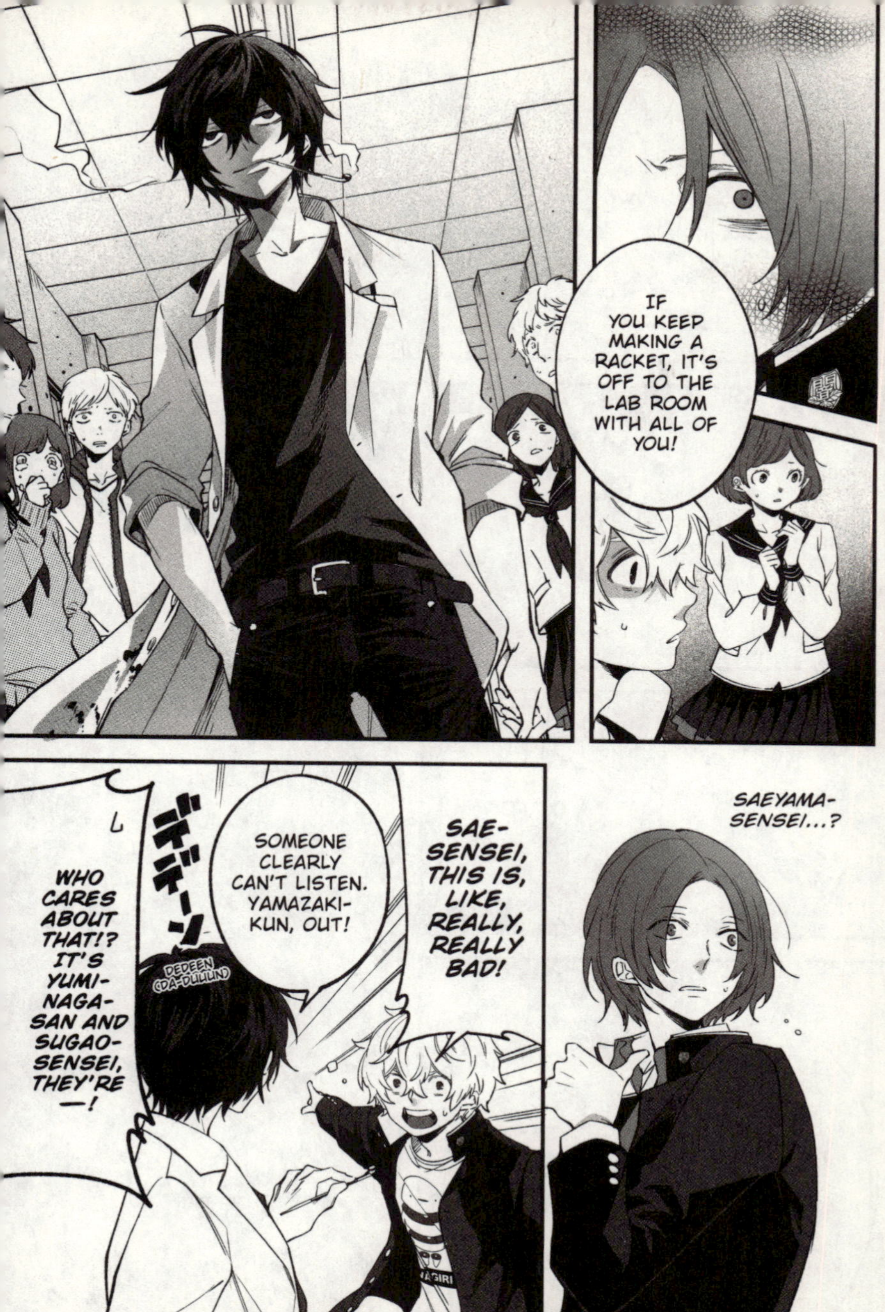
IF YOU KEEP MAKING A RACKET, IT'S OFF TO THE LAB ROOM WITH ALL OF YOU!
SAEYAMA-SENSEI...?
SAE-SENSEI, THIS IS, LIKE, REALLY, REALLY BAD!
SOMEONE CLEARLY CAN'T LISTEN. YAMAZAKI-KUN, OUT!
DEDEEN (DA-DUUUN)
WHO CARES ABOUT THAT!? IT'S YUMINAGA-SAN AND SUGAO-SENSEI, THEY'RE—!

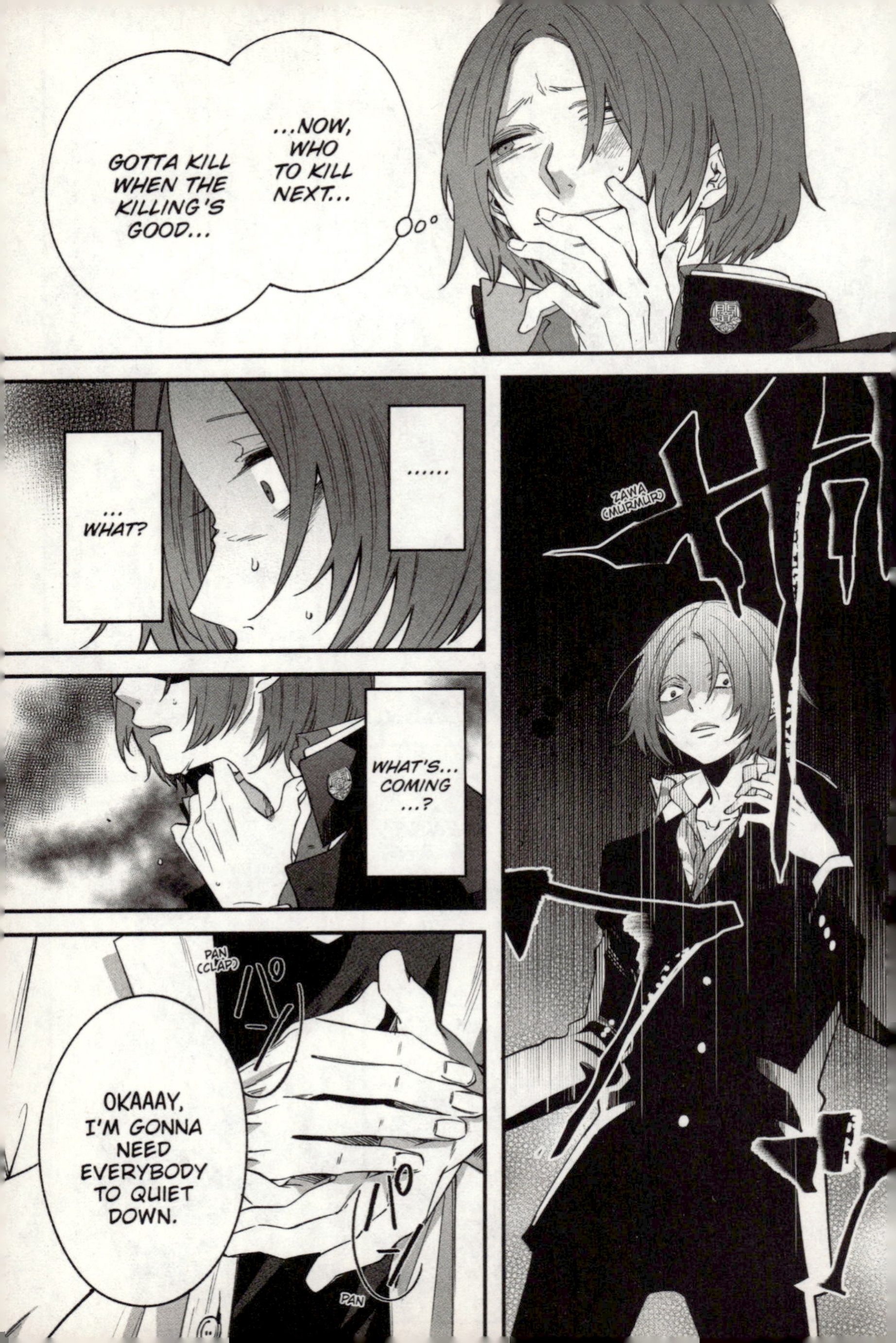
...NOW, WHO TO KILL NEXT...
GOTTA KILL WHEN THE KILLING'S GOOD...
ZAWA (MURMUR)
......
... WHAT?
WHAT'S... COMING ...?
PAN (CLAP)
OKAAAY, I'M GONNA NEED EVERYBODY TO QUIET DOWN.
PAN

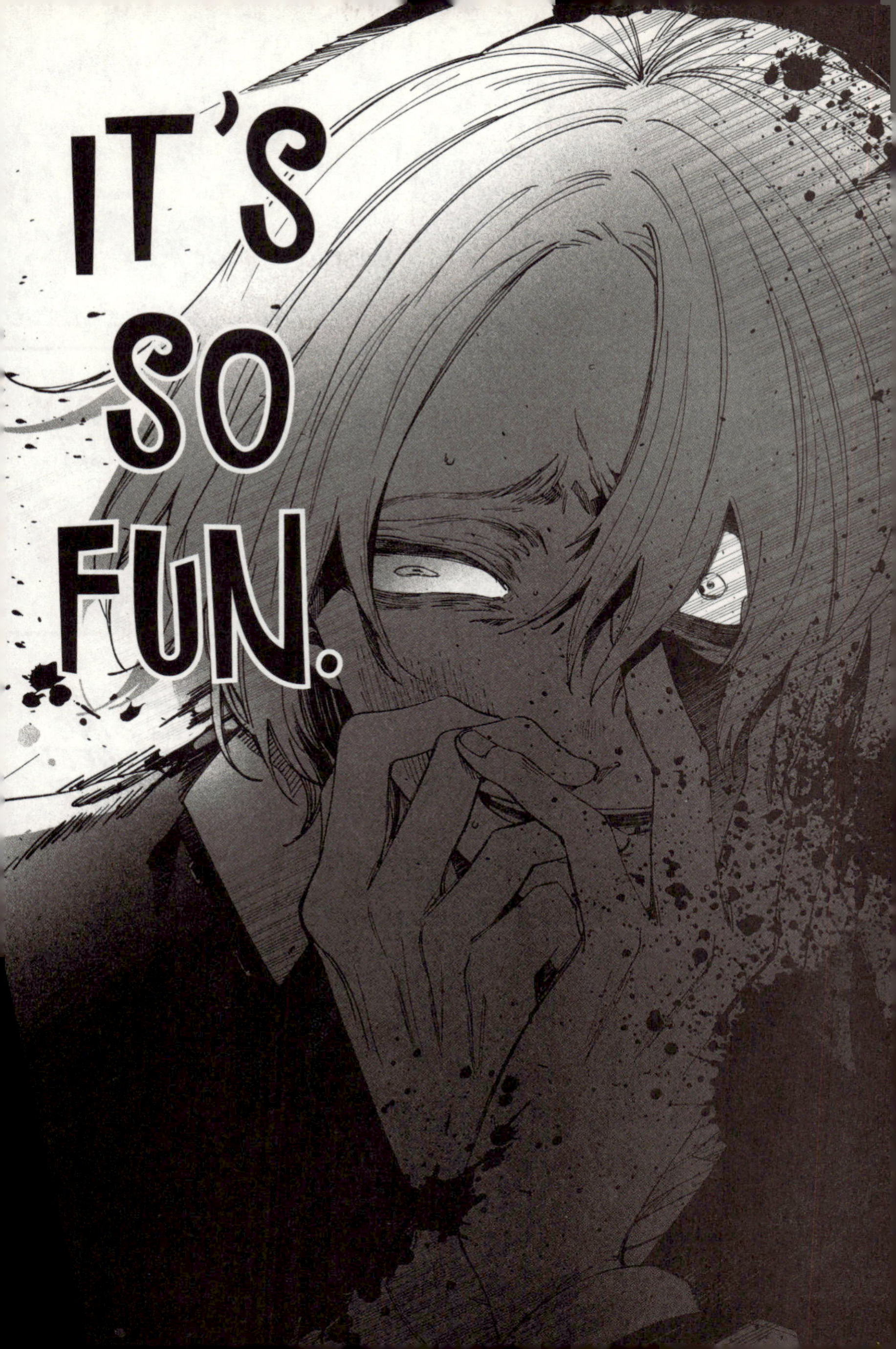
IT'S SO FUN.

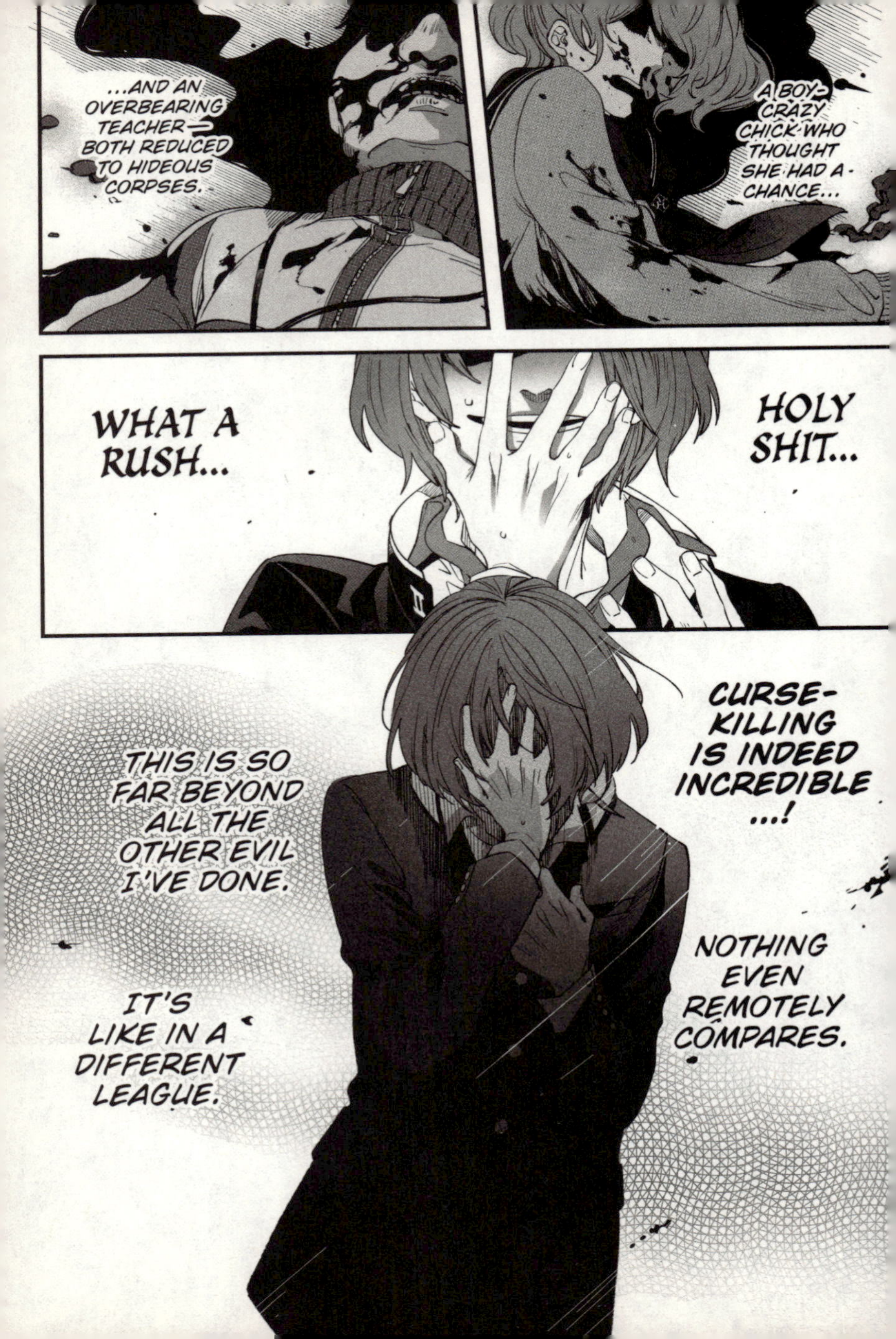
A BOY-CRAZY CHICK WHO THOUGHT SHE HAD A CHANCE...
...AND AN OVERBEARING TEACHER—BOTH REDUCED TO HIDEOUS CORPSES.
HOLY SHIT...
WHAT A RUSH...
CURSE-KILLING IS INDEED INCREDIBLE...!
THIS IS SO FAR BEYOND ALL THE OTHER EVIL I'VE DONE.
NOTHING EVEN REMOTELY COMPARES.
IT'S LIKE IN A DIFFERENT LEAGUE.

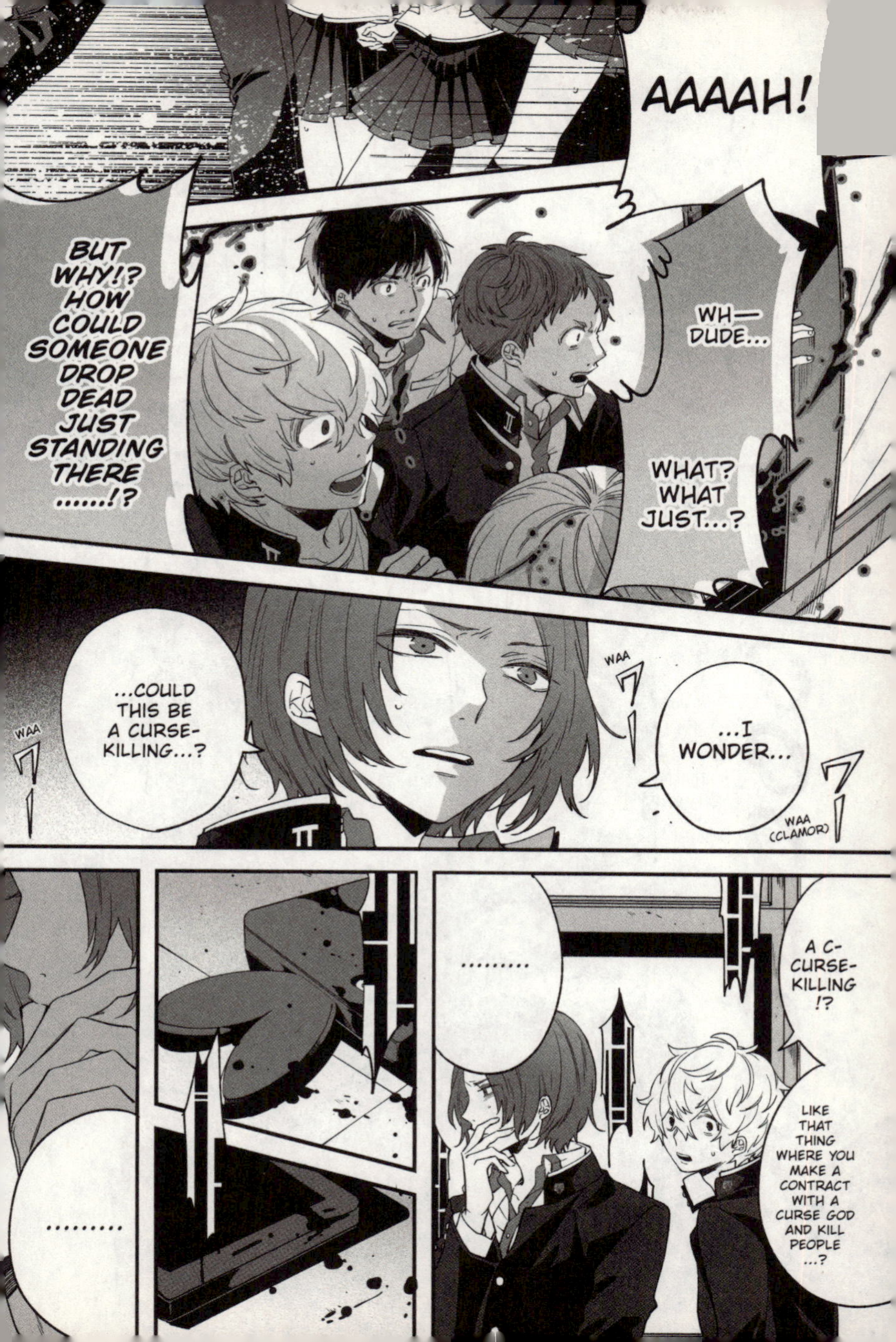
AAAAH!
WH— DUDE...
WHAT? WHAT JUST...?
BUT WHY!? HOW COULD SOMEONE DROP DEAD JUST STANDING THERE......!?
WAA (CLAMOR)
...I WONDER...
WAA
...COULD THIS BE A CURSE-KILLING...?
WAA
A C-CURSE-KILLING!?
LIKE THAT THING WHERE YOU MAKE A CONTRACT WITH A CURSE GOD AND KILL PEOPLE...?
....
....

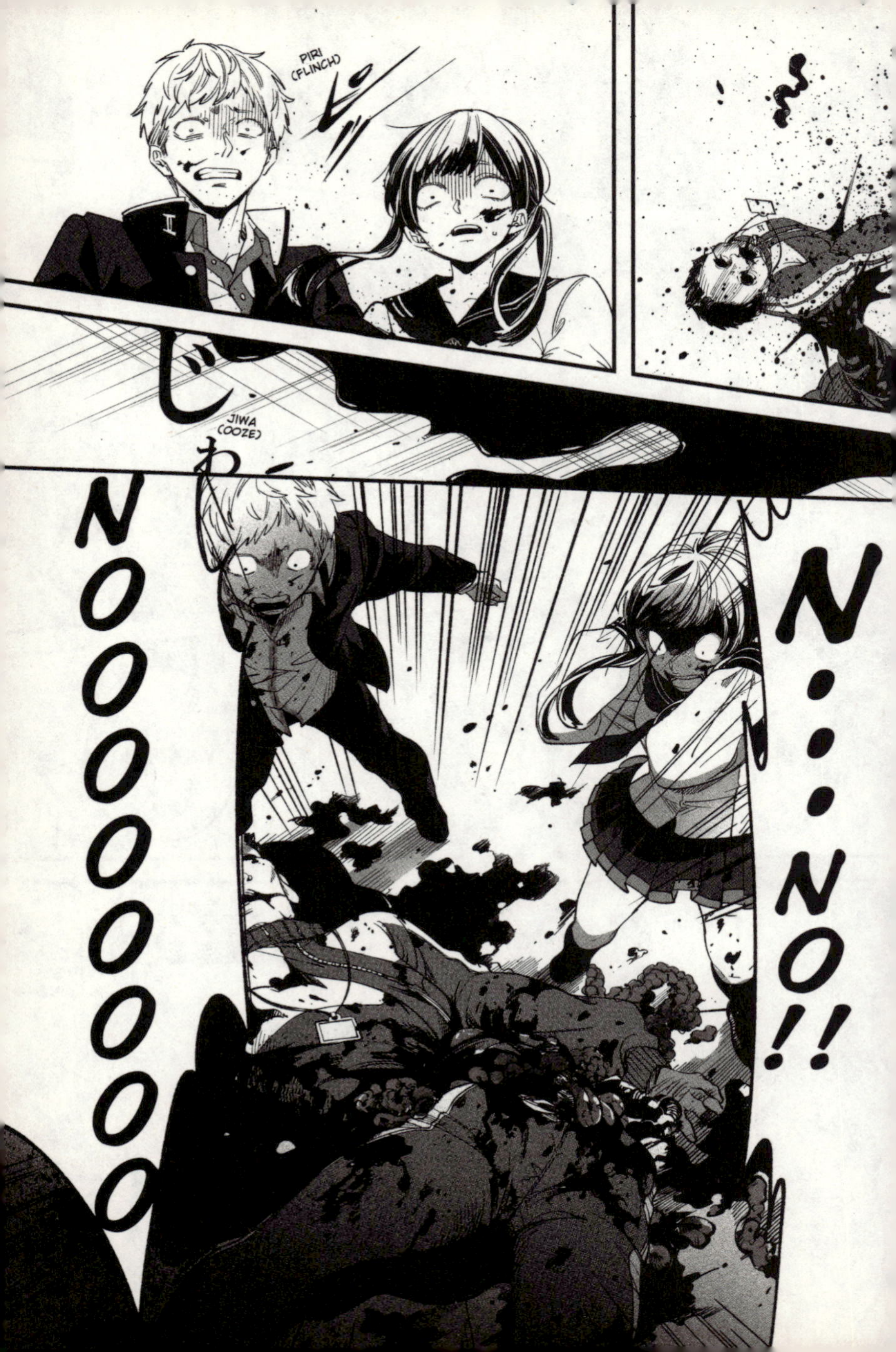
PIRI (FLINCH)
じわ
JIWA (OOZE)
N...NO!!
NOOOOOOOO

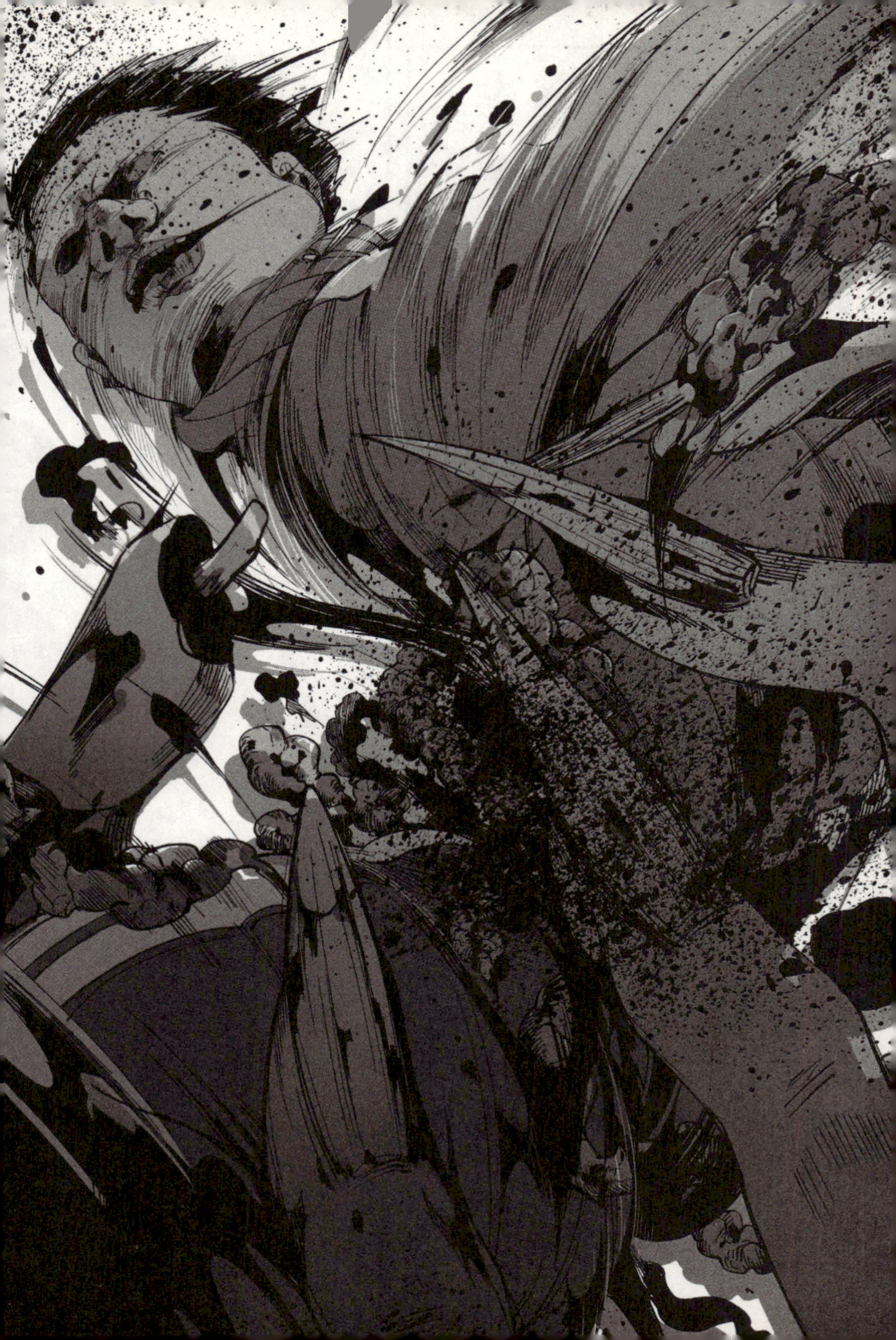

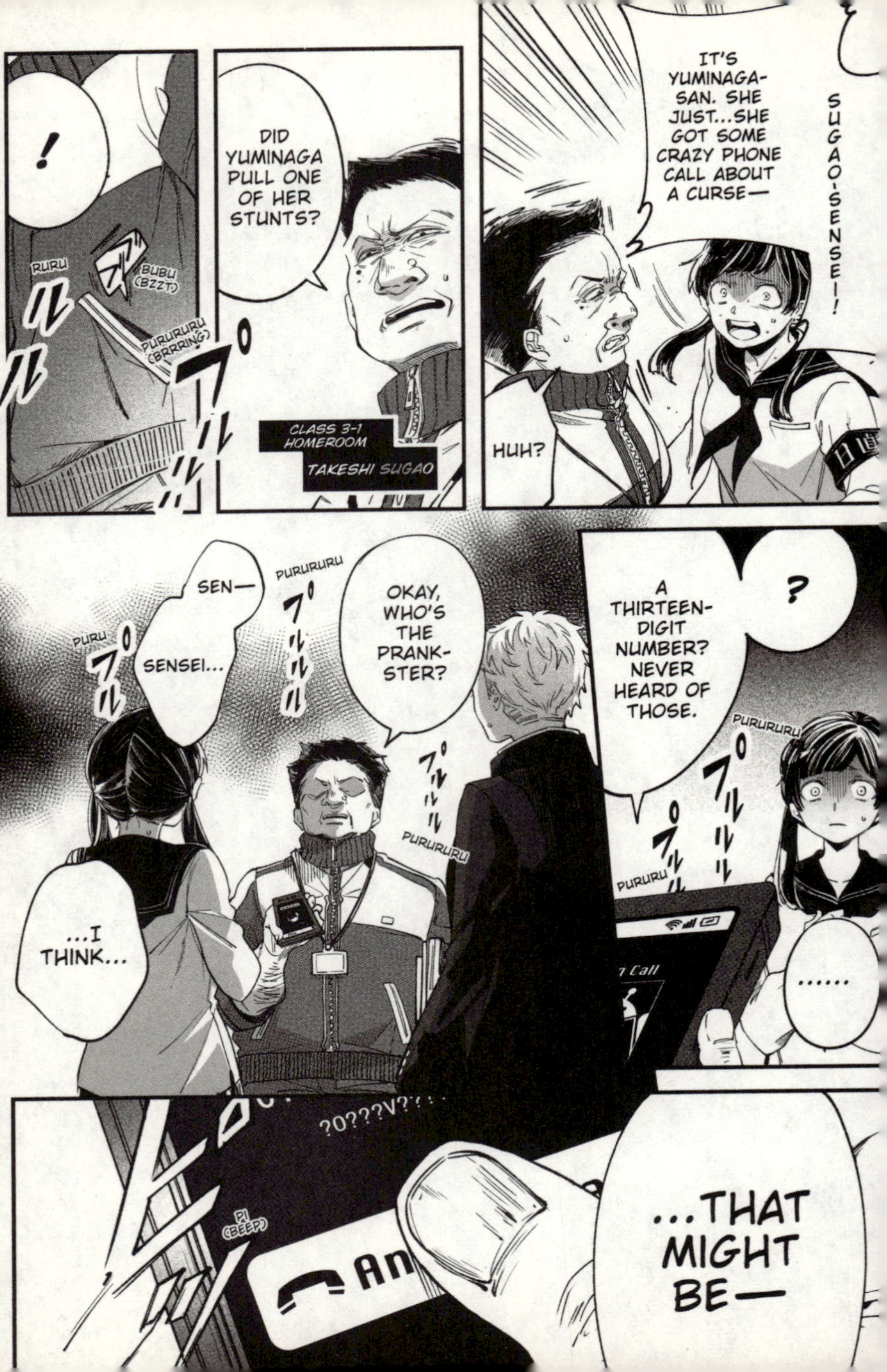
SUGAO-SENSEI!
IT'S YUMINAGA-SAN. SHE JUST...SHE GOT SOME CRAZY PHONE CALL ABOUT A CURSE—
HUH?
DID YUMINAGA PULL ONE OF HER STUNTS?
CLASS 3-1 HOMEROOM
TAKESHI SUGAO
!
RURU
BUBU (BZZT)
PURURURU (BRRRING)
?
A THIRTEEN-DIGIT NUMBER? NEVER HEARD OF THOSE.
PURURURU
PURURU
......
OKAY, WHO'S THE PRANKSTER?
PURURURU
PURURURU
SEN—
SENSEI...
PURU
...I THINK...
...THAT MIGHT BE—
?0???V?
PI (BEEP)
An

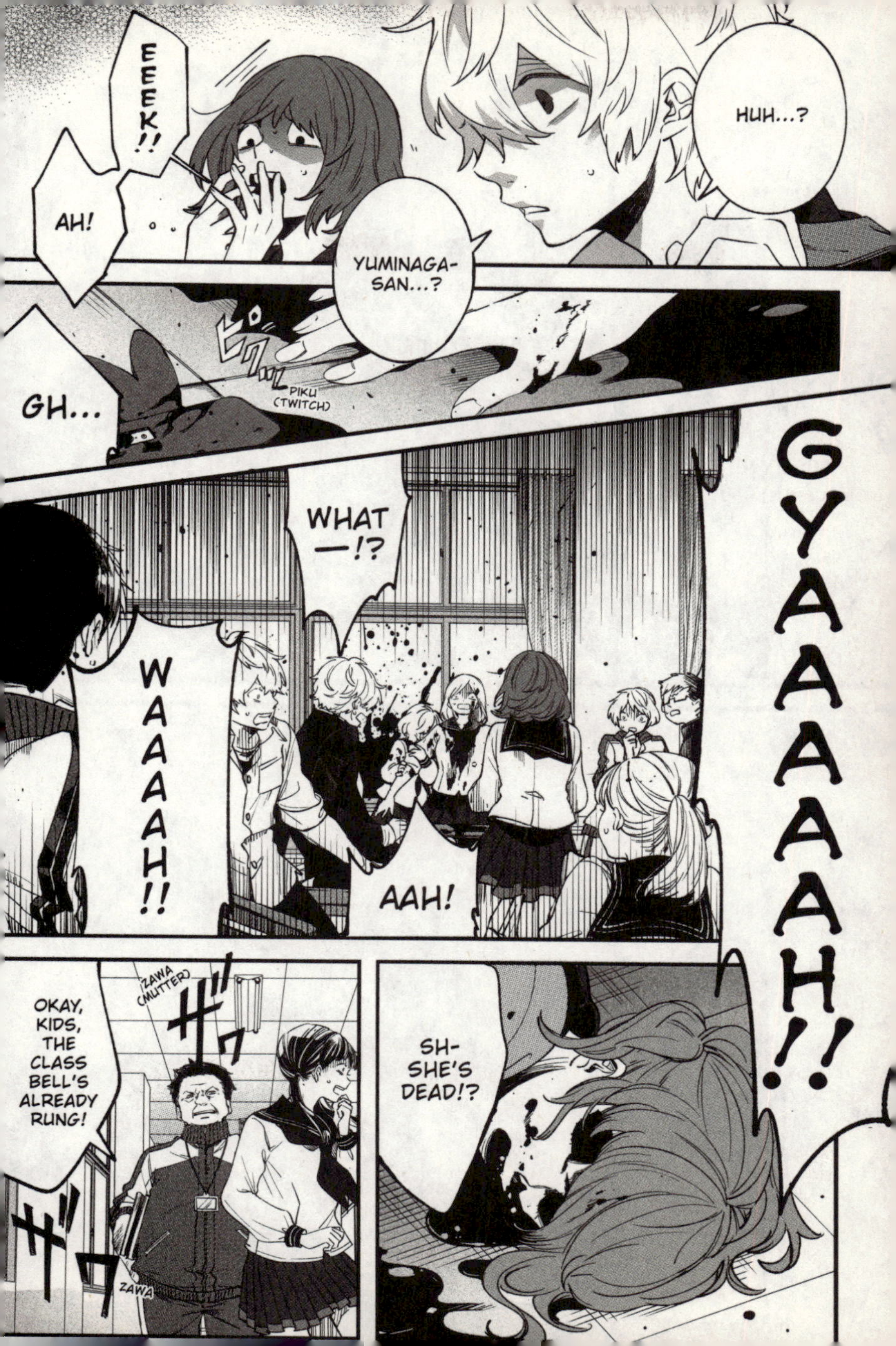
HUH...?
YUMINAGA-SAN...?
EEEK!!
AH!
ピクッ
PIKU (TWITCH)
GH...
GYAAAAAH!!
WHAT—!?
WAAAAAH!!
AAH!
SH-SHE'S DEAD!?
ZAWA (MUTTER)
ザワ
OKAY, KIDS, THE CLASS BELL'S ALREADY RUNG!
ザワ
ZAWA

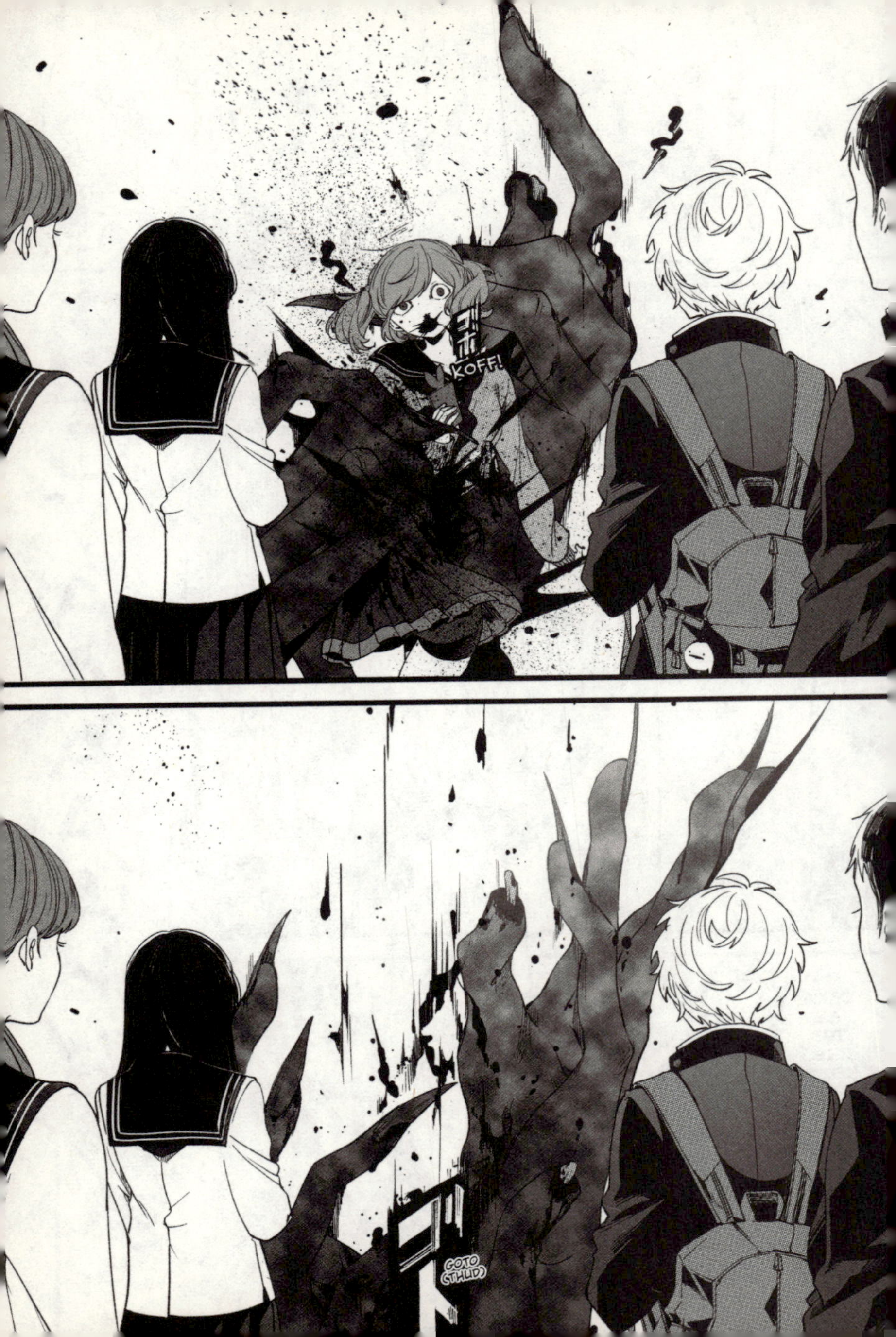
KOFF!
GOTO
(THUD)

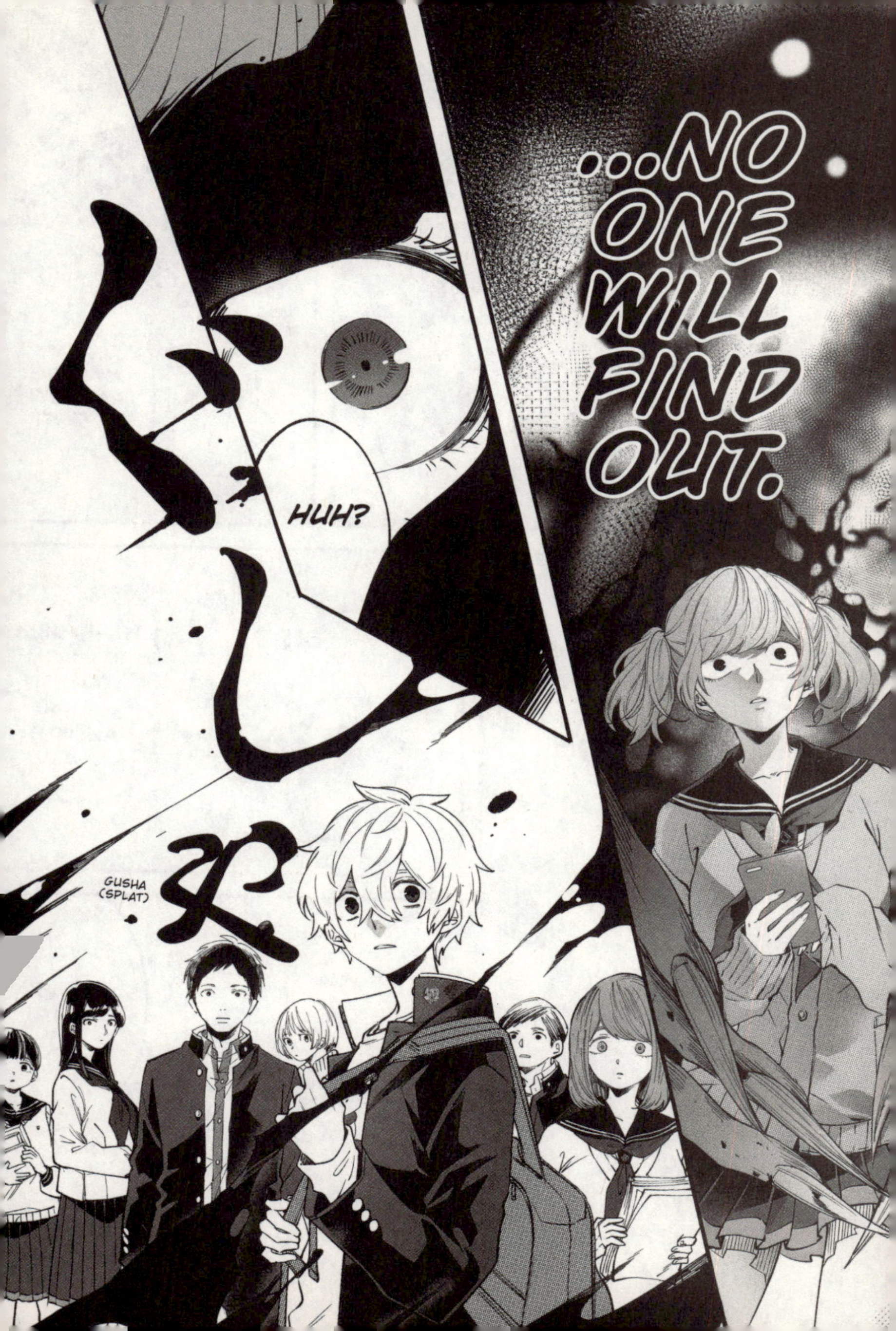
...NO ONE WILL FIND OUT.
HUH?
GUSHA (SPLAT)

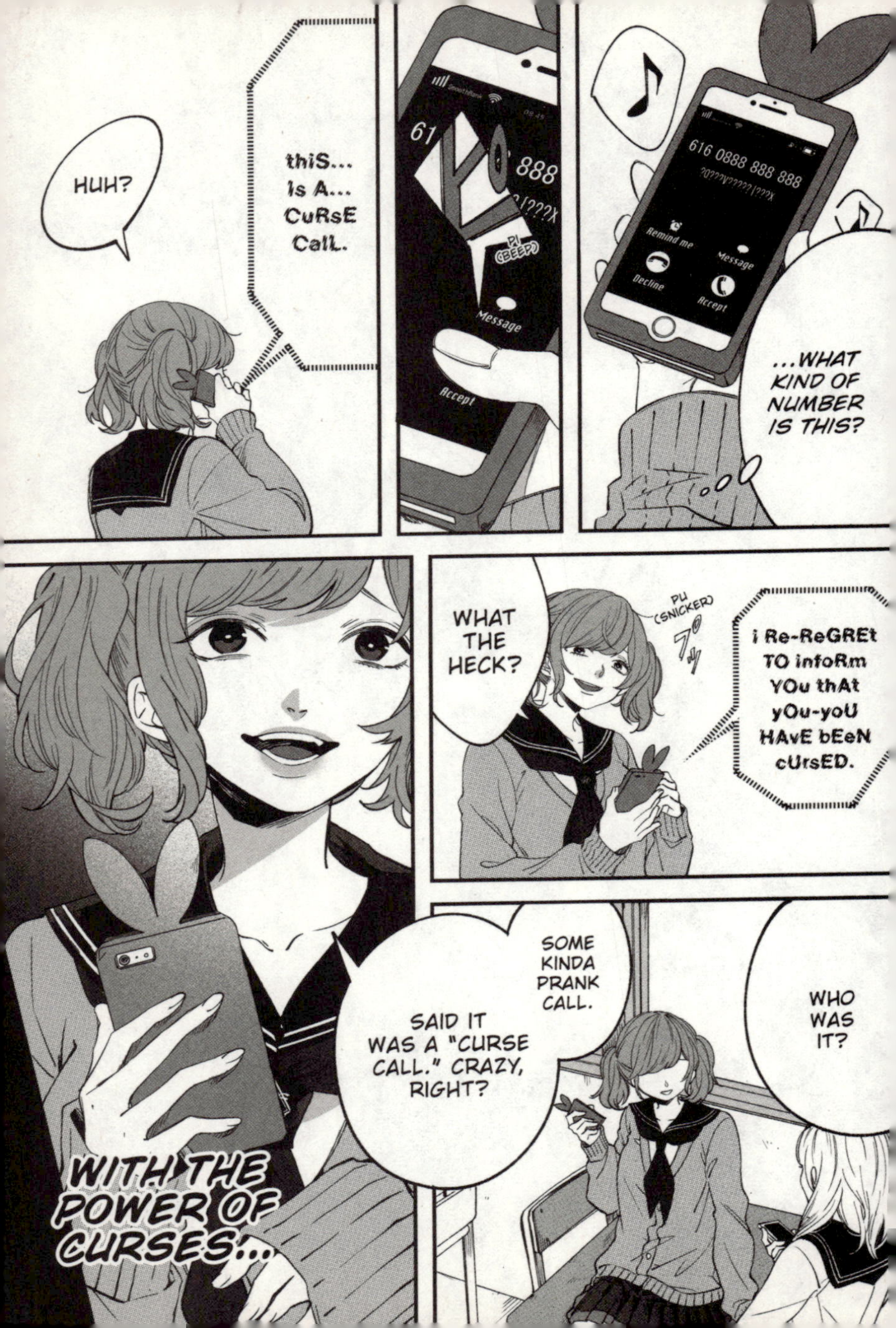
616 0888 888 888
?0???Y?????!???X
Remind me
Message
Decline
Accept
...WHAT KIND OF NUMBER IS THIS?
61
888
PI (BEEP?)
Message
Accept
thiS... Is A... CuRsE Call.
HUH?
i Re-ReGREt TO infoRm YOu thAt yOu-yoU HAvE bEeN cUrsED.
PU (SNICKER)
WHAT THE HECK?
WHO WAS IT?
SOME KINDA PRANK CALL.
SAID IT WAS A "CURSE CALL." CRAZY, RIGHT?
WITH THE POWER OF CURSES...

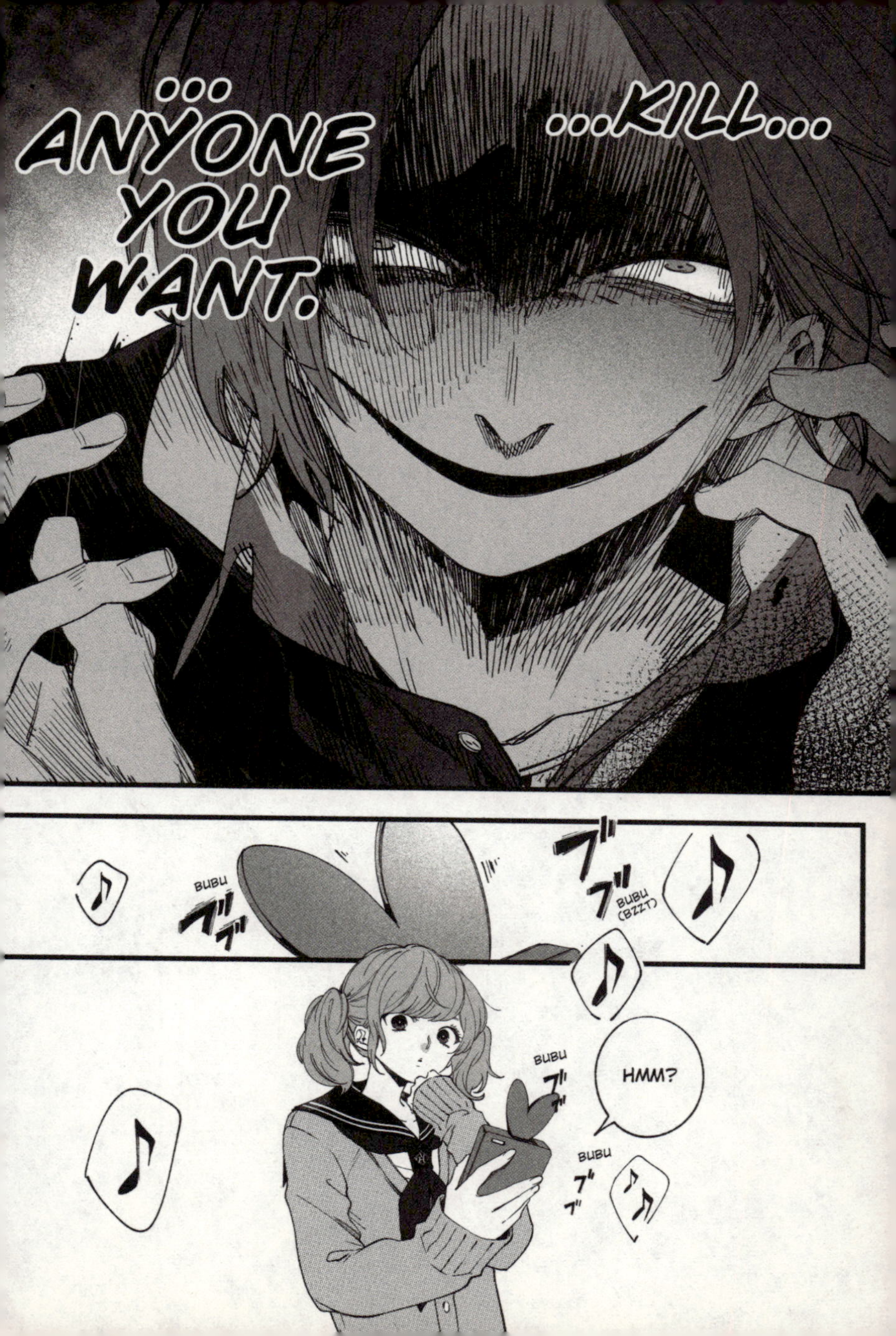
...KILL...
...ANYONE YOU WANT.
BUBU (BZZT)
BUBU
BUBU
HMM?
BUBU

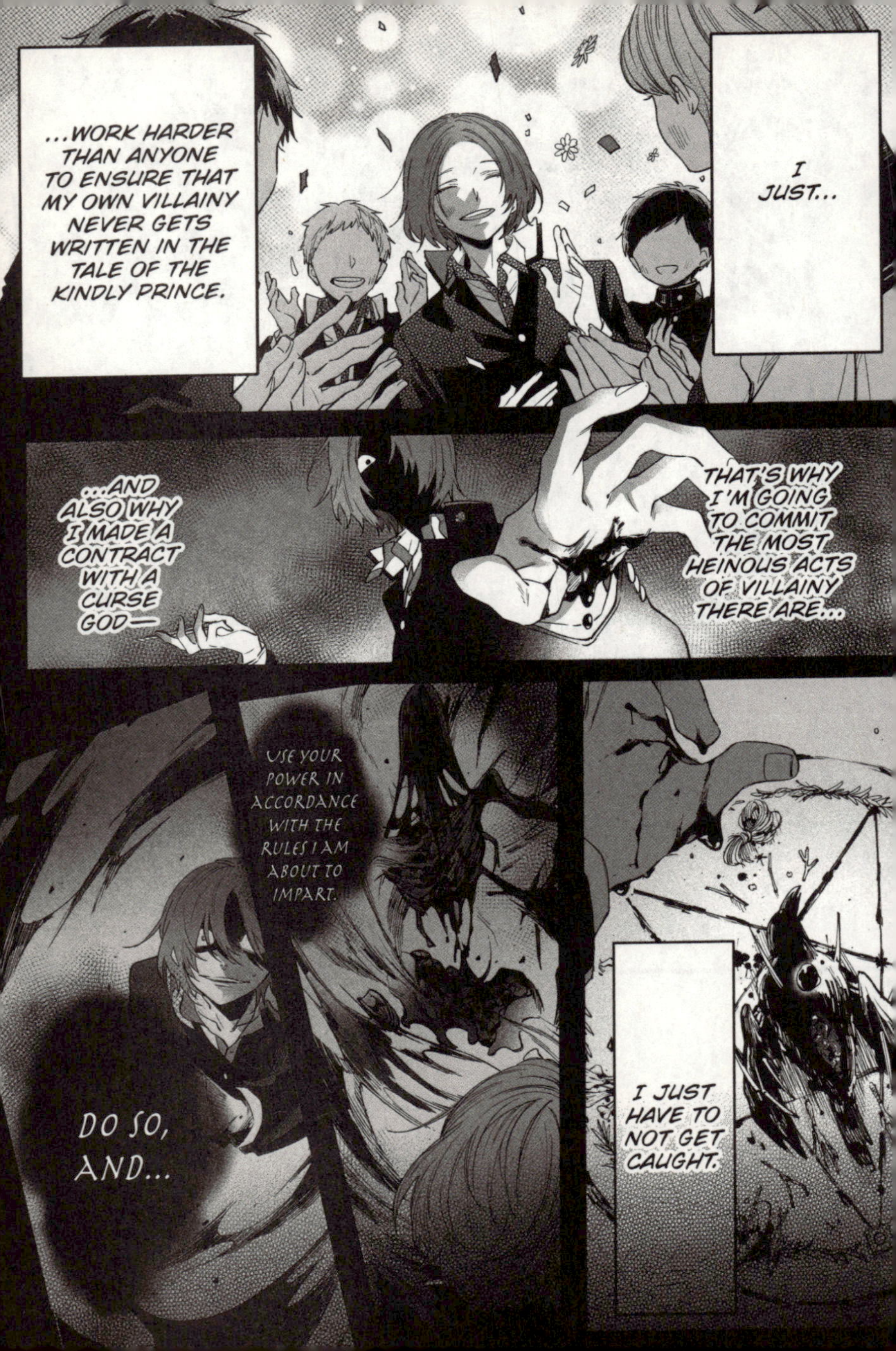
I JUST...
...WORK HARDER THAN ANYONE TO ENSURE THAT MY OWN VILLAINY NEVER GETS WRITTEN IN THE TALE OF THE KINDLY PRINCE.
THAT'S WHY I'M GOING TO COMMIT THE MOST HEINOUS ACTS OF VILLAINY THERE ARE...
...AND ALSO WHY I MADE A CONTRACT WITH A CURSE GOD—
I JUST HAVE TO NOT GET CAUGHT.
USE YOUR POWER IN ACCORDANCE WITH THE RULES I AM ABOUT TO IMPART.
DO SO, AND...

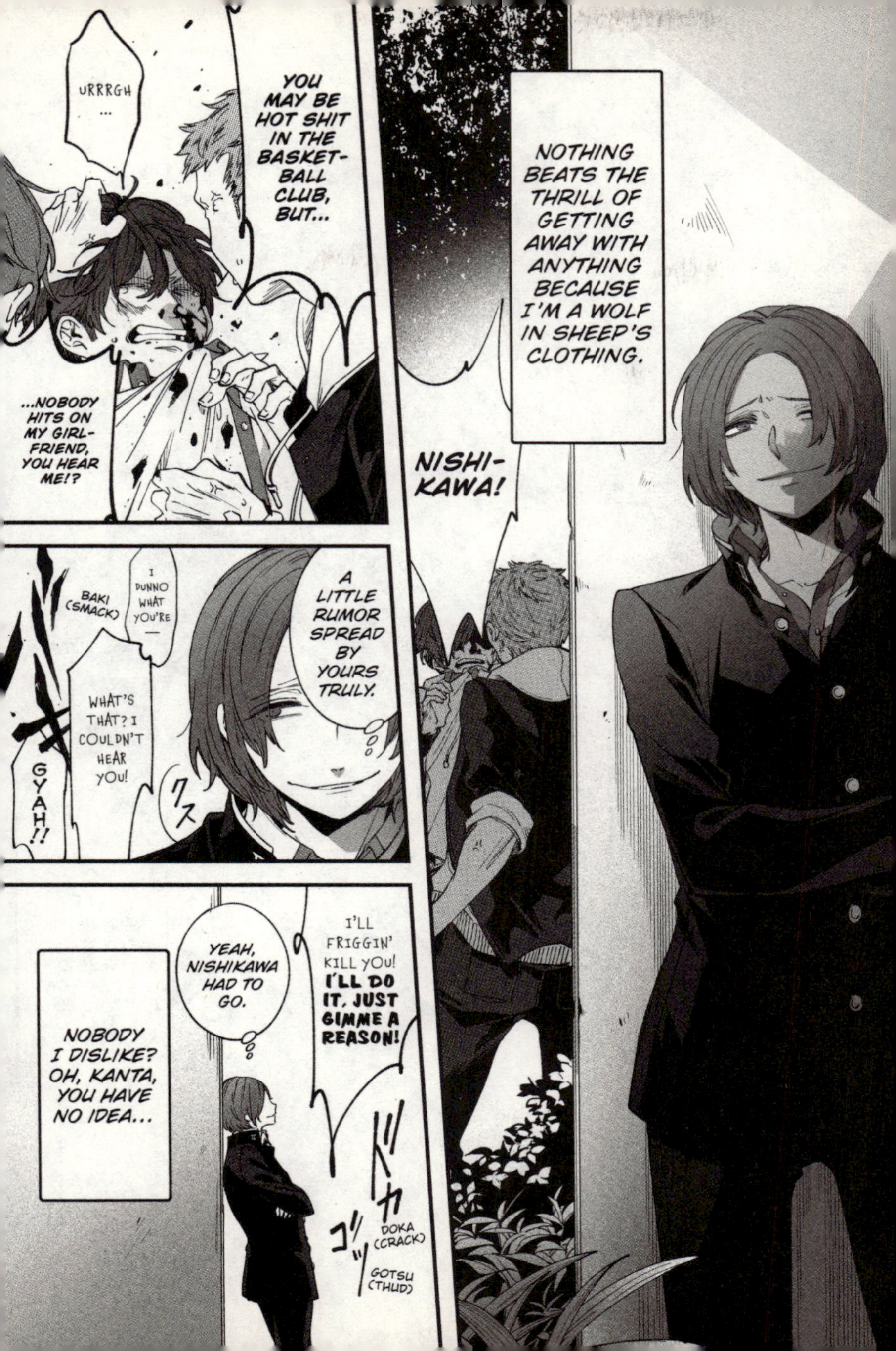
NOTHING BEATS THE THRILL OF GETTING AWAY WITH ANYTHING BECAUSE I'M A WOLF IN SHEEP'S CLOTHING.
NISHI-KAWA!
YOU MAY BE HOT SHIT IN THE BASKET-BALL CLUB, BUT...
URRRGH ...
...NOBODY HITS ON MY GIRL-FRIEND, YOU HEAR ME!?
A LITTLE RUMOR SPREAD BY YOURS TRULY.
I DUNNO WHAT YOU'RE —
BAKI (SMACK)
WHAT'S THAT? I COULDN'T HEAR YOU!
GYAH!!
I'LL FRIGGIN' KILL YOU! I'LL DO IT, JUST GIMME A REASON!
YEAH, NISHIKAWA HAD TO GO.
NOBODY I DISLIKE? OH, KANTA, YOU HAVE NO IDEA...
DOKA (CRACK)
GOTSU (THUD)

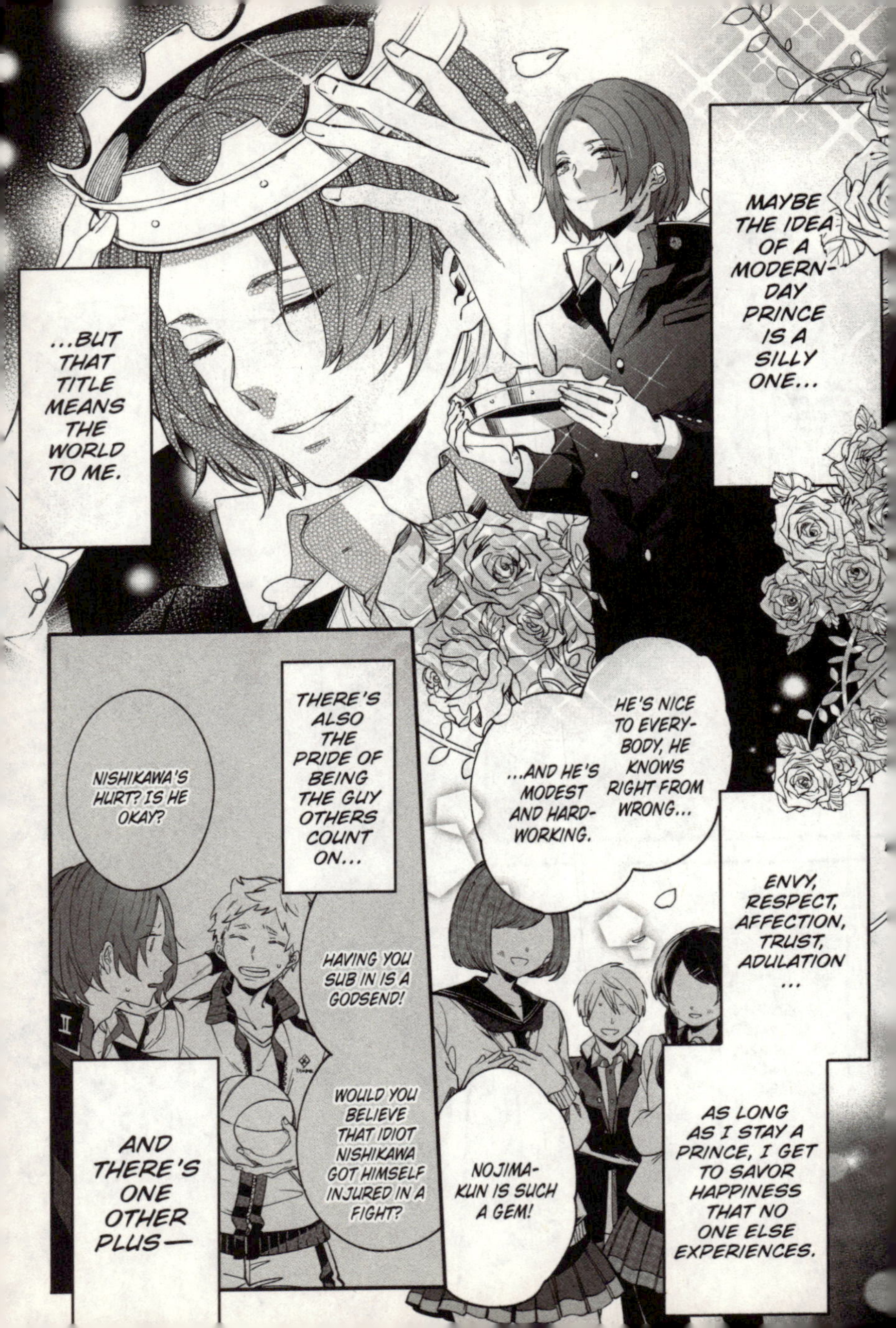
MAYBE THE IDEA OF A MODERN-DAY PRINCE IS A SILLY ONE...
...BUT THAT TITLE MEANS THE WORLD TO ME.
HE'S NICE TO EVERY-BODY, HE KNOWS RIGHT FROM WRONG...
...AND HE'S MODEST AND HARD-WORKING.
ENVY, RESPECT, AFFECTION, TRUST, ADULATION...
NOJIMA-KUN IS SUCH A GEM!
AS LONG AS I STAY A PRINCE, I GET TO SAVOR HAPPINESS THAT NO ONE ELSE EXPERIENCES.
THERE'S ALSO THE PRIDE OF BEING THE GUY OTHERS COUNT ON...
NISHIKAWA'S HURT? IS HE OKAY?
HAVING YOU SUB IN IS A GODSEND!
WOULD YOU BELIEVE THAT IDIOT NISHIKAWA GOT HIMSELF INJURED IN A FIGHT?
AND THERE'S ONE OTHER PLUS—

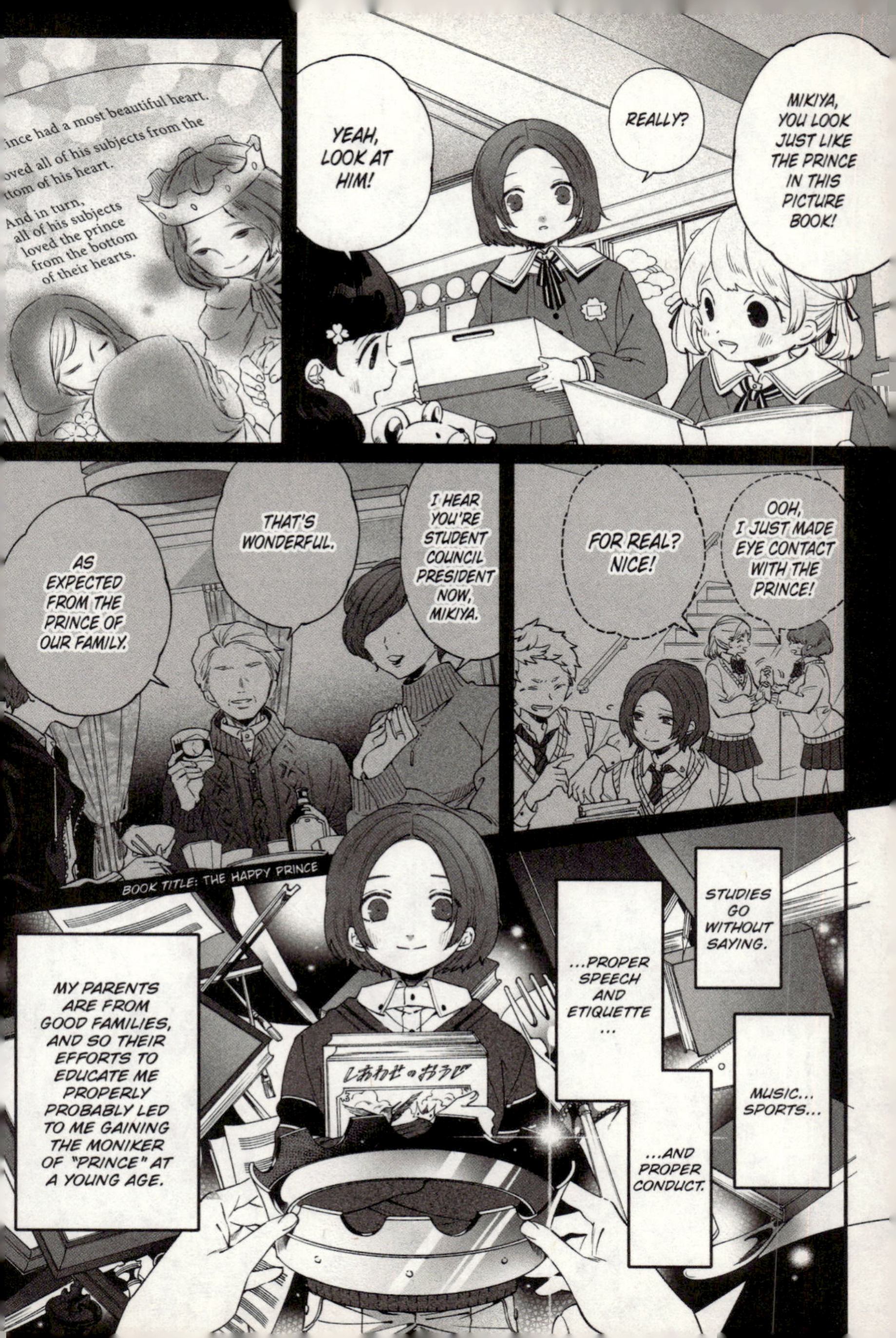

MIKIYA, YOU LOOK JUST LIKE THE PRINCE IN THIS PICTURE BOOK!
REALLY?
YEAH, LOOK AT HIM!
ince had a most beautiful heart.
oved all of his subjects from the ttom of his heart.
And in turn, all of his subjects loved the prince from the bottom of their hearts.
OOH, I JUST MADE EYE CONTACT WITH THE PRINCE!
FOR REAL? NICE!
I HEAR YOU'RE STUDENT COUNCIL PRESIDENT NOW, MIKIYA.
THAT'S WONDERFUL.
AS EXPECTED FROM THE PRINCE OF OUR FAMILY.
BOOK TITLE: THE HAPPY PRINCE
STUDIES GO WITHOUT SAYING.
...PROPER SPEECH AND ETIQUETTE...
MUSIC... SPORTS...
...AND PROPER CONDUCT.
しあわせのおうじ
MY PARENTS ARE FROM GOOD FAMILIES, AND SO THEIR EFFORTS TO EDUCATE ME PROPERLY PROBABLY LED TO ME GAINING THE MONIKER OF "PRINCE" AT A YOUNG AGE.

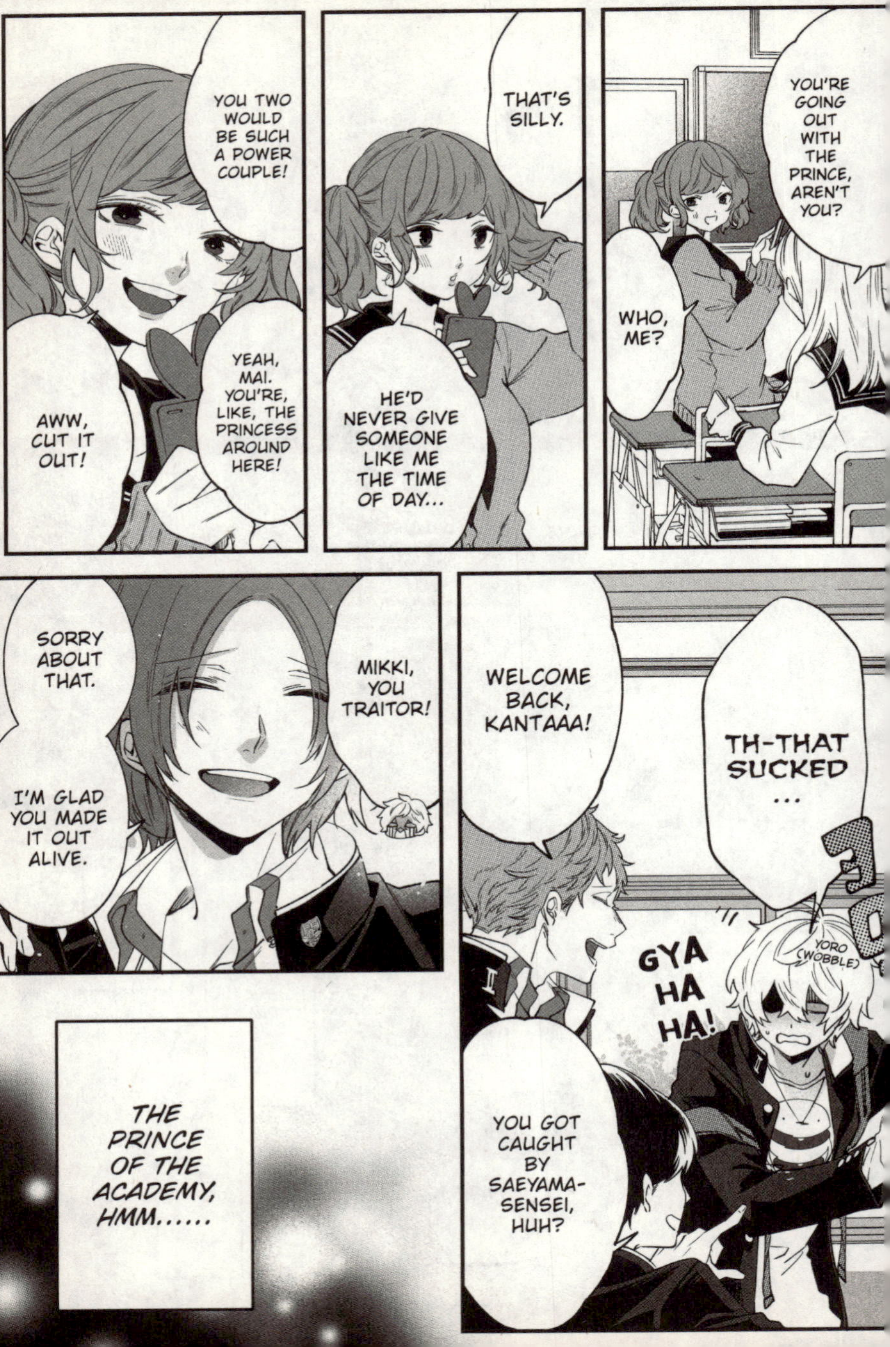
YOU'RE GOING OUT WITH THE PRINCE, AREN'T YOU?
WHO, ME?
THAT'S SILLY.
HE'D NEVER GIVE SOMEONE LIKE ME THE TIME OF DAY...
YOU TWO WOULD BE SUCH A POWER COUPLE!
YEAH, MAI. YOU'RE, LIKE, THE PRINCESS AROUND HERE!
AWW, CUT IT OUT!
TH-THAT SUCKED...
YORO (WOBBLE)
WELCOME BACK, KANTAAA!
GYA HA HA!
YOU GOT CAUGHT BY SAEYAMA-SENSEI, HUH?
MIKKI, YOU TRAITOR!
SORRY ABOUT THAT.
I'M GLAD YOU MADE IT OUT ALIVE.
THE PRINCE OF THE ACADEMY, HMM......

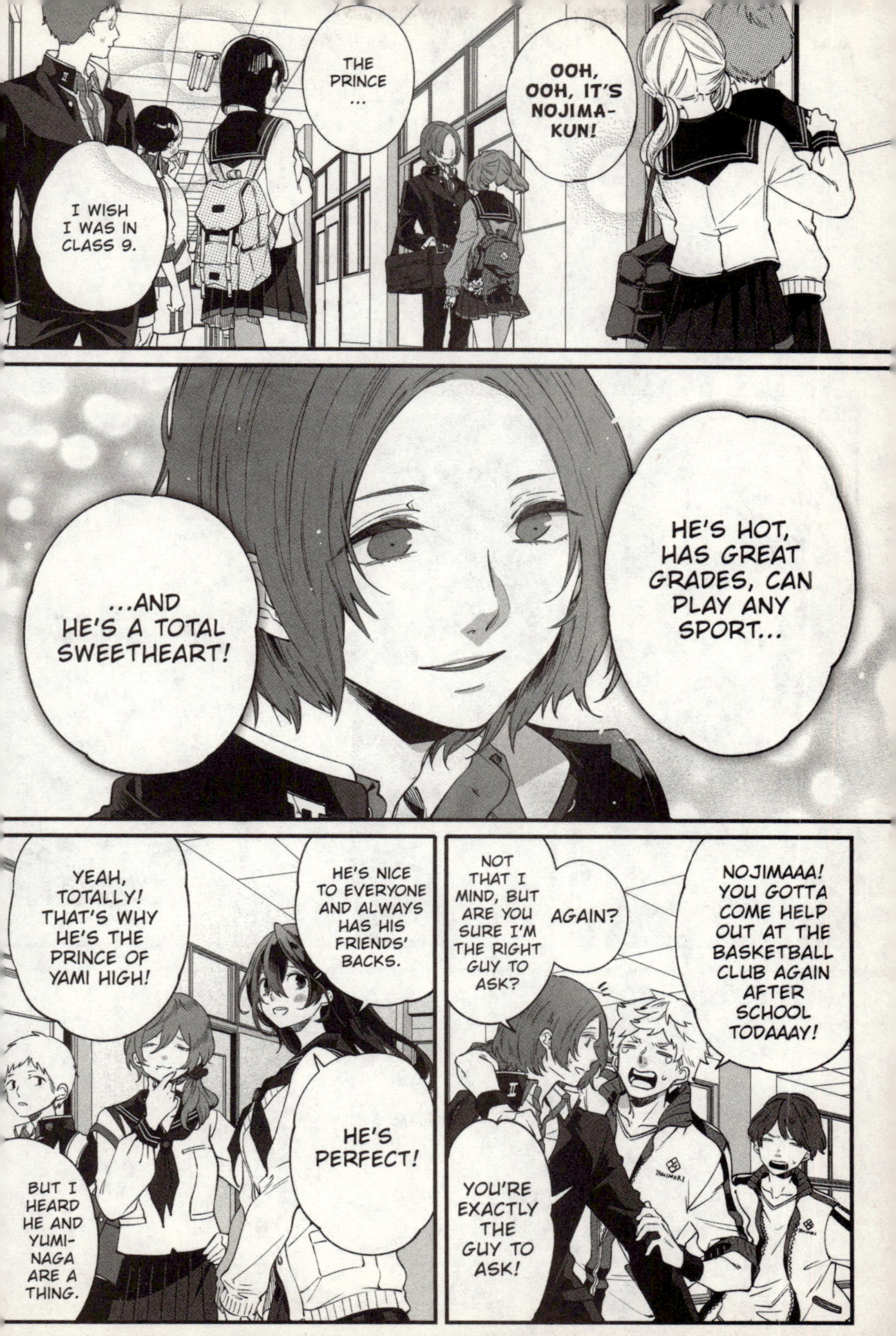
OOH, OOH, IT'S NOJIMA-KUN!
THE PRINCE...
I WISH I WAS IN CLASS 9.
HE'S HOT, HAS GREAT GRADES, CAN PLAY ANY SPORT...
...AND HE'S A TOTAL SWEETHEART!
NOJIMAAA! YOU GOTTA COME HELP OUT AT THE BASKETBALL CLUB AGAIN AFTER SCHOOL TODAAAY!
AGAIN?
NOT THAT I MIND, BUT ARE YOU SURE I'M THE RIGHT GUY TO ASK?
YOU'RE EXACTLY THE GUY TO ASK!
HE'S NICE TO EVERYONE AND ALWAYS HAS HIS FRIENDS' BACKS.
YEAH, TOTALLY! THAT'S WHY HE'S THE PRINCE OF YAMI HIGH!
HE'S PERFECT!
BUT I HEARD HE AND YUMINAGA ARE A THING.

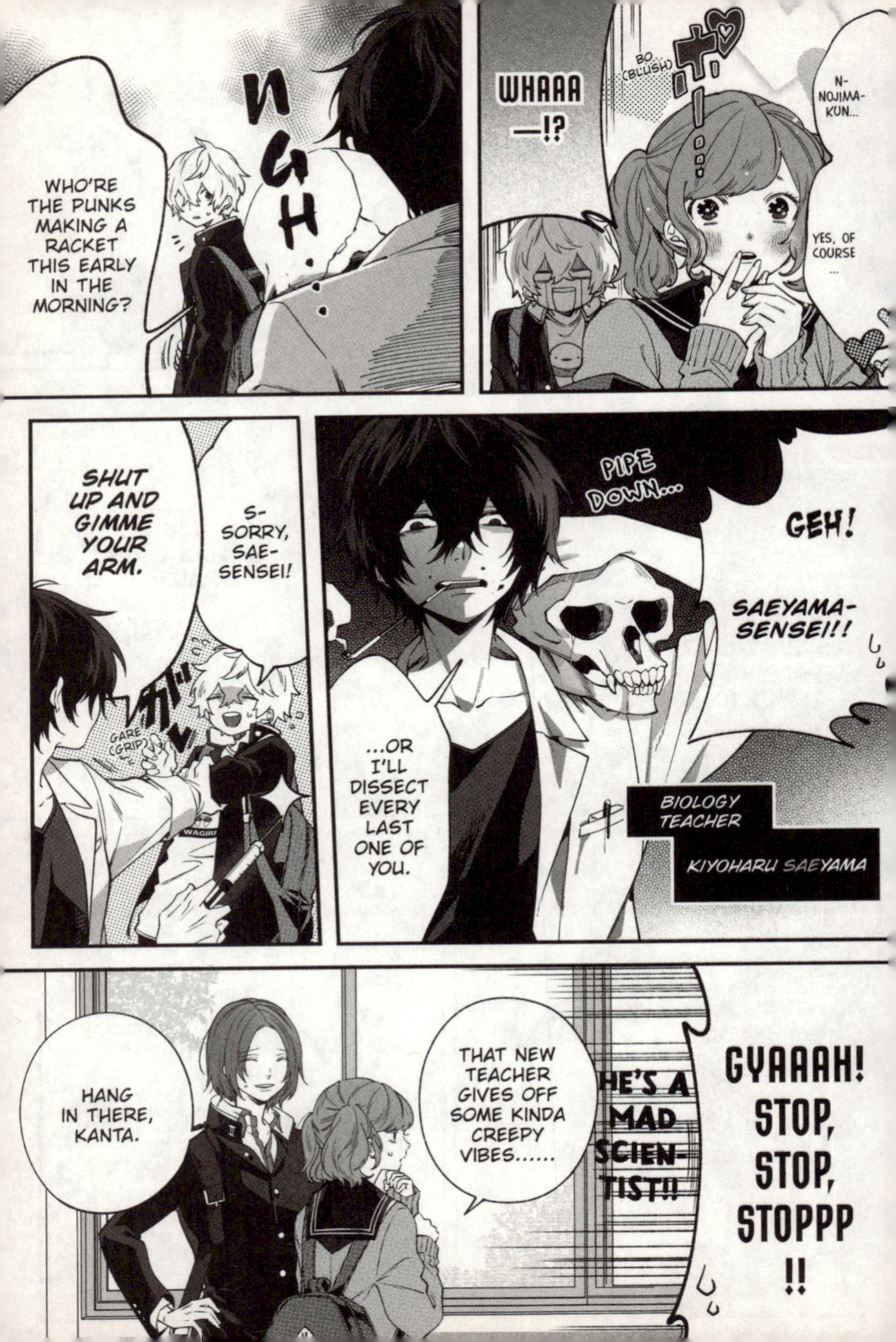
N-NOJIMA-KUN...
BO (BLUSH)
WHAAA—!?
YES, OF COURSE...
NGH...
WHO'RE THE PUNKS MAKING A RACKET THIS EARLY IN THE MORNING?
PIPE DOWN...
GEH!
SAEYAMA-SENSEI!!
...OR I'LL DISSECT EVERY LAST ONE OF YOU.
BIOLOGY TEACHER
KIYOHARU SAEYAMA
S-SORRY, SAE-SENSEI!
SHUT UP AND GIMME YOUR ARM.
GARE (GRIP)
GYAAAH! STOP, STOP, STOPPP!!
HE'S A MAD SCIENTIST!!
THAT NEW TEACHER GIVES OFF SOME KINDA CREEPY VIBES......
HANG IN THERE, KANTA.

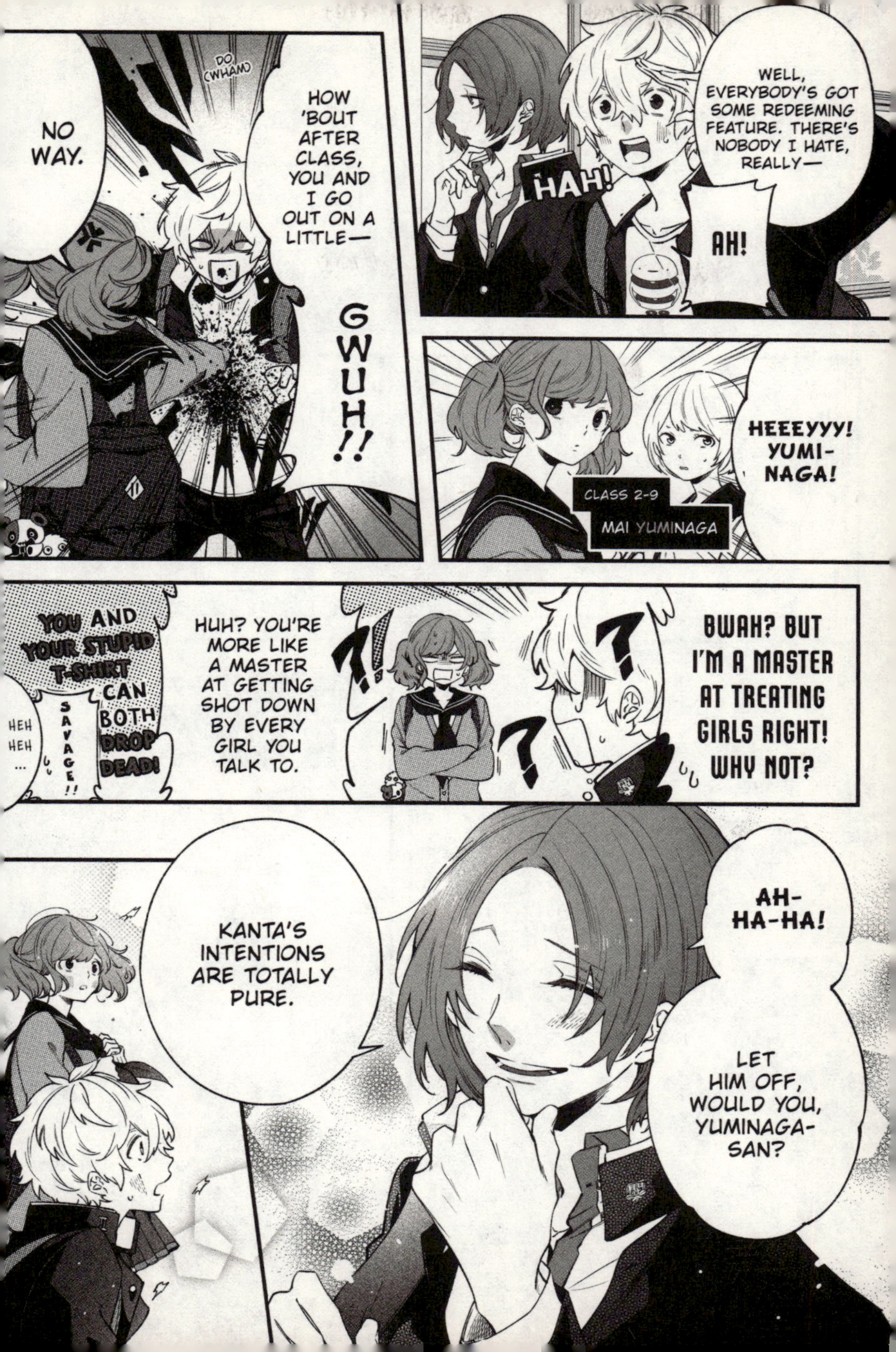
WELL, EVERYBODY'S GOT SOME REDEEMING FEATURE. THERE'S NOBODY I HATE, REALLY—
HAH!
AH!
HEEEYYY! YUMINAGA!
CLASS 2-9
MAI YUMINAGA
HOW 'BOUT AFTER CLASS, YOU AND I GO OUT ON A LITTLE—
DO (WHAM)
NO WAY.
GWUH!!
BWAH? BUT I'M A MASTER AT TREATING GIRLS RIGHT! WHY NOT?
HUH? YOU'RE MORE LIKE A MASTER AT GETTING SHOT DOWN BY EVERY GIRL YOU TALK TO.
YOU AND YOUR STUPID T-SHIRT CAN BOTH DROP DEAD!
SAVAGE!!
HEH HEH ...
AH-HA-HA!
LET HIM OFF, WOULD YOU, YUMINAGA-SAN?
KANTA'S INTENTIONS ARE TOTALLY PURE.

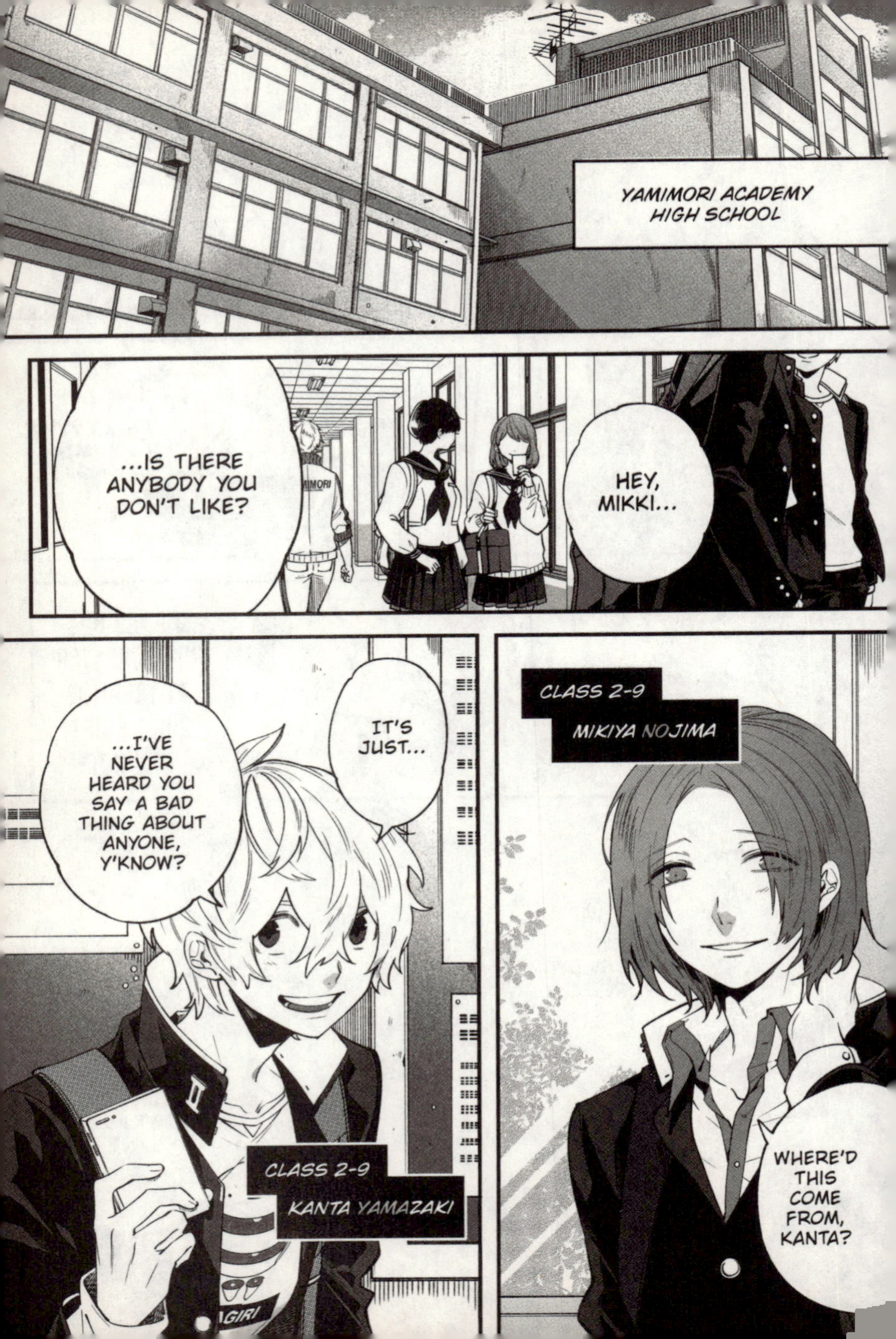
YAMIMORI ACADEMY HIGH SCHOOL
HEY, MIKKI...
...IS THERE ANYBODY YOU DON'T LIKE?
CLASS 2-9
MIKIYA NOJIMA
WHERE'D THIS COME FROM, KANTA?
IT'S JUST...
...I'VE NEVER HEARD YOU SAY A BAD THING ABOUT ANYONE, Y'KNOW?
CLASS 2-9
KANTA YAMAZAKI

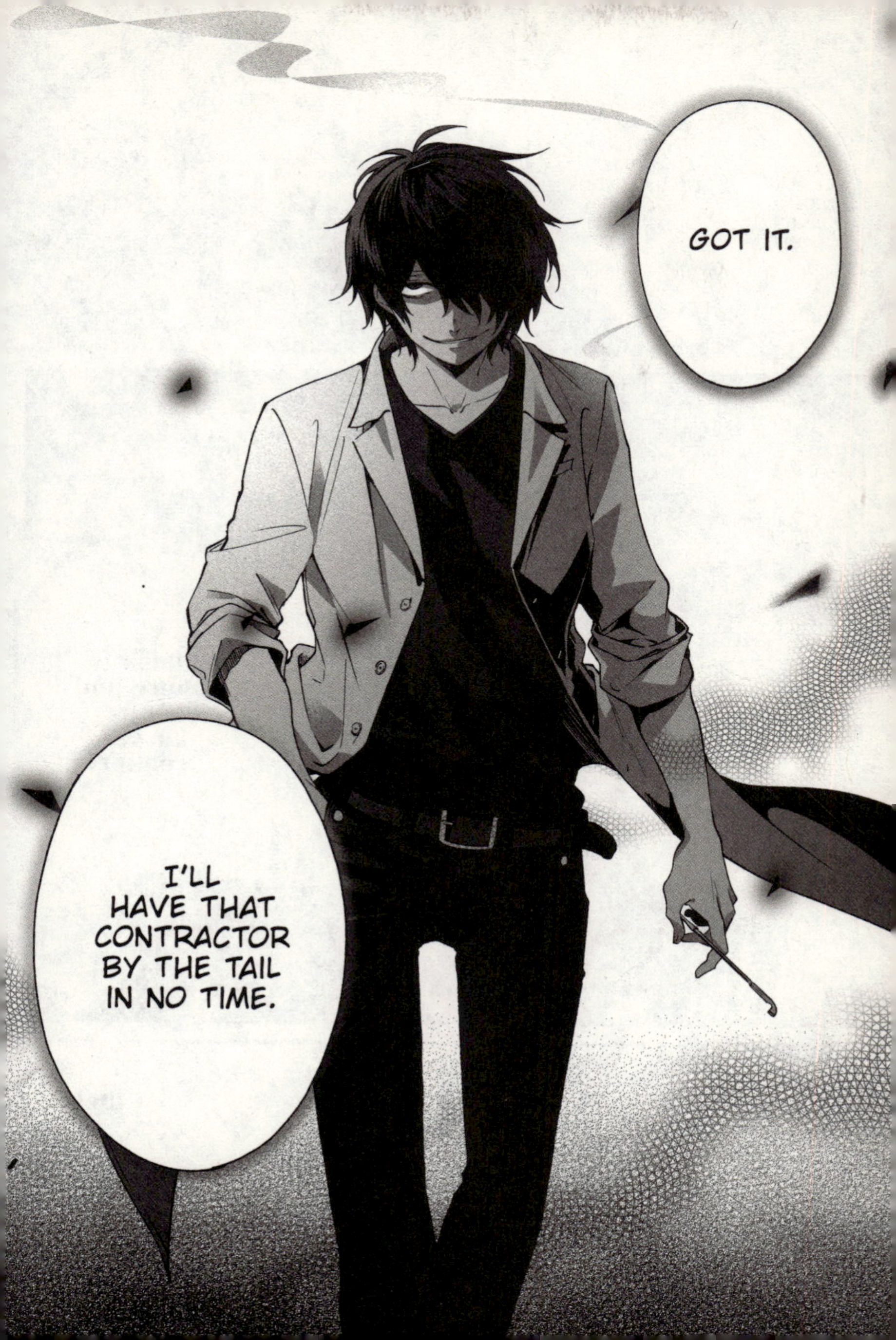
GOT IT.
I'LL HAVE THAT CONTRACTOR BY THE TAIL IN NO TIME.

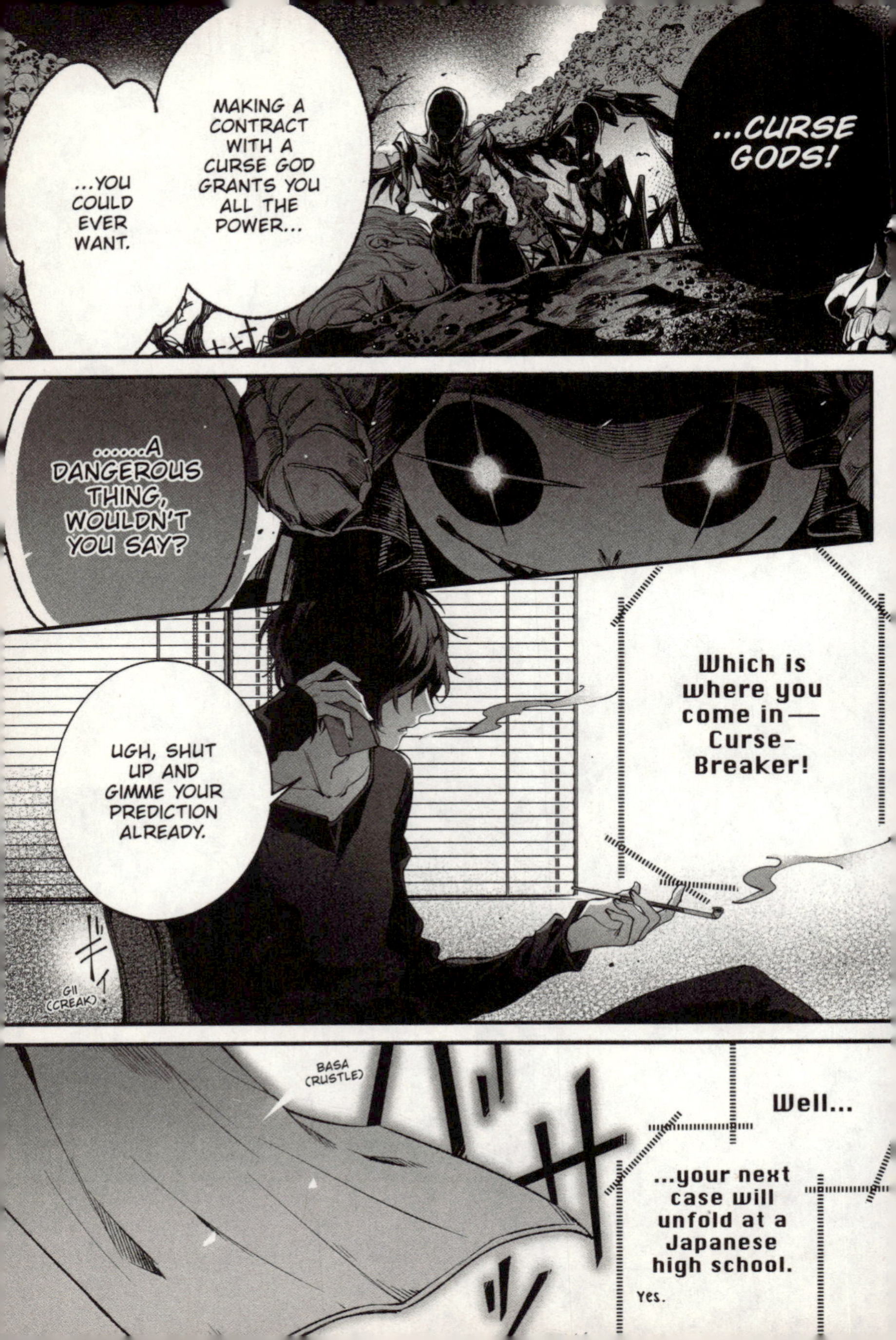
...CURSE GODS!
MAKING A CONTRACT WITH A CURSE GOD GRANTS YOU ALL THE POWER...
...YOU COULD EVER WANT.
......A DANGEROUS THING, WOULDN'T YOU SAY?
Which is where you come in— Curse-Breaker!
UGH, SHUT UP AND GIMME YOUR PREDICTION ALREADY.
GII (CREAK)
Well...
...your next case will unfold at a Japanese high school.
Yes.
BASA (RUSTLE)

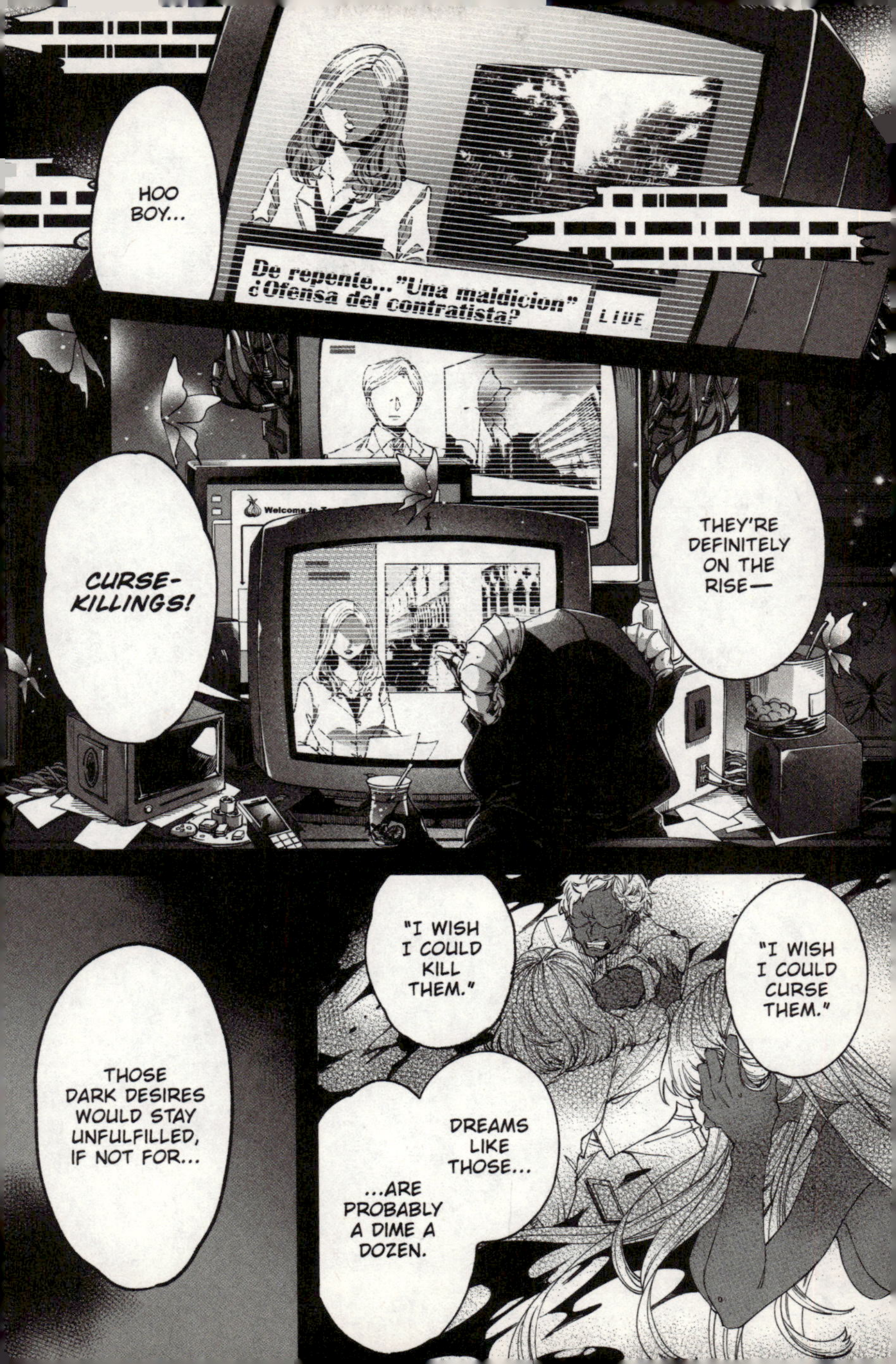
De repente..."Una maldicion" ¿Ofensa del contratista?
LIVE
HOO BOY...
THEY'RE DEFINITELY ON THE RISE—
CURSE-KILLINGS!
"I WISH I COULD CURSE THEM."
"I WISH I COULD KILL THEM."
DREAMS LIKE THOSE...
...ARE PROBABLY A DIME A DOZEN.
THOSE DARK DESIRES WOULD STAY UNFULFILLED, IF NOT FOR...

CHAPTER 1 | THE KINDLY PRINCE SMILES BENEATH HIS MASK

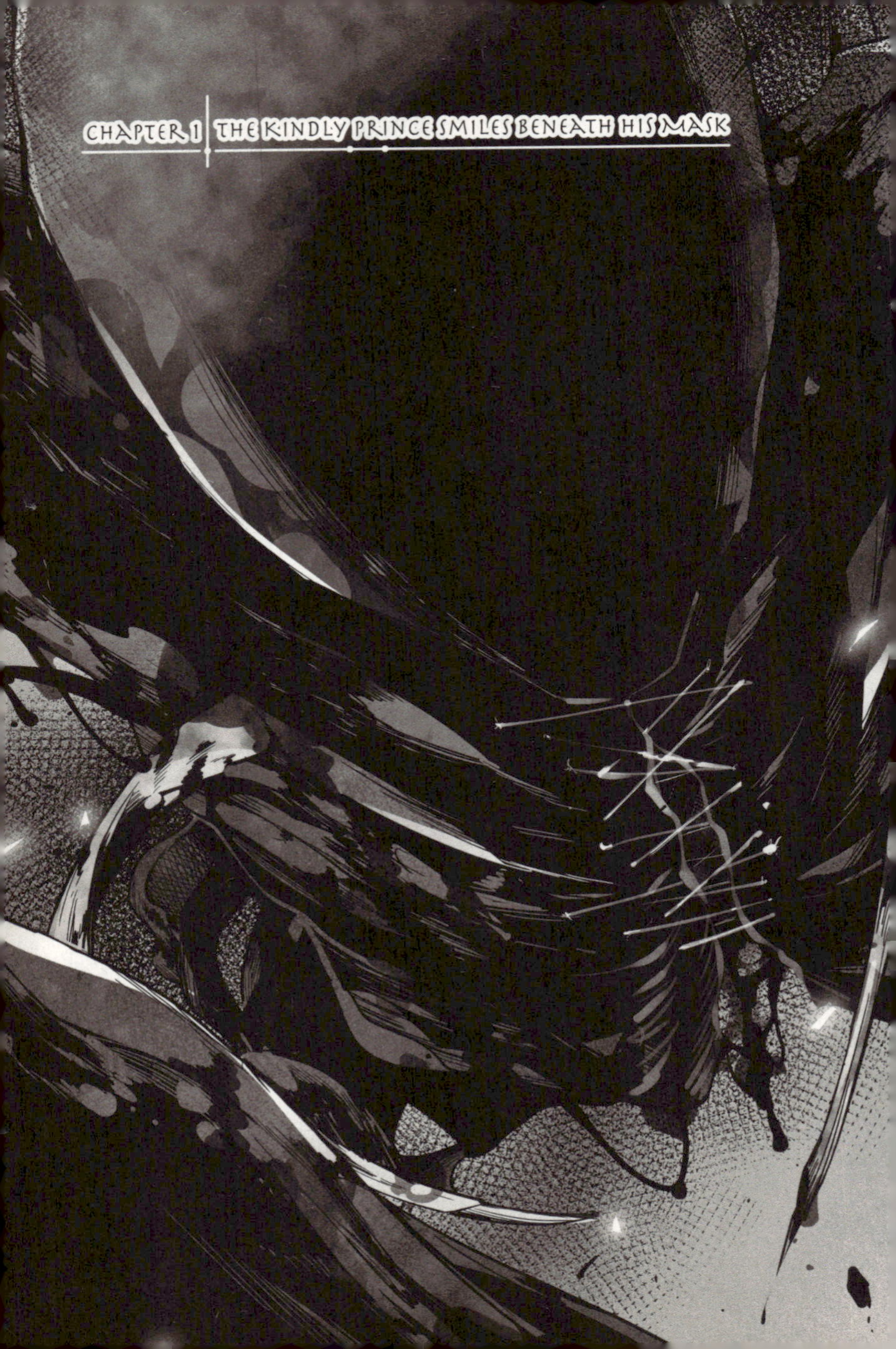

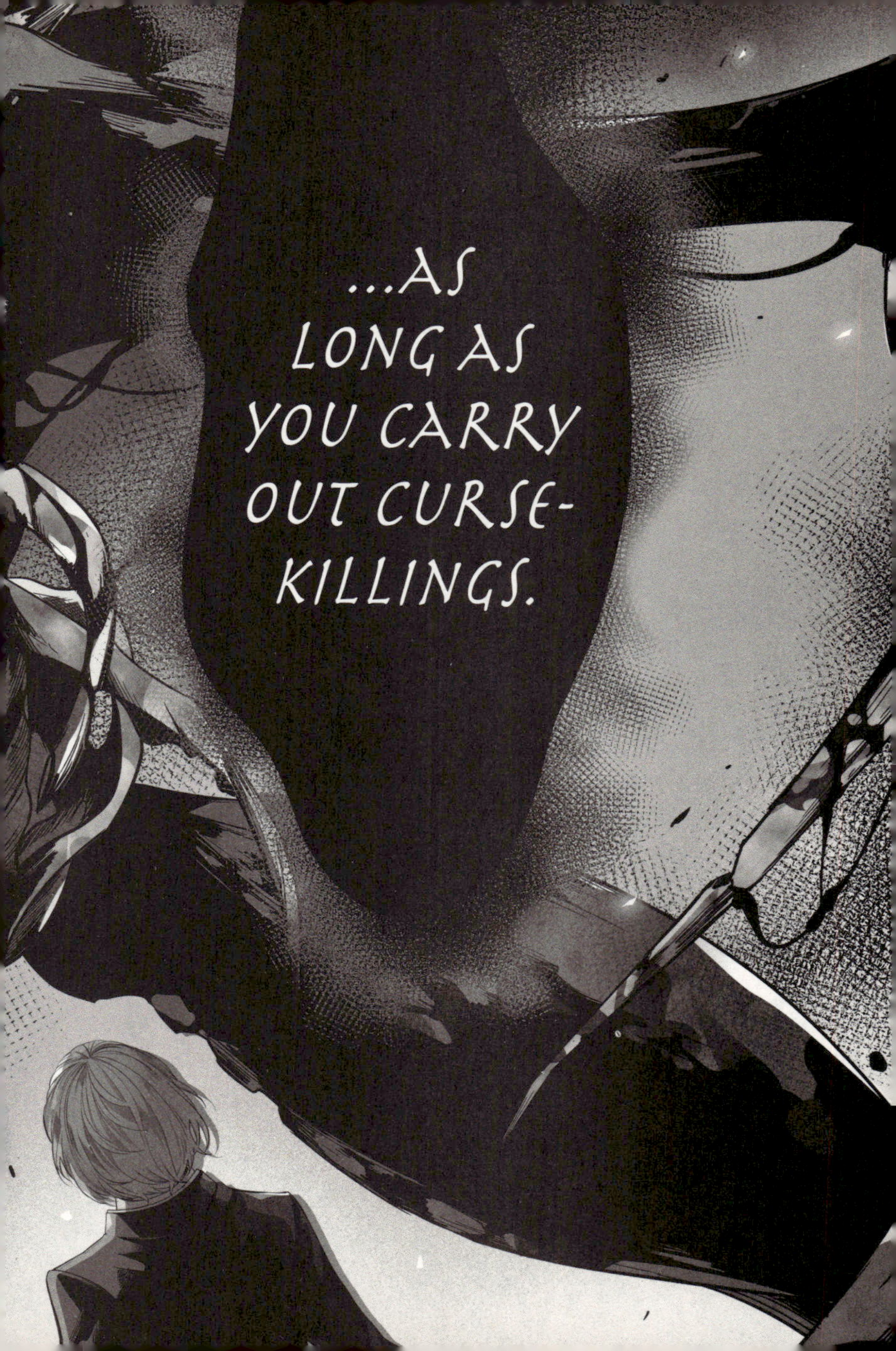
...AS LONG AS YOU CARRY OUT CURSE-KILLINGS.

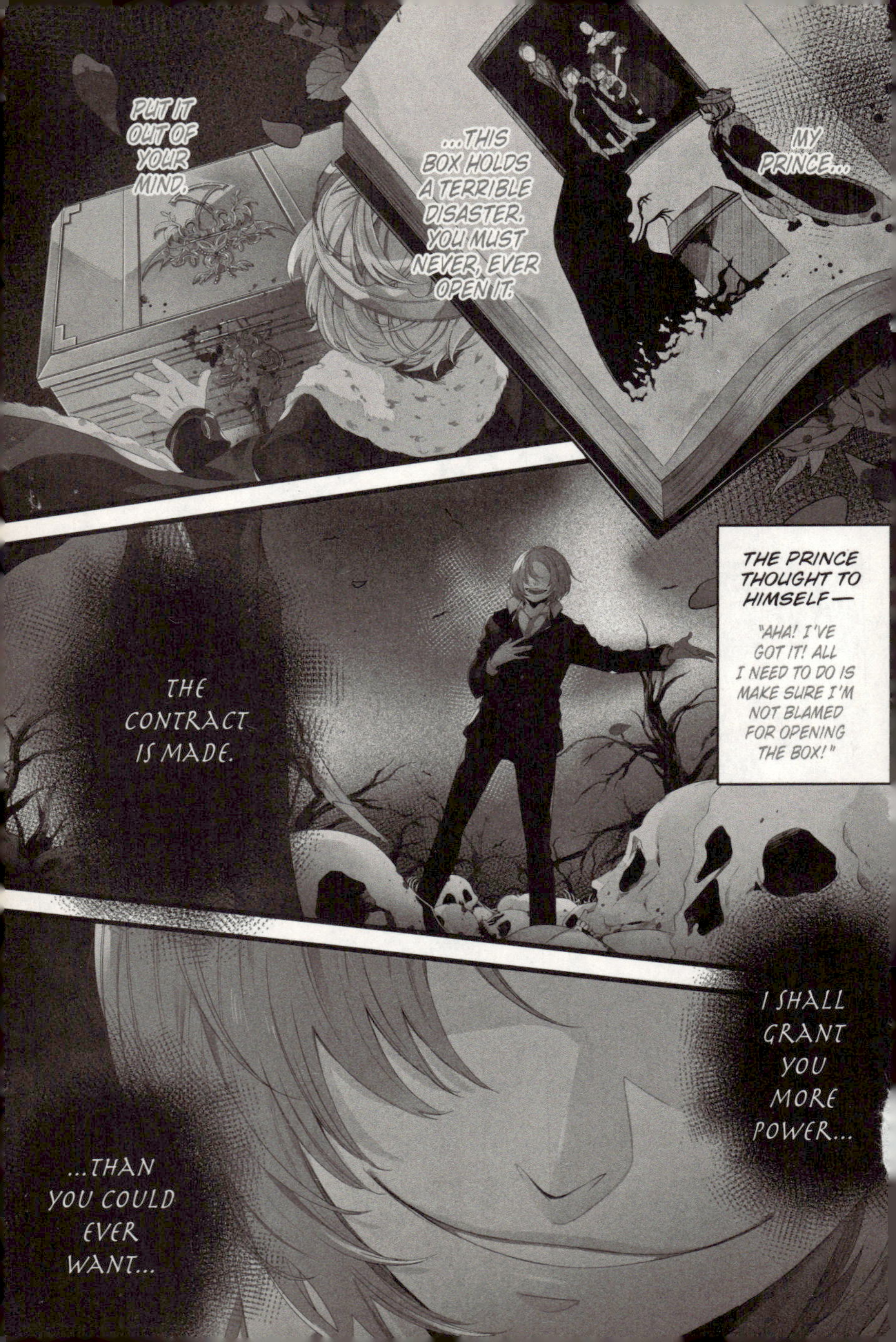
MY PRINCE...
...THIS BOX HOLDS A TERRIBLE DISASTER. YOU MUST NEVER, EVER OPEN IT.
PUT IT OUT OF YOUR MIND.
THE PRINCE THOUGHT TO HIMSELF—
"AHA! I'VE GOT IT! ALL I NEED TO DO IS MAKE SURE I'M NOT BLAMED FOR OPENING THE BOX!"
THE CONTRACT IS MADE.
I SHALL GRANT YOU MORE POWER...
...THAN YOU COULD EVER WANT...